W9-AOP-165

CORTINA DICTIONARY SERIES

TRAVELER'S GERMAN DICTIONARY

ENGLISH-GERMAN / GERMAN-ENGLISH

by
Josefa Zotter, M.A.
St. Mary's College
Notre Dame, Indiana

•

SERIES GENERAL EDITORS
Dilaver Berberi, Ph.D.
Edel A. Winje, Ed.D.

CORTINA LEARNING INTERNATIONAL, INC.
Publishers • WESTPORT, CT 06880

Library of Congress Cataloging-in-Publication Data

Zotter, Josefa.
    Cortina traveler's German dictionary: English-German/German-
English / by Josefa Zotter; series general editors, Dilaver
Berberi, Edel A. Winje.
        p.   cm.
    ISBN 0-8327-0723-6 (paper): $6.95
    1. German language—Dictionaries—English. 2. English language
—Dictionaries—German. I. Title. II. Title: Traveler's German
dictionary.
PF3640.Z66   1993   93-3679
433'.21—dc20   CIP

Printed in the United States of America

HH Editions 9 8 7 6 5 4 3 2 1   9307-16

Contents

How to Use This Dictionary

Here is a handy, pocket-sized Dictionary that will put German at your fingertips. Whether you are a beginner or already have a working knowledge of German, whether you are a student, a businessperson, or a tourist—this Dictionary will give you what you need to get along in German.

The entries are the heart of the Dictionary; they number almost 11,000 (5000-plus in the English-German section, 5000-plus in the German-English section). On the English side, entries were chosen for their usefulness and applicability to common everyday situations. German entries were selected from words that occur most frequently in the course of everyday life in German-speaking countries. Thus, you will find here the words you will actually hear and speak when using German, whether at home or abroad. In addition, this Dictionary is unique in providing the pronunciation of the German words *on both sides,* so that whenever you encounter them you can immediately pronounce them.

Additional Special Features

In addition to the entries themselves, this Dictionary includes the following extra features to enable you to actually use the German language in a variety of different situations.

Guide to Pronunciation. The pronunciation of each German entry is given in simple English alphabet transcriptions. Thus, the user can pronounce a new word immediately, just by following the simple guide which appears with each entry. The "Key to German Pronunciation," found on page viii, explains German sounds and gives examples of each one, and shows how they compare with English.

Phrases for Use Abroad (page 319). Everyday expressions, requests, statements, questions and answers for specific situations—each with its pronunciation—let you communicate easily.

Menu Reader (page 330). A comprehensive list of food and drink, complete with pronunciation, takes the mystery out of German menus.

Concise German Grammar (page 337). For the user who wishes a quick overview of German grammar, or who wants an explanation of how verbs are conjugated or noun plurals formed, this grammar section is an invaluable aid. It is divided into sections treating nouns, verbs, adjectives, adverbs, sentence formation, etc., for easy reference and use.

Helpful Notes for the Reader

1. *All verbs* are marked *v.*, and irregular verbs are marked *irreg.* There are tables of irregular verbs showing their conjugation at the end of the Dictionary, and the "Concise Grammar" explains the conjugation of regular verbs.

2. *Separable prefixes* are a feature of German verbs explained in the "Concise Grammar." In the Dictionary entries, a hyphen is shown between separable prefix and stem. This lexicographical hyphen does not occur in written German.

3. *Reflexive verbs* are preceded by *sich*. See the "Concise Grammar" for an explanation of the use of these verbs.

4. *Gender* is a feature of every German noun (and of

adjectives and pronouns), and each is masculine, feminine, or neuter and declined through four separate cases, both singular and plural. Genders must be memorized, though there are endings in each of the genders that are regularly masculine, feminine, or neuter. The gender of every noun is marked in the Dictionary. For the adjectives, the nominative of the masculine singular is given, and the other cases and genders can be derived from it.

5. *Plurals* of German nouns are formed in various ways. The plural may *(a)* be the same as the singular; *(b)* take an umlaut over the stem vowel; *(c)* take an ending, such as *-e, -en, -er, -ien, -s;* or *(d)* take an umlaut and ending. These are indicated in the Dictionary after the entry word in this way: *(a)* -; *(b)* ¨; *(c)* -e; *(d)* ¨er. For examples:

(a) **Lehrer,-**	The plural is **Lehrer.**
(b) **Garten,** ¨	The plural is **Gärten.**
(c) **Tisch, -e**	The plural is **Tische.**
(d) **Buch,** ¨er	The plural is **Bücher.**

6. *The parts of speech* of entries (except verbs) are not marked unless the translation does not indicate the part of speech or unless the word appears more than once as different parts of speech.

7. *Many common or idiomatic expressions* are included in the Dictionary, along with their pronunciation, so that the reader can use them correctly.

8. In the "Key to German Pronunciation" the sounds of High German have been used. Though there are many regional dialects in Germany, Austria, and Switzerland, the pronunciations given here will be understood everywhere.

Using this Dictionary is sure to make your contact with German-speaking people and their language much more pleasurable and satisfying, whether at home or abroad.

vii

Key to German Pronunciation

Vowels

The vowel sounds in German are "purer" than those in English. They are pronounced more tensely in the throat.

The five basic vowel sounds in German — *a, e, i, o, u* — can be either long or short. A vowel that is followed by only one consonant (including *h*) is usually long. Long vowels will be indicated in the transcription of words in this dictionary by *ah, eh, ee, oh,* and *oo.* A vowel followed by two or more consonants is short. The vowel also is short in a few one-syllable words even though it is followed by only one consonant: *am, ab, in, um.*

German spelling	Phonetic symbol	Sound description & Examples
a	*a*	pronounced as *a* in p*a*rt. *Ex.:* **kalt** [*kalt*] cold
a, aa, ah	*ah*	as *a* in f*a*ther. *Ex.:* **kam** [*kahm*] came
e	*e*	as *e* in m*e*t. *Ex.:* **helfen** [*hel'-fən*] to help
e, ee, eh	*eh*	as *a* in d*a*y. *Ex.:* **geht** [*geht*] goes
e	*ə*	unstressed *e,* as *u* in c*u*t. *Ex.:* **verlangen** [*fer-lang'-ən*] to desire
i	*i*	as *i* in f*i*t, h*i*t. *Ex.:* **Wind** [*vint*] wind
i, ie, ih, ieh	*ee*	as *i* in mach*i*ne or *ee* in f*ee*t. *Ex.:* **die** [*dee*] the; **Maschine** [*ma-shee'-nə*] machine
o	*o*	as *o* in c*o*st. *Ex.:* **Kosten** [*ko'-stən*] costs.
o, oo, oh	*oh*	as *o* in g*o.* *Ex.:* **Boot** [*boht*] boat
u	*u*	as *u* in p*u*t or *oo* in b*oo*k. *Ex.:* **Mutter** [*mu'-tər*] mother

| u, uh | oo | as *u* in r*u*le or *oo* in b*oo*t. *Ex.*: **Buch** [*bookh*] book |
| y | *i* or *ü* | usually pronounced as short German *i* (see above) but may also be pronounced as short *ü* (see below). *Ex.*: **Typistin** [*ti-pi'-stin*] or [*tü-pi'-stin*] typist; **Typus** [*tü'-pus*] type |

Umlaut Vowels

Graphically, an umlaut vowel consists of an *a*, *o*, or *u* with two dots over it: *ä*, *ö*, *ü*. The two dots indicate a change in the pronunciation of the vowel, in the following way:

> *ä* is pronounced as *e* (see above)
> *ö* is pronounced as *e* with rounded lips
> *ü* is pronounced as *i* with rounded lips

Umlaut vowels, like plain vowels, may be short or long:

ä	e	as short German *e*. *Ex.*: **Bäcker** [*be'-kər*] baker
ä, äh	eh	as long German *eh*. *Ex.*: **fähig** [*feh'-iç*] able, capable
ö	ö	as short German *e* but with lips rounded, or approximately as *i* in g*i*rl. *Ex.*: **göttlich** [*göt'-liç*] divine
ö, öh	öh	as long German *e* but with lips rounded. *Ex.*: **Höhe** [*höh'-ə*] height
ü	ü	as short German *i* but with lips rounded. *Ex.*: **füllen** [*fü'-lən*] to fill; **Mütter** [*mü'-tər*] mothers
ü, üh	üh	as long German *i* but with lips rounded. *Ex.*: **müde** [*müh'-də*] tired; **rühren** [*rüh'-rən*] to stir

Diphthongs

A diphthong is a compound vowel sound made up of two simple vowels. German diphthongs are always long and are tenser than their English counterparts.

| au | ou | as *ou* in h*ou*se or *ow* in c*ow*, h*ow*. *Ex.*: **Haus** [*hous*] house; **kauft** [*kouft*] buys |

German spelling	Phonetic symbol	Sound description & Examples

ei, ai   *ai*   as *i* in k*i*te or *y* in m*y*. *Ex.*: **rein** [*rain*] pure; **Kaiser** [*kai'-zǝr*] emperor

eu, äu   *oi*   as *oi* in *oi*l or *oy* in b*oy*. *Ex.*: **neun** [*noin*] nine; **Fräulein** [*froi'-lain*] Miss

Consonants

The German consonants *p*, *b*, *t*, *d*, *k*, *g* (hard), *f*, *v*, *s*, *z*, *h*, *m*, *n*, and *x* are pronounced approximately as their English counterparts. However, *b*, *d*, *g* at the end of a word and before another consonant are pronounced as *p*, *t*, *k* respectively. The following consonants have a different pronounciation from the same consonants in English, or do not exist in English at all.

German spelling	Phonetic symbol	Sound description & Examples
ch	*kh*	pronounced as a strongly aspirated *h* in *h*ot, *ch* in Scottish word Lo*ch*, or as in gargling. It occurs after vowels *a*, *o*, *u* and *au*. *Ex.*: **Koch** [*kokh*] cook; **Nacht** [*nakht*] night
ch	*ç*	pronounced as a strongly aspirated *k* as in *c*ue, or close to *h*ue, *h*uman. It occurs at beginning of words before *e*, *i*. It occurs after vowels *i*, *e*, *ä*, *ai*, *äu*, *ei*, but not *a*, *o*, *u;* and after a consonant. *Ex.*: **ich** [*iç*] I; **lächerlich** [*le'-çǝr-liç*] ridiculous; **solcher** [*zol'-çer*] such; **Chemie** [*çe'-mee*] chemistry; **mutig** [*moo'-tiç*] courageous; **siebzig** [*zeep'-tsiç*] seventy
ch	*sh*	as *sh* in *sh*ip in words of French origin *Ex.*: **Chef** [*shef*] chief, master cook
ch	*k*	as *k* in *k*ing, generally in words of Greek origin. *Ex.*: **chronisch** [*kroh'-nish*] chronic
g	*g*	as *g* in *g*old, except at the end of a
g	*k*	word when it becomes *k* and after
g	*ç*	*i* at the end of a word when it be-

		comes *ç*. *Ex*.: **Geld** [*gelt*] money; **Tag** [*tahk*] day; **geizig** [*gai'-tsiç*] stingy
g	zh	as *s* in plea*s*ure before *e* and *i* in words of French origin. *Ex*.: **Genie** [*zhe-nee'*] genius; **girieren** [*zhi-ree'-rən*] endorse
j	y	as *y* in *y*es. *Ex*.: **Jahre** [*yah'-rə*] years
j	zh	as *s* in plea*s*ure in words of French origin. *Ex*.: **Journalist** [*zhur-nah-list'*] reporter
s	z	as *z* in *z*one at the beginning of a word and between and before vowels. *Ex*.: **so** [*zoh*] thus; **Hosen** [*hoh'-zən*] trousers
s, ss, sz, c	s	as *s* in *s*in at the end of a syllable and before a consonant (including itself). *Ex*.: **Haus** [*hous*] house; **Mass** [*mahs*] measure; **kostbar** [*kost'-bar*] precious
v	f	generally as English *f*. *Ex*.: **von** [*fon*] of, by
v	v	as *v* in *v*et between vowels and before vowels in words of foreign origin. *Ex*.: **Novelle** [*no-ve'-lə*] novella; **Vase** [*vah'-zə*] vase
w	v	approximately as English *v*. *Ex*.: **Wasser** [*va'-sər*] water; **Wurst** [*voorst*] sausage
z	ts	Pronounced as *ts* in ca*ts*. *Ex*.: **verzeihen** [*fər-tsai'-ən*] forgive, v.
l	l	always pronounced as the first *l* in *l*ittle but not as the second *l*. *Ex*.: **Liebe** [*lee'-bə*] love
r	r	generally pronounced as an uvular French *r*, but also as a trill *r* vibrating the tip of the tongue. *Ex*.: **rot** [*roht*] red; **braun** [*broun*] brown
h	h	as in *h*ouse. *h* also serves to lengthen a preceding vowel. After a

xi

		consonant, it is not pronounced. *Ex.*: **Haus** [*hous*] house; **nehmen** [*neh'-mən*] take; **Rhein** [*rain*] Rhine
chs	*ks*	as *x* in si*x*. *Ex.*: **sechs** [*zeks*] six
ck	*k*	as *k* in bac*k*. *Ex.*: **Bäcker** [*be'-kər*] baker
dt	*t*	as *t* in *t*ip. *Ex.*: **verwandt** [*fer-vant'*] related
ng	*ng*	as *ng* in ri*ng*. *Ex.*: **Wange** [*vang'-ə*] cheek
pf	*pf*	as *pf* in hel*pf*ul. *Ex.*: **Pferd** [*pfehrt*] horse
ps	*ps*	as *ps* in rha*ps*ody. *Ex.*: **Psalm** [*psalm*] psalm
ph	*f*	as *f* in *f*ee. *Ex.*: **Philosophie** [*fi-lo-zo-fee'*] philosophy
qu	*kv*	as *k* followed by German *w* or English *v*. *Ex.*: **quer** [*kvehr*] across
sch	*sh*	as *sh* in *sh*ip. *Ex.*: **schmutzig** [*shmu'-tsiç*] dirty
tsch	*ch*	as *ch* in *ch*ip. *Ex.*: **Deutschland** [*doich'-lant*] Germany
sp	*shp*	as *sh* in *sh*ip followed by *p* as in *p*it. *Ex.*: **spielen** [*shpee'-lən*] play
st	*sht, st*	as *sh* in *sh*ip followed by *t* as in *t*ip. Or as *st*. *Ex.*: **Stuhl** [*shtool*] chair; **Kost** [*kost*] food, fare
th	*t*	always as *t* in *t*ip, never as English *th*. *Ex.*: **Theorie** [*te-o-ree'*] theory
tz	*ts*	always as *ts* in oa*ts*. *Ex.*: **Hitze** [*hi'-tsə*] heat
tion	*tsi-ohn*	close to the *ts* in oa*ts* followed by *o* as in ow*n*. *Ex.*: **Nation** [*na-tsi-ohn'*] nation

Accent

The main accent of words is indicated in the phonetic transcription by an accent mark (') following the stressed syllable.

xii

Abbreviations Used in This Dictionary

acc.	accusative	*irreg.*	irregular
adj.	adjective	*m.*	masculine
adv.	adverb	*masc.*	masculine
anat.	anatomy	*n.*	noun, neuter
arch.	architecture	*naut.*	nautical
art.	article	*neut.*	neuter
Aux.	auxiliary	*nom.*	nominative
conj.	conjunction	*obj.*	object
dat.	dative	*pers.*	person, personal
dem.	demonstrative	*pl.*	plural
eccl.	ecclesiastic	*prep.*	preposition
f.	feminine	*pron.*	pronoun
fem.	feminine	*rel.*	relative
gen.	genitive	*sing.*	singular
interj.	interjection	*subj.*	subject
interr.	interrogative	*v.*	verb
invar.	invariable		

English/German

A

a, an, ein, eine, ein [*ain, ai'-nə, ain*]
abandon *v.*, auf-geben (irreg) [*ouf'-geh-bən*]
ability, Fähigkeit, -en (f) [*feh'-iç-kait*]
able *adj.*, fähig [*feh'-iç*]
  be able *v.*, können (irreg) [*kö'-nən*]
aboard, an Bord [*an bort*]
  All aboard! Einsteigen! [*ain'-shtai-gən*]
abolish *v.*, auf-heben (irreg) [*ouf'-heh-bən*]
about *prep.*, über (plus dat) [*üh'-bər*]
about *adv.*, ungefähr [*un'-gə-fehr*]
above *prep.*, über (plus dat; plus acc for motion) [*üh'-bər*]
  above all, vor allem [*fohr a'-ləm*]
abroad, im Ausland [*im ous'-lant*]
absence, Abwesenheit (f) [*ap'-veh-zən-hait*]
absent *adj.*, abwesend [*ap'-veh-zənt*]
absent-minded, zerstreut [*tser-shtroit'*]
absolute, absolut [*ap-zo-loot'*]
absolutely, unbedingt [*un'-bə-dingt*]
absorb *v.*, auf-saugen [*ouf'-zou-gən*]
abstract *v.*, abstrahieren [*ap-stra-hee'-rən*]
abstraction, Abstraktion, -en (f) [*ap-strak-tsi-ohn'*]
absurd, absurd [*ap-zurt'*]
abundance, Überfluss (m) [*üh'-bər-flus*]
abuse *v.*, missbrauchen [*mis-brou'-khən*]
academy, Akademie, -n (f) [*a-ka-də-mee'*]
accent *n.*, Akzent, -e (m) [*ak-tsent'*]
accent *v.*, betonen [*bə-toh'-nən*]
accept *v.*, an-nehmen (irreg) [*an'-neh-mən*]
acceptance, Annahme (f) [*an'-nah-mə*]
access, Zugang, ⸗e (m) [*tsoo'-gang, tsoo'-geng-ə*]
accessible, zugänglich [*tsoo'-geng-liç*]
accident, Zufall, ⸗e (m) [*tsoo'-fal, tsoo'-fe-lə*]

1

accidental, zufällig [*tsoo'-fe-liç*]

accommodation, Unterkunft, ⸗e (f) [*un'-tər-kunft, un'-tər-künf-tə*]

accompany *v.*, begleiten [*bə-glai'-tən*]

accomplish *v.*, vollenden [*fo-len'-dən*]

accomplishment, Leistung, -en (f) [*lai'-stung*]

accord *n.*, Übereinstimmung, -en (f) [*üh-bər-ain'-shti-mung*]

according to, gemäss (plus dat) [*gə-mehss'*]

account *n.*, Rechnung, -en (f) [*reç'-nung*]

   pay on account, eine Rechnung bezahlen [*ai'-nə reç'-nung bə-tsah'-lən*]

accuracy, Genauigkeit (f) [*gə-nou'-iç-kait*]

accurate, genau [*gə-nou'*]

accusation, Anklage, -n (f) [*an'-klah-gə*]

accuse *v.*, an-klagen [*an'-klah-gən*]

ache *n.*, Schmerz, -en (m) [*shmerts*]

   headache, Kopfschmerzen (m, pl) [*kopf'-shmert-sən*]

ache *v.*, schmerzen [*shmert'-sən*]

achieve *v.*, erreichen [*er-rai'-çən*]

acid *n.*, Säure, -n (f) [*zoi'-rə*]

acknowledge *v.*, an-erkennen (irreg) [*an'-er-ke-nən*]

acquaint *v.*, bekanntmachen [*bə-kant'-ma-khən*]

acquaintance, Bekanntschaft, -en (f) [*bə-kant'-shaft*]

acquire *v.*, erwerben (irreg) [*er-ver'-bən*]

acquit *v.*, frei-sprechen (irreg) [*frai'-shpre-çən*]

acre, Acker, ⸗ (m) [*a'-kər, e'-kər*]

act [deed] *n.*, Tat, -en (f) [*taht*]

act [of a play] *n.*, Akt, -e (m) [*akt*]

act [do] *v.*, handeln [*han'-dəln*]

act [represent] *v.*, spielen [*shpee'-lən*]

active, aktiv [*ak-teef'*]

activity, Tätigkeit, -en (f) [*teh'-tiç-kait*]

actor, Schauspieler, - (m) [*shou'-shpee-lər*]

actress, Schauspielerin, -nen (f) [*shou'-shpee-lə-rin*]

actual, wirklich [*virk'-liç*]

actually, tatsächlich [*taht'-zeç-liç*]

add *v.*, hinzu-fügen [*hin-tsoo'-füh-gən*]

addition, Zusatz, ⸗e (m) [*tsoo'-zats, tsoo'-zetz-ə*]

additional, zusätzlich [*tsoo'-zets-liç*]

address [place] *n.*, Adresse, -n (f) [*a-dre'-sə*]

address [speech] *n.*, Ansprache, -n (f) [*an'-shprah-khə*]

address [a letter] *v.*, adressieren [*a-dre-see'-rən*]

address [speak] *v.*, an-reden [*an'-reh-dən*]

addressee, Empfänger, - (m) [*em-pfeng'-ər*]

adept, geschickt [*gə-shikt'*]

adequate, angemessen [*an'-gə-me-sən*]

adjacent, anliegend [*an-lee'-gənt*]

adjective, Adjektiv, -e (n) [*at'-yek-teef, at'-yek-tee-və*]

adjust *v.*, sich an-passen (plus dat) [*ziç an'-pa-sən*]

adjustment, Ausgleichung, -en (f) [*ous'-glai-çung*]

administration, Verwaltung, -en (f) [*fer-val'-tung*]

admirable, bewundernswert [*bə-vun'-dərns-vehrt*]

admiration, Bewunderung (f) [*bə-vun'-də-rung*]

admire *v.*, bewundern [*bə-vun'-dərn*]

admission [fee], Eintrittsgeld, -er (n) [*ain'-trits-gelt, ain'-trits-gel-dər*]

admission [concession], Zugeständnis, -se (n) [*tsoo'-gə-shtent-nis*]

admit *v.*, eintreten lassen (irreg) [*ain'-treh-tən la'-sən*]

admittance, Zutritt (m) [*tsoo'-trit*]

  No admittance! Zutritt verboten! [*tsoo'-trit fer-boh'-tən*]

adoption, Annahme, -n (f) [*an'-nah-mə*]

adorn *v.*, schmücken [*shmü'-kən*]

advance *v.*, vor-rücken (*Aux:* SEIN) [*fohr'-rü-kən*]

  in advance, im voraus [*im foh'-rous*]

advancement, Fortschritt, -e (m) [*fort'-shrit*]

advantage, Vorteil, -e (m) [*for'-tail*]

  have the advantage, im Vorteil sein [*im for'-tail zain*]

adventure, Abenteuer, - (n) [*ah'-bən-toi-ər*]

adversary, Gegner, - (m) [*gehg'-nər*]

adverse, widrig [*vid'-riç*]

advertise *v.*, Reklame machen für (plus acc) [*re-klah'-mə ma'-khən führ*]

advertisement, Reklame, -n (f) [*re-klah'-mə*]

advice, Rat (m, sing), Ratschläge (pl) [*raht, raht'-shleh-gə*]

advise *v.*, beraten (irreg) [*bə-rah'-tən*]

affair [love], Liebschaft, -en (f) [*leep'-shaft*]

affair [matter], Angelegenheit, -en (f) [*an'-gə-leh-gən-hait*]

affected, affektiert [*a-fek-teert'*]

affection, Zuneigung, -en (f) [*tsoo'-nai-gung*]

affectionate, liebevoll [*lee'-bə-fol*]

affirm v., bejahen [*bə-yah'-ən*]

affirmative n., Bejahung, -en (f) [*bə-yah'-ung*]

afflict v., plagen [*plah'-gən*]

afford v., sich leisten [*ziç lai'-stən*]

   I can't afford it, Ich kann es mir nicht leisten [*iç kan es
     meer niçt-lai'stən*]

afraid: be afraid of, Angst haben vor (plus dat) [*angst hah'-
   ben fohr*]

Africa, Afrika (n) [*a'-fri-kah*]

after adv., nachher [*nakh-hehr'*]

after prep., nach (plus dat) [*nakh*]

after all, schliesslich [*shlees'-liç*]

afternoon, Nachmittag, -e (m) [*nakh'-mi-tahk, nakh'-mi-
   tah-gə*]

   every afternoon, jeden Nachmittag [*yeh'-dən nakh'-mi-
     tahk*]

afterwards, später [*shpeh'-tər*]

again, wieder [*vee'-dər*]

   again and again, immer wieder [*i'-mer vee'-dər*]

   never again, nie wieder [*nee vee'-dər*]

   once again, noch einmal [*nokh ain'-mahl*]

age [of a person] n., Alter (n) [*al'-tər*]

age v., altern (*Aux:* SEIN) [*al'-tərn*]

agency, Agentur, -en (f) [*a-gen-toor'*]

   travel agency, Reisebüro, -s (n) [*rai'-zə-bü-roh, rai'-zə-
     bü-rohs*]

agent, Agent, -en (m) [*a-gent'*]

aggravate v., ärgern [*er'-gərn*]

aggression, Angriff, -e (m) [*an'-grif*]

ago, vor (plus dat) [*fohr*]

   a year ago, vor einem Jahre [*fohr ai'-nəm yah'-rə*]

   long ago, lange her [*lang'-ə hehr*]

   How long ago? Wie lange ist es her? [*vee lang'-ə ist es* *hehr?*]

agony, Qual, -en (f) [*kvahl*]

agree *v.*, überein-stimmen [*üh-bər-ain'-shti-mən*]

agreement, Übereinstimmung, -en (f) [*üh-bər-ain'-shti-mung*]

agriculture, Landwirtschaft (f) [*lant'-virt-shaft*]

ahead, voraus [*fo-rous'*]

   straight ahead, geradeaus [*gə-rah-də-ous'*]

aid *n.*, Hilfe (f) [*hil'-fə*]

   first aid, erste Hilfe [*ehr'-ste hil'-fə*]

aim *n.*, Ziel, -e (n) [*tseel*]

aim (at) *v.*, zielen auf (plus acc) [*tsee'-lən ouf*]

air, Luft, ⸗e (f) [*luft, lüf'-te*]

air-conditioning, Klimaanlage (f) [*klee'-mah-an-lah-gə*]

airline, Luftlinie, -n (f) [*luft'-lee-ni-ə*]

airmail *n.*, Luftpost (f) [*luft'-post*]

   by airmail, mit Luftpost [*mit luft'-post*]

airplane, Flugzeug, -e (n) [*flook'-tsoik, flook'-tsoi-gə*]

airport, Flughafen, ⸗ (m) [*flook'-hah-fən, flook'-heh-fən*]

alarm *n.*, Alarm, -e (m) [*a-larm'*]

alarm *v.*, beunruhigen [*bə-un'-roo-i-gən*]

alarm clock, Wecker, - (m) [*ve'-kər*]

alcohol, Alkohol, -e (m) [*al'-ko-hol*]

alcoholism, Alkoholismus (m) [*al-ko-ho-lis'-mus*]

alert *adj.*, auf der Hut [*ouf dehr hoot*]

alike *adv.*, gleich [*glaiç*]

alike *adj.*, ähnlich (plus dat) [*ehn'-liç*]

alive, lebendig [*lə-ben'-diç*]

all *adj.*, all [*al*]

all *pron.*, alles, alle [*a'-ləs, a'-lə*]

all *adv.*, ganz [*gants*]

   not at all, gar nicht [*gahr niçt*]

All right! In Ordnung! [*in ord'-nung*]

allied (with) *adj.*, verbunden (mit) [*fer-bun'-dən (mit)*]

Allies, die Alliierten (m, pl) [*dee a-li-eer'-tən*]

allow *v.*, erlauben [*er-lou'-bən*]

allowance [money], Taschengeld (n) [*ta'-shən-gelt*]

almost, fast [*fast*]

alone, allein [*a-lain'*]
along *adv.*, mit [*mit*]
along *prep.*, entlang (plus acc) [*ent-lang'*]
aloud, laut [*lout*]
already, schon [*shohn*]
also, auch [*oukh*]
altar, Altar, =e (m) [*al-tahr', al-teh'rə*]
alter *v.*, ändern [*en'-dərn*]
alter *v.*, sich verändern [*ziç fer-en'-dərn*]
although, obgleich [*op-glaiç'*]
altitude, Höhe, -n (f) [*höh'-ə*]
always, immer [*i'-mər*]
ambition, Ehrgeiz (m) [*ehr'-gaits*]
ambitious, ehrgeizig [*ehr'-gait-siç*]
ambulance, Krankenwagen, - (m) [*kran'-kən-vah-gən*]
America, Amerika (n) [*a-meh-ri-kah'*]
  North America, Nordamerika (n) [*nort'-a-meh-ri-kah*]
  South America, Südamerika (n) [*züht'-a-meh-ri-kah*]
American [female], Amerikanerin, -nen (f) [*a-me-ri-kah'-ne-rin*]
American [male], Amerikaner, - (m) [*a-me-ri-kah'-nər*]
American *adj.*, amerikanisch [*a-me-ri-kah'-nish*]
ammunition, Munition (f) [*mu-ni-tsi-ohn'*]
among, unter (plus dat) [*un'-tər*]
ample, reichlich [*raiç'-liç*]
amuse *v.*, amüsieren [*a-mü-zee'-rən*]
amusement, Unterhaltung, -en (f) [*un-tər-hal'-tung*]
analysis, Analyse, -n (f) [*a-na-lüh'-zə*]
ancestor, Vorfahr, -en (m) [*fohr'-fahr*]
anchor *n.*, Anker, - (m) [*an'-kər*]
ancient, uralt [*oor'-alt*]
and, und [*unt*]
anecdote, Anekdote, -en (f) [*a-nek-doh'-tə*]
angel, Engel, - (m) [*eng'-el*]
anger *n.*, Zorn (m) [*tsorn*]
angry, zornig [*tsor'-niç*]
anguish, Pein (f) [*pain*]
animal, Tier, -e (n) [*teer*]

animate v., beleben [bə-leh'-bən]

anniversary, Jahrestag, -e (m) [yah'-rəs-tahk, yah'-rəs-tah-
gə]

ankle, Fussknöchel, - (m) [fus'-knö-çəl]

announce v., an-kündigen [an'-kün-di-gən]

annoy v., ärgern [er'-gərn]

annoying, ärgerlich [er'-gər-liç]

annual, jährlich [yehr'-liç]

anonymous, anonym [a-no-nühm']

another, ein anderer [ain an'-dər-ər]

answer n., Antwort, -en (f) [ant'-vort]

answer v., antworten (plus dat) [ant'-vor-tən]

ant, Ameise, -n (f) [ah'-mai-zə]

antidote, Gegengift, -e (n) [geh'-gən-gift]

anticipate v., vorweg-nehmen (irreg) [fohr-vek'-neh-mən]

antiquity, Altertum (n) [al'-tər-toom]

anxious, ängstlich [engst'-liç]

any, irgendein, irgendeine [ir'-gənd-ain, ir'-gənd-ai-nə]

    Have you any money? I have no money, Haben Sie Geld?
Ich habe kein Geld [hah'-bən zee gelt? iç hah'-bə kain
gəlt]

anybody, jemand [yeh'-mant]

anyhow, irgendwie [ir'-gənt-vee]

anything, (irgend) etwas [(ir'-gənt) et'-vas]

anyway, ohnehin [oh-nə-hin']

anywhere, irgendwo(hin) [ir-gənt-voh', ir-gənt-voh(hin')]

apart, getrennt [gə-trent']

apartment, Wohnung, -en (f) [voh'-nung]

apology, Entschuldigung, -en (f) [ent-shul'-di-gung]

apparatus, Apparat, -e (m) [a-pa-raht']

apparent, offenbar [o'-fən-bahr]

appeal n., Anziehungskraft (f) [an'-tsee-ungs-kraft]

appeal (to) v., sich wenden (irreg) an (plus acc) [ziç ven'-dən
an]

    This doesn't appeal to me, Dies reizt mich nicht [dees raitst
miç niçt]

appear v., erscheinen (irreg; Aux: SEIN) [er-shai'-nən]

appearance, Erscheinung, -en (f) [er-shai'-nung]

appendicitis, Blinddarmentzündung, -en (f) [*blint'-darm-ent-tsün-dung*]

appetite, Appetit (m) [*a-pe-teet'*]

applause, Beifall (m) [*bai'-fal*]

apple, Apfel, ⸗ (m) [*a'-pfəl, e'-pfəl*]

apple pie, Apfelkuchen, - (m) [*a'-pfəl-ku-khən*]

apple tree, Apfelbaum, ⸗e (m) [*a'-pfəl-boum, a'-pfəl-boi-mə*]

applicant [female], Bittstellerin, -nen (f) [*bit'-shte-lə-rin*]

applicant [male], Bittsteller, - (m) [*bit'-shte-lər*]

application, Bewerbung, -en (f) [*bə-ver'-bung*]

apply (for) *v.*, sich bewerben (um plus acc) (irreg) [*ziç bə-ver'-bən (um)*]

appoint *v.*, ernennen (irreg) [*er-ne'-nən*]

appointment, Ernennung, -en (f) [*er-ne'-nung*]

appreciate *v.*, schätzen [*shet'-sən*]

apprentice, Lehrling, -e (m) [*lehr'-ling*]

approach *v.*, sich nähern [*ziç neh'-ərn*]

appropriate *adj.*, passend (für, plus acc) [*pa'-sənt (führ)*]

appropriate *v.*, sich an-eignen [*ziç an'-aig-nən*]

approval, Billigung, -en [*bi'-li-gung*]

approve *v.*, billigen [*bi'-li-gən*]

approximately, ungefähr [*un'-gə-fehr*]

April, April (m) [*a-pril'*]

apron, Schürze, -n (f) [*shürt'-sə*]

Arab [male], Araber, - (m) [*ah'-ra-bər*]

Arab [female], Araberin, -nen (f) [*ah'-ra-bə-rin*]

Arabic, arabisch [*a-rah'-bish*]

arbitrary, willkürlich [*vil'-kühr-liç*]

arch, Bogen, ⸗ (m) [*boh'-gen, böh'-gen*]

architect, Architekt, -en (m) [*ar-çi-tekt'*]

architecture, Architektur (f) [*ar-çi-tek-toor'*]

are, sind [*zint*]

   you, they are, Sie, sie sind [*zee, zee zint*]

   we are, wir sind [*veer zint*]

area, Gebiet, -e (m) [*gə-beet'*]

Argentine, Argentinien (n) [*ar-gen-tee'-ni-ən*]

arise *v.*, auf-stehen (irreg; *Aux:* SEIN) [*ouf'-shteh-ən*]

aristocrat, Aristokrat, -en (m) [*a-ri-sto-kraht'*]
aristocratic, aristokratisch [*a-ri-sto-krah'-tish*]
arm *m.*, Arm, -e (m) [*arm*]
arm *v.*, bewaffnen [*bə-vaf'-nən*]
army, Armee, -n (f) [*ar-meh'*]
around *prep.*, um (plus acc) [*um*]
 (all) around, rundherum [*runt'-he-rum*]
arrange *v.*, ordnen [*ord'-nən*]
arrangement, Anordnung, -en (f) [*an'-ord-nung*]
arrest *n.*, Verhaftung, -en (f) [*fer-haf'-tung*]
arrest *v.*, verhaften [*fer-haf'-tən*]
arrival, Ankunft (f) [*an'-kunft*]
arrive *v.*, an-kommen (irreg; *Aux:* SEIN) [*an'-ko-mən*]
arrogance, Überheblichkeit (f) [*üh-bər-hehp'-liç-kait*]
art, Kunst, ⸗e (f) [*kunst, kün'-stə*]
artery, Arterie, -n (f) [*ar-teh'-ri-ə*]
article, Artikel, - (m) [*ar-tee'-kəl*]
artificial, künstlich [*künst'-liç*]
artist [female], Künstlerin, -nen (f) [*künst'-lə-rin*]
artist [male], Künstler, - (m) [*künst'-lər*]
artistic, künstlerisch [*künst'-lə-rish*]
as . . . as, so . . . wie [*zo . . . vee*]
as for, was . . . [acc form] . . . betrifft [*vas . . . bə-trift'*]
 Insofar as it concerns me, Soweit es mich betrifft [*zo-vait' es miç bə-trift'*]
as much as, soviel wie [*zo-feel' vee*]
as soon as, sobald [*zo-balt'*]
ascent, Aufstieg, -e (m) [*ouf'-shteek, ouf'-shtee-gə*]
ash, Asche, -n (f) [*a'-shə*]
ashamed, beschämt [*bə-shemt'*]
ashtray, Aschenbecher, - (m) [*a'-shən-be-çər*]
Asia, Asien (n) [*ah'-zi-ən*]
aside, beiseite [*bai-zai'-tə*]
ask *v.*, fragen [*frah'-gən*]
 ask a question, eine Frage stellen [*ai'-nə frah'-gə shte'-lən*]
asleep, schlafend [*shlah'-fənt*]
 fall asleep *v.*, ein-schlafen (irreg; *Aux:* SEIN) [*ain'-shlah-fən*]

aspiration, Bestrebung, -en (f) [*be-shtreh'-bung*]

assault *n.*, Angriff, -e (m) [*an'-grif*]

assemble *v.*, versammeln [*fer-za'-məln*]

assembly, Versammlung, -en (f) [*fer-zam'-lung*]

assignment, Auftrag, ≈e (m) [*ouf'-trahk, ouf'-treh-gə*]

assist *v.*, bei-stehen (irreg) [*bai'-shteh-ən*]

assistance, Beistand, ≈e [*bai'-shtant, bai'-shten-də*]

assistant [female], Assistentin, -nen (f) [*a-sis-ten'-tin*]

assistant [male], Assistent, -en (m) [*a-sis-tent'*]

associate *n.*, Teilhaber, - (m) [*tail'-hah-bər*]

associate (with) *v.*, Umgang haben (mit) [*um'-gang hah'-ben (mit)*]

assortment, Auswahl (f) [*ous'-vahl*]

assume *v.*, an-nehmen (irreg) [*an'-neh-mən*]

assumption, Annahme, -n (f) [*an'-nah-mə*]

assurance, Versicherung, -n (f) [*fer-zi'-çə-rung*]

assure *v.*, versichern [*fer-zi'-çərn*]

astonish *v.*, in Erstaunen setzen [*in er-shtou'-nən zet'-sən*]

astonishing, erstaunlich [*er-shtoun'-liç*]

astronaut, Astronaut, -en (m) [*a-stro-nout'*]

astronomy, Astronomie (f) [*a-stro-no-mee'*]

at *prep.*, in, an, auf, bei, durch, vor, zu, nach, mit, um [*in, an, ouf, bai, durç, fohr, tsu, nahkh, mit, um*]

  at first, zuerst [*tsu-ehrst'*]

  at once, sofort [*zo-fort'*]

athletic, athletisch [*at-leh'-tish*]

athletics, Athletik (f) [*at-leh'-tik*]

atmosphere, Atmosphäre, -n (f) [*at-mo-sfeh'-rə*]

atonement, Sühne (f) [*züh'-nə*]

attack *n.*, Angriff, -e (m) [*an'-grif*]

attack *v.*, an-greifen (irreg) [*an'-grai-fən*]

attain *v.*, erreichen [*er-rai'-çən*]

attempt *v.*, versuchen [*fer-zoo'-khən*]

attend *v.*, bei-wohnen (plus dat) [*bai'-voh-nən*]

attendant, Begleiter, - (m) [*bə-glai'-tər*]

attention, Aufmerksamkeit (f) [*ouf'-merk-sam-kait*]

attentive, aufmerksam [*ouf'-merk-sam*]

attic, Dachstube, -n (f) [*dakh'-shtoo-bə*]
attire, Kleidung (f) [*klai'-dung*]
attitude, Stellung, -en (f) [*shte'-lung*]
attorney [female], Anwältin, -nen (f) [*an'-vel-tin*]
attorney [male], Anwalt, ≈e (m) [*an'-valt, an'-vel-tə*]
attract *v.*, an-ziehen (irreg) [*an'-tsee-ən*]
attraction, Anziehungskraft (f) [*an'-tsee-ungs-kraft*]
attractive, anziehend [*an'-tsee-ənt*]
audience, Publikum (n) [*poo'-bli-kum*]
August, August (m) [*ou-gust'*]
aunt, Tante, -n (f) [*tan'-tə*]
Australia, Australien (m) [*ous-trah'-li-ən*]
Australian, australisch [*ous-trah'-lish*]
Austria, Österreich (n) [*öh'-stə-raiç*]
Austrian [female], Österreicherin, -nen [*öh'-stə-rai-çə-rin*]
Austrian [male], Österreicher, - (m) [*öh'-stə-rai-çər*]
Austrian *adj.*, Österreichisch [*öh'-stə-rai-çish*]
authentic, authentisch [*ou-ten'-tish*]
author [female], Verfasserin, -nen [*fer-fa'-sə-rin*]
author [male], Verfasser, - (m) [*fer-fa'-sər*]
authority, Autorität, -en [*ou-to-ri-teht'*]
automatic, automatisch [*ou-to-mah'-tish*]
automobile, Auto, -s (n) [*ou'-toh, ou-tohs*]
autumn, Herbst, -e (m) [*herpst*]
available, verfügbar [*fer-fühk'-bahr*]
avenge *v.*, rächen [*re'-çən*]
avenue, Allee, -n (f) [*a-leh'*]
average *n.*, Durchschnitt, -e (m) [*durkh'-shnit*]
  on the average, im Durchschnitt, [*im durkh'-shnit*]
avoid *v.*, vermeiden (irreg) [*fer-mai'-dən*]
awaken *v.*, wecken [*ve'-kən*]
award *v.*, gewähren [*gə-veh'-rən*]
(be) aware, wissen (von) (irreg) [*vi'-sən (fon)*]
away, fort [*fort*]
awful, furchtbar [*furkht'-bahr*]
awkward, ungeschickt [*un'-gə-shikt*]
axe, Axt, ≈e (f) [*akst, ek'-stə*]
axle, Achse, -n (f) [*ak'-sə*]

B

baby, Baby, Babies (n) [*beh'-bi, beh'-bis*]
back *n.*, Rücken, - (m) [*rü'-kən*]
  behind his back, heimlich [*haim'-liç*]
  on her back, auf dem Rücken [*ouf dehm rü'-kən*]
back *adj.*, Hinter (prefix) [*hin'-tər*]
back *adv.*, zurück [*tsu-rük'*]
back out of *v.*, zurück-treten von (irreg; *Aux:* SEIN) [*tsu-rük'-treh-tən fon*]
back room, Hinterstube, -n (f) [*hin'-tər-shtoo-bə*]
backward, rückständig [*rük'-shten-diç*]
bacon, Speck (m) [*shpek*]
bad, schlecht [*shleçt*]
  in a bad temper, schlechtgelaunt [*shleçt'-gə-lount*]
badge, Abzeichen, - (n) [*ap'-tsai-çən*]
baggage, Gepäck (n) [*gə-pek'*]
bait, Köder (m) [*köh'-dər*]
bake *v.*, backen [*ba'-kən*]
bakery, Bäckerei, -en (f) [*be-kə-rai'*]
balance *n.*, Bilanz, -en (f) [*bi-lants'*]
balance *v.*, wägen [*veh'-gən*]
balcony, Balkon, -e (m) [*bal-kon'*]
bald, kahl [*kahl*]
ball, Ball, ⸗e [*bal, be'-lə*]
ballet, Ballett, -e (n) [*ba-let'*]
band, Band, ⸗er [*bant, ben'-der*]
bandage *n.*, Binde, -n (f) [*bin'-də*]
bandage *v.*, verbinden (irreg) [*fer-bin'-dən*]
bank *n.*, Bank, -en (f) [*bank*]
bank [money] *v.*, (Geld) auf die Bank legen [*(gelt) ouf dee bank leh'-gən*]
bank account, Bankkonto, Bankkonten (n) [*bank'-kon-toh, bank'-kon-tən*]

banknote, Banknote, -n (f) [*bank'-no-tə*]
baptism, Taufe, -n (f) [*tou'-fə*]
bar *n.*, Bar, -s (f) [*bahr, bahrs*]
bar *v.*, sperren [*shpe'-rən*]
barber, Friseur, -e (m) [*fri-zöhr'*]
bare, nackt [*nakt*]
barefoot, barfuss [*bahr'-foos*]
bareheaded, barhäuptig [*bahr'-hoip-tiç*]
bargain *n.*, Geschäft, -e (n) [*ge-sheft'*]
bargain *v.*, handeln [*han'-dəln*]
barn, Scheune, -n (f) [*shoi'-nə*]
baron, Baron, -e (m) [*ba-rohn'*]
barrel, Fass, ⸗er (n) [*fas, fe'-sər*]
barricade, Barrikade, -n (f) [*ba-ri-kah'-də*]
base, Basis, Basen (f) [*bah'-zis, bah'-zən*]
basement, Kellergeschoss, -e (n) [*ke'-lər-gə-shos*]
basic, grundlegend [*grunt'-leh-gənt*]
basin, Becken, - (n) [*be'-kən*]
basket, Korb, ⸗e (m) [*korp, kör'-bə*]
bath, Bad, ⸗er (n) [*baht, beh'-dər*]
   take a bath, ein Bad nehmen (irreg) [*ain baht neh'-mən*]
bathe *v.*, baden [*bah'-dən*]
bathroom, Badezimer, - (n) [*bah'-də-tsi-mər*]
bathtub, Badewanne, -n (f) [*bah'-də-va-nə*]
bathing suit, Badeanzug, ⸗e (m) [*bah'-də-an-tsook, bah'-də-an-tsüh-gə*]
battle, Schlacht, -en (f) [*shlakht*]
be *v.*, sein (irreg; *Aux:* SEIN) [*zain*]
bead, Perle, -n (f) [*per'-lə*]
beach, Strand, ⸗e (m) [*shtrant, shtren'-də*]
bear [carry] *v.*, tragen (irreg) [*trah'-gən*]
bear [give birth] *v.*, gebären (irreg; *Aux:* SEIN) [*gə-beh'-rən*]
beard, Bart, ⸗e (m) [*bahrt, behr'-tə*]
beardless, bartlos [*bahrt'-lohs*]
beast, Vieh (n) [*fee*]
beat [pulse], Pulsschlag, ⸗e (m) [*puls'-shlahk, puls'-shleh-gə*]
beat [hit, win] *v.*, schlagen (irreg) [*shlah'-gən*]
   Beat it! [slang], Hau ab! [*hou ap*]

beautiful, schön [*shöhn*]
beauty, Schönheit, -en (f) [*shöhn'-hait*]
beauty parlor, Damensalon, -s (m) [*dah'-mən-sa-lon*]
because, weil [*vail*]
because of, wegen (plus gen) [*veh'-gən*]
become *v.*, werden (irreg; *Aux:* SEIN) [*vehr'-dən*]
bed, Bett, -en (n) [*bet*]
bedroom, Schlafzimmer, - (n) [*shlaf'-tsi-mər*]
bee, Biene, -n (f) [*bee'-nə*]
beef, Rindfleisch (n) [*rint'-flaish*]
beefsteak, Beefsteak, -s (n) [*beef-stehk, beef'-stehks*]
beer, Bier, -e (n) [*beer*]
before *adv.*, vorher [*fohr'-her*]
before *prep.*, vor (plus dat; plus acc for motion) [*fohr*]
beforehand, vorher [*fohr'-her*]
beg *v.*, betteln; an-flehen [*bet'-əln; an'-fleh-ən*]
begin *v.*, beginnen (irreg); an-fangen (irreg) [*bə-gi'-nən, an'-fan-gən*]
    Begin again! Fangen Sie wieder an! [*fan'-gən zee vee'-dər an*]
beginning *n.*, Anfang, ⸗e (m) [*an'-fang, an'-fen-gə*]
behave *v.*, sich benehmen (irreg) [*ziç bə-neh'-mən*]
behavior, Benehmen (n) [*bə-neh'-mən*]
behind *adv.*, hinten [*hin'-tən*]
behind *prep.*, hinter (plus dat; plus acc for motion) [*hin'-tər*]
being *n.*, Sein (n); Wesen, - (n) [*zain; veh'-zən*]
Belgian, belgisch [*bel'-gish*]
Belgium, Belgien (n) [*bel'-gi-ən*]
belief, Glaube (m) [*glou'-bə*]
bell, Glocke, -n (f) [*glo'-kə*]
bellboy, Hotelpage, -n (m) [*ho-tel'-pah-zhə*]
belong (to) *v.*, gehören (plus dat) [*gə-höh'-rən*]
below *adv.*, unten [*un'-tən*]
below *prep.*, unter (plus dat; plus acc for motion) [*un'-tər*]
belt, Gürtel, - (m) [*gür'-təl*]
bend *v.*, (sich) biegen (irreg) [*(ziç) bee'-gən*]
beneath, unter [*un'-tər*]

beside, neben (plus dat; plus acc for motion) [*neh'-bən*]
   beside the point, nicht zur Sache gehörig [*niçt tsur za'-khə gə-höh'-riç*]
besides, ausserdem [*ou'-ser-dehm*]
best, best- [*best-*]
bet *n.,* Wette, -n (f) [*ve'-tə*]
bet *v.,* wetten [*ve'-tən*]
better, besser [*be'-sər*]
   She is better, Es geht ihr besser [*es geht eer be'-sər*]
beware (of) *v.,* sich hüten (vor, plus dat) [*ziç hüh'-tən (fohr)*]
between, zwischen (plus dat; plus acc for motion) [*tsvi'-shən*]
beyond, jenseits (plus gen) [*yehn'-zaits*]
Bible, Bibel, -n (f) [*bee'-bəl*]
bicycle *n.,* Fahrrad, ̈er (n) [*fahr'-raht, fahr'-reh-dər*]
bicycle *v.,* rad-fahren (irreg; *Aux:* SEIN) [*raht'-fah-rən*]
bid, Angebot, -e (n) [*an'-gə-boht*]
bill, Rechnung, -en (f) [*reç'-nung*]
   pay the bill *v.,* die Rechnung bezahlen [*dee reç'-nung bə-tsah'-lən*]
bill of fare, Speise karte, -n (f) [*shpai'-zə-kar-tə*]
bird, Vogel, ̈ (m) [*foh'-gəl, föh'-gəl*]
birth, Geburt, -en (f) [*gə-boort'*]
birthday, Geburtstag, -e (m) [*gə-boorts'-tahk, gə-boorts'-tah-gə*]
   Happy Birthday!, Herzlichen Glückwunsch zum Geburtstag! [*herts'-li-çən glük'-vunsh tsum gə-boorts'-tahk*]
biscuit, Zwieback (m) [*tsvee'-bak*]
bishop, Bischof, ̈e (m) [*bi'-shohf, bi'-shöh-fə*]
bite *v.,* beissen (irreg) [*bai'-sən*]
bitter, bitter [*bi'-tər*]
black, schwarz [*shvarts*]
blame *n.,* Schuld (f) [*shult*]
blame *v.,* tadeln [*tah'-dəln*]
blank *adj.,* blank; leer [*blank; lehr*]
blanket, Decke, -n (f) [*de'-kə*]
bleed *v.,* bluten [*bloo'-tən*]

bless v., segnen [*zehg'-nən*]

blessing, Segen, - (m) [*zeh'-gən*]

blind adj., blind [*blint*]

blindness, Blindheit (f) [*blint'-hait*]

blister, Blase, -n (f) [*blah'-zə*]

blonde, blond [*blont*]

blood, Blut (n) [*bloot*]

blossom n., Blüte, -n (f) [*blüh'-tə*]

blossom v., blühen (*blüh'-ən*]

blouse, Bluse, -n (f) [*bloo'-zə*]

blow n., Schlag, ⸗e (m) [*shlahk, shleh'-gə*]

blow v., blasen (irreg); wehen [*blah'-zən; veh'-ən*]

blue, blau [*blou*]

board n., Brett, -er (n) [*bret, bre'-tər*]

board v., ein-steigen in (plus acc) (irreg; *Aux:* SEIN) [*ain'-shtai-gən in*]

boarding house, Pension, -en (f) [*pen-zi-ohn'*]

boat, Boot, -e (n); Schiff, -e (n) [*boht; shif*]

body, Körper, - (m) [*kör'-pər*]

boil v., sieden; kochen [*zee'-dən; ko'-khən*]

bold, kühn [*kühn*]

bond, Band, -e (n) [*bant, ban'-de*]

bone, Knochen, - (m) [*kno'-khən*]

book, Buch, ⸗er [*bookh, büh'-çər*]

bookcase, Bücherschrank, ⸗e (m) [*büh'-çər-shrank, büh'-çər-shren-kə*]

bookstore, Buchhandlung, -en (f) [*bookh'-hand-lung*]

boot, Stiefel, - (m) [*shtee'-fəl*]

border, Grenze, -n (f); Rand, ⸗er (m) [*gren'-tsə; rant, ren'-dər*]

bore v., langweilen [*lang'-vai-lən*]

  be bored stiff, sich tödlich langweilen [*ziç töt'-liç lang'-vai-lən*]

bore [person], ein langweiliger Mensch [*ain lang'-vai-li-gər mensh*]

boring, langweilig [*lang'-vai-liç*]

borrow v., borgen [*bor'-gən*]

boss, Boss, -e (m) [*bos*]

both, beide [*bai'-də*]
bother *n.*, Plage, -n (f) [*plah'-gə*]
   Don't bother!, Bemühen Sie sich nicht! [*bə-müh'-ən zee ziç niçt*]
   Don't bother me!, Stören Sie mich nicht! [*shtöh'-rən zee miç niçt*]
bottle, Flasche, -n (f) [*fla'-shə*]
bottle-opener, Flaschenöffner, - (m) [*fla'-shən-öf-nər*]
bottom, Boden ⁼ (m) [*boh'-dən, böh'-dən*]
boundary, Grenze, -n (f) [*gren'-tsə*]
bow, Bogen, ⁼ (m) [*boh'-gən, böh'-gən*]
box [container] *n.*, Schachtel, -n (f) [*shakh'-təl*]
boxing [sport], Boxen (n) [*bok'-sən*]
box office, Theaterkasse, -n (f) [*te-ah'-tər-ka-sə*]
boy, Junge, -n [*yung'-ə*]
boyfriend, Freund, -e (m) [*froint, froin'-də*]
bracelet, Armband, ⁼er (n) [*arm'-bant, arm'-ben-dər*]
brag *v.*, prahlen [*prah'-lən*]
braggart, Prahler, - (m) [*prah'-lər*]
brain, Gehirn, -e (n) [*gə-hirn'*]
brake *n.*, Bremse, -n (f) [*brem'-zə*]
brake *v.*, bremsen [*brem'-zən*]
branch, Zweig, -e (m) [*tsvaik, tsvai'-gə*]
brand, Marke, -n (f) [*mar'-kə*]
brand-new, nagelneu [*nah'-gəl-noi*]
brandy, Kognak, -s (m) [*kon'-yak, kon'-yaks*]
brass, Messing (n) [*me'-sing*]
brassiere, Büstenhalter, - (m) [*bü'-stən-hal-tər*]
brave, tapfer [*ta'-pfər*]
bravery, Tapferkeit (f) [*ta'-pfər-kait*]
Brazil, Brasilien (n) [*bra-zee'-li-ən*]
Brazilian, brasilisch [*bra-zee'-lish*]
bread, Brot, -e (n) [*broht*]
break *v.*, brechen (irreg; *Aux:* HABEN or SEIN) [*bre'-çən*]
breakfast, Frühstück, -e (n) [*früh'-shtük*]
breast, Brust, ⁼e (f) [*brust, brü'-stə*]
breath, Atemzug, ⁼e (m) [*ah'-təm-tsook, ah'-təm-tsüh-gə*]
breathe *v.*, atmen [*aht'-mən*]

breeze, Brise, -n (f) [*bree'-zə*]
bribe *v.,* bestechen (irreg) [*bə-shte'-çən*]
bribe *n.,* Bestechungsgeld, -er (n) [*bə-shte'-çungz-gelt,
    bə-shte'-çungz-gel-dər*]
brick, Ziegel, - (m) [*tsee'-gəl*]
bride, Braut, ‡e (f) [*brout, broi'-tə*]
bridegroom, Bräutigam, -e (m) [*broi'-ti-gam*]
bridesmaid, Brautjungfer, -n (f) [*brout'-yung-fər*]
bridge *n.,* Brücke, -n (f) [*brü'-kə*]
bridge *v.,* überbrücken [*üh-bər-brü'-kən*]
brief, kurz [*kurts*]
bright, hell; begabt [*hel; bə-gahpt'*]
brilliant, glänzend [*glent'-sənt*]
bring *v.,* bringen (irreg) [*bring'-ən*]
  bring in, herein-bringen (irreg) [*he-rain'-bring-ən*]
  bring together, zusammen-bringen (irreg) [*tsu-za'-mən-
    bring-ən*]
  bring up [a topic], auf-bringen (irreg) [*ouf'-bring-ən*]
  bring up [rear], erziehen (irreg) [*er-tsee'-ən*]
brisk, lebhaft [*lehp'-haft*]
Britain, Britannien (n) [*bri-ta'-ni-ən*]
British, britisch [*bri'-tish*]
broad, breit; weit [*brait; vait*]
broadcast, Rundfunksendung, -en (f) [*runt'-funk-zen-dung*]
broil *v.,* auf dem Rost braten [*ouf dem rost brah'-tən*]
bronze, Bronze (f) [*bron'-tsə*]
brook, Bach, ‡e (m) [*bakh, be'-çə*]
broom, Besen, - (m) [*beh'-zən*]
broth, Fleischbrühe (f) [*flaish'-brüh-ə*]
brother, Bruder, ‡ (m) [*broo'-dər, brüh'-dər*]
brother-in-law, Schwager, ‡ (m) [*shvah'-gər, shveh'-gər*]
brow, Stirn, -en (f); Augenbraue, -n (f) [*shtirn; ou'-gən-
    brou-ə*]
brown, braun [*broun*]
bruise, Quetschung, -en (f) [*kvet'-shung*]
brunette, Brünette, -n (f) [*brü-ne'-tə*]
brush *n.,* Bürste, -n (f) [*bür'-stə*]
bucket, Eimer, - (m) [*ai'-mər*]

buckle *n.*, Schnalle, -n (f) [*shna'-lə*]
budget *n.*, Haushaltsplan, ̈e (m) [*hous'-halts-plahn, hous'-halts-pleh-nə*]
build *v.*, bauen [*bou'-ən*]
bulb [light], Glühbirne, -n (f) [*glüh'-bir-nə*]
bulb [plant], Knolle, -n (f) [*kno'-lə*]
Bulgaria, Bulgarien (n) [*bul-gah'-ri-ən*]
Bulgarian, bulgarisch [*bul-gah'-rish*]
bulky, unhandlich [*un'-hant-liç*]
bull, Stier, -e (m) [*shteer*]
bullfight, Stierkampf, ̈e (m) [*shteer'-kampf, shteer'-kem-pfə*]
bundle, Bündel, - (n) [*bün'-dəl*]
burden *n.*, Last, -en (f) [*last*]
burden *v.*, belasten [*bə-la'-stən*]
burglar, Einbrecher, - (m) [*ain'-bre-çər*]
burial, Begräbnis, -se (n) [*bə-grehp'-nis*]
burn *v.*, brennen (irreg) [*bre'-nən*]
burn *n.*, Brandwunde, -n (f) [*brant'-vun-də*]
burst *v.*, bersten (irreg; *Aux:* SEIN); platzen (*Aux:* SEIN) [*ber'-stən; plat'-sən*]
bury *v.*, begraben (irreg) [*bə-grah'-bən*]
bus, Autobus, -se (m); Bus, -se (m) [*ou'-to-bus; bus*]
bush, Gebüsch, -e (n) [*gə-büsh*]
business, Geschäft, -e (n) [*gə-sheft'*]
businessman, Geschäftsmann (m, sing), Geschäftsleute (pl) [*gə-shefts'-man, gə-shefts'-loi-tə*]
busy, beschäftigt [*bə-shef'-tiçt*]
but, aber; sondern [*ah'-bər; zon'-dərn*]
butcher, Metzger, - (m); Fleischer, - (m); Schlächter, - (m) [*mets'-gər; flai'-shər; shleç'-tər*]
butcher shop, Metzgerei, -en (f) [*mets-gə-rai'*]
butter, Butter (f) [*bu'-tər*]
buy *v.*, kaufen [*kou'-fən*]
by, bei; an; neben; durch; über; von [*bai; an; neh'-bən; durç; üh'-bər; fon*]
  by and by, bald [*balt*]
  by airplane, mit dem Flugzeug [*mit dem flook'-tsoik*]
  by car, mit dem Auto [*mit dem ou'-toh*]

by chance, zufällig [*tsoo'-fe-liç*]
by experience, aus Erfahrung [*ous er-fah'-rung*]

C

cab, Taxi, -s (n) [*tak'-see, tak'-sees*]
cabbage, Kohl (m) [*kohl*]
cabin, Hütte, -n (f) [*hü'-tə*]
cable n., Kabel, - (n) [*kah'-bəl*]
cable v., telegraphieren [*te-le-gra-fee'-rən*]
cafe, Café, -s (n); Kaffeehaus, ¨er [*ka-feh', ka-fehs'; ka'-feh-hous, ka'-feh-hoi-zər*]
cage, Käfig, -e (m) [*keh'-fiç, keh'-fi-gə*]
cake, Kuchen, - (m) [*ku'-khən*]
calendar, Kalender, - (m) [*ka-len'-dər*]
call v., rufen (irreg); an-rufen (irreg) [*roo'-fən; an'-roo-fən*]
  call forth, hervor-rufen (irreg) [*her-fohr'-roo-fən*]
  call in, herein-rufen (irreg) [*he-rain'-roo-fən*]
  call off, ab-rufen (irreg) [*ap'-roo-fən*]
  call out, aus-rufen (irreg) [*ous'-roo-fən*]
  call together, zusammen-rufen (irreg) [*tsu-za'-mən-roo-fən*]
  call up, auf-rufen (irreg); an-rufen (irreg) [*ouf'-roo-fən; an'-roo-fən*]
call n., Ruf, -e (m) [*roof*]
  telephone call, Anruf, -e (m) [*an'-roof*]
calm, gelassen; ruhig [*gə-la'-sən; roo'-iç*]
camera, Kamera, -s (f) [*ka'-mə-ra, ka'-mə-ras*]
camp, Lager, - (n) [*lah'-gər*]
can n., Büchse, -n (f); Dose, -n (f) [*bük'-sə; doh'-zə*]
can opener, Dosenöffner, - (m) [*doh'-zen-öf-nər*]
can, können; dürfen [*köhn'-nən, dühr'-fən*]
  I can come, Ich kann kommen [*iç kan ko'-mən*]
Canada, Kanada (n) [*ka'-na-da*]
Canadian, kanadisch [*ka-nah'-dish*]

canal, Kanal, ⸗e (m) [*ka-nahl', ka-neh'-lə*]

cancel *v.*, ab-sagen [*ap'-zah-gən*]

candle, Kerze, -n (f) [*ker'-tsə*]

candlestick, Leuchter, - (m) [*loiç'-tər*]

candy, Süsswaren (f, pl) [*zühs'-vah-rən*]

candy store, Süsswarenladen, ⸗ (m) [*zühs'-vah-rən-lah-dən, zühs'-vah-rən-leh-dən*]

cane, Stock, ⸗e (m) [*shtok, shtö'-kə*]

cap, Mütze, -n (f) [*mü'-tsə*]

capable, fähig [*feh'-iç*]

capacity, Fähigkeit, -en (f) [*feh'-iç-kait*]

cape, Cape, -s (n) [*kehp, kehps*]

capital [money], Kapital, -ien (n) [*ka-pi-tahl', ka-pi-tah'-li-ən*]

capitalism, Kapitalismus (m) [*ka-pi-ta-lis'-mus*]

captain, Kapitän, -e (m) [*ka-pi-tehn'*]

car, Auto, -s (n); Wagen, - (m) [*ou'-toh, ou'-tohs; vah-gən*]
    streetcar, Strassenbahn, -en (f) [*shtrah'-sən-bahn*]

card, Karte, -n (f) [*kar'-tə*]
    calling card, Visitenkarte, -n (f) [*vi-zee'-tən-kar-tə*]
    Christmas card, Weihnachtskarte, -n (f) [*vai'-nakhts-kar-tə*]
    playing cards, Spielkarten (f, pl) [*shpeel'-kar-tən*]

cardboard, Karton, -s (m) [*kar-tohn', kar-tohns'*]

care (for) *v.*, sorgen (für, plus acc) [*zor'-gən (für)*]

career, Karriere, -n (f) [*kar-yeh'-rə*]

careful, vorsichtig [*fohr'-siç-tiç*]
    Be careful! Seien Sie vorsichtig! [*zai'-ən zee fohr'-ziç-tiç*]

careless, sorglos [*zorg'-lohs*]

cares, Sorgen (f, pl) [*zor'-gən*]

cargo, Ladung, -en (f) [*lah'-dung*]

carnival, Karneval, -e (m) [*kar'-ne-val*]

carpenter, Zimmermann (m, sing), Zimmerleute (pl) [*tsi'-mər-man, tsi'-mər-loi-tə*]

carpet, Teppich, -e (m) [*te'-piç*]

carry *v.*, tragen (irreg); bringen (irreg) [*trah'-gən; bring'-ən*]
    carry out, durch-setzen [*durç'-zet-sən*]
    carry through, durch-führen [*durç'-füh-rən*]

carve v., schnitzen [*shnit'-sən*]

carving, Schnitzerei, -en (f) [*shnit-sə-rai'*]

case [circumstance], Fall, ⸗e (m) [*fal, fe'-lə*]

   in any case, auf jeden Fall [*ouf yeh'-dən fal*]

   in case, im Falle [*im fa'-lə*]

cash [ready], Bargeld, -er (n) [*bahr'-gelt, bahr'-gel-dər*]

cash v., ein-wechseln [*ain'-vek-səln*]

cashier, Kassierer, - (m) [*ka-see'-rər*]

castle, Schloss, ⸗er (n) [*shlos, shlö'-sər*]

cat, Katze, -n (f) [*ka'-tsə*]

catalogue, Katalog, -e (m) [*ka-ta-lohk', ka-ta-loh'-gə*]

catch v., fangen (irreg) [*fang'-ən*]

   catch up with [overtake], ein-holen [*ain'-hoh-lən*]

cathedral, Kathedrale, -n (f); Dom, -e (m) [*ka-te-drah'-lə; dohm*]

Catholic, katholisch [*ka-toh'-lish*]

cause n., Ursache, -n (f) [*oor'-za-khə*]

cause v., verursachen [*fer-oor'-za-khən*]

caution n., Vorsicht (f) [*fohr'-ziçt*]

cave, Höhle, -n (f) [*höh'-lə*]

cease (from) v., auf-hören (mit) [*ouf'-höh-rən (mit)*]

ceiling, Decke, -n (f) [*de'-kə*]

celebrate v., feiern [*fai'-ərn*]

celebration, Feier, -n (f); Fest, -e (n) [*fai'-ər; fest*]

cell, Zelle, -n (f) [*tse'-lə*]

cellar, Keller, - (m) [*ke'-lər*]

   salt cellar, Salzfass, ⸗er (n) [*zalts'-fas, zalts'-fe-sər*]

cement, Zement (m) [*tse-ment'*]

cemetery, Friedhof, ⸗e (m) [*freed'-hohf, freed'-höh-fə*]

censorship, Zensur (f) [*tsen-zoor'*]

center, Mittelpunkt, -e (m) [*mi'-təl-punkt*]

century, Jahrhundert, -e (n) [*yahr-hun'-dərt*]

ceremony, Zeremonie, -n (f) [*tse-re-mo-nee'*]

certain, sicher; gewiss [*zi'-çər; gə-vis'*]

certainly, gewiss [*gə-vis'*]

certificate, Bescheinigung, -en (f) [*bə-shai'-ni-gung*]

chain, Kette, -n (f) [*ke'-tə*]

chair, Stuhl, ⸗e (m) [*shtool, shtüh'-lə*]

challenge v., heraus-fordern [he-rous'-for-dərn]
chambermaid, Stubenmädchen, - (n) [shtoo'-bən-meht-çən]
champagne, Champagner (m) [sham-pan'-yər]
champion, Vorkämpfer, - (m) [fohr'-kem-pfər]
chance, Zufall, ⸗e (m) [tsoo'-fal, tsoo'-fe-lə]
  by chance, durch Zufall [durç tsoo'-fal]
  take a chance v., es darauf ankommen lassen (irreg)
    [es da-rouf' an'-ko-mən la'-sən]
change, Veränderung, -en (f) [fer-en'-də-rung]
character, Charakter, -e (m) [ka-rak'-tər, ka-rak-teh'-rə]
characteristic n., Kennzeichen, - (n) [ken'-tsai-çən]
charm n., Zauber, - (m); Reiz, -e (m) [tsou'-bər; raits]
charming, reizend [rait'-sənt]
chart, Tabelle, -n (f) [ta-be'-lə]
charter [a ship] v., chartern [tshar'-tərn]
chase v., jagen [yah'-gən]
chat n., Geplauder (n) [gə-plou'-dər]
chat v., plaudern [plou'-dərn]
chauffeur, Chauffeur, -e (m) [shoh-föhr']
cheap, billig [bi'-liç]
cheat v., betrügen (irreg) [bə-trüh'-gən]
check v., hemmen [he'-mən]
check [money], Scheck, -s (m) [shek, sheks]
  baggage check, Gepäckschein, -e (m) [gə-pek'-shain]
  bank check, Bankanweisung, -en (f) [bank'-an-vai-zung]
checking account, Bankkonto, Bankkontos [bank'-kon-toh,
  bank'-kon-tohs]
cheek, Backe, -n (f) [ba'-kə]
cheer [of applause] n., Beifallsruf, -e (m) [bai'-fals-roof]
cheer v., Beifall spenden; zujubeln [bai'-fal shpen'-dən;
  tsoo'-yoo-bəln]
cheerful, heiter [hai'-tər]
cheese, Käse (m) [keh'-zə]
chest [anat.], Brust, ⸗e (f); Brustkasten (m, pl) [brust, brü'-stə;
  brust'-ka-stən]
chest of drawers, Kommode, -n (f) [ko-moh'-də]
chew v., kauen [kou'-ən]
chicken, Huhn, ⸗er (n) [hoon, hüh'-nər]

chief *n.*, Haupt, ⸗er (n) [*houpt, hoip'-tər*]
child, Kind, -er (n) [*kint, kin'-dər*]
childbirth, Niederkunft (f) [*nee'-dər-kunft*]
childhood, Kindheit (f) [*kint'-hait*]
Chile, Chile (n) [*çi'-leh*]
Chilean, chilenisch [*çi-leh'-nish*]
chilly, kühl [*kühl*]
chimney, Schornstein, -e (m) [*shorn'-shtain*]
chin, Kinn, -e (n) [*kin*]
China, China (n) [*çee'-nah*]
chinaware, Porzellan (n) [*port-se-lahn'*]
Chinese *adj.*, chinesisch [*çi-neh'-zish*]
chocolate, Schokolade (f) [*sho-ko-lah'-də*]
choice, Wahl, -en (f) [*vahl*]
choose *v.*, wählen [*veh'-lən*]
Christian *adj.*, christlich [*krist'-liç*]
Christian name, Taufname, -n (m); Vorname, -n (m) [*touf'-nah-mə; fohr'-nah-mə*]
Christmas, Weihnacht (f); Weihnachten (pl) [*vai'-nakht*]
 Merry Christmas! Fröhliche Weihnachten! [*fröh'-li-çə vai'-nakh-tən*]
church, Kirche, -n (f) [*kir'-çə*]
cider, Apfelwein, -e [*a'-pfəl-vain*]
cigar, Zigarre, -n (f) [*tsi-ga'-rə*]
cigarette, Zigarette, -n (f) [*tsi-ga-re'-tə*]
circle, *n.*, Kreis, -e (m) [*krais, krai'-zə*]
circle *v.*, um-kreisen [*um-krai'-zən*]
circulation, Umlauf, ⸗e (m); Kreislauf (m) [*um'-louf, um'-loi-fə; krais'-louf*]
circumstance, Umstand, ⸗e (m) [*um'-shtant; um'-shten-də*]
circus, Zirkus, -se (m) [*tsir'-kus*]
citizen [female], Staatsbürgerin, -nen (f) [*shtahts'-bür-gə-rin*]
citizen [male], Staatsbürger, - (m) [*shtahts'-bür-gər*]
citizenship, Staatsangehörigkeit (f) [*shtahts'-an-gə-höh-riç-kait*]
city, Stadt, ⸗e [*shtat, shte'-tə*]
city hall, Rathaus, ⸗er (n) [*raht'-hous, raht'-hoi-zər*]
civilization, Zivilisation, -en (f); Kultur, -en (f) [*tsi-vi-li-za-*

tsi-ohn'; kul-toor']

claim v., fordern; behaupten [*for'-dərn*; *bə-houp'-tən*]

claim n., Anspruch, ⸗e (m) [*an'-shprukh, an'-shprü-çə*]

class, Klasse, -n (f) [*kla'-sə*]

classmate, Mitschüler, - (m) [*mit'-shüh-lər*]

classroom, Klassenzimmer, - (n) [*kla'-sən-tsi-mər*]

classic, klassisch [*kla'-sish*]

clean v., reinigen; säubern [*rai'-ni-gən; zoi'-bərn*]

clean adj., rein; sauber [*rain; zou'-bər*]

cleaner's shop, Reinigungsanstalt, -en (f) [*rai'-ni-gungs-an-shtalt*]

cleaning, Reinigung, -en (f) [*rai'-ni-gung*]

cleaning woman, Aufwartefrau, -en (f) [*ouf'-var-tə-frou*]

clear adj., hell; klar [*hel; klahr*]

clearance, Freilegung (f)[*frai'-leh-gung*]

clergy, Geistlichkeit (f) [*gaist'-liç-kait*]

clerk, Büroangestellte, -n (m, f) [*bü-roh'-an-gə-shtel-tə*]

clever, klug [*klook*]

client [female], Klientin, -nen (f) [*kli-en'-tin*]

client [male], Klient, -en (m) [*kli-ent'*]

climate, Klima (n) [*klee'-mah*]

climb v., hinauf-steigen auf (plus acc) (irreg; *Aux:* SEIN) [*hin-ouf'-shtai-gən ouf*]

clock, Uhr, -en (f) [*uhr*]
   It's ten o'clock, Es ist zehn Uhr [*es ist tsehn uhr*]

close [exact], genau [*gə-nou'*]

closet, Wandschrank, ⸗e (m) [*vant'-shrank, vant'-shren-kə*]

clothes, Kleider (n, pl); Kleidung (f) [*klai'-dər; klai'-dung*]

cloud, Wolke, -n (f) [*vol'-kə*]

cloudy, bewölkt [*bə-völkt'*]

coach, Trainer, - (m) [*treh'- nər*]

coal, Kohle, -n (f) [*koh'-lə*]

coal mine, Kohlenbergwerk, -e (n) [*koh'-lən-berk-verk*]

coarse, roh; grob [*roh; grohp*]

coast, Küste, -n (f) [*kü'-stə*]

coat, Rock, ⸗e (m); Mantel, ⸗ (m) [*rok, rö'-kə; man'-təl, men'-təl*]

cocoa, Kakao (m) [*ka-kah'-o*]

coconut, Kokosnuss, ⸗e (f) [*koh'-kos-nus, koh'-kos-nü-sə*]
coffee, Kaffee (m) [*ka-feh'*]
coin, Münze, -n (f) [*mün'-tsə*]
cold *adj.,* kalt [*kalt*]
  I'm cold, Mir ist kalt [*meer ist kalt*]
cold *n.,* Kälte (f) [*kel'-tə*]
  catch a cold *v.,* sich erkälten [*ziç er-kel'-tən*]
collapse *v.,* zusammen-fallen (irreg; *Aux:* SEIN) [*tsu-za'-mən-fa-lən*]
collar [of a dress], Kragen, - (m) [*krah'-gən*]
colleague, Kollege, -n (m) [*ko-leh'-gə*]
collect *v.,* sammeln [*za'-məln*]
collection, Sammlung, -en (f) [*zam'-lung*]
college, College, -s (n); Hochschule, -n (f) [*ko'-lidzh, ko'-li-dzhəs; hohkh'-shoo-lə*]
colony, Kolonie, -n (f) [*ko-lo-nee'*]
color, Farbe, -n (f) [*far'-bə*]
column [arch.], Säule, -n (f) [*zoi'-lə*]
comb *n.,* Kamm, ⸗e (m) [*kam, ke'-mə*]
comb *v.,* kämmen [*ke'-mən*]
come *v.,* kommen (irreg; *Aux:* SEIN) [*ko'-mən*]
  come about, sich ereignen [*ziç er-raig'-nən*]
  come back, zurück-kommen (irreg; *Aux:* SEIN) [*tsu-rük'-ko-mən*]
  come down [lose face], herunter-kommen (irreg; *Aux:* SEIN) [*hə-run'-tər-ko-mən*]
  come for, ab-holen [*ap'-hoh-lən*]
  come forward, hervor-treten (irreg; *Aux:* SEIN) [*her-fohr'-treh-tən*]
  come from [arise from], kommen von; her-kommen von (plus dat) (irreg; *Aux:* SEIN) [*ko'-mən fon; hehr'-ko-mən fon*]
  come out, heraus-kommen (irreg; *Aux:* SEIN) [*he-rous'-ko-mən*]
comedian, Komödiant, -en (m) [*ko-mö-di-ant'*]
comedy, Komödie, -n (f) [*ko-möh'-di-ə*]
comfortable, gemütlich; bequem [*gə-müht'-liç; bə-kvehm'*]
command, Befehl, -e (m); Gebot, -e (n) [*bə-fehl'; gə-boht'*]

the Ten Commandments, die zehn Gebote (pl) [*dee tsehn gə-boh′-tə*]

command *v.*, befehlen (irreg) [*bə-feh′-lən*]

comment *n.*, Kommentar, -e (m) [*ko-mən-tahr′*]

comment *v.*, Erklärungen geben (irreg) [*er-kleh′-rung-ən geh′-bən*]

commercial, kommerziell [*ko-mer-tsi-el′*]

commit *v.*, begehen (irreg) [*bə-geh′-ən*]

common, gewöhnlich; gemeinsam [*gə-vöhn′-liç; gə-main′-zam*]

commotion, Tumult, -e (m) [*tu-mult′*]

communicate *v.*, mit-teilen [*mit′-tai-lən*]

communication, Mitteilung, -en [*mit′-tai-lung*]

communism, Kommunismus (m) [*ko-mu-nis′-mus*]

communist, Kommunist, -en (m) [*ko-mu-nist′*]

community, Gemeinde, -n (f); Gemeinschaft, -en (f) [*gə-main′-də; gə-main′-shaft*]

companion [female], Gefährtin, -nen (f) [*gə-fehr′-tin*]

companion [male], Gefährte, -n (m) [*gə-fehr′-tə*]

company [business], Handelsgesellschaft, -en (f) [*han′-dəls-gə-zel-shaft*]

company [social], Gesellschaft, -en (f) [*gə-zel′-shaft*]

comparison, Vergleichung, -en (f) [*fer-glai′-çung*]

compartment, Abteil, -e (n) [*ap′-tail*]

compel *v.*, zwingen (irreg) [*tsving′-ən*]

compensation, Ersatz (m) [*er-zats′*]

competent, zuständig; fähig [*tsoo′-shten-diç; feh′-iç*]

competition, Konkurrenz (f) [*kon-ku-rents′*]

complain *v.*, klagen [*klah′-gən*]

complaint, Klage, -n (f) [*klah′-gə*]

complete *adj.*, vollständig [*fol′-shten-diç*]

complete *v.*, vollenden [*fol-en′-dən*]

complexion, Teint, -s (m) [*tent, tents*]

compliment, Kompliment, -e (n) [*kom-pli-ment′*]

compose *v.*, komponieren; verfassen [*kom-po-nee′-rən; fer-fa′-sən*]

composer, Komponist, -en (m) [*kom-po-nist′*]

composure, Fassung (f) [*fa′-sung*]

comprehend *v.*, begreifen (irreg) [*bə-grai′-fən*]

compromise v., kompromittieren [kom-pro-mi-tee'-rən]
compulsion, Zwang, ⸗e (m) [tsvang, tsveng'-ə]
conceal v., verbergen (irreg) [fer-ber'-gən]
conceit, Einbildung (f) [ain'-bil-dung]
conceited, eingebildet [ain'-gə-bil-dət]
concentrate v., konzentrieren [kon-tsən-tree'-rən]
concept, Begriff, -e (m) [bə-grif']
concerning, betreffend (plus acc) [bə-tre'-fənt]
concert, Konzert, -e (n) [kon-tsərt']
concise, knapp [knap]
conclusion, Schluss, ⸗e (m) [shlus, shlü'-sə]
condemn v., verurteilen [fer-ur'-tai-lən]
condemnation, Verurteilung, -en (f) [fer-ur'-tai-lung]
condition, Zustand, ⸗e (m); Bedingung, -en (f) [tsoo'-shtant, tsoo'-shten-də; bə-ding'-ung]
  in good condition, in gutem Zustande [in goo'-təm tsoo'-shtan-də]
conduct v., führen; leiten [füh'-rən; lai'-tən]
conduct [behavior] n., Benehmen (n) [bə-neh'-mən]
conductor, Führer, - (m); Schaffner, - (m); Leiter, - (m) [füh'-rər; shaf'-nər; lai'-tər]
conference, Beratung, -en (f); Sitzung, -en (f) [bə-rah'-tung; zit'-sung]
confess v., gestehen (irreg) [gə-shteh'-ən]
confession, Geständnis, -se (n) [gə-shtent'-nis]
confident, zuversichtlich [tsoo'-fer-ziçt-liç]
confidentially, im Vertrauen [im fer-trou'-ən]
confirm v., bestätigen [bə-shteh'-ti-gən]
conflict, Konflikt, -e (m) [kon-flikt']
confusion, Verwirrung, -en (f) [fer-vi'-rung]
congratulations, Glückwünsche (pl) [glük'-vün-shə]
congress, Kongress, -e (m) [kon-gres']
connection, Verbindung, -en (f) [fer-bin'-dung]
conquer v., besiegen; erobern [bə-zee'-gən; e-roh'-bərn]
conscience, Gewissen (n) [gə-vi'-sən]
conscientious, gewissenhaft [gə-vi'-sən-haft]
conscious, bewusst [bə-vust']
consent [to] v., ein-willigen (in, plus acc) [ain'-vi-li-gen (in)]

consent *n.*, Zustimmung, -en (f) [*tsoo'-shti-mung*]
consequence, Folge, -n (f) [*fol'-gə*]
conspicuous, auffallend [*ouf'-fa-lənt*]
constant, beständig [*bə-shten'-diç*]
consul, Konsul, -n (m) [*kon'-zul*]
construction, Bau, -ten (m) [*bou, bou'-tən*]
consulate, Konsulat, -e (n) [*kon-zu-laht'*]
consume *v.*, verbrauchen [*fer-brou'-khən*]
contagious, ansteckend [*an'-shte-kənt*]
contain *v.*, enthalten (irreg) [*ent-hal'-tən*]
container, Behälter, - (m) [*bə-hel'-tər*]
contemporary *n.*, Zeitgenosse, -n (m) [*tsait'-gə-no-sə*]
contempt, Verachtung (f) [*fer-akh'-tung*]
contest *n.*, Wettkampf, ⸗e (m) [*vet'-kampf, vet'-kem-pfə*]
continent, Kontinent, -e (m); Erdteil, -e (m) [*kon'-ti-nənt; ehrt'-tail*]
continue *v.*, fort-fahren (irreg) [*fort'-fah-rən*]
contradiction, Widerspruch, ⸗e (m) [*vee'-dər-shprukh, vee'-dər-shprü-çə*]
contrary *adj.*, entgegengesetzt [*ent-gəh'-gen-gə-zetst*]
  on the contrary, im Gegenteil [*im geh'-gən-tail*]
contrast *n.*, Gegensatz, ⸗e (m) [*geh'-gən-zats, geh'-gən-se-tsə*]
control *n.*, Kontrolle, -n (f) [*kon-tro'-lə*]
control *v.*, kontrollieren [*kon-tro-lee'-rən*]
controversy, Streit (m, sing), Streitigkeiten (pl) [*shtrait, shtrai'-tiç-kai-tən*]
convenient for, passend für (plus acc) [*pa'-sənt führ*]
convent, Kloster, ⸗ (n) [*kloh'-stər, klöh'-stər*]
conversation, Gespräch, -e (n) [*gə-shprehç'*]
convert *v.*, bekehren [*bə-keh'-rən*]
convert *n.*, Bekehrte, -n (m, f) [*bə-kehr'-tə*]
convict *n.*, Sträfling, -e (m) [*shtrehf'-ling*]
convict of *v.*, überführen (plus gen) (irreg) [*üh-bər-füh'-rən*]
convince *v.*, überzeugen [*üh-bər-tsoi'-gən*]
cook *v.*, kochen [*ko'-khən*]
cook [female], Köchin, -nen (f) [*kö'-çin*]
cook [male], Koch, ⸗e (m) [*kokh, kö'-çə*]
cool *adj.*, kühl [*kühl*]

cool *v.*, ab-kühlen [*ap'-küh-lən*]

cooperation, Zusammenarbeit (f) [*tsu-za'-mən-ar-bait*]

copper, Kupfer (n) [*ku'-pfər*]

copy *v.*, ab-schreiben (irreg); vervielfältigen [*ap'-shrai-bən; fer-feel'-fel-ti-gən*]

copy *n.*, Kopie, -n (f); Exemplar, -e (n); Manuskript, -e (n) [*ko-pee'; ek-sem-plahr'; ma-nu-skript'*]

cord, Seil, -e (n) [*zail*]

corkscrew, Korkzieher, - (m) [*kork'-tsee-ər*]

corn [Indian], Mais (m) [*mais*]

corner, Ecke, -n (f) [*e'-kə*]

corporation, Körperschaft, -en (f); Gesellschaft, -en (f) [*kör'-pər-shaft; gə-zel'-shaft*]

correct *adj.*, richtig [*riç'-tiç*]

correct *v.*, korrigieren [*ko-ri-gee'-rən*]

correspondence, Briefwechsel, - (m) [*breef'-vek-səl*]

corridor, Korridor, -e (m) [*ko'-ri-dohr*]

corrupt *v.*, bestechen (irreg) [*bə-shte'-çən*]

cosmetic, Schönheitsmittel, - (n) [*shöhn'-haits-mi-təl*]

cost *n.*, Preis, -e (m); Kosten (pl) [*prais, prai'-zə; ko'-stən*]

cost *v.*, kosten [*ko'-stən*]

cottage, Hütte, -n (f); Bungalow, -s (m) [*hü'-tə; bung'-gə-loh, bung'-gə-lohs*]

cotton, Baumvolle (f) [*boum'-vo-lə*]

couch, Couch, -es (f) [*kouch, kou'-chəs*]

cough *v.*, husten [*huh'-stən*]

cough, Husten (m) [*huh'-stən*]

could, konnte; könnte [*kon'-tə; kön'-tə*]

  I could go, Ich konnte (könnte) gehen [*iç kon'-tə (kön'-tə) gəh'-ən*]

  I couldn't go, Ich konnte (könnte) nicht gehen [*iç kon'-tə (kön'-tə) niçt geh'-ən*]

count *n.*, Graf, -en (m) [*grahf*]

countess, Gräfin, -nen (f) [*greh'-fin*]

count *v.*, zählen; rechnen [*tseh'-lən; reç'-nən*]

count on, zählen auf (plus acc) [*tseh'-lən ouf*]

country, Land, ⸗er (n) [*lant, len'-dər*]

countryman, Landsmann (m, sing), Landsleute (pl) [*lants'-*

  man, *lants'-loi-tə*]

couple, Paar, -e (n) [*pahr*]

coupon, Gutschein, -e (m) [*guht'-shain*]

courageous, mutig [*moo'-tiç*]

course, Bahn, -en (f); Kursus, Kurse (m) [*bahn; kur'-zus, kur'-zə*]

 of course, natürlich [*na-tühr'-liç*]

 matter of course, Selbstverständlichkeit (f) [*zelpst'-fer-shtent-liç-kait*]

court *n.*, Hof, ⸗e (m) [*hohf, höh'-fə*]

court *v.*, werben um (plus acc) (irreg) [*ver'-bən um*]

courteous, höflich [*höhf'-liç*]

courtyard, Hof, ⸗e (m) [*hohf, höh'-fə*]

cousin [female], Kusine, -n (f) [*ku-zee'-nə*]

cousin [male], Vetter, -n (m) [*fe'-tər*]

cover *v.*, bedecken [*bə-de'-kən*]

cover *n.*, Decke, -n (f) [*de'-kə*]

coward, Feigling, -e (m) [*faig'-ling*]

crab, Krabbe, -n (f) [*kra'-bə*]

crack *n.*, Krach (m) [*krakh*]

cradle, Wiege, -n (f) [*vee-'gə*]

craftsman, Handwerker, - (m) [*hant'-ver-kər*]

crash *v.*, krachen [*kra'-khən*]

crawl *v.*, kriechen (irreg; *Aux:* SEIN) [*kree'-çən*]

crazy, verrückt [*fer-riikt'*]

cream, Sahne (f) [*zah'-nə*]

create *v.*, schaffen (irreg) [*sha'-fən*]

creation, Schöpfung, -en (f) [*shö'-pfung*]

creature, Geschöpf, -e (n) [*gə-shöpf'*]

credit *n.*, Kredit, -e (m) [*kre-deet'*]

creditor, Gläubiger, - (m) [*gloi'-bi-gər*]

crew, Mannschaft, -en (f) [*man'-shaft*]

crib, Krippe, -n (f); Kinderbett, -en (n) [*kri'-pə; kin'-dər-bet*]

crime, Verbrechen, - (n) [*fer-bre'-çən*]

criminal [male], Verbrecher, - (m) [*fer-bre'-çər*]

criminal [female], Verbrecherin, -nen (f) [*fer-bre'-çə-rin*]

crisis, Krise, -n (f) [*kree'-zə*]

crisscross v., kreuzen [*kroi'-tsən*]
critical, kritisch [*kree'-tish*]
criticize v., kritisieren [*kri-ti-zee'-rən*]
crook [criminal], Gauner, - (m) [*gou'-nər*]
crooked, schief; krumm [*sheef; krum*]
crop, Ernte, -n (f) [*ern'-tə*]
cross n., Kreuz, -e (n) [*kroits*]
cross v., kreuzen [*kroi'-tsən*]
crossing, Übergang, ⁼e (m) [*üh'-bər-gang, üh'-bər-geng-ə*]
crossroad, Kreuzweg, -e (m) [*kroits'-vehk, kroits'-veh-gə*]
crowd, Menge, -n (f) [*meng'-ə*]
crowded (with), angefüllt (mit, plus dat) [*an'-gə-fült (mit)*]
crown, Krone, -n (f) [*kroh'-nə*]
cruel, grausam [*grou'-zam*]
cruelty, Grausamkeit, -en (f) [*grou'-zam-kait*]
cruise, Seereise, -n (f) [*zeh'-rai-zə*]
cruiser, Kreuzer, - (m) [*kroi'-tsər*]
crumb, Krume, -n (f) [*kruh'-mə*]
crush v., zerdrücken [*tser-drü'-kən*]
cry v., weinen; rufen (irreg) [*vai'-nən; roo'-fən*]
cucumber, Gurke, -n (f) [*gur'-kə*]
culture, Kultur, -en (f) [*kul-toor'*]
cunning adj., schlau [*shlou*]
cup, Tasse, -n (f) [*ta'-sə*]
cupboard, Speiseschrank, ⁼e (m) [*shpai'-zə-shrank, shpai'-zə-shren-kə*]
cure v., heilen [*hai'-lən*]
cure n., Heilung, -en (f) [*hai'-lung*]
curiosity, Neugier(de) (f) [*noi'-geer-(də)*]
curl n., Locke, -n (f) [*lo'-kə*]
curl v., kräuseln [*kroi'-zəln*]
currency [money], Währung, -en (f) [*veh'-rung*]
curse n., Fluch, ⁼e (m) [*flukh, flü'-çə*]
curse v., verfluchen [*fer-flu'-khən*]
curtain, Vorhang, ⁼e (m) [*fohr'-hang, fohr'-heng-ə*]
curve n., Kurve, -n (f) [*kur'-və*]
    dangerous curve, gefährliche Kurve [*gə-fehr'-li-çə kur'-və*]
cushion, Polster, -(n); Kissen, - (n) [*pol'-stər; ki'-sən*]

custom, Sitte, -n (f) [*zi'-tə*]
customary, üblich [*ühp'-liç*]
customer [female], Kundin, -nen (f) [*kun'-din*]
customer [male], Kunde, -n (m) [*kun'-də*]
customhouse, Zollhaus, ⁼er (n) [*tsol'-hous, tsol'-hoi-zər*]
customs, Zoll, ⁼e (m) [*tsol, tsö'-lə*]
customs duty [charge], Zollgebühr, -en (f) [*tsol'-gə-bühr*]
customs officer, Zollbeamte, -n (m) [*tsol'-be-am-tə*]
cut *v.*, schneiden (irreg) [*shnai'-dən*]
cut [of dress], Schnitt, -e (m) [*shnit*]
cypress, Zypresse, -n (f) [*tsü-pre'-sə*]

D

daily *adj.*, täglich [*tehk'-liç*]
dainty, lecker; fein [*le'-kər; fain*]
dairy, Molkerei, -en (f) [*mol-kə-rai'*]
dam *n.*, Damm, ⁼e (m) [*dam, de'-mə*]
damage *n.*, Schaden, ⁼ (m) [*shah'-dən, sheh'-dən*]
damaged, beschädigt [*bə-sheh'-diçt*]
damp, feucht [*foiçt*]
dance *v.*, tanzen [*tan'-tsən*]
dance *n.*, Tanz, ⁼e (m) [*tants, ten'-tsə*]
   May I have this dance? Darf ich um den Tanz bitten?
   [*darf iç um dehn tants bi'-tən*]
dancer [male], Tänzer, - (m) [*ten'-tsər*]
dancer [female], Tänzerin, -nen (f) [*ten'-tse-rin*]
danger, Gefahr, -en (f) [*gə-fahr'*]
   out of danger, ausser Gefahr [*ou'-sər gə-fahr'*]
dangerous, gefährlich [*gə-fehr'-liç*]
Danish, dänisch [*deh'-nish*]
dare *v.*, wagen [*vah'-gən*]
daring *n.*, Kühnheit (f) [*kühn'-hait*]
dark, dunkel [*dun'-kəl*]
darkness, Dunkelheit (f) [*dun'-kəl-hait*]

dash [strike] v., schlagen (irreg) [*shlah'-gən*]
date [engagement], Verabredung, -en (f) [*fer-ap'-reh-dung*]
date [day of month], Datum, Daten, (n) [*dah'-tum, dah'-tən*]
date [fruit], Dattel, -n (f) [*da'-təl*]
daughter, Tochter, ≈ (f) [*tokh'-tər, töç'-tər*]
daughter-in-law, Schwiegertochter, ≈ (f) [*shvee'-gər-tokh-tər, shvee'-gər-töç-tər*]
dawn, Dämmerung (f) [*dem'-ə-rung*]
day, Tag, -e (m) [*tahk, tah'-gə*]
  all day long, den ganzen Tag [*dehn gant'-sən tahk*]
  everyday, jeden Tag [*yeh'-dən tahk*]
  twice a day, zweimal täglich [*tsvai'- mahl tehk'-liç*]
dead, tot [*toht*]
deadly, tödlich [*töht'-liç*]
deaf, taub [*toup*]
deal [business], Handel (m) [*han'-dəl*]
  a good deal, ziemlich viel [*tseem'-liç feel*]
deal [cards] v., (Karten) geben (irreg) [(*kar'-tən) geh'-bən*]
deal with [a subject], behandeln [*bə-han'-dəln*]
dealer, Händler, - (m) [*hend'-lər*]
dear [expensive], teuer [*toi'-ər*]
death, Tod (m) [*toht*]
debt, Schuld, -en (f) [*shult, shul'-dən*]
decade, Jahrzehnt, -e (n) [*yahr-tsehnt'*]
decay n., Verfall (m) [*fər-fal'*]
decay v., verfallen (irreg; Aux: SEIN) [*fer-fa'-lən*]
deceased, verstorben [*fər-shtor'-bən*]
deceit, Täuschung, -en (f) [*toi'-shung*]
deceive v., täuschen [*toi'-shən*]
December, Dezember (m) [*de-tsem'-bər*]
decency, Anstand, ≈e (m) [*an'-shtant, an'-shten-də*]
decent, anständig [*an'-shten-diç*]
deception, Betrug (m) [*bə-trook'*]
decide v., entscheiden (irreg) [*ent-shai'-dən*]
decision, Entscheidung, -en (f) [*ent-shai'-dung*]
deck [of ship], Deck, -e (n) [*dek*]
declaration, Erklärung, -en (f) [*er-kleh'-rung*]
declare v., erklären [*er-kleh'-rən*]

decorate *v.*, schmücken [*shmü'-kən*]

decoration, Verzierung, -en (f) [*fer-tsee'-rung*]

decrease *v.*, vermindern [*fer-min'-dərn*]

dedicate *v.*, widmen [*vid'-mən*]

deed [act], Tat, -en (f) [*taht*]

deep, tief [*teef*]

defeat *n.*, Niederlage, -n (f) [*nee'-dər-lah-gə*]

defend *v.*, verteidigen [*fer-tai'-di-gən*]

defense, Verteidigung, -en (f) [*fer-tai'-di-gung*]

defiant, trotzig [*trot'-siç*]

deficient, mangelhaft [*man'-gəl-haft*]

define *v.*, bestimmen [*bə-shtim'-ən*]

definite, bestimmt [*bə-shtimt'*]

definition, Definition, -en (f) [*de-fi-ni-tsi-ohn'*]

degree [temperature], Grad, -e (m) [*graht, grah'-də*]

delay, Verzögerung, -en (f) [*fer-tsöh'-gə-rung*]

deliberate *adj.*, absichtlich [*ap'-ziçt-liç*]

delicate, fein; zart [*fain; tsahrt*]

delicious, köstlich [*köst'-liç*]

delight *n.*, Lust, ⸗e (f) [*lust, lü'-stə*]

delight *v.*, ergötzen [*er-gö'-tsən*]

delightful, entzückend [*ent-tsü'-kənt*]

deliver *v.*, liefern [*lee'-fərn*]

demand *v.*, verlangen [*fer-lang'-ən*]

demand *n.*, Verlangen, - (n) [*fer-lang'-ən*]

  on demand, auf Verlangen [*ouf fer-lang'-ən*]

democracy, Demokratie, -n (f) [*de-mo-kra-tee'*]

democratic, demokratisch [*de-mo-krah'-tish*]

demonstrate *v.*, vor-führen [*fohr'-füh-rən*]

demonstration, Demonstration, -en (f) [*de-mon-stra-tsi-ohn'*]

denial, Verneinung, -en (f) [*fer-nai'-nung*]

Denmark, Dänemark (n) [*deh'-nə-mark*]

dense, dicht [*diçt*]

density, Dichte (f) [*diç'-tə*]

dentist [female], Zahnärztin, -nen (f) [*tsahn'-ehrt-stin*]

dentist [male], Zahnarzt, ⸗e (m) [*tsahn'-ahrtst, tsahn'-ehrt-stə*]

deny *v.*, verneinen [*fer-nai'-nən*]

depart *v.*, ab-fahren (irreg; *Aux:* SEIN) [*ap'-fah-rən*]

department, Abteilung, -en (f) [*ap-tai'-lung*]

department store, Warenhaus, ⸗er (n) [*vah'-rən-hous, vah'-rən-hoi-zər*]

departure, Abreise, -n (f); Abfahrt, -en (f) [*ap'-rai-zə; ap'-fahrt*]

depend (on) *v.*, ab-hängen (von) (irreg) [*ap'-heng-ən (fon)*]
   That depends, Das hängt davon ab [*das hengt da'-fon ap*]

dependent (on), abhängig (von) [*ap'-heng-iç (fon)*]

deposit *n.*, Einzahlung, -en (f) [*ain'-tsah-lung*]

deposit *v.*, ein-zahlen [*ain'-tsah-lən*]

depot, Bahnhof, ⸗e (m) [*bahn'-hohf, bahn'-höh-fə*]

deprive *v.*, (einem etwas) nehmen (irreg) [(*ai'-nem et'-vahs) neh'-mən*]

depth, Tiefe, -n (f) [*tee'-fə*]

deputy, Abgeordnete, -n (m, f) [*ap'-gə-ord-nə-tə*]

descend *v.*, ab-steigen (irreg; *Aux:* SEIN) [*ap'-shtai-gən*]

describe *v.*, beschreiben (irreg) [*bə-shrai'-bən*]

description, Beschreibung, -en (f) [*bə-shrai'-bung*]

desert *n.*, Wüste, -n (f) [*vüh'-stə*]

desert *v.*, verlassen (irreg) [*fer-la'-sən*]

deserve *v.*, verdienen [*fer-dee'-nən*]

design, Zeichnung, -en (f) [*tsaiç'-nung*]

desirable, wünschenswert [*vün'-shəns-vehrt*]

desire *v.*, wünschen [*vün'-shən*]

desire *n.*, Wunsch, ⸗e (n) [*vunsh, vün'-shə*]

desk, Schreibtisch, -e (m) [*shraip'-tish*]

despair *v.*, verzweifeln [*fer-tsvai'-fəln*]

despair *n.*, Verzweiflung (f) [*fer-tsvaif'-lung*]

desperate, verzweifelt [*fer-tsvai'-fəlt*]

despite, trotz (plus gen) [*trots*]

dessert, Nachtisch (m) [*nakh'-tish*]

destitute, notleidend [*noht'-lai-dənt*]

destroy *v.*, zerstören [*tser-shtöh'-rən*]

destruction, Zerstörung, -en (f) [*tser-shtöh'-rung*]

detail, Einzelheit, -en (f) [*ain'-tsel-hait*]

detain *v.*, auf-halten (irreg); in Haft behalten (irreg) [*ouf'-hal-tən; in haft bə-hal'-tən*]

detained, aufgehalten [*ouf'-gə-hal-tən*]

detective, Detektiv, -e (m) [*de-tek-teef´*, *de-tek-tee´-və*]

determine *v.*, bestimmen [*bə-shti´-mən*]

detour, Unweg, -e (m) [*um´-vehk*, *um´-veh-gə*]

develop *v.*, entwickeln [*ent-vi´-kəln*]

development, Entwicklung, -en (f) [*ent-vik´-lung*]

device, Vorrichtung, -en (f) [*fohr´-riç-tung*]

devil, Teufel, - (m) [*toi´-fəl*]

devoted to *adj.*, ergeben (plus dat) [*er-geh´-bən*]

devotion, Ergebenheit (f) [*er-geh´-bən-hait*]

dew, Tau (m) [*tou*]

diagnosis, Diagnose, -n (f) [*di-ag-noh´-zə*]

dialect, Dialekt, -e [*di-a-lekt´*]

dialogue, Dialog, -e (m) [*di-a-lohk´*, *di-a-loh´-gə*]

diameter, Durchmesser, - (m) [*durkh´-me-sər*]

diamond, Diamant, -en (m) [*di-a-mant´*]

diary, Tagebuch, ¨er (n) [*tah´-gə-bookh*, *tah´-gə-bü-çər*]

dice, Würfel (m, pl) [*vür´-fəl*]

dictate *v.*, diktieren [*dik-tee´-rən*]

dictation, Diktat, -e (n) [*dik-taht´*]

dictionary, Wörterbuch, ¨er [*vör´-tər-bookh*, *vör´-tər-büh-çər*]

die *v.*, sterben (irreg; *Aux:* SEIN) [*shter´-bən*]

diet *n.*, Diät (f) [*di-eht´*]

   be on a diet *v.*, diät leben [*di-eht´ le´-bən*]

difference, Unterschied, -e (m) [*un´-tər-sheet*, *un´-tər-shee-də*]

   It does not make any difference, Das macht nichts aus
     [*das makht niçts ous*]

   What difference does it make? Was macht das aus?
     [*vas makht das ous*]

different, verschieden [*fer-shee´-dən*]

difficult, schwierig [*shvee´-riç*]

difficulty, Schwierigkeit, -en (f) [*shvee´-riç-kait*]

dig *v.*, graben (irreg) [*grah´-bən*]

digestion, Verdauung (f) [*fer-dou´-ung*]

dignity, Würde (f) [*vühr´-də*]

diminish *v.*, vermindern [*fer-min´-dərn*]

dine *v.*, zu Mittag essen (irreg) [*tsu mi´-tahk e´-sən*]

dining car, Speisewagen, - (m) [*shpai´-zə-vah-gən*]

dining room, Speisezimmer, - (n) [*shpai´-zə-tsi-mər*]

dinner, Abendessen (n) [*ah'-bənt-e-sən*]
  Dinner is ready! Das Essen steht auf dem Tische! [*das e'-sən shteht ouf dehm ti'-shə*]
diploma, Diplom, -e (n) [*di-plohm'*]
diplomat, Diplomat, -en (m) [*di-ploh-maht'*]
diplomatic, diplomatisch [*di-ploh-mah'-tish*]
direct adj., direkt [*di-rekt'*]
direct [show the way] v., den Weg zeigen [*dehn vehk tsai'-gən*]
direction, Richtung, -en [*riç'-tung*]
director [female], Direktorin, -nen (f) [*di-rek-toh'-rin*]
director [male], Direktor, -en (m) [*di-rek'-tohr*]
dirty, schmutzig [*shmut'-siç*]
disabled soldier, Kriegsbeschädigte, -n (m) [*kreeks'-bə-sheh-diç-tə*]
disadvantage, Nachteil, -e (m) [*nakh'-tail*]
disagree v., anderer Meinung sein [*an'-də-rər mai'-nung zain*]
disagreeable, unangenehm [*un'-an-gə-nehm*]
disappear v., verschwinden (irreg; Aux: SEIN) [*fer-shvin'-dən*]
disappoint v., enttäuschen [*ent-toi'-shən*]
disappointed, enttäuscht [*ent-toisht'*]
disapprove v., missbilligen [*mis-bi'-li-gən*]
disaster, Katastrophe, -n (f) [*ka-ta-stroh'-fə*]
discipline n., Disziplin (f) [*dis-tsi-pleen'*]
disclose v., auf-decken [*ouf'-de-kən*]
discomfort, Unbehagen (n) [*un'-bə-hah-gən*]
disconnect v., trennen [*tre'-nən*]
discovery, Entdeckung, -en (f) [*ent-de'-kung*]
discontinue v., auf-hören [*ouf'-höh-rən*]
discount n., Preisnachlass, ⸗e (m) [*prais'-nakh-las, prais'-nakh-le-sə*]
discourage v., entmutigen [*ent-moo'-ti-gən*]
discover v., entdecken [*ent-de'-kən*]
discuss v., besprechen (irreg) [*bə-shpre'-çən*]
discussion, Diskussion, -en (f) [*dis-ku-si-ohn'*]
disease, Krankheit, -en (f) [*krank'-hait*]

disgrace *n.*, Ungnade (f); Schande (f) [*un'-gnah-də; shan'-də*]

disgrace *v.*, in Ungnade stürzen; in Schande stürzen [*in un'-gnah-də shtür'-tsən; in shan'-də shtür'-tsən*]

disguise *n.*, Verkleidung, -en (f) [*fer-klai'-dung*]

disgusting, ekelhaft [*eh'-kəl-haft*]

dish, Schüssel, -n (f); Gericht, -e (n) [*shü'-səl; gə-riçt'*]

dishonest, unehrlich [*un'-ehr-liç*]

dislike *n.*, Abneigung, -en (f) [*ap'-nai-gung*]

   I dislike it, Ich mag es nicht [*iç mahk es niçt*]

dismiss *v.*, entlassen (irreg) [*ent-la'-sən*]

disobey *v.*, missachten [*mis-akh'-tən*]

disorder, Unordnung, -en (f) [*un'-ord-nung*]

display *v.*, aus-stellen [*ous'-shte-lən*]

display *n.*, Schaustellung, -en (f) [*shou'-shte-lung*]

dispute, Streit (m, sing), Streitigkeiten (pl) [*shtrait, shtrai'-tiç-kai-tən*]

dissolve *v.*, auf-lösen [*ouf'-löh-zən*]

distance, Entfernung, -en (f) [*ent-fer'-nung*]

distant, fern; entfernt [*fern; ent-fernt'*]

distinguish (from) *v.*, unterscheiden (von, plus dat) (irreg) [*un-tər-shai'-dən (fon)*]

distress *n.*, Not, ⸗e [*noht, nöh'-tə*]

distress *v.*, quälen [*kveh'-lən*]

distribute *v.*, verteilen [*fer-tai'-lən*]

distribution, Verteilung, -en (f) [*fer-tai'-lung*]

district, Bezirk, -e (m) [*bə-tsirk'*]

distrust *v.*, misstrauen [*mis-trou'-ən*]

distrust *n.*, Misstrauen (n) [*mis'-trou-ən*]

disturb *v.*, stören [*shtöh'-rən*]

disturbance, Störung, -en (f) [*shtöh'-rung*]

ditch, Graben, ⸗ (m) [*grah'-bən, greh'-bən*]

dive *v.*, tauchen [*tou'-khən*]

divide *v.*, teilen [*tai'-lən*]

divine, göttlich [*göt'-liç*]

divorce, Scheidung, -en (f) [*shai'-dung*]

   He divorced his wife, Er liess sich von seiner Frau scheiden [*er lees ziç fon zai'-nər frou shai'-dən*]

dizzy, schwindlig [*shvind'-liç*]

do *v.*, tun (irreg) [*toon*]
    How do you do? [at introductions] Guten Tag! Wie geht es
    Ihnen? [*goo'-tən tahk. vee geht es ee'-nən*]
    How do you do? [reply at introductions] Sehr angenehm
    [*zehr an'-gə-nehm*]
dock *n.*, Dock, -s (n) [*dok, doks*]
dock *v.*, docken [*do'-kən*]
doctor [female], Ärztin, -nen (f) [*ehrt'-stin*]
doctor [male] Arzt, ⸗e [*ahrtst, ehrt-stə*]
document, Dokument, -e (n) [*do-ku-ment'*]
dog, Hund, -e (m) [*hunt, hun'-də*]
doll, Puppe, -n [*pu'-pə*]
dollar, Dollar, -s (m) [*do'-lar, do'-lars*]
dome, Kuppel, -n (f) [*ku'-pəl*]
domestic *adj.*, inländisch [*in'-len-dish*]
domestic animal, Haustier, -e (n) [*hous'-teer*]
donkey, Esel, - (m) [*eh'-səl*]
door, Tür, -en (f) [*tühr*]
    Close the door! Schliessen Sie die Tür! [*shlee'-sən zee
    dee tühr*]
    Open the door! Öffnen Sie die Tür! [*öf'-nən zee dee
    tühr*]
dormitory, Schlafsaal, Schlafsäle (m) [*shlahf'-zahl, shlahf'-
    zeh-lə*]
dose, Dosis (f, sing), Dosen (pl) [*doh'-zis, doh'-zən*]
double, doppelt [*do'-pəlt*]
doubt *n.*, Zweifel, - (m) [*tsvai'-fəl*]
doubt *v.*, zweifeln [*tsvai'-fəln*]
doubtful, zweifelhaft [*tsvai'-fəl-haft*]
doubtless, zweifellos [*tsvai'-fə-lohs*]
down *adv.*, nieder; unten [*nee'-dər, oon'-tən*]
    be down on a person *v.*, streng sein gegen einen [*shtreng
    zain geh'-gən ai'-nən*]
    lie down *v.*, sich hin-legen [*ziç hin'-leh-gən*]
    sit down *v.*, sich setzen [*ziç zet'-sən*]
downfall, Sturz, ⸗e (m) [*shturts, shtür'-tsə*]
downhearted, niedergeschlagen [*nee'-dər-gə-shlah-gən*]
downstairs, (nach) unten [(*nakh) un'-tən*]

doze *v.*, schlummern [*shlu'-mərn*]

dozen, Dutzend, -e (n) [*du'-tsənt, du'-tsen-də*]

draft [air], Durchzug (m) [*durkh'-tsook*]

draft [army], Einberufung, -en (f) [*ain'-bə-roo-fung*]

drag *v.*, ziehen (irreg) [*tsee'-ən*]

drain *v.*, entwässern [*ent-ve'-sərn*]

drama, Drama (n, sing), Dramen (pl) [*drah'-ma, drah'-mən*]

dramatic, dramatisch [*dra-mah'-tish*]

draw [a picture] *v.*, zeichnen [*tsaiç'-nən*]

draw [a weapon] *v.*, ziehen (irreg) [*tsee'-ən*]

draw up *v.*, verfassen [*fer-fa'-sən*]

drawer, Schublade, -n (f) [*shoop'-lah-də*]

dreadful, schrecklich [*shrek'-liç*]

dream *n.*, Traum, ⸗e (m) [*troum, troi'-mə*]

dream *v.*, träumen [*troi'-mən*]

dress *n.*, Kleid, -er [*klait, klai'-dər*]

   evening dress, Abendkleid, -er (n) [*ah'-bənt-klait, ah'-bənt-klai-dər*]

   get dressed *v.*, sich an-ziehen (irreg) [*ziç an'-tsee-ən*]

dressmaker, Schneiderin, -nen (f) [*shnai'-də-rin*]

dresser, Anrichte, -n (f) [*an'-riç-tə*]

drink *v.*, trinken (irreg) [*trin'-kən*]

drink *n.*, Getränk, -e (n) [*gə-trenk'*]

drip *v.*, tröpfeln [*trö'-pfəln*]

drive [a car] *v.*, fahren (irreg) [*fah'-rən*]

driver, Fahrer, - (m) [*fah'-rər*]

drop *n.*, Tropfen, - (m) [*tro'-pfən*]

drop *v.*, fallen lassen (irreg) [*fa'-lən la'-sən*]

drown *v.*, ertrinken (irreg; *Aux:* SEIN) [*er-trin'-kən*]

drug [medical], Droge, -n (f) [*droh'-gə*]

drug [narcotic], Rauschgift, -e (n) [*roush'-gift*]

druggist, Apotheker, - (m) [*a-po-teh'-kər*]

drugstore, Apotheke, - n (f) [*a-po-teh'-kə*]

drum, Trommel, -n (f) [*tro'-məl*]

dry *adj.*, trocken; herb [*tro'-kən; herp*]

dry *v.*, trocknen [*trok'-nən*]

dry-clean *v.*, chemisch reinigen [*çeh'-mish rai'-ni-gən*]

duchess, Herzogin, -nen (f) [*her'-tsoh-gin*]
duck, Ente, -n [*en'-tə*]
due, fällig [*fe'-liç*]
  fall due *v.*, fällig werden (irreg; *Aux:* SEIN) [*fe'-liç vehr'-dən*]
duke, Herzog, ⸗e [*her'-tsohk, her'-tsöh-gə*]
dull, langweilig [*lang'-vai-liç*]
dumb [stupid], dumm [*dum*]
dumb [mute], stumm [*shtum*]
durable, dauerhaft [*dou'-ər-haft*]
during, während (plus gen) [*veh'-rənt*]
dusk, Dämmerung (f) [*de'-mə-rung*]
dust, Staub (m) [*shtoup*]
dusty, staubig [*shtou'-biç*]
Dutch, holländisch [*ho'-len-dish*]
duty [obligation], Pflicht, -en (f) [*pfliçt*]
  be on duty *v.*, Dienst haben (irreg) [*deenst ha'-bən*]
duty [customs], Zoll, ⸗e (m) [*tsol, tsö'-lə*]
duty-free, zollfrei [*tsol'-frai*]
dye *v.*, färben [*fer'-bən*]
dye *n.*, Farbe, -n (f) [*far'-bə*]
dynamite, Dynamit (n) [*dü-na-meet'*]
dysentery, Ruhr (f) [*roor*]

E

each, jeder; jede; jedes [*yeh'-dər, yeh'-də, yeh'-dəs*]
each other, einander [*ai-nan'-dər*]
each time, jedesmal [*yeh'-dəs-mal*]
eager, eifrig [*ai'-friç*]
eagle, Adler, - (m) [*ahd'-lər*]
ear, Ohr, -en (n) [*ohr*]
early, früh [*früh*]
earn *v.*, verdienen [*fer-dee'-nən*]
earring, Ohrring, -e (m) [*ohr'-ring*]

earth, Erde (f) [*ehr'-də*]

earthquake, Erdbeben, -(n) [*ehrt'-beh-bən*]

ease, Bequemlichkeit, -en (f) [*bə-kvehm'-liç-kait*]

east, Osten (m) [*o'-stən*]

  Far East, der Ferne Osten [*dehr fer'-nə o'-stən*]

  Near East, der Nahe Osten [*dehr nah'-ə o'-stən*]

Easter, Ostern (pl) [*oh'-stərn*]

Easter Bunny, Osterhase, -n (m) [*oh'-stər-hah-zə*]

easy, leicht [*laiçt*]

  That's very easy! Das ist sehr leicht! [*das ist sehr laiçt*]

easygoing, leichtlebig [*laiçt'-leh-biç*]

eat *v.*, essen (irreg) [*e'-sən*]

economical, wirtschaftlich; sparsam [*virt'-shaft-liç; spahr'-zam*]

edge, Kante, -n (f) [*kan'-tə*]

edible, essbar [*es'-bar*]

edition, Ausgabe, -n (f) [*ous'-gah-bə*]

editor, Redakteur, -e (m) [*re-dak-töhr'*]

education, Erziehung (f) [*er-tsee'-ung*]

effect *n.*, Wirkung, -en (f) [*vir'-kung*]

effective, wirksam [*virk'-sam*]

effort, Anstrengung, -en (f) [*an'-shtreng-ung*]

egg, Ei, -er (n) [*ai, ai'-ər*]

  fried eggs, Spiegeleier [*shpee'-gel-ai-ər*]

  hard-boiled eggs, hartgekochte Eier [*hart'-gə-kokh-tə ai'-ər*]

  scrambled eggs, Rührei, -er (n) [*rüh'-rai*]

  soft-boiled eggs, weich gekochte Eier [*vaiç gə-kokh'-tə ai'-ər*]

Egypt, Ägypten (n) [*e-güp'-tən*]

Egyptian, ägyptisch [*e-güp'-tish*]

eight, acht [*akht*]

eighteen, achtzehn [*akht'-tsehn*]

eighty, achtzig [*akht'-tsiç*]

either . . . or, entweder . . . oder [*ent-veh'-dər . . . oh'-dər*]

elaborate *v.*, aus-arbeiten [*ous'-ar-bai-tən*]

elastic *adj.*, elastisch [*e-la'-stish*]

elbow, Ellbogen, - (m) [*el'-boh-gən*]

elder, älter [*el'-tər*]
elderly, bejahrt [*bə-yahrt'*]
elect *v.*, wählen [*veh'-lən*]
election, Wahl, -en (f) [*vahl*]
electric, elektrisch [*e-lek'-trish*]
electricity, Elektrizität (f) [*e-lek-tri-tsi-teht'*]
elegance, Eleganz (f) [*e-le-gants'*]
elegant, elegant [*e-le-gant'*]
element, Element, -e (n) [*e-lə-ment'*]
elementary, elementar [*e-lə-men-tahr'*]
elephant, Elefant, -en (m) [*e-lə-fant'*]
elevator, Aufzug, ⸗e (m) [*ouf'-tsook, ouf'-tsüh-gə*]
eleven, elf [*elf*]
else, sonst [*zonst*]
   Anything else? Sonst noch etwas? [*zonst nokh et'-vas*]
   Nothing else, Sonst nichts [*zonst niçts*]
   someone else, jemand anders [*yeh'-mant an'-dərs*]
   somewhere else, woanders [*voh-an'-dərs*]
embarass *v.*, verlegen machen [*fer-leh'-gən ma'-khən*]
embarrassed *adj.*, verlegen [*fer-leh'-gən*]
embassy, Botschaft, -en (f) [*boht'-shaft*]
embrace *n.*, Umarmung, -en (f) [*um-ar'-mung*]
embrace *v.*, umarmen [*um-ar'-mən*]
emerald, Smaragd, -e (m) [*sma-rakt', sma-rak'-də*]
emergency, Notfall, ⸗e (m) [*noht'-fal, noht'-fe-lə*]
   in case of emergency, im Notfalle [*im noht'-fa-lə*]
emigrant, Auswanderer, - (m) [*ous'-van-də-rər*]
emigration, Auswanderung (f) [*ous'-van-də-rung*]
emotional, gefühlsbetont [*gə-fühls'-bə-tohnt*]
emperor, Kaiser, - (m) [*kai'-zər*]
emphasis, Betonung, -en (f) [*bə-toh'-nung*]
emphasize *v.*, betonen [*bə-toh'-nən*]
empire, Reich, -e (n) [*raiç*]
employ *v.*, an-stellen [*an'-shte-lən*]
employee [male], Arbeitnehmer, - (m) [*ar'-bait-neh-mər*]
employee [female], Arbeitnehmerin, -nen (f) [*ar'-bait-neh-me-rin*]
employer [male], Arbeitgeber, - (m) [*ar'-bait-geh-bər*]

employer [female], Arbeitgeberin, -nen (f) [*ar'-bait-geh-be-rin*]

employment, Anstellung, -en (f) [*an'-shte-lung*]

empty, leer [*lehr*]

encourage v., ermutigen; zu-reden (plus dat) [*er-moo'-ti-gən; tsoo'-reh-dən*]

encouragement, Aufmunterung (f) [*ouf'-mun-tə-rung*]

end v., beenden [*bə-en'-dən*]

end n., Ende, -n (n) [*en'-də*]

endless, endlos [*ent'-lohs*]

endure v., aus-halten (irreg) [*ous'-hal-tən*]

enemy, Feind, -e (m) [*faint, fain'-də*]

energetic, energisch [*e-ner'-gish*]

energy, Energie, -n (f) [*e-ner-gee'*]

engaged [busy], beschäftigt [*bə-shef'-tiçt*]

engaged [to be married], verlobt [*fer-lohpt'*]

engagement [to marry], Verlobung, -en (f) [*fer-loh'-bung*]

engagement [appointment], Verabredung, -en (f) [*fer-ap'-reh-dung*]

engine, Maschine, -n (f) [*ma-shee'-nə*]

engineer, Ingenieur, -e (m) [*in-zhe-ni-öhr'*]

England, England (n) [*eng'-lant*]

English, englisch [*eng'-lish*]

enjoy v., geniessen [*gə-nee'-sən*]
  Enjoy yourself! Amüsieren Sie sich! [*a-mü-zee'-rən zee ziç*]

enjoyment, Genuss, ⸗e (m) [*gə-nus', gə-nü'-sə*]

enormous, ungeheuer [*un'-gə-hoi-ər*]

enough, genug [*gə-nook'*]
  more than enough, mehr als genug [*mehr als gə-nook'*]
  That's enough, Das ist genug [*das ist gə-nook'*]

enter v., ein-treten (irreg; *Aux:* SEIN) [*ain'-treh-tən*)
  Do not enter! Eintritt verboten! [*ain'-trit fer-boh'-tən*]

enterprise, Unternehmen, - (n) [*un-tər-neh'-mən*]

entertain [amuse] v., unterhalten (irreg) [*un-tər-hal'-tən*]

entertaining, unterhaltend [*un-tər-hal'-tənt*]

entertainment, Unterhaltung, -en (f) [*un-tər-hal'-tung*]

enthusiasm, Begeisterung (f) [*bə-gai'-stə-rung*]

entire, ganz [*gants*]

entirely, gänzlich [*gents'-liç*]

entrance, Eingang, ⸗e [*ain'-gang, ain'-geng-ə*]

envelope, Umschlag, ⸗e (m) [*um'-shlahk, um'-shleh-gə*]

environment, Umwelt (f) [*um'-velt*]

envy *v.,* beneiden [*bə-nai'-dən*]

equal, gleich [*glaiç*]

equality, Gleichheit (f) [*glaiç'-hait*]

  equality of rights, Gleichberechtigung (f) [*glaiç'-bə-reç-ti-gung*]

equipment, Ausrüstung (f) [*ous'-rü-stung*]

equivalent *n.,* Gegenwert, -e (m) [*geh'-gən-vehrt*]

erase *v.,* aus-radieren [*ous'-ra-dee-rən*]

eraser, Radiergummi, -s (m) [*ra-deer'-gu-mi, ra-deer'-gu-mis*]

error, Irrtum, ⸗er (m) [*ir'-tum, ir'-tü-mər*]

escape *n.,* Flucht, -en (f) [*flukht*]

escape *v.,* entfliehen (plus dat) (irreg; *Aux:* SEIN) [*ent-flee'-ən*]

especially, besonders [*bə-zon'-dərs*]

essential, wesentlich [*vee'-zent-liç*]

establish *v.,* errichten [*er-riç'-tən*]

estimate *v.,* schätzen [*shet'-sən*]

et cetera, und so weiter [*unt zo vai'-tər*]

eternal, ewig [*eh'-viç*]

Europe, Europa (n) [*oi-roh'-pa*]

European *adj.,* europäisch [*oi-roh-peh'-ish*]

eve, Vorabend, -e (m) [*fohr'-ah-bent, fohr'-ah-ben-də*]

  Christmas Eve, Heiliger Abend, -e (m) [*hai'-li-gər ah'-bent*]

even *adj.,* eben; gleich; gerade [*eh'-bən; glaiç; gə-rah'-də*]

even *adv.,* sogar [*zo-gahr'*]

  even I, sogar ich [*zo-gahr' iç*]

  not even, nicht einmal [*niçt ain'-mahl*]

evening, Abend, -e (m) [*ah'-bənt, ah'-bən-də*]

  Good evening! Guten Abend! [*guh'-tən ah'-bəntı*]

  in the evening, am Abend [*am ah'-bənt*]

  tomorrow evening, morgen abend [*mor'-gən ah'-bənt*]

  yesterday evening, gestern abend [*gə'-stərn ah'-bənt*]

even number, gerade Zahl [*gə-rah'-də tsahl*]

event, Ereignis, -se (n) [*e-raig'-nis*]
  in the event that, im Falle dass [*im fa'-lə das*]
ever, je; jemals [*yeh; yeh'-mahls*]
  as ever, wie immer [*vee i'-mər*]
  for ever, für immer [*führ i'-mər*]
every, jeder; jede; jedes [*yeh'-dər; yeh'-də; yeh'-dəs*]
  every day, jeden Tag [*yeh'-dən tak*]
  every other day, jeden zweiten Tag [*yeh'-dən tsvai'-tən tahk*]
  every time, jedesmal [*yeh'-dəs-mahl*]
everybody, jeder; jedermann [*yeh'-dər; yeh'-dər-man*]
everything, alles [*a'-ləs*]
everywhere, überall [*üh'-bər-al*]
evidence [material], Beweis, -e (m) [*bə-vais', bə-vai'-zə*]
evidently, offenbar [*of'-ən-bahr*]
evil *adj.,* übel; böse; schlimm [*üh'-bəl; böh'-sə; shlim*]
exact, exactly, genau [*gə-nou'*]
  Exactly! Ganz richtig! [*gants riç'-tiç*]
exaggerate *v.,* übertreiben (irreg) [*üh-bər-trai'-bən*]
exaggeration, Übertreibung, -en (f) [*üh-bər-trai'-bung*]
examination, Prüfung, -en (f) [*prüh'-fung*]
examine *v.,* prüfen [*prüh'-fən*]
example, Beispiel, -e (n) [*bai'-shpeel*]
exceed *v.,* übertreffen (irreg) [*üh-bər-tre'-fən*]
excellent, ausgezeichnet [*ous'-gə-tsaiç-net*]
except *prep.,* ausser (plus dat) [*ou'-sər*]
exception, Ausnahme, -n (f) [*ous'-nah-mə*]
excess, Übermass (n) [*üh'-bər-mahs*]
exchange *v.,* aus-tauschen [*ous'-tou-shən*]
exchange *n.,* Austausch (m) [*ous'-toush*]
excited, aufgeregt [*ouf'-gə-rehkt*]
  Don't get excited! Regen Sie sich nicht auf! [*reh'-gən zee ziç niçt ouf*]
exclusive, ausschliesslich; exklusiv [*ous'-shlees-liç; eks-klu-zeef'*]
excursion, Ausflug, ⸗e (m) [*ous'-fluhk, ous'-flüh-gə*]
excuse *n.,* Entschuldigung, -en (f) [*ent-shul'-di-gung*]
excuse *v.,* entschuldigen [*ent-shul'-di-gən*]

Excuse me, Verzeihung! [*fer-tsai'-ung*]

exercise *n.*, Übung, -en (f); Bewegung, -en (f) [*üh'-bung; bə-veh'-gung*]

exercise [body or mind] *v.*, üben [*üh'-bən*]

exercise [power or a profession] *v.*, aus-üben [*ous'-üh-bən*]

exhausted, erschöpft [*er-shöpft'*]

exhibit *v.*, aus-stellen [*ous'-shte-lən*]

exhibition, Ausstellung, -en (f) [*ous'-shte-lung*]

exist *v.*, bestehen (irreg) [*bə-shteh'-ən*]

existence, Existenz, -en (f) [*ek-sis-tents'*]

exit *n.*, Ausgang, ⸗e (m) [*ous'-gang, ous'-geng-ə*]

expect *v.*, erwarten [*er-var'-tən*]

expedition, Expedition, -en (f) [*eks-pe-di-tsi-ohn'*]

expense, Ausgabe, -n (f) [*ous'-gah-bə*]

expensive, teuer [*toi'-ər*]

experience *n.*, Erfahrung, -en (f) [*er-fah'-rung*]

experiment, Versuch, -e (m) [*fer-zookh'*]

expert, Fachmann (m, sing), Fachleute (pl) [*fakh'-man, fakh'-loi-tə*]

explain *v.*, erklären [*er-kleh'-rən*]

   Please explain! Erklären Sie bitte [*er-kleh'-rən zee bi'-tə*]

explanation, Erklärung, -en (f) [*er-kleh'-rung*]

explore *v.*, erforschen [*er-for'-shən*]

explosion, Explosion, -en (f) [*eks-plo-zi-ohn'*]

export *v.*, exportieren [*eks-por-tee'-rən*]

express [train], Schnellzug, ⸗e (f) [*shnel'-tsook, shnel'-tsüh-gə*]

express [mail], durch Eilboten [*durkh ail'-boh-tən*]

express *v.*, aus-drücken [*ous'-drü-kən*]

exquisite, köstlich [*köst'-liç*]

extend *v.*, verlängern [*fer-leng'-ərn*]

exterior *n.*, Äussere (n) [*oi'-sə-rə*]

external, äusserlich [*oi'-sər-liç*]

extinguish *v.*, aus-löschen [*ous'-lö-shən*]

extra, extra [*ek'-stra*]

extract [a tooth] *v.*, aus-ziehen (irreg) [*ous'-tsee-ən*]

extraordinary, aussergewöhnlich [*ou'-sər-gə-vöhn-liç*]

extravagant [ridiculous], überspannt [*üh-bər-shpant'*]

extravagant [with money] verschwenderisch [*fer-shven'-də-rish*]

extreme *adj.*, äusserst [*oi'-serst*]

extremely, ausserordentlich [*ou'-sər-or-dənt-liç*]

eye, Auge, -n (n) [*ou'-gə*]

eyebrow, Augenbraue, -n (f) [*ou'-gən-brou-ə*]

eye doctor, Augenarzt, ⸗e (m) [*ou'-gən-ahrtst, ou'-gən-ehrt-stə*]

eyeglasses, Brille, -n (f) [*bri'-lə*]

eyelash, Augenwimper, -n (f) [*ou'-gən-vim-pər*]

eyelid, Augenlid, -er (n) [*ou'-gən-leet, ou'-gən-lee-dər*]

F

fable, Fabel, -n (f) [*fah'-bəl*]

fabric, Stoff, -e (m) [*shtof*]

face, Gesicht, -er (n) [*gə-ziçt', gə-ziç'-tər*]

fact, Tatsache, -n (f) [*taht'-za-khə*]
   in fact, tatsächlich [*taht'-zeç-liç*]

factory, Fabrik, -en (f) [*fa-breek'*]

faculty [university], Fakultät, -en (f) [*fa-kul-teht'*]

fad, Mode, -n (f); Modetorheit, -en (f) [*moh'-də; moh'-də-tohr-hait*]

fade [lose color] *v.*, verblassen [*fer-bla'-sən*]

fail *v.*, fehl-schlagen (irreg; *Aux:* SEIN) [*fehl'-shlah-gən*]

faint *n.*, Ohnmacht (f) [*ohn'-makht*]

faint *v.*, in Ohnmacht fallen (irreg) [*in ohn'-makht fa'-lən*]

fair [just], gerecht; fair [*gə-reçt'; fehr*]

fair [light], blond [*blont*]

faith [belief], Glaube (m) [*glou'-bə*]

faithful, treu [*troi*]

fall *v.*, fallen (irreg; *Aux:* SEIN) [*fa'-lən*]
   fall in love, sich verlieben [*ziç fer-lee'-bən*]
   fall back, zurück-fallen (irreg; *Aux:* SEIN) [*tsu-rük'-fa-lən*]

fall *n.*, Sturz, ⁼e (m) [*shturts, shtür'-tsə*]

fall [autumn], Herbst, -e (m) [*herpst*]

false, falsch [*falsh*]

falsehood, Falschheit, -en (f); Lüge, -n (f) [*falsh'-hait; lüh'-gə*]

fame, Ruhm (m) [*room*]

familiar, bekannt [*bə-kant'*]

family, Familie, -n (f) [*fa-mee'-li-ə*]

famous, berühmt [*bə-rühmt'*]

fan [mechanical], Ventilator, -en (m) [*ven-ti-lah'-tor, ven-ti-la-toh'-rən*]

fantastic, phantastisch [*fan-ta'-stish*]

far, weit [*vait*]

  far away, weit weg [*vait vek*]

  how far? wie weit [*vee vait*]

fare [traveling] *n.*, Fahrpreis, -e (m) [*fahr'-prais, fahr'-prai-zə*]

  What is the fare? Was habe ich zu bezahlen? [*vas hah'-bə iç tsu bə-tsah'-lən*]

farewell *n.*, Abschied, -e (m) [*ap'-sheet, ap'-shee-də*]

farm *n.*, Bauernhof, ⁼e (m) [*bou'-ərn-hohf, bou'-ərn-höh-fə*]

farmer, Bauer, -n (m) [*bou'-ər*]

farmer's wife, Bäuerin, -nen (f) [*boi'-ə-rin*]

farmyard, Wirtschaftshof, ⁼e (m) [*virt'-shafts-hohf, virt'-shafts-höh-fə*]

fascinate *v.*, bezaubern; faszinieren [*bə-tsou'-bərn; fas-tsi-nee'-rən*]

fascinating, bezaubernd [*bə-tsou'-bərnt*]

fashion, Mode, -n (f) [*moh'-də*]

fashionable, modern [*mo-dern'*]

fast *adj.*, schnell [*shnel*]

fast *v.*, fasten [*fa'-stən*]

fasten *v.*, befestigen [*bə-fe'-sti-gən*]

fat *adj.*, fett [*fet*]

fatal, tödlich [*töht'-liç*]

fate, Schicksal, -e (n) [*shik'-zahl*]

father, Vater, ⁼ (m) [*fah'-tər, feh'-tər*]

father-in-law, Schwiegervater, ⁼ (m) [*shvee'-gər-fah-tər,* *shvee'-gər-feh-tər*]

faucet, Hahn, ⸗e (m) [*hahn, heh'-nə*]

fault *n.*, Fehler, - (m) [*feh'-lər*]

  It's my fault, Das ist mein Fehler [*das ist main feh'-lər*]

favor *n.*, Gefallen (m, sing), Gefälligkeiten (pl) [*gə-fa'-lən, gə-fe'-liç-kai-tən*]

favorable, günstig [*gün'-stiç*]

favorite, Günstling, -e (m) [*günst'-ling*]

fear *n.*, Furcht (f) [*furçt*]

fear *v.*, fürchten [*fürç'-tən*]

fearful, furchtbar; furchtsam [*furçt'-bahr; furçt'-sam*]

fearless, furchtlos [*furçt'-los*]

feast *n.*, Festmahl, -e (n) [*fest'-mahl*]

feather, Feder, -n (f) [*feh'-dər*]

feature [face], Gesichtszug, ⸗e (m) [*gə-siçts'-tsook, gə-siçts'-tsüh'-gə*]

February, Februar (m) [*feh'-bru-ahr*]

federal, föderalistisch; Bundes- [*fö-də-ra-li'-stish; bun'-dəs-*]

Federal Republic, Bundesrepublik (f) [*bun'-dəs-re-pub-leek'*]

fee, Gebühr, -en (f) [*gə-bühr'*]

feed [cattle] *v.*, füttern [*fü'-tərn*]

feel *v.*, fühlen [*füh'-lən*]

feeling *n.*, Gefühl, -e (n) [*gə-fühl'*]

fellow, Gefährte, -n (m) [*gə-fehr'-tə*]

female, feminine, weiblich [*vaip'-liç*]

fence, Zaun, ⸗e [*tsoun, tsoi'-nə*]

fencing *n.*, Fechten (n) [*feç'-tən*]

fender, Kotflügel, - (m) [*koht'-flüh-gəl*]

festival, Fest, -e (n) [*fest*]

fetch *v.*, holen [*hoh'-lən*]

fever, Fieber, - (n) [*fee'-bər*]

feverish, fieberisch [*fee'-bə-rish*]

few, wenige [*veh'-ni-gə*]

fewer, weniger [*veh'-ni-gər*]

fiance, Verlobte, -n (m) [*fer-lohp'-tə*]

fiancee, Verlobte, -n (f); Braut, ⸗e (f) [*fer-lohp'-tə; brout, broi'-tə*]

field, Feld, -er (n) [*felt, fel'-dər*]

fierce, wild [*vilt*]
fifteen, fünfzehn [*fünf'-tsehn*]
fifty, fünfzig [*fünf'-tsiç*]
fig, Feige, -n (f) [*fai'-gə*]
fight *n.,* Kampf, ⁼e (m) [*kampf, kem'-pfə*]
fight *v.,* kämpfen [*kem'-pfən*]
figure, Figur, -en (f) [*fi-goor'*]
file [tool], Feile, -n (f) [*fai'-lə*]
fill *v.,* füllen [*fü'-lən*]
   fill up, voll machen [*fol ma'-khən*]
film *n.,* Film, -e (m) [*film*]
filter *n.,* Filter, - (m) [*fil'-tər*]
filthy, schmutzig [*shmoot'-siç*]
final *adj.,* endgültig [*ent'-gül-tiç*]
finally, schliesslich; endlich [*shlees'-liç; ent'-liç*]
financially, finanziell [*fi-nan-tsi-el'*]
find *v.,* finden (irreg) [*fin'-dən*]
fine [good], schön [*shöhn*]
fine [penalty], Geldstrafe, -n (f) [*gelt'-shtrah-fə*]
finger, Finger, - (m) [*fin'-gər*]
finish *v.,* beenden [*bə-en'-dən*]
fire, Feuer, - (n) [*foi'-ər*]
fireproof, feuerfest [*foi'-ər-fest*]
fireplace, Kamin, -e (m) [*ka-meen'*]
firm *adj.,* fest [*fest*]
firm [company], Firma (f, sing), Firmen (pl) [*fir'-mah, fir'-mən*]
first *adj.,* erst [*ehrst*]
first aid, erste Hilfe [*ehr'-stə hil'-fə*]
first name, Vorname, -n (m) [*fohr'-nah-mə*]
fish *n.,* Fisch, -e (m) [*fish*]
fish *v.,* fischen; angeln [*fi'-shən; ang'-əln*]
fisherman, Fischer, - (m) [*fi'-shər*]
fishing *n.,* Fischen (n) [*fi'-shən*]
fishing boat, Fischerboot, -e (n) [*fi'-shər-boht*]
fist, Faust, ⁼e (f) [*foust, foi'-stə*]
fit *v.,* passen [*pa'-sən*]
fit [clothes] *v.,* an-probieren [*an'-pro-bee-rən*]

five, fünf [*fünf*]

fix [fasten] *v.*, fest-machen [*fest'-ma-khən*]

fix [repair] *v.*, reparieren [*re-pa-ree'-rən*]

fixed price, (der) feste Preis [(*dehr) fe'-stə prais*]

flag, Fahne, -n (f) [*fah'-nə*]

flame, Flamme, -n (f) [*fla'-mə*]

flask, Flasche, -n (f) [*fla'-shə*]

flat *adj.*, flach [*flakh*]

flatiron, Bügeleisen, - (n) [*büh'-gəl-ai-zən*]

flatter *v.*, schmeicheln [*shmai'-çəln*]

flavor *n.*, Geschmack, ≈e (m) [*gə-shmak', gə-shme'-kə*]

flavor *v.*, würzen [*vür'-tsən*]

flea, Floh, ≈e (m) [*floh, flöh'-ə*]

flee *v.*, fliehen (irreg; *Aux:* SEIN) [*flee'-ən*]

flesh, Fleisch (n) [*flaish*]

flight [fleeing], Flucht (f) [*flukht*]

flight [flying], Flug, ≈e (m) [*fluhk, flüh'-gə*]

fling *v.*, werfen (irreg) [*ver'-fən*]

float *v.*, schwimmen (irreg; *Aux:* SEIN) [*shvi'-mən*]

flood, Flut, -en (f) [*floot*]

flour, Mehl (n) [*mehl*]

flow *v.*, fliessen (irreg; *Aux:* SEIN) [*flee'-sən*]

flower, Blume, -n (f) [*bloo'-mə*]

flowershop, Blumengeschäft, -e (n) [*bloo'-mən-gə-sheft'*]

fluently, fliessend [*flee'-sənt*]

flush *v.*, aus-spülen [*ous'-shpüh-lən*]

flute, Flöte, -n (f) [*flöh'-tə*]

fly *n.*, Fliege, -n (f) [*flee'-gə*]

fly *v.*, fliegen (irreg; *Aux:* SEIN) [*flee'-gən*]

foam, Schaum, ≈e (m) [*shoum, shoi'-mə*]

foe, Feind, -e (m) [*faint, fain'-də*]

fog, Nebel, - (m) [*neh'-bəl*]

foggy, nebelig [*neh'-bə-liç*]

fold *n.*, Falte, -n (f) [*fal'-tə*]

follow *v.*, folgen (plus dat) (*Aux:* SEIN) [*fol'-gən*]

   Follow me! Folgen Sie mir! [*fol'-gən zee meer*]

fond [loving], zärtlich [*tsehrt'-liç*]

food, Speise, -n (f); Nahrung (f) [*shpai'-zə; nah'-rung*]

fool, Dummkopf, ≠e (m) [*dum'-kopf, dum'-kö-pfə*]

foolish, albern [*al'-bərn*]

foot, Fuss, ≠e (m) [*foos, füh'-sə*]

football, Fussball, ≠e (m) [*foos'-bal, foos'-be-lə*]

football player, Fussballspieler, - (m) [*foos'-bal-shpee-lər*]

for, für [*führ*]

    for example, zum Beispiel [*tsum bai'-shpeel*]

    for me; for you, für mich; für Sie [*führ miç; führ zee*]

    what for? wofür [*voh-führ'*]

forbid *v.*, verbieten (irreg) [*fer-bee'-tən*]

force *n.*, Gewalt, -en (f) [*gə-valt'*]

force *v.*, zwingen (irreg) [*tsvin'-gən*]

forehead, Stirn, -en (f) [*shteern*]

foreign, ausländisch [*ous'-len-aish*]

foreign policy, Aussenpolitik (f) [*ou'-sən-po-li-teek*]

foreigner [male], Ausländer, - (m) [*ous'-len-dər*]

foreigner [female], Ausländerin, -nen (f) [*ous'-len-də-rin*]

forest, Wald, ≠er (m) [*valt, vel'-dər*]

forever, auf immer [*ouf i'-mər*]

forget *v.*, vergessen (irreg) [*fer-ge'-sən*]

forgive *v.*, verzeihen (irreg) [*fer-tsai'-ən*]

fork, Gabel, -n (f) [*gah'-bəl*]

form *n.*, Form, -en (f) [*form*]

form *v.*, bilden [*bil'-dən*]

formal, formell [*for-mel'*]

formality, Formalität, -en (f) [*for-ma-li-teht'*]

former, früher [*früh'-ər*]

formula, Formel, -n (f) [*for'-məl*]

fortunate, glücklich [*glük'-liç*]

fortunately, glücklicherweise [*glük'-liç-ər-vai-zə*]

fortune [wealth], Vermögen, - (n) [*fer-möh'-gən*]

forty, vierzig [*fir'-tsiç*]

forum, Forum (n, sing), Foren (pl) [*foh'-rum, foh'-rən*]

forward *adv.*, vorwärts [*fohr'-verts*]

found *v.*, gründen [*grün'-dən*]

foundation, Gründung, -en (f); Stiftung, -en (f);
    Fundament, -e (n) [*grün'-dung; shtif'-tung; fun-da-ment'*]

fountain, Quelle, -n (f); Brunnen, - (m) [*kve'-lə; bru'-nən*]
fountain pen, Füllfeder, -n (f) [*fül'-feh-dər*]
four, vier [*feer*]
fourteen, vierzehn [*fir'-tsehn*]
fourth, vierte [*feer'-tə*]
fracture, Bruch, ⸗e (m) [*brukh, brü'-çə*]
fragrance, Duft, ⸗e (m) [*duft, düf'-tə*]
frail, schwach [*shvakh*]
frame, Rahmen, - (m) [*rah'-mən*]
France, Frankreich (n) [*frank'-raiç*]
frank *adj.,* offen [*o'-fən*]
fraud, Betrug (m) [*bə-trook'*]
free *adj.,* frei [*frai*]
free *v.,* befreien [*bə-frai'-ən*]
freedom, Freiheit, -en (f) [*frai'-hait*]
freeze *v.,* frieren (irreg; *Aux:* HABEN, SEIN) [*free'-rən*]
freight, Fracht (f) [*frakht*]
French, französisch [*fran-tsöh'-zish*]
Frenchman, Franzose, -n (m) [*fran-tsoh'-zə*]
Frenchwoman, Französin -nen (f) [*fran-tsöh'-zin*]
frequently, häufig [*hoi'-fiç*]
fresh, frisch [*frish*]
Friday, Freitag, -e (m) [*frai'-tahk, frai'-tah-gə*]
fried, gebraten [*gə-brah'-tən*]
friend [female], Freundin, -nen (f) [*froin'-din*]
friend [male], Freund, -e (m) [*froint, froin'-də*]
friendship, Freundschaft, -en (f) [*froint'-shaft*]
frighten *v.,* erschrecken [*er-shre'-kən*]
frog, Frosch, ⸗e (m) [*frosh, frö'-shə*]
from, von (plus dat) [*fon*]
  from now on, von jetzt an [*fon yetst an*]
  From where do you come? Woher kommen Sie? [*voh-hehr' ko'-mən zee*]
front, Front, -en (f) [*front*]
frost, Frost, ⸗e (m) [*frost, frö'-stə*]
frozen, gefroren [*gə-froh'-rən*]
fruit, Frucht, ⸗e (f); Obst (m) [*frukht, früç'-tə; ohpst*]
fruit salad, Obstsalat, -e (m) [*ohpst'-za-laht*]

fruit market, Obstmarkt, ¨e (m) [*ohpst'-markt, ohpst'-merk-tə*]
fry *v.*, braten (irreg) [*brah'-tən*]
frying pan, Bratpfanne, -n (f) [*braht'-pfa-nə*]
fuel [of rocket], Treibstoff, -e (m) [*traip'-shtof*]
full, voll [*fol*]
fun, Spass, ¨e (m) [*shpahs, shpeh'-sə*]
function *n.*, Funktion, -en (f) [*funk-tsi-ohn'*]
funds, Geldmittel (n, pl) [*gelt'-mi-təl*]
funeral, Begräbnis, -se (n) [*bə-grehp'-nis*]
funny, komisch [*koh'-mish*]
fur, Pelz, -e (m) [*pelts*]
fur coat, Pelzmantel, ¨ (m) [*pelts'-man-təl, pelts'-men-təl*]
furious, wütend [*vüh'-tənt*]
furnish [a house] *v.*, ein-richten [*ain'-riç-tən*]
furniture, Möbel (n, pl) [*möh'-bəl*]
further *adv.*, weiter [*vai'-tər*]
future, Zukunft (f) [*tsoo'-kunft*]
  in the future, in Zukunft [*in tsoo'-kunft*]

G

gag *n.*, Witz, -e (m) [*vits*]
gaiety, Heiterkeit (f) [*hai'-tər-kait*]
gain *n.*, Gewinn, -e (m) [*gə-vin'*]
gain *v.*, gewinnen (irreg) [*gə-vi'-nən*]
gallon, Gallone, -n (f) [*ga-loh'-nə*]
gamble *v.*, spielen [*shpee'-lən*]
game, Spiel, -e (n) [*shpeel*]
garage, Garage, -n (f) [*ga-rah'-zhə*]
garbage, Abfall, ¨e (m) [*ap'-fal, ap'-fe-lə*]
garden, Garten, ¨ (m) [*gar'-tən, ger'-tən*]
gardener [male], Gärtner, - (m) [*gert'-nər*]
garlic, Knoblauch (m) [*knohp'-loukh*]
garment, Gewand, ¨er (n) [*gə-vant', gə-ven'-dər*]

gas, Gas, -e (n) [*gahs, gah'-zə*]

gasoline, Benzin (n) [*ben-tseen'*]

gasoline station, Tankstelle, -n (f) [*tank'-shte-lə*]

gate, Tor, -e (n) [*tohr*]

gather *v.*, sammeln [*za'-məln*]

gay, fröhlich [*fröh'-liç*]

gear [motor], Gang, ⸗e (m) [*gang, geng'-ə*]
  first (second) gear, erster (zweiter) Gang [*ehr'-stər (tsvai'-tər) gang*]

gem, Edelstein, -e (m) [*eh'-dəl-shtain*]

gender, Geschlecht, -er (n) [*gə-shleçt', gə-shleç'-tər*]

general *adj.*, allgemein [*al'-gə-main*]
  in general, im allgemeinen [*im al-gə-mai'-nən*]

general delivery, postlagernd [*post'-lah-gərnt*]

general *n.*, General, -e [*ge-nə-rahl*]

generation, Generation, -en (f) [*ge-nə-ra-tsi-ohn'*]

generous, freigebig [*frai'-geh-biç*]

genius, Genie, -s (n) [*zhe-nee', zhe-nees'*]

gentle, sanft [*zanft*]

gentleman, Herr, -en (m) [*her*]

genuine, echt [*eçt*]

geography, Geographie (f) [*ge-o-gra-fee'*]

germ [bot.], Keim (m) [*kaim*]

German *adj.*, deutsch [*doich*]

German [male, female], Deutsche, -n (m, f) [*doi'-chə*]

Germany Deutschland (n) [*doich'-lant*]

get [become] *v.*, werden (irreg; *Aux:* SEIN) [*vehr'-dən*]

get [receive] *v.*, bekommen (irreg) [*bə-ko'-mən*]
  get in, ein-steigen (irreg; *Aux:* SEIN) [*ain'-shtai-gən*]
  get married, sich verheiraten [*ziç fer-hai'-rah-tən*]
  get off, aus-steigen (irreg; *Aux:* SEIN) [*ous'-shtai-gən*]
  get to, erreichen [*er-rai'-çən*]

get up, auf-stehen (irreg; *Aux:* SEIN) [*ouf'-shteh-ən*]

ghost, Gespenst, -er (n) [*gə-shpenst', gə-shpen'-stər*]

gift, Geschenk, -e (n) [*gə-shenk'*]

gifted, begabt [*be-gahpt'*]

gigantic, riesig [*ree'-ziç*]

girdle, Gürtel, - (m) [*gür'-təl*]

girl, Mädchen, - (n) [*meht'-çən*]
give *v.*, geben (*irreg*) [*geh'-bən*]
  give back, zurück-geben (irreg) [*tsu-rük'-geh-bən*]
  Give it to her (him, me, them, us), Geben Sie es ihr
    (ihm, mir, ihnen, uns) [*geh'-bən zee es eer (eem, meer,
    ee'-nən, uns)*]
  give in [admit], zu-geben (irreg) [*tsoo'-geh-bən*]
  give up, auf-geben (irreg) [*ouf'-geh-bən*]
glad, froh [*froh*]
glamour, Zauber (m) [*tsou'-bər*]
glass, Glas, ⁼er (n) [*glahs, gleh'-zər*]
glasses, Brille, -n (f) [*bri'-lə*]
globe, Kugel, -n (f) [*koo'-gəl*]
globetrotter, Weltenbummler, - (m) [*vel'-tən-bum-lər*]
gloomy, düster [*düh'-stər*]
glory, Ruhm (m) [*room*]
glove, Handschuh, -e (m) [*hant'-shoo*]
glow *n.*, Glut (f) [*gloot*]
glow *v.*, glühen [*glüh'-ən*]
go *v.*, gehen (irreg; *Aux:* SEIN) [*geh'-ən*]
  go away, weg-gehen (irreg; *Aux:* SEIN) [*vek'-geh-ən*]
  Go back! Gehen Sie zurück! [*geh'-ən zee tsu-rük'*]
  go for [fetch], holen [*hoh'-lən*]
  go in, hinein-gehen (irreg; *Aux:* SEIN) [*hi-nain'-geh-ən*]
  go on [advance], weiter-gehen (irreg; *Aux:* SEIN) [*vai'-tər-
    geh-ən*]
  go on [continue], fort-fahren (irreg; *Aux:* SEIN) [*fort'-
    fah-rən*]
  go out, aus-gehen (irreg; *Aux:* SEIN) [*ous'-geh-ən*]
  go to bed, schlafen gehen (irreg; *Aux:* SEIN) [*shlah'-fən
    geh'-ən*]
goal, Ziel, -e (n) [*tseel*]
God, Gott, ⁼er (m) [*got, gö'-tər*]
godchild, Patenkind, -er (n) [*pah'-tən-kint, pah'-tən-kin-dər*]
godfather, Pate, -n (m) [*pah'-tə*]
godmother, Patin, -nen (f) [*pah'-tin*]
gold, Gold (n) [*golt*]
gold [made of gold], aus Gold [*ous golt*]

golden, golden [*gol'-dən*]

golf, Golf (n) [*golf*]

good, gut [*goot*]

   Good day! Guten Tag! [*goo'-tən tahk*]

   Good evening! Guten Abend! [*goo'-tən ah'-bənt*]

   Good luck! Viel Glück! [*feel glük*]

   Good morning! Guten Morgen! [*goo'-tən mor'-gən*]

   Good night! Gute Nacht! [*goo'-tə nakht*]

   Good bye! Auf Wiedersehen! [*ouf vee'-dər-zeh-ən*]

goodlooking, gut aussehend [*goot ous'-zeh-ənt*]

goodness, Güte (f) [*güh'-tə*]

goods, Waren (f, pl) [*vah'-rən*]

goose, Gans, ⸗e (f) [*gans, gen'-zə*]

gorgeous, prächtig [*preç'-tiç*]

gossip, *n.*, Klatsch (m) [*klatch*]

gossip *v.*, schwatzen [*shvat'-sən*]

gothic, gotisch [*goh'-tish*]

government, Regierung, -en (f) [*re-gee'-rung*]

grace, Anmut (f) [*an'moot*]

grade, Grad, -e (m) [*graht, grah'-də*]

grade [academic], Note, -n (f) [*noh'-tə*]

gradually, stufenweise [*shtoo'-fən-vai-zə*]

graduation [from high school], Reifeprüfung, -en (f) [*rai'-fə-prüh-fung*]

grammar, Grammatik, -en (f) [*gra-ma'-tik*]

grandchild, Enkelkind, -er (n) [*en'-kəl-kint, en'-kəl-kin-dər*]

granddaughter, Enkelin, -nen (f) [*en'-kə-lin*]

grandfather, Grossvater, ⸗ (m) [*grohs'-fah-tər, grohs'-feh-tər*]

grandmother, Grossmutter, ⸗ (f) [*grohs'-mu-tər, grohs'-mü-tər*]

grandparents, Grosseltern (pl) [*grohs'-el-tərn*]

grandson, Enkel, - (m) [*en'-kəl*]

grape, Traube, -n (f) [*trou'-bə*]

grapefruit, Pampelmuse, -n (f) [*pam-pel-moo'-zə*]

grass, Gras, ⸗er [*grahs, greh'-zər*]

grateful, dankbar [*dank'-bahr*]

gratis, gratis [*grah'-tis*]
grave *n.*, Grab, ⁼er (n) [*grahp, greh'-bər*]
grave *adj.*, ernst [*ernst*]
grease, Fett, -e (n) [*fet*]
great, gross [*grohs*]
   a great deal, sehr viel [*zehr feel*]
   a great many, sehr viele [*zehr fee'-lə*]
greatness, Grösse (f) [*gröh'-sə*]
Great Britain, Grossbritannien (f) [*grohs-bri-ta'-ni-ən*]
Greece, Griechenland (n) [*gree'-çən-lant*]
Greek *adj.*, griechisch [*gree'-çish*]
green, grün [*grühn*]
greet *v.*, grüssen [*grüh'-sən*]
greetings, Grüsse (m, pl) [*grüh'-sə*]
grey, grau [*grou*]
grief, Kummer (m) [*ku'-mər*]
grind [coffee, corn] *v.*, mahlen (reg & irreg) [*mah'-lən*]
ground, Boden, ⁼ (m) [*boh'-dən, böh'-dən*]
ground floor, Erdgeschoss, -e (n) [*ehrt'-gə-shos*]
group, Gruppe, -n (f) [*gru'-pə*]
grow [become] *v.*, werden (irreg; Aux: SEIN) [*vehr'-dən*]
   grow old, alt werden (irreg; Aux: SEIN) [*alt vehr'-dən*]
grow [increase] *v.*, wachsen (irreg; Aux: SEIN) [*vak'-sən*]
guarantee, Garantie, -n (f) [*ga-ran-tee'*]
guard *n.*, Wächter, - (m) [*veç'-tər*]
guardian, Hüter, - (m); Vormund, -e (m) [*hüh'-tər; fohr'-munt, fohr'-mun-də*]
guess *v.*, erraten (irreg) [*er-rah'-tən*]
guest, Gast, ⁼e (m) [*gast, ge'-stə*]
guide, Führer, - (m) [*füh'-rər*]
guilty, schuldig [*shul'-diç*]
guitar, Gitarre, -n (f) [*gi-ta'-rə*]
gum [teeth], Zahnfleisch (n) [*tsahn'-flaish*]
gun, Gewehr, -e (n); Kanone, -n (f); Pistole, -n (f) [*gə-vehr'; ka-noh'-nə; pi-stoh'-lə*]
gymnasium, Turnhalle, -n (f) [*turn'-ha-lə*]
gypsy, Zigeuner, - (m) [*tsi-goi'-nər*]

H

habit, Gewohnheit, -en (f) [gə-vohn'-hait]

hair, Haar, -e (n) [hahr]

hairbrush, Haarbürste, -n (f) [hahr'-bür-stə]

haircut, Haarschnitt, - (m) [hahr'-shnit]
   I had a haircut yesterday, Ich liess mir gestern die Haare
   schneiden [iç lees mir ge'-stərn dee hah'-rə shnai'-dən]

hairdresser, Friseur, -e (m) [fri-zöhr']

hair tonic, Haarwasser, = (n) [hahr'-va-sər, hahr'-ve-sər]

half n., Hälfte, -n (f) [helf'-tə]

half adj., halb [halp]
   half past two, halb drei [halp drai]

halfway, halbwegs [halp'-vehks]

hall [entrance], Flur, -e (m); Diele, -n (f) [fluhr; dee'-lə]

Halt! Halt! [halt]

ham, Schinken, - (m) [shin'-kən]

hammer, Hammer, = (m) [ha'-mər, he'-mər]

hand n., Hand, =e (f) [hant, hen'-də]
   on the other hand, anderseits [an'-dər-zaits]

hand v., reichen [rai'-çən]

handbag, Handtasche, -n (f) [hant'-ta-shə]

handkerchief, Taschentuch, =er (n) [ta'-shən-tukh, ta'-shən-
   tüh-çər]

handsewn, handgenäht [hant'-gə-neht]

handle n., Handgriff, -e (m) [hant'-grif]

handsome, gut aussehend [goot ous'-seh-ent]

hang [a person] v., erhängen [er-heng'-ən]

hang [an object] v., hängen [heng'-ən]

happen v., geschehen (irreg; Aux: SEIN) [gə-sheh'-ən]
   What is happening? Was ist los? [vas ist lohs]
   When did it happen? Wann ist das geschehen? [van ist
   das gə-sheh'-ən]

happy, glücklich [glük'-liç]

Happy Birthday! Viel Glück zu Ihrem Geburtstag!
[*feel glük tsu ee'-rəm gə-burts'-tahk*]
Happy New Year! Prosit Neujahr! [*proh'-zit noi'-yahr*]
harbor *n.*, Hafen, ˮ (m) [*hah'-fən, heh'-fən*]
hard [difficult], schwer [*shvehr*]
hard [not soft], hart [*hart*]
hardhearted, hartherzig [*hart'-her-tsiç*]
hardly, kaum [*koum*]
harm *v.*, schaden [*shah'-dən*]
harmful, schädlich [*sheht'-liç*]
harp, Harfe, -n (f) [*har'-fə*]
harvest *n.*, Ernte, -n (f) [*ern'-tə*]
haste, Eile (f) [*ai'-lə*]
hat, Hut, ˮe (m) [*hoot, hüh'-tə*]
hate *v.*, hassen [*ha'-sən*]
hate *n.*, Hass (m) [*has*]
have *v.*, haben (irreg) [*hah'-bən*]
   have to, müssen (mod aux) [*mü'-sən*]
   I have to go, Ich muss gehen [*iç mus geh'-ən*]
he, er [*ehr*]
head [anat.], Kopf, ˮe (m) [*kopf, kö'-pfə*]
head [chief], Oberhaupt, ˮer (n) [*oh'-bər-houpt, oh'-bər-houp-tər*]
headache, Kopfschmerzen (m, pl) [*kopf'-shmer-tsən*]
headquarters [army], Hauptquartier, -e (n) [*houpt-kvar-teer'*]
headquarters [business], Zentrale, -n (f) [*tsen-trah'-lə*]
health, Gesundheit (f) [*gə-zunt'-hait*]
   be in good health *v.*, bei guter Gesundheit sein [*bai goo'-tər gə-zunt'-hait zain*]
   To your health! Auf Ihr Wohl! [*ouf eer vohl*]
healthy, gesund [*gə-zunt'*]
hear *v.*, hören [*höh'-rən*]
heart, Herz, -en (n) [*herts*]
   by heart, auswendig [*ous'-ven-diç*]
heart disease, Herzkrankheit, -en (f) [*herts'-krank-hait*]
heat *n.*, Hitze (f) [*hit'-sə*]
heat *v.*, heizen [*hait'-sən*]
heating *n.*, Heizung, -en [*hait'-sung*]

heaven, Himmel, - (m) [*hi'-məl*]
   Heavens! Lieber Himmel! [*lee'-bər hi'-məl*]
heavy, schwer [*shvehr*]
heavy industry, Schwerindustrie, -n (f) [*shvehr'-in-du-stree*]
Hebrew, hebräisch [*he-breh'-ish*]
heel [foot], Ferse, -n (f) [*fehr'-zə*]
heel [shoe], Absatz, ⁼e [*ap'-zats, ap'-ze-tsə*]
height, Höhe, -n (f) [*höh'-ə*]
heir, Erbe, -n (m) [*er'-bə*]
heiress, Erbin, -nen (f) [*er'-bin*]
hell, Hölle, -n (f) [*hö'-lə*]
Hello! Hallo! [*ha-loh'*]
help *n.*, Hilfe (f) [*hil'-fə*]
help *v.*, helfen (irreg) [*hel'-fən*]
   Help! Hilfe! [*hil'-fə*]
helpful, behilflich [*bə-hilf'-liç*]
hen, Henne, -n (f) [*he'-nə*]
her [as indirect obj. and poss.], ihr [*eer*]
her [as direct obj. or acc.], sie [*zee*]
herself, sich selbst (dat, acc); sie selbst (nom) [*ziç zelpst; zee zelpst*]
here, hier [*heer*]
   Come here! Kommen Sie her! [*ko'-mən zee hehr*]
   Here it is, Hier ist es [*heer ist es*]
hero, Held, -en (m) [*helt, hel'-dən*]
hers, ihr, ihre, ihres [*eer, ee'-re, ee'-rəs*]
hesitate *v.*, zögern [*tsöh'-gərn*]
hide *v.*, verstecken [*fer-shte'-kən*]
hideous, scheusslich [*shois'-liç*]
high, hoch [*hokh*]
higher, höher [*höh'-ər*]
highest, höchst [*höhçst*]
high school, höhere Schule (f) [*höh'-ə-re shoo'-lə*]
high school certificate, Reifezeugnis, -se (n) [*rai'-fə-tsoik-nis*]
highway, Landstrasse, -n (f) [*lant'-shtra-sə*]
hill, Hügel, - (m) [*hüh'-gəl*]
him [direct obj. or acc.], ihn [*een*]

him [as indirect obj.], ihm [*eem*]
himself, sich selbst (dat, acc) ; er selbst (nom) [*ziç zelpst; ehr zelpst*]
   He dresses himself, Er zieht sich an [*ehr tseet ziç an*]
hip, Hüfte, -n (f) [*hüf'-tə*]
hire [rent], *v.*, mieten [*mee'-tən*]
his, sein, seine [*zain, zai'-nə*]
history, Geschichte, -n (f) [*gə-shiç'-tə*]
hit *v.*, schlagen (irreg) [*shlah'-gən*]
hitch-hike *v.*, per Anhalter fahren (irreg; *Aux:* SEIN) [*per an'-hal-tər fah'-rən*]
hold *v.*, halten (irreg) [*hal'-tən*]
hole, Loch, ⸗er (n) [*lokh, lö'-çər*]
holiday, Feiertag, -e (m) [*fai'-ər-tahk, fai'-ər-tah-gə*]
Holland, Holland (n) [*ho'-lant*]
holy, heilig [*hai'-liç*]
home *n.*, Heim, -e (n) [*haim*]
   at home, zu Hause [*tsu hou'-zə*]
   Make yourself at home! Fühlen Sie sich wie zu Hause! [*füh'-lən zee ziç vee tsu hou'-zə*]
honest, ehrlich [*ehr'-liç*]
honey [from bees], Honig (m) [*hoh'-niç*]
honey [word of endearment], Liebling!, Schatz! [*leep'-ling, shats*]
honeymoon, Flitterwochen (f, pl) [*fli'-tər-vo-khən*]
honor *n.*, Ehre, -n (f) [*eh'-rə*]
hope *n.*, Hoffnung, -en (f) [*hof'-nung*]
hope *v.*, hoffen [*ho'-fən*]
hopeful, hoffnungsvoll [*hof'-nungs-fol*]
hopeless, hoffnungslos [*hof'-nungs-lohs*]
horizon, Horizont, -e (m) [*ho-ri-tsont'*]
horn [on animal], Horn, ⸗er (n) [*horn, hör'-nər*]
horn [on auto], Hupe, -n (f) [*hoo'-pə*]
horrible, schrecklich [*shrek'-liç*]
horse, Pferd, -e (n) [*pfehrt, pfehr'-də*]
hospital, Krankenhaus, ⸗er (n) [*kran'-kən-hous, kran'-kən-hoi-zər*]
hospitality, Gastfreundschaft (f) [*gast'-froint-shaft*]

host, Gastgeber, - (n) [*gast'-geh-bər*]
hostess, Gastgeberin, -nen (f) [*gast'-geh-bə-rin*]
hostile, feindlich [*faint'-liç*]
hot, heiss [*hais*]
hotel, Hotel, -s (n) [*ho-təl', ho-təls'*]
hotel room, Hotelzimmer, - (n) [*ho-tel'-tsi-mər*]
hour, Stunde, -n (f) [*shtun'-də*]
hourly, stündlich [*shtünt'-liç*]
house, Haus, ‟er [*hous, hoi'-zər*]
housekeeper, Haushälterin, -nen (f) [*hous'-hel-tə-rin*]
housewife, Hausfrau, -en (f) [*hous'-frou*]
how, wie [*vee*]
　　How do you do? Wie geht es Ihnen? [*vee geht es ee'-nən*]
　　how far? wie weit? [*vee vait*]
　　how long [a time]? wie lange? [*vee lan'-gə*]
　　how much? wieviel? [*vee-feel'*]
however, aber; jedoch [*ah'-bər; ye-dokh'*]
huge, ungeheuer [*un'-gə-hoi-ər*]
human, menschlich [*mensh'-liç*]
humble, demütig [*deh'-müh-tiç*]
humid, feucht [*foiçt*]
humorous, humoristisch [*hu-mo-ri'-stish*]
hundred, hundert [*hun'-dərt*]
Hungarian *adj.*, ungarisch [*ung'-ga-rish*]
Hungary, Ungarn (n) [*ung'-garn*]
hunger, Hunger (m) [*hung'-ər*]
　　I'm hungry, Ich habe Hunger [*iç hah'-bə hung'-ər*]
hunt *v.*, jagen [*yah'-gən*]
hunter, Jäger, - (m) [*yeh'-gər*]
hurry *v.*, sich beeilen [*ziç bə-ai'-lən*]
　　Hurry up! Beeilen Sie sich!, (Machen Sie) schnell! [*bə-ai'-lən zee ziç, (ma'-khən zee) shnel*]
　　be in a hurry, es eilig haben [*es ai'-liç hah'-bən*]
hurt [somebody] *v.*, weh tun (irreg) [*veh toon*]
hurt [ache] *v.*, schmerzen [*shmert'-sən*]
husband, Gatte, -n (m); Mann, ‟er (m) [*ga'-tə; man, me'-nər*]
hysterical, hysterisch [*hü-steh'-rish*]

I

I, ich [*iç*]
I myself, ich selbst [*iç zelpst*]
ice, Eis (n) [*ais*]
ice cream, Eis (n); Speiseeis (n) [*ais; shpai'-zə-ais*]
idea, Idee, -n (f) [*i-deh'*]
ideal *adj.,* ideal [*i-de-ahl'*]
identical, identisch [*i-den'-tish*]
identification card, Personalausweis, -e (m) [*per-zo-nahl'-ous-vais*]
identify *v.,* identifizieren [*i-den-ti-fi-tsee'-rən*]
idle *adj.,* müssig [*miih'-siç*]
idiot, Idiot, -en (m) [*i-di-oht'*]
if, wenn [*ven*]
  even if, sogar wenn [*zo-gahr' ven*]
ignorant, unwissend [*un'-vi-sənt*]
ill, krank [*krank*]
illegal, gesetzwidrig [*gə-zets'-veed-riç*]
illegible, unleserlich [*un'-leh-zər-liç*]
illness, Krankheit, -en (f) [*krank'-hait*]
imagination, Phantasie (f) [*fan-ta-zee'*]
imagine [to have an idea] *v.,* sich vor-stellen [*ziç fohr'-shte-lən*]
  Just imagine! Stellen Sie sich vor! [*shte'-lən zee ziç fohr*]
imitate *v.,* nach-ahmen [*nakh'-ah-mən*]
imitation, Nachahmung, -en (f) [*nakh'-ah-mung*]
immature, unreif [*un'-raif*]
immediate, unmittelbar [*un'-mi-təl-bahr*]
immediately, sofort [*zo-fort'*]
immigration, Einwanderung, -en (f) [*ain'-van-də-rung*]
immoral, unmoralisch [*un'-mo-rah-lish*]
impatient, ungeduldig [*un'-gə-dul-diç*]
imperfect *adj.,* unvollkommen [*un'-fol-ko-mən*]

66

implement [tool], Gerät, -e (n) [*gə-reht'*]

impolite, unhöflich [*un'-höhf-liç*]

import *v.*, importieren [*im-por-tee'-rən*]

importance, Wichtigkeit (f) [*viç'-tiç-kait*]

important, wichtig [*viç'-tiç*]

imported, importiert [*im-por-teert'*]

impossible, unmöglich [*un'-möhk-liç*]

impression, Eindruck, ⸗e (m) [*ain'-druk, ain'-drü-kə*]

improve *v.*, verbessern [*fer-be'-sərn*]

improvement, Verbesserung, -en (f) [*fer-be'-sə-rung*]

in *prep.*, in (plus dat; plus acc for motion) [*in*]

    in back of, hinter (plus dat) [*hin'-tər*]

    in front of, vor (plus dat) [*fohr*]

    Is Miss Bauer in? Ist Fräulein Bauer da? [*ist froi'-lain bou'-ər dah*]

inch, Zoll, - (m) [*tsol*]

incident, Vorfall, ⸗e (m) [*fohr'-fal, fohr'-fe-lə*]

incidentally, übrigens [*üh'-bri-gəns*]

inclination, Neigung (f) [*nai'-gung*]

include *v.*, ein-schliessen (irreg) [*ain'-shlee-sən*]

income, Einkommen, - (n) [*ain'-ko-mən*]

income tax, Einkommensteuer, -n (f) [*ain'-ko-mən-shtoi-ər*]

incomparable, unvergleichlich [*un-fer-glaiç'-liç*]

incomplete, unvollständig [*un'-fol-shten-diç*]

incorrect, unrichtig [*un'-riç-tiç*]

increase *n.*, Vermehrung, -en (f) [*fer-meh'-rung*]

increase *v.*, vermehren [*fer-meh'-rən*]

incredible, unglaublich [*un-gloup'-liç*]

indecent, unanständig [*un'-an-shten-diç*]

indeed, tatsächlich [*taht'-zeç-liç*]

    Yes, indeed! Jawohl! [*ya-vohl'*]

indefinite, unbestimmt [*un'-bə-shtimt*]

independence, Unabhängigkeit (f) [*un'-ap-heng-iç-kait*]

independent, unabhängig [*un'-ap-heng-iç*]

India, Indien (n) [*in'-di-ən*]

Indian [Asia] *adj.*, indisch [*in'-dish*]

Indian [America] *adj.*, indianisch [*in-di-ah'-nish*]

indifferent, gleichgültig [*glaiç'-gül-tiç*]

indigestion, Verdauungsstörung, -en (f) [_fer-dou'-ungs-shtöh-rung_]

indirect, indirekt [_in'-di-rekt_]

indiscreet, indiskret [_in'-dis-kreht_]

individual _adj.,_ individuell [_in-di-vi-du-el'_]

individual _n.,_ Individuum (n, sing), Individuen (pl) [_in-di-vee'-du-um, in-di-vee'-du-ən_]

indoors, im Hause [_im hou'-zə_]

industrial, industriell [_in-dus-tri-el'_]

industry, Industrie, -n (f) [_in-du-stree'_]

infantry, Infanterie (f) [_in-fan-tə-ree'_]

infection, Entzündung, -en (f) [_ent-tsün'-dung_]

inferior, minderwertig [_min'-dər-vehr-tiç_]

infinite, unendlich [_un-ent'-liç_]

influence _n.,_ Einfluss, ⸗e (m) [_ain'-flus, ain'-flü-sə_]

influence _v.,_ beeinflussen [_bə-ain'-flu-sən_]

information, Auskunft, ⸗e (f) [_ous'-kunft, ous'-künf-tə_]

inhabitant, Einwohner, - (m) [_ain'-voh-nər_]

inherit _v.,_ erben [_er'-bən_]

inheritance, Erbschaft, -en (f) [_erp'-shaft_]

initial, anfänglich [_an'-feng-liç_]

injection, Spritze, -n (f) [_shprit'-sə_]

injure _v.,_ verletzen [_fer-let'-sən_]

injured, verletzt [_fer-letst'_]

injury, Verletzung, -en [_fer-let'-sung_]

injustice, Ungerechtigkeit, -en (f) [_un'-gə-reç-tiç-kait_]

ink, Tinte, -n (f) [_tin'-tə_]

inn, Wirtshaus, ⸗er (n) [_virts'-hous, virts'-hoi-zər_]

innocent, unschuldig [_un'-shul-diç_]

innumerable, unzählig [_un-tseh'-liç_]

inquire _v.,_ sich erkundigen [_ziç er-kun'-di-gən_]

insane, wahnsinnig [_vahn'-zi-niç_]

insect, Insekt, -en (n) [_in-zekt'_]

inside _adv.,_ drinnen [_dri'-nən_]

insist on _v.,_ bestehen auf (plus dat) (irreg) [_bə-shteh'-ən ouf_]

inspection [examination], Untersuchung, -en (f) [_un-tər-suh'-khung_]

inspector, Inspektor, -en (m) [_in-spek'-tor_]

inspiration, Eingebung, -en (f) [*ain'-geh-bung*]
instance, Beispiel [*bai'-shpeel*]
  for instance, zum Beispiel [*tsum bai'-shpeel*]
instead of, anstatt [*an-shtat'*]
instinct, Instinkt, -e (m) [*in-stinkt'*]
institution, Institut, -e (n) [*in-sti-toot'*]
instruct v., unterrichten [*un-tər-riç'-tən*]
instruction, Unterricht (m) [*un'-tə-riçt*]
instructor [male], Lehrer, - (m) [*leh'-rər*]
instructor [female], Lehrerin, -nen (f) [*leh'-rə-rin*]
instrument, Instrument, -e (n) [*in-stru-ment'*]
insufficient, ungenügend [*un'-gə-nüh-gənt*]
insult n., Beleidigung, -en (f) [*bə-lai'-di-gung*]
insult v., beleidigen [*bə-lai'-di-gən*]
insurance, Versicherung, -en (f) [*fer-zi'-çə-rung*]
insurance policy, Police, -n (f) [*po-lee'-sə*]
intact, unversehrt [*un'-fer-zehrt*]
intellectual adj., intellektuell [*in-te-lek-tu-el'*]
intelligent, intelligent [*in-te-li-gent'*]
intense, intensiv [*in-ten-zeef'*]
intention, Absicht, -en (f) [*ap'-ziçt*]
interest [on debt], Zinsen (m, pl) [*tsin'-zən*]
interest [concern], Interesse, -n (n) [*in-te-re'-sə*]
interesting, interessant [*in-te-re-sant'*]
interior n., Innere (n) [*i'-nər-ə*]
intermission, Unterbrechung, -en (f); Pause, -n (f) [*un-tər-bre'-çung; pou'-zə*]
internal, inner [*i'-nər*]
international, international [*in-tər-na-tsi-o-nahl'*]
interpreter, Dolmetscher, - (m) [*dol'-met-chər*]
interview n., Interview, -s (n) [*in-tər-vyoo', in-tər-vyoos'*]
intimate adj., intim [*in-teem'*]
into, in (plus acc) [*in*]
introduce [people] v., vor-stellen [*fohr'-shte-lən*]
introduction, Vorstellung, -en (f) [*fohr'-shte-lung*]
invalid n., Kranke, -n (m, f) [*kran'-kə*]
invasion, Invasion, -en (f) [*in-va-zi-ohn'*]
invention, Erfindung, -en (f) [*er-fin'-dung*]

inventor, Erfinder, - (m) [*er-fin'-dər*]
invest [money] *v.,* an-legen [*an'-leh-gən*]
investigate *v.,* untersuchen [*un-tər-zuh'-khən*]
invisible, unsichtbar [*un'-ziçt-bahr*]
invitation, Einladung, -en (f) [*ain'-lah-dung*]
invite *v.,* ein-laden (irreg) [*ain'-lah-dən*]
invoice, Rechnung, -en (f) [*reç'-nung*]
iodine, Jod (n) [*yoht*]
Ireland, Irland (n) [*ir'-lant*]
Irish *adj.,* irisch [*eer'-ish*]
iron [metal] *n.,* Eisen, - (n) [*ai'-zən*]
iron [for clothes] *n.,* Bügeleisen, - (n) [*büh'-gəl-ai-zən*]
iron *v.,* bügeln [*büh'-gəln*]
irrational, irrational [*ir-ra-tsi-oh-nahl'*]
irrigation, Bewässerung (f) [*bə-ve'-sə-rung*]
irritation, Reizung, -en (f) [*rait'-sung*]
is *v.,* ist [*ist*]
island, Insel, -n (f) [*in'-zəl*]
it [subj. of verb], er, sie, es [*er, zee, es*]
it [obj. of verb] ihn, sie, es [*een, zee, es*]
it [pers. pron.], es [*es*]
it [demons. pron.], das [*das*]
  Have you the newspaper? Yes, I have it, Haben Sie die
    Zeitung? Ja, ich habe sie [*hah'-bən zee dee zai'-tung?
    yah iç hah'-bə zee*]
  It isn't so, Das ist nicht so [*das ist niçt zoh*]
  It is late, Es ist spät [*es ist shpeht*]
  Is it raining? Regnet es? [*reg'-nət es*]
Italian *adj.,* italienisch [*i-ta-li-eh'-nish*]
Italy, Italien (n) [*i-tah'-li-ən*]
itch *v.,* jucken [*yu'-kən*]
itinerary, Reiseplan, ⸗e (m) [*rai'-zə-plahn, rai'-zə-pleh-nə*]
ivory, Elfenbein (n) [*el'-fən-bain*]

J

jacket, Rock, ⸗e (m); Jacke, -n (f) [*rok, rö'-kə*; *ya'-kə*]
jail, Gefängnis, -se (n) [*gə-feng'-nis*]
jam *n.*, Marmelade, -n (f) [*mar-mə-lah'-də*]
janitor, Pförtner, - (m); Portier, -s (m) [*pfört'-nər*; *port-yeh'*, *port-yehs'*]
January, Januar (m) [*ya'-nu-ahr*]
Japan, Japan (n) [*yah'-pan*]
Japanese *adj.*, japanisch [*ya-pah'-nish*]
jar *n.*, Krug, ⸗e (m) [*krook, krüh'-gə*]
jaw, Kinnbacken, - (m) [*kin'-ba-kən*]
jazz, Jazz (m) [*dzhahz*]
jealous, eifersüchtig [*ai'-fər-züç-tiç*]
jelly, Gelee, -s (n) [*zhe-leh'*, *zhe-lehs'*]
Jew, Jude, -n (m) [*yoo'-də*]
jewel, Juwel, -en (n) [*yoo-vehl'*]
jewelry, Schmuck (m, sing), Schmucksachen (pl) [*shmuk, shmuk'-za-khən*]
Jewess, Jüdin, -nen (f) [*yüh'-din*]
Jewish, jüdisch [*yüh'-dish*]
job, Arbeit, -en (f); Stellung, -en (f) [*ar'-bait, shte'-lung*]
joke *n.*, Witz, -e (m) [*vits*]
joke *v.*, scherzen [*shert'-sən*]
journal, Journal, -e (n) [*zhur-nahl'*]
journalist, Journalist, -en (m) [*zhur-na-list'*]
journey, Reise, -n (f) [*rai'-zə*]
joy, Freude, -n (f) [*froi'-də*]
joyful, freudig [*froi'-diç*]
judge *n.*, Richter, - (m) [*riç'-tər*]
judge *v.*, urteilen [*ur'-tai-lən*]
judgment, Urteil, -e (n) [*ur'-tail*]
juice, Saft, ⸗e (m) [*zaft, zef'-tə*]
July, Juli (m) [*yoo'-lee*]

jump v., springen (irreg; *Aux:* SEIN) [*shpring'-ən*]
June, Juni (m) [*yoo'-nee*]
jury, Geschworenen (pl) [*gə-shvoh'-rə-nən*]
just adj., gerecht [*gə-reçt'*]
just adv., eben; gerade [*eh'-bən; gə-rah'-də*]
just as, gerade wie [*gə-rah'-də vee*]
justice, Gerechtigkeit (f) [*gə-reç'-tiç-kait*]
justify v., rechtfertigen [*reçt'-fer-ti-gən*]

K

keen, scharf [*sharf*]
keep v., halten (irreg) [*hal'-tən*]
  Keep out! Bleiben Sie draussen! [*blai'-bən zee drou'-sən*]
  Keep quiet! Seien Sie ruhig! [*zai'-ən zee roo'-iç*]
kettle, Kessel, - (m) [*ke'-səl*]
key, Schlüssel, - (m) [*shlü'-səl*]
kick v., (mit dem Fuss) stossen (irreg) [*(mit dem foos) shtoh'-sən*]
kidnap v., entführen [*ent-füh'-rən*]
kidney, Niere, -n (f) [*nee'-rə*]
kill v., töten [*töh'-tən*]
kind adj., gütig; liebenswürdig [*güh'-tiç; lee'-bəns-vür-diç*]
  That is very kind of you, Das ist sehr liebenswürdig von Ihnen [*das ist zehr lee'-bəns-vür-diç fon ee'-nən*]
kindness, Liebenswürdigkeit, -en (f) [*lee'-bəns-vür-diç-kait*]
king, König, -e (m) [*köh'-niç, köh'-ni-gə*]
kingdom, Königreich, -e (n) [*köh'-nik-raiç*]
kiss n., Kuss, ⸚e (m) [*kus, kü'-sə*]
kiss v., küssen [*kü'-sən*]
kitchen, Küche, -n (f) [*kü'-çə*]
knee, Knie, - (n) [*knee*]
kneel v., knien [*knee'-ən*]
knife, Messer, - (n) [*me'-sər*]
knight, Ritter, - (m) [*ri'-tər*]

knock [at door] *v.*, klopfen [*klo'-pfən*]
knot *n.*, Knoten, - (m) [*knoh'-tən*]
know [a fact] *v.*, wissen (irreg) [*vi'-sən*]
  I don't know where she is, Ich weiss nicht, wo sie ist
    [*iç vais niçt, voh zee ist*]
know [be acquainted with] *v.*, kennen (irreg) [*ke'-nən*]
  Do you know this film? Kennen Sie diesen Film? [*ke'-nen
    zee dee'-zən film*]
know [something thoroughly, as a language] *v.*, können
    (mod aux, irreg) [*kö'-nən*]
  I know English, Ich kann Englisch [*iç kan eng'-lish*]
knowledge, Kenntnis (f) [*kent'-nis*]
known *adj.*, bekannt [*bə-kant'*]

L

labor [work] *n.*, Arbeit, -en (f) [*ar'-bait*]
labor *v.*, arbeiten [*ar'-bai-tən*]
laboratory, Laboratorium (n, sing), Laboratorien (pl)
    [*la-bo-ra-toh'-ri-um, la-bo-ra-toh'-ri-ən*]
laborer, Arbeiter, - (m) [*ar'-bai-tər*]
lack *v.*, fehlen [*feh'-lən*]
ladder, Leiter, -n (f) [*lai'-tər*]
ladies' room, Damentoilette, -n (f) [*dah'-mən-to-a-le-tə*]
lady, Dame, -n (f) [*dah'-mə*]
lake, See, -n (m) [*zeh*]
lamb [food], Lammfleisch (n) [*lam'-flaish*]
lame *adj.*, lahm [*lahm*]
lamp, Lampe, -n (f) [*lam'-pə*]
land [plane & ship] *v.*, landen [*lan'-dən*]
land *n.*, Land, ⸗er (n) [*lant, len'-dər*]
landlady, Wirtin, -nen (f) [*vir'-tin*]
landlord, Wirt, -e (m) [*virt*]
landmark, Landmarke, -n (f) [*lant'-mar-kə*]
landscape, Landschaft, -en (f) [*lant'-shaft*]

language, Sprache, -n (f) [*shprah'-khə*]
large, gross [*grohs*]
last *adj.*, letzt [*letsı*]
   at last, endlich [*ent'-liç*]
   last night, gestern abend [*ge'-stərn ah'-bənt*]
   last week, vorige Woche [*foh'-ri-gə vo'-khə*]
last *v.*, dauern [*dou'-ərn*]
late, spät [*shpeht*]
lately, kürzlich [*kürts'-liç*]
lateness, Verspätung, -en (f) [*fer-shpeh'-tung*]
later, später [*shpeh'-tər*]
   (at the) latest, spätestens [*shpeh'-təs-təns*]
Latin *n.*, Latein (n) [*la-tain'*]
Latin *adj.*, lateinisch [*la-tai'-nish*]
laugh, lachen [*la'-khən*]
laughter, Gelächter (n) [*gə-leç'-tər*]
laundry, Wäscherei, -en (f); Wäsche (f) [*ve-shə-rai'; ve'-shə*]
law, Gesetz, -e (n) [*gə-zets'*]
lawful, rechtmässig [*reçt'-meh-siç*]
lawn, Rasen, - (m) [*rah'-zən*]
lawyer [female], Rechtsanwältin, -nen (f) [*reçts'-an-vel-tin*]
lawyer [male], Rechtsanwalt, ⸗e (m) [*reçts'-an-valt, reçts'-an-vel-tə*]
lay *v.*, legen [*leh'-gən*]
lazy, faul [*foul*]
lead [metal], Blei (n) [*blai*]
lead *v.*, führen [*füh'-rən*]
leader, Führer, - (m) [*füh'-rər*]
leading *adj.*, führend [*füh'-rənt*]
leaf, Blatt, ⸗er (n) [*blat, ble'-tər*]
lean *adj.*, mager [*mah'-gər*]
lean *v.*, lehnen [*leh'-nən*]
learn *v.*, lernen [*ler'-nən*]
learned *adj.*, gelehrt [*gə-lehrt'*]
learning *n.*, Gelehrsamkeit (f) [*gə-lehr'-sam-kait*]
lease *n.*, Mietvertrag, ⸗e (n) [*meet'-fer-trahk, meet'-fer-treh-gə*]
lease *v.*, vermieten [*fer-mee'-tən*]

least, geringst [*gə-ringst'*]
  at least, wenigstens [*veh'-niç-stəns*]
leather, Leder, - (n) [*leh'-dər*]
leave [abandon] *v.*, verlassen (irreg) [*fer-la'-sən*]
lecture, Vorlesung, -en (f) [*fohr'-leh-zung*]
  give a lecture *v.*, eine Vorlesung halten [*ai'-nə fohr'-leh-zung hal'-tən*]
left *adj.*, links [*links*]
  to the left, zur Linken [*tsur lin'-kən*]
  the left hand, die linke Hand [*dee lin'-kə hant*]
leg, Bein, -e (n) [*bain*]
legal, gesetzlich [*gə-zets'-liç*]
leisure, Musse (f) [*moo'-sə*]
lemon, Zitrone, -n (f) [*tsi-troh'-nə*]
lemonade, Limonade, -n (f) [*li-mo-nah'-də*]
lend *v.*, leihen (irreg) [*lai'-ən*]
length, Länge, -n (f) [*leng'-ə*]
lens, Linse, -n (f) [*lin'-zə*]
less, weniger [*veh'-ni-gər*]
  more or less, mehr oder weniger [*mehr oh'-dər veh'-ni-gər*]
lesson, Stunde, -n (f) [*shtun'-də*]
let [permit] *v.*, lassen (irreg) [*la'-sən*]
  let alone, in Ruhe lassen [*in roo'-ə la'-sən*]
let [rent] *v.*, vermieten [*fer-mee'-tən*]
  room to let, Zimmer zu vermieten [*tsi'-mər tsu fer-mee'-tən*]
letter [alphabet], Buchstabe, -n (m) [*bookh'-shtah-bə*]
letter [correspondence], Brief, -e (m) [*breef*]
lettuce, Kopfsalat, -e (m) [*kopf'-za-laht*]
liar, Lügner, - (m) [*lühg'-nər*]
liberal *adj.*, liberal [*li-bə-rahl'*]
liberty, Freiheit, -en (f) [*frai'-hait*]
library, Bibliothek, -en (f) [*beeb-li-o-tehk'*]
license, Lizenz, -en (f) [*li-tsents'*]
lie *n.*, Lüge, -n (f) [*lüh'-gə*]
lie [rest] *v.*, liegen (irreg) [*lee'-gən*]
lie [tell untruth] *v.*, lügen [*lüh'-gən*]

lie down *v.*, sich hin-legen [*ziç hin'-leh-gən*]
life, Leben (n, sing), Menschenleben (pl) [*leh'-bən, men'-shən-leh-bən*]
life insurance, Lebensversicherung, -en (f) [*leh'-bəns-ferzi'-çə-rung*]
lifeboat, Rettungsboot, -e (n) [*re'-tungz-boht*]
lift *v.*, heben (irreg) [*heh'-bən*]
light *n.*, Licht, -er (n) [*liçt, liç'-tər*]
light *adj.*, leicht [*laiçt*]
light *v.*, an-zünden [*an'-tsün-dən*]
lighter [cigarette], Feuerzeug, -e (n) [*foi'-ər-tsoik, foi'-ər-tsoi-gə*]
lightning, Blitz, -e (m) [*blits*]
like *prep.*, wie [*vee*]
like *v.*, gern haben (irreg) [*gərn hah'-bən*]
  I'd like to, Ich möchte [*iç möç'-tə*]
  Would you like, Möchten Sie [*möç'-tən zee*]
  I don't like it, Ich mag es nicht [*iç mahk es niçt*]
likewise, ebenso [*eh'-bən-zoh*]
lily, Lilie, -n (f) [*lee'-li-ə*]
limb, Glied, -er (n) [*gleet, glee'-dər*]
limit, Grenze, -n (f) [*gren'-tsə*]
line *n.*, Linie, -n (f); Zeile, -n (f) [*lee'-ni-ə; tsai'-lə*]
linen, Leinen (n) [*lai'-nən*]
liner [ship], Ozeandampfer, - (m) [*oh'-tse-ahn-dam-pfər*]
lingerie, Wäsche (f) [*ve'-shə*]
lion, Löwe, -n (m) [*löh'-və*]
lip, Lippe, -n (f) [*li'-pə*]
lipstick, Lippenstift, -e (m) [*li'-pən-shtift*]
liquor, Schnaps, ⸗e (m) [*shnaps, shnep'-sə*]
list *n.*, Liste, -n (f) [*li'-stə*]
listen *v.*, zu-hören [*tsoo'-höh-rən*]
literal, wörtlich [*vört'-liç*]
literature, Literatur, -en (f) [*li-tə-ra-toor'*]
little *adj.*, klein [*klain*]
  a little bit, ein bisschen [*ain bis'-çən*]
  very little, sehr wenig [*zehr veh'-niç*]
  little by little, allmählich [*al-meh'-liç*]

little *adv.*, wenig [*veh'-niç*]
live *v.*, leben [*leh'-bən*]
lively, lebendig [*le-ben'-diç*]
liver, Leber, -n (f) [*leh'-bər*]
living room, Wohnzimmer, - (n) [*vohn'-tsi-mər*]
load *v.*, laden (irreg) [*lah'-dən*]
loaf *v.*, bummeln [*bu'-məln*]
loan *n.*, Anleihe, -n (f) [*an'-lai-ə*]
lobby *n.*, Vorhalle, -n (f) [*fohr'-ha-lə*]
lobster, Hummer, - (m) [*hu'-mər*]
location, Lage, -n (f) [*lah'-gə*]
lock *v.*, ab-schliessen (irreg) [*ap'-shlee-sən*]
locomotive, Lokomotive, -n (f) [*lo-ko-mo-tee'-və*]
lodging *n.*, Unterkunft, ⸗e (f) [*un'-tər-kunft, un'-tər-künf-tə*]
logical, logisch [*loh'-gish*]
lonely, einsam [*ain'-zam*]
long *adj. & adv.*, lang [*lang*]
   a long time, (eine) lange Zeit [(ai-nə) *lang'-ə tsait*]
   long ago, vor langer Zeit [*fohr lang'-ər tsait*]
   How long? Wie lange? [*vee lang'-ə*]
long for *v.*, sich sehnen nach (plus dat) [*ziç zeh'-nən nakh*]
longest *adv.*, am längsten [*am leng'-stən*]
longing *n.*, Sehnsucht (f) [*zehn'-zukht*]
look *v.*, sehen (irreg) [*zeh'-ən*]
   Look! Schauen Sie! [*shou'-ən zee*]
   look at, an-sehen (irreg) [*an'-zeh-ən*]
   look for, erwarten [*er-var'-tən*]
   Look out! Passen Sie auf!, Vorsicht! [*pa'-sən zee ouf; fohr'-ziçt*]
loosen *v.*, lose machen [*loh'-zə ma'-khən*]
lord, Herr, -en (m) [*her*]
Lord [God], der Herr [*dehr her*]
lose *v.*, verlieren (irreg) [*fer-lee'-rən*]
loss, Verlust, -e (m) [*fer-lust'*]
loud, laut [*lout*]
loudspeaker, Lautsprecher, - (m) [*lout'-shpre-çər*]
love *n.*, Liebe (f) [*lee'-bə*]
love *v.*, lieben [*lee'-bən*]

lovely, lieblich [*leep'-liç*]
lover [male], Liebhaber, - (m) [*leep'-hah-bər*]
low, niedrig [*need'-riç*]
loyal, treu [*troi*]
lubrication, Schmieren (n) [*shmee'-rən*]
lubricate v., schmieren [*shmee'-rən*]
luck, Glück (n) [*glük*]
  be lucky v., Glück haben (irreg) [*glük hah'-bən*]
luggage, Gepäck (n) [*gə-pek'*]
lunch, Mittagessen (n) [*mi'-tahk-e-sən*]
  have lunch v., zu Mittag essen (irreg) [*tsu mi'-tahk e'-sən*]
lung, Lunge, -n (f) [*lung'-ə*]
luxurious, luxuriös [*luk-su-ri-öhs'*]

M

machine, Maschine, -n (f) [*ma-shee'-nə*]
machinery, Maschinen (f, pl) [*ma-shee'-nən*]
mad [insane], verrückt [*fer-rükt'*]
Madam [form of address], gnädige Frau (f) [*gneh'-di-gə
  frou*]
magazine [literary], Zeitschrift, -en (f) [*tsait'-shrift*]
magical, zauberhaft [*tsau'-bər-haft*]
magnificent, grossartig [*grohs'-ar-tiç*]
maid, Mädchen, - (n) [*meht'-çən*]
mail n., Post (f) [*post*]
mail v., senden [*zen'-dən*]
mailbox, Briefkasten, ⸗n (m) [*breef'-ka-stən, breef'-ke-stən*]
mailman, Briefträger, - (m) [*breef'-treh-gər*]
main, Haupt- [*houpt*-]
main street, Hauptstrasse, -n (f) [*houpt'-shtra-sə*]
mainly, hauptsächlich [*houpt'-zeç-liç*]
majesty, Majestät, -en (f) [*ma-ye-steht'*]
majority, Mehrzahl (f) [*mehr'-tsahl*]
make v., machen [*ma'-khən*]

make a mistake, einen Fehler machen [*ai'-nən feh'-lər ma'-khən*]

make a speech, eine Rede halten (irreg) [*ai'-nə reh'-də hal'-tən*]

make ready, sich fertig machen [*ziç fer'-tiç ma'-khən*]

male, männlich [*men'-liç*]

man, Mann, ≃er (m) [*man, me'-nər*]

manage *v.,* leiten [*lai'-tən*]

manager, Leiter, - (m); Manager, - (m) [*lai'-tər; me'-nə-dzhər*]

manner, Art, -en (f) [*art*]

manners, Manieren (f, pl) [*ma-nee'-rən*]

manufacture *v.,* her-stellen [*hehr'-shte-lən*]

manufacturer, Fabrikant, -en (m) [*fa-bri-kant'*]

manuscript, Manuskript, -e (n) [*ma-nu-skript'*]

many, viele [*fee'-lə*]

  how many? wie viele? [*vee fee'-lə*]

  very many, sehr viele [*zehr fee'-lə*]

map, Karte, -n (f) [*kar'-tə*]

marble, Marmor (m) [*mar'-mor*]

March [month], März (m) [*merts*]

march *v.,* marschieren [*mar-shee'-rən*]

mark *n.,* Zeichen, - (f) [*tsai'-çən*]

  German mark, Deutsche Mark, - (f) [*doi'-chə mark*]

mark *v.,* bezeichnen [*bə-tsaiç'-nən*]

market, Markt, ≃e (m) [*markt, merk'-tə*]

marriage, Heirat, -en (f) [*hai'-raht*]

marry *v.,* heiraten [*hai'-rah-tən*]

  get married, sich verheiraten [*ziç fer-hai'-rah-tən*]

marvelous, wunderbar [*vun'-dər-bahr*]

mask, Maske, -n (f) [*mas'-kə*]

mass [church], Messe, -n (f) [*me'-sə*]

mass [quantity], Masse, -n (f) [*ma'-sə*]

mass production, Massenproduktion (f) [*ma'-sən-pro-duk-tsi-ohn*]

massage *n.,* Massage, -n (f) [*ma-sah'-zhə*]

master *n.,* Meister, - (m) [*mai'-stər*]

masterpiece, Meisterwerk, -e (n) [*mai'-stər-verk*]

match [cigarette], Streichholz, ⸗er (n) [*straiç'-holts, straiç'-höl-tsər*]

match [sport], Spiel, -e (n) [*shpeel*]

maternal, mütterlich [*mü'-tər-liç*]

maternity, Mutterschaft (f) [*mu'-tər-shaft*]

mathematics, Mathematik (f) [*ma-te-ma-teek'*]

matter, Sache, -n (f) [*za'-khə*]

  What's the matter? Was ist los? [*vas ist lohs*]

  It doesn't matter, Das macht nichts aus [*das makht niçts ous*]

matter-of-fact [prosaic], prosaisch [*pro-zah'-ish*]

mattress, Matratze, -n (f) [*ma-tra'-tsə*]

mature *adj.*, reif [*raif*]

May, Mai (m) [*mai*]

may *mod. aux.*, mögen, können, dürfen [*möh'-gən, köh'-nən, dühr'-fən*]

  It may be, Es kann sein [*es kan zain*]

  May I come in? Darf ich eintreten? [*darf iç ain'-treh-tən*]

maybe, vielleicht [*fee-laiçt'*]

mayor, Bürgermeister, - (m) [*bür'-gər-mai-stər*]

me, mich [*miç*]

  to me, mir [*meer*]

  with me, mit mir [*mit meer*]

meal, Mahlzeit, -en (f) [*mahl'-tsait*]

mean *v.*, meinen [*mai'-nən*]

  What does it mean? Was bedeutet das? [*vas bə-doi'-tət das*]

  What do you mean? Was meinen Sie? [*vas mai'-nən zee*]

means [income], Mittel (n, pl) [*mi'-təl*]

  by means of, mittels [*mi'-təls*]

  by no means, keineswegs [*kai'-nəs-vehks*]

measles, Masern (pl) [*mah'-zərn*]

measure, Mass, -e (n) [*mahs*]

meat, Fleisch (n) [*flaish*]

mechanic, Mechaniker, - (m) [*me-çah'-ni-kər*]

mechanical, mechanisch [*me-çah'-nish*]

medical, medizinisch [*me-di-tsee'-nish*]

medicine, Arznei, -en (f) [*arts'-nai*]

Mediterranean, Mittelmeer (n) [*mi'-təl-mehr*]
meet [become acquainted] *v.*, kennen-lernen [*ke'-nən-ler-nən*]
   Delighted to meet you! Es freut mich, Sie kennenzulernen.
   [*es froit miç, zee ke'-nən-tsu-ler-nən*]
meet [definite appointment] *v.*, treffen (irreg) [*tre'-fən*]
meeting, Versammlung, -en (f) [*fer-zam'-lung*]
melody, Melodie, -en (f) [*me-lo-dee'*]
melon, Melone, -n (f) [*me-loh'-nə*]
melt *v.*, schmelzen (irreg; *Aux:* HABEN, SEIN) [*shmel'-tsən*]
member, Mitglied, -er (n) [*mit'-gleet, mit'-glee-dər*]
memory, Gedächtnis (n) [*gə-deçt'-nis*]
mend [matters] *v.*, besser machen [*be'-sər ma'-khən*]
mental, geistig [*gai'-stiç*]
mention *v.*, erwähnen [*er-veh'-nən*]
menu, Speisekarte, -n (f) [*shpai'-zə-kar-tə*]
merchandise, Ware, -n (f) [*vah'-rə*]
merchant, Kaufmann (m, sing), Kaufleute (pl) [*kouf'-man, kouf'-loi-tə*]
merely, bloss [*blohs*]
merit *n.*, Verdienst, -e (n) [*fer-deenst'*]
merry, lustig [*lu'-stiç*]
message, Botschaft, -en (f) [*boht'- shaft*]
messenger, Bote, -n (m) [*boh'-tə*]
metal, Metall, -e (n) [*me-tal'*]
meter, Meter, - (m) [*meh'-tər*]
method, Methode, -n (f) [*me-toh'-də*]
metric system, Dezimalsystem (n) [*de-tsi-mahl'-sü-stehm*]
Mexican *adj.*, mexikanisch [*me-ksi-kah'-nish*]
Mexico, Mexiko (n) [*me'-ksi-koh*]
middle, Mitte (f) [*mi'-tə*]
midnight, Mitternacht (f) [*mi'-tər-nakht*]
mild, mild [*milt*]
mile, Meile, -n [*mai'-lə*]
military *adj.*, militärisch [*mi-li-teh'-rish*]
military service, Wehrdienst (m) [*vehr'-deenst*]
milk, Milch (f) [*milç*]
million, Million, -en (f) [*mi-li-ohn'*]

millionaire, Millionär, -e (m) [*mi-li-o-nehr'*]

mind, Verstand (m) [*fer-shtant'*]

mine *pron.*, mein; meine [*main; mai'-nə*]

   This book is mine, Das ist mein Buch [*das ist main bookh*]

mine *n.*, Mine, -n (f) [*mee'-nə*]

mineral *adj.*, mineralisch [*mi-nə-rah'-lish*]

miniskirt, Minirock, ⸗e (m) [*mi'-ni-rok, mi'-ni-rö-kə*]

minister [church], Geistliche, -n (m) [*gaist'-li-çə*]

mink, Nerz, -e (m) [*nerts*]

minor [age], minderjährig [*min'-dər-yeh-riç*]

minus, weniger [*veh'-ni-gər*]

minute *n.*, Minute, -n (f) [*mi-noo'-tə*]

   Wait a minute! Warten Sie einen Moment! [*var'-tən zee ai'-nən mo-ment'*]

mirror, Spiegel, - (m) [*shpee'-gəl*]

miserable, elend [*eh'-lent*]

misery, Elend (n) [*eh'-lent*]

Miss, Fräulein, - (n) [*froi'-lain*]

miss [someone] *v.*, vermissen [*fer-mi'-sən*]

   be missing, fehlen [*feh'-lən*]

mission, Mission, -en (f) [*mi-si-ohn'*]

missionary, Missionar, -e (m) [*mi-si-o-nahr'*]

mistake *n.*, Fehler, - (m) [*feh'-lər*]

   be mistaken *v.*, sich irren [*ziç i'-rən*]

mistrust *n.*, Misstrauen (n) [*mis'-trou-ən*]

mistrust *v.*, misstrauen [*mis-trou'-ən*]

misunderstanding *n.*, Missverständis, -se (n) [*mis'-fer-shtent-nis*]

mix *v.*, mischen [*mi'-shən*]

mixed, gemischt [*gə-misht'*]

model, Modell, -e (n) [*mo-del'*]

modern, modern [*mo-dern'*]

modest, bescheiden [*bə-shai'-dən*]

modesty, Bescheidenheit (f) [*bə-shai'-dən-hait*]

moment, Moment, -e (m) [*mo-ment'*]

monarchy, Monarchie, -n (f) [*mo-nar-çee'*]

monastery, Kloster, ⸗ (n) [*kloh'-stər, klöh'-stər*]

Monday, Montag, -e (m) [*mohn'-tahk, mohn'-tah-gə*]

money, Geld, -er (n) [*gelt, gel'-dər*]

monk, Mönch, -e (m) [*mönç*]

monkey, Affe, -n (m) [*a'-fə*]

monotonous, monoton [*mo-no-tohn'*]

month, Monat, -e (m) [*moh'-nat*]

monthly, monatlich [*moh'-nat-liç*]

monument, Denkmal, ⸗er (n) [*denk'-mahl, denk'-meh-lər*]

mood [feeling], Laune, -n (f) [*lou'-nə*]

   She's in a good mood, Sie ist (bei) guter Laune [*zee ist (bai) goo'-tər lou'-nə*]

   He's in a bad mood, Er ist (bei) schlechter Laune [*er ist (bai) shleç'-tər lou'-nə*]

moon, Mond, -e (m) [*mohnt, mohn'-də*]

moonlight, Mondschein (m) [*mohnt'-shain*]

moral *n.*, Moral (f) [*mo-rahl'*]

more, mehr [*mehr*]

   once more, noch einmal [*nokh ain'-mahl*]

   more or less, mehr oder weniger [*mehr oh'-dər veh'-ni-gər*]

morning, Morgen, - (m) [*mor'-gən*]

   Good morning! Guten Morgen! [*goo'-tən mor'-gən*]

   in the morning, morgens [*mor'-gəns*]

mortgage, Hypothek, -en (f) [*hü-po-tehk'*]

mosquito, Mücke, -n (f) [*mü'-kə*]

most *adv.*, am meisten [*am mai'-stən*]

mother, Mutter, ⸗ (f) [*mu'-tər, mü'-tər*]

mother-in-law, Schwiegermutter, ⸗ (f) [*shvee'-gər-mu-tər, shvee'-gər-mü-tər*]

motherhood, Mutterschaft (f) [*mu'-tər-shaft*]

motion, Bewegung, -en (f) [*bə-veh'-gung*]

motive [intent], Absicht, -en (f) [*ap'-ziçt*]

motor, Motor, -en (m) [*moh'-tor, mo-toh'-rən*]

motorcycle, Motorrad, ⸗er (n) [*moh'-tor-raht, moh'-tor-reh-dər*]

mount *v.*, besteigen (irreg) [*bə-shtai'-gən*]

mountain, Berg, -e (m) [*berk, ber'-gə*]

mountain range, Gebirgskette, -n (f) [*gə-birks'-ke-tə*]

mourn *v.*, trauern um (plus acc) [*trou'-ərn um*]

in mourning, in Trauer [*in trou'-ər*]
mouse, Maus, ⸗e (f) [*mous, moi'-zə*]
mouth, Mund, ⸗er (m) [*munt, mün'-dər*]
move [one's dwelling] *v.*, um-ziehen (irreg; *Aux:* SEIN) [*um'-tsee-ən*]
move [motion] *v.*, bewegen [*bə-veh'-gən*]
move [the feelings] *v.*, rühren [*rüh'-rən*]
movies, Kino, -s (n) [*kee'-noh, kee'-nohs*]
Mr. [form of address], Herr [*her*]
Mrs. [form of address], Frau [*frou*]
much, viel [*feel*]
  as much as, soviel wie [*zo-feel' vee*]
  How much? Wieviel? [*vee-feel'*]
  too much, zuviel [*tsu-feel'*]
  very much, sehr viel [*zehr feel*]
mud, Schlamm (m) [*shlam*]
mug *n.*, Becher, - (m) [*be'-çər*]
murder *v.*, morden [*mor'-dən*]
murderer, Mörder, - (m) [*mör'-dər*]
muscle, Muskel, -n (m) [*mus'-kəl*]
museum, Museum (n, sing), Museen (pl) [*mu-zeh'-um, mu-zeh'-ən*]
mushroom, Pilz, -e (m) [*pilts*]
music, Musik (f) [*mu-zeek'*]
musical *adj.*, musikalisch [*mu-zi-kah'-lish*]
musician, Musiker, - (m) [*moo'-zi-kər*]
must *v.*, müssen [*müs'-sən*]
  I must go, Ich muss gehen [*iç mus geh'-ən*]
  You must come, Sie müssen kommen [*zee mü'-sən ko'-mən*]
mustache, Schnurrbart, ⸗e (m) [*shnur'-bahrt, shnur'-behr-tə*]
mustard, Senf (m) [*zenf*]
mutual, gegenseitig [*geh'-gən-zai-tiç*]
my, mein, meine [*main, mai'-nə*]
myself, ich selbst; mir; mich [*iç zelpst; meer; miç*]
  I dress myself, Ich ziehe mich an [*iç tsee'-ə miç an*]
mysterious, geheimnisvoll [*gə-haim'-nis-fol*]

mystery, Geheimnis, -se (n) [gə-haim'-nis]
mystic adj., mystisch [müs'-tish]

N

nail n., Nagel, ⁼ (m) [nah'-gəl, neh'-gəl]
nail (on) v., an-nageln [an'-nah-gəln]
naive, naiv [na-eef']
naked, nackt [nakt]
name, Name, -n (m) [nah'-mə]
   first name, Vorname, -n (m) [fohr'-nah-mə]
   last name, Zuname, -n (m) [tsoo'-nah-mə]
   What is your name? Wie heissen Sie? [vee hai'-sən zee]
namely, nämlich [nehm'-liç]
nap [sleep] n., Schläfchen, - (n) [shlehf'-çən]
   take a nap v., ein Schläfchen machen [ain shlehf'-çən
   ma'-khən]
napkin, Serviette, -n (f) [zer-vi-e'-tə]
narrate v., erzählen [er-tseh'-lən]
narrative, Erzählung, -en (f) [er-tseh'-lung]
narrow, eng [eng]
nation, Nation, -en (f) [na-tsi-ohn']
national, national [na-tsi-o-nahl']
nationality, Nationalität, -en (f) [na-tsi-o-na-li-teht']
native land, Heimatland, ⁼ er (n) [hai'-mat-lant, hai'-mat-
   len-dər]
natural, natürlich [na-tühr'-liç]
nature, Natur (f) [na-toor']
navy, Marine (f) [ma-ree'-nə]
near, nearby, nahe [nah'-ə]
   Which is nearer? Was ist näher? [vas ist neh'-ər]
nearly, fast [fast]
necessary, notwendig [noht'-ven-diç]
neck, Hals, ⁼e (m) [hals, hel'-zə]
necklace, Halskette, -n (f) [hals'-ke-tə]

necktie, Kravatte, -n (f) [*kra-va'-tə*]

need *n.,* Not, ⸗e (f) [*noht, növ'-tə*]

need *v.,* brauchen [*brou'-khən*]

needle, Nadel, -n (f) [*nah'-dəl*]

negative *adj.,* negativ [*ne-ga-teef'*]

neglect [of duty, guests], Vernachlässigung (f) [*fer-nahkh'-le-si-gung*]

Negress, Negerin, -nen (f) [*neh'-gə-rin*]

Negro, Neger, - (m) [*neh'-gər*]

neighbor [male], Nachbar, -n (m) [*nakh'-bahr*]

neighbor [female], Nachbarin, -nen (f) [*nakh'-ba-rin*]

neighborhood, Nachbarschaft (f) [*nakh'-bahr-shaft*]

neither . . . nor, weder . . . noch [*veh'-dər nokh*]
   Neither you nor I, Weder Sie noch ich [*veh'-dər zee nokh iç*]

nephew, Neffe, -n (m) [*ne'-fə*]

nerve, Nerv, -en (m) [*nerf, ner'-fən*]

nervous, nervös [*ner-vöhs'*]

nest, Nest, -er (n) [*nest*]

net [fishing], Netz, -e (n) [*nets*]

net [hair], Haarnetz, -e (n) [*hahr'-nets*]

neutral, neutral [*noi-trahl'*]

never, nie [*nee*]
   Never mind! Macht nichts! [*makht niçts*]

nevertheless, trotzdem [*trots'-dehm*]

new, neu [*noi*]
   Happy New Year! Prosit Neujahr! [*proh'-zit noi'-yahr*]

news *pl.,* Nachricht, -en (f) [*nakh'-riçt*]

newspaper, Zeitung, -en (f) [*tsai'-tung*]

newsstand, Zeitungsstand, ⸗e (m) [*tsai'-tungs-shtant, tsai'-tungs-shten-də*]

next, nächst [*nehçst*]
   next month, nächsten Monat [*nehç'-stən moh'-nat*]
   next week, nächste Woche [*nehç'-stə vo'-khə*]
   next time, das nächste Mal [*das nehç'-stə mahl*]

next to, gleich neben [*glaiç neh'-bən*]

nice [pleasing], nett [*net*]

nickname, Spitzname, -n (m) [*shpits'-nah-mə*]

niece, Nichte, -n (f) [*niç'-tə*]

night, Nacht, ⁼e (f) [*nakht, neç'-tə*]

   Good night! Gute Nacht! [*goo'-tə nakht*]

   last night, vorige Nacht; gestern abend [*foh'-ri-gə nakht; ge'-stərn ah'-bent*]

nightclub, Nachtlokal, -e (n) [*nakht'-lo-kahl*]

nightfall, Einbruch der Nacht [*ain'-brukh dehr nakht*]

nightgown, Nachthemd, -en (n) [*nakht'-hemt, nakht'-hem-dən*]

nightmare, Alpdrücken (n) [*alp'-drü-kən*]

nine, neun [*noin*]

nineteen, neunzehn [*noin'-tsehn*]

ninth, neunt [*noint*]

ninety, neunzig [*noin'-tsiç*]

no *adj.,* kein [*kain*]

   by no means, keineswegs [*kai'-nəs-vehks*]

no *adv.,* nicht [*niçt*]

   no more, nicht mehr [*niçt mehr*]

   It's no good, Das taugt nichts [*das toukt niçts*]

no [opposite of yes], nein [*nain*]

noble *adj.,* edel [*eh'-dəl*]

nobody, niemand [*nee'-mant*]

noise, Geräusch, -e (n); Lärm (m) [*gə-roish'; lerm*]

noisy, laut [*lout*]

none, keiner, keine, keines [*kai'-nər, kai'-nə, kai'-nəs*]

   Any coffee left? There is none, Ist noch Kaffee übrig? Es ist keiner da [*ist nokh ka'-fe üh'-briç? es ist kai'-nər da*]

nonsense, Unsinn (m) [*un'-zin*]

noodle, Nudel, -n (f) [*noo'-dəl*]

noon, Mittag, -e (m) [*mit'-tahk, mit'-tah-gə*]

normal, normal [*nor-mahl'*]

north, Norden (m) [*nor'-dən*]

North America, Nordamerika [*nort'-ah-meh-ri-kah*]

northeast, Nordosten (m) [*Nort-ost'-ən*]

northern, nördlich [*nört'-liç*]

northwest, Nordwesten (m) [*nort-vest'-ən*]

Norway, Norwegen (n) [*nor'-veh-gən*]

Norwegian *adj.,* norwegisch [*nor'-veh-gish*]

nose, Nase, -n (f) [*nah'-zə*]
not, nicht [*niçt*]
   not any, kein [*kain*]
   not at all, durchaus nicht [*durç-ous' niçt*]
   not one, nicht einer [*niçt ai'-nər*]
note *n.*, Notiz, -en (f) [*no-teets'*]
note *v.*, notieren [*no-tee'-rən*]
notebook, Notizbuch, ⸗er (n) [*no-teets'-bookh, no-teets'-büh-çər*]
nothing, nichts [*niçts*]
   nothing new, nichts Neues [*niçts noi'-əs*]
notice *v.*, bemerken [*bə-mer'-kən*]
notion, Begriff, -e (m) [*bə-grif'*]
noun, Hauptwort, ⸗er (n) [*houpt'-vort, houpt'-vör-tər*]
novel [work of fiction], Roman, -e (m) [*ro-mahn'*]
novelist, Romanschriftsteller, - (m) [*ro-mahn'-shrift-shte-lər*]
novelty, Neuheit, -en (f) [*noi'-hait*]
November, November (m) [*no-vem'-bər*]
now, jetzt [*yetst*]
   now and then, hin und wieder [*hin unt vee'-dər*]
   from now on, von jetzt an [*fon yetst an*]
   until now, bis jetzt [*bis yetst*]
nowadays, heutzutage [*hoit'-tsu-tah-gə*]
nowhere, nirgendwo [*nir'-gənt-voh*]
number *n.*, Nummer, -n (f) [*nu'-mər*,
numerous, zahlreich [*tsahl'-raiç*]
nun, Nonne, -n (f) [*no'-nə*]
nurse *n.*, Krankenschwester, -n (f) [*kran'-kən-shve-stər*]
nurse [an infant] *v.*, säugen; stillen [*zoi'-gən; shti'-lən*]
nursemaid, Kindermädchen, - (n) [*kin'-dər-meht-çən*]
nursery, Kinderzimmer, - (n) [*kin'-dər-tsi-mər*]
nut [food], Nuss, ⸗e [*nus, nü'-sə*]
nylon, Nylon (n) [*nai'-lon*]
nylons [stockings], Nylonstrümpfe (m, pl) [*nai'-lon-shtrüm-pfə*]

O

oak, Eiche, -e (f) [*ai'-çə*]

oath, Eid, -e (m) [*ait, ai'-də*]

obedient, gehorsam [*gə-hohr'-zahm*]

obey *v.,* gehorchen [*gə-hor'-çən*]

object *n.,* Gegenstand, ⸗e (m) [*geh'-gən-shtant, geh'-gən-shten-də*]

objection, Einwand, ⸗e (m) [*ain'-vant, ain'-ven-də*]

obligatory, obligatorisch [*ob-li-ga-toh'-rish*]

oblige [compel] *v.,* verpflichten [*fer-pfliç'-tən*]

   Much obliged, Sehr verbunden [*zehr fer-bun'-dən*]

observation, Beobachtung, -en (f) [*bə-oh'-bakh-tung*]

observe [watch] *v.,* beobachten [*bə-oh'-bakh-tən*]

obstacle, Hindernis, -se (n) [*hin'-der-nis*]

obtain *v.,* erhalten (irreg) [*er-hal'-tən*]

obvious, klar [*klahr*]

occasion, Gelegenheit, -en (f) [*gə-leh'-gən-hait*]

occasionally, gelegentlich [*gə-leh'-gənt-liç*]

occupation [work], Beschäftigung, -en (f) [*bə-shef'-ti-gung*]

occupied [seat], besetzt [*bə-zetst'*]

occupy *v.,* besetzen [*bə-ze'-tsən*]

occur *v.,* vor-kommen (irreg; *Aux:* SEIN) [*fohr'-ko-mən*]

occurence, Ereignis, -se (n) [*er-aik'-nis*]

ocean, Ozean, -e (m) [*oh'-tse-ahn*]

October, Oktober (m) [*ok-toh'-bər*]

oculist, Augenarzt, ⸗e (f) [*ou'-gən-ahrtst, ou'-gən-ehrts-tə*]

odd [uneven], ungerade [*un'-gə-rah-də*]

odd [unusual], sonderbar [*zon'-dər-bahr*]

odor, Geruch, ⸗e (m) [*gə-rukh', gə-rü'-çə*]

of, von (plus dat) [*fon*]

   of course, natürlich [*na-tühr'-liç*]

off *adv.,* weg [*vehk*]

offend *v.,* beleidigen [*bə-lai'-di-gən*]

offensive [insulting], beleidigend [*bə-lai'-di-gənt*]
offensive [invasion], Angriff, -e (m) [*an'-grif*]
offer *n.*, Angebot, -e (n) [*an'-gə-boht*]
offer *v.*, an-bieten (irreg) [*an'-bee-tən*]
office, Büro, -s (n) [*bü-roh', bü-rohs'*]
officer [mil.], Offizier, -e (m) [*o-fi-tseer'*]
often, oft [*oft*]
oil, Öl, -e (n) [*öhl*]
oil crisis, Ölkrise, -n (f) [*öhl'-kree-zə*]
oil field, Ölfeld, -er (n) [*öhl'-felt, öhl'-fel-dər*]
oil painting, Ölgemälde, - (n) [*öhl-gə-mehl'-də*]
oil well, Ölbohrloch, ⸚er (n) [*öhl'-bohr-lokh, öhl'-bohr-lö-çər*]
old, alt [*alt*]
   How old are you? Wie alt sind Sie? [*vee alt zint zee*]
olive, Olive, -n (f) [*o-lee'-və*]
olive oil, Olivenöl (n) [*o-lee'-vən-öhl*]
omelet, Omelett, -e (n) [*om-e-let'*]
omission, Unterlassung, -en (f) [*un-tər-la'-sung*]
omit *v.*, unterlassen (irreg) [*un-tər-la'-sən*]
on, an; auf (plus dat; acc for motion) [*an; ouf*]
   on duty, im Dienst [*im deenst*]
   on foot, zu Fuss [*tsu foos*]
   on my part, meinerseits [*mai'-nər-zaits*]
   on purpose, absichtlich [*ap'-ziçt-liç*]
   on the contrary, im Gegenteil [*im geh'-gən-tail*]
   on the left, links [*links*]
   on time, pünktlich [*pünkt'-liç*]
once, einmal [*ain'-mahl*]
   at once, sofort [*zo-fort'*]
one [counting], eins [*ains*]
one *adj.*, ein; einer, eine, eines [*ain; ai'-nər, ai'-nə, ai'-nəs*]
one-way street, Einbahnstrasse, -n (f) [*ain'-bahn-shtrah-sə*]
onion, Zwiebel, -n (f) [*tsvee'-bəl*]
only *adv.*, nur [*noor*]
only *adj.*, einzig [*ain'-tsiç*]
open *v.*, öffnen [*öf'-nən*]
open *adj.*, offen [*o'-fən*]
open-handed, freigebig [*frai'-geh-biç*]

opening *n.*, Öffnung, -en (f) [*öf'-nung*]

opera, Oper, -n (f) [*oh'-pər*]

operate [a vehicle] *v.*, fahren (irreg; *Aux:* HABEN) [*fah'-rən*]

operate [medical] *v.*, operieren [*o-pe-ree'-rən*]

operation, Operation, -en (f) [*o-pe-ra-tsi-ohn'*]

operator [telephone-girl], Telephonistin, -nen (f) [*te-le-fo-ni'-stin*]

opinion, Meinung, -en (f) [*mai'-nung*]

opportunity, Gelegenheit, -en (f) [*gə-leh'-gən-hait*]

opposite *adv.*, gegenüber [*geh-gən-üh'-bər*]

optimist, Optimist, -en (m) [*op-ti-mist'*]

optimistic, optimistisch [*op-ti-mis'-tish*]

optional, wahlfrei [*vahl'-frai*]

or, oder [*oh'-dər*]

orange, Apfelsine, -n (f) [*a-pfəl-zee'-nə*]

orange juice, Orangensaft (m) [*o-ran'-zhən-zaft*]

orchard, Obstgarten, ╝ (m) [*ohpst'-gahr-tən, ohpst'-ger-tən*]

orchestra, Orchester, - (n) [*or-ke'-stər*]

orchid, Orchidee, -n (f) [*or-çi-dee'-ə*]

order [arrangement] *n.*, Ordnung, -en (f) [*ord'-nung*]

order [command] *n.*, Befehl, -e (m) [*bə-fehl'*]

order [someone] *v.*, befehlen (irreg) [*bə-feh'-lən*]

order [something] *v.*, bestellen [*bə-shte'-lən*]

ordinary, gewöhnlich [*gə-vöhn'-liç*]

ordinarily, im allgemeinen [*im al-gə-mai'-nən*]

ore, Erz, -e (n) [*ehrts*]

organ [music], Orgel, -n (f) [*or'-gəl*]

organic, organisch [*or-gah'-nish*]

organization, Organisation, -en (f) [*or-ga-ni-za-tsi-ohn'*]

oriental, orientalisch [*o-ri-en-tah'-lish*]

original *adj.*, originell [*o-ri-gi-nel'*]

originally, ursprünglich [*oor-shprüng'-liç*]

orphan, Waisenkind, -er (n) [*vai'-zən-kint, vai'-zən-kin-dər*]

other, ander [*an'-der*]

   on the other hand, anderseits [*an'-dər-zaits*]

otherwise, sonst [*zonst*]

ought to, sollte, sollten [*zol'-tə, zol'-tən*]

   I ought to do it, Ich sollte es eigentlich tun [*iç zol'-tə es* *ai'-gənt-liç toon]*

You ought to go, Sie sollten gehen [*zee zol'-tən geh'-ən*]
ounce, Unze, -n (f) [*un'-tsə*]
our, unser, unsere [*un'-zər, un'-zə-rə*]
ours, der (die, das) unsere [*dehr (dee, das) un'-zə-rə*]
out *adv.,* aus; heraus [*ous; he-rous'*]
out-of-date, veraltet [*fer-al'-tət*]
outdoors, draussen [*drou'-sən*]
outfit *n.,* Ausstattung, -en (f) [*ous'-shta-tung*]
outside *prep.,* ausserhalb (plus gen) [*ou'-sər-halp*]
outstanding, hervorragend [*her-fohr'-rah-gənt*]
oven, Ofen, ¤ (m) [*oh'-fən, öh'-fən*]
over [finished], vorbei [*fohr-bai'*]
over *prep.,* über (plus dat; acc for motion) [*üh'-bər*]
overboard, über Bord [*üh'-bər bort*]
overcoat, Mantel, ¤ (m) [*man'-təl, men'-təl*]
overcome *v.,* überwinden (irreg) [*üh-bər-vin'-dən*]
overflow [flood] *v.,* über-fliessen (irreg; *Aux:* SEIN) [*üh'-bər-flee-sən*]
overnight, die Nacht über [*dee nakht üh'-bər*]
oversight, Versehen, - (n) [*fer-zeh'-ən*]
overturn *v.,* um-stürzen [*um'-shtür-tsən*]
owe *v.,* schulden [*shul'-dən*]
How much do I owe you? Wieviel schulde ich Ihnen? [*vee-feel' shul'-də iç ee'-nən*]
own *adj.,* eigen [*ai'-gən*]
own *v.,* besitzen (irreg) [*bə-zi'-tsən*]
owner, Besitzer, - (m) [*bə-zi'-tsər*]
ox, Ochse, -n (m) [*ok'-sə*]
oxygen, Sauerstoff (m) [*zou'-ər-shtof*]
oyster, Auster, -n (f) [*ou'-stər*]

P

pace *n.,* Schritt, -e (m) [*shrit*]
pack *v.,* packen [*pa'-kən*]

pack of cigarettes, Schachtel (-n, f) Zigaretten [*shakh'-təl tsi-ga-re'-tən*]

pack of playing cards, Spielkarten (pl) [*shpeel'-kar-tən*]

package, Paket, -e (n) [*pa-keht'*]

packing *n.,* Packen (n) [*pa'-kən*]

page, Seite, -n (f) [*zai'-tə*]

pail, Eimer, - (m) [*ai'-mər*]

pain, Schmerz, -en (m) [*shmerts*]

painful, schmerzhaft [*shmerts'-haft*]

paint *v.,* malen [*mah'-lən*]

painter [male], Maler, - (m) [*mah'-lər*]

painter [female], Malerin, -nen (f) [*mah'-lə-rin*]

painting [picture], Gemälde, - (n) [*gə-mehl'-də*]

pair *n.,* Paar, -e (n) [*pahr*]

palace, Palast, ⸗e (m) [*pa-last', pa-le'-stə*]

pale *adj.,* bleich [*blaiç*]

palm [bot.], Palme, -n (f) [*pal'-mə*]

pants, Hosen (f, pl) [*hoh'-zən*]

paper, Papier, -e (n) [*pa-peer'*]

parachute, Fallschirm, -e (m) [*fal'-shirm*]

parade, Parade, -n (f) [*pa-rah'-də*]

paradise, Paradies, -e (n) [*pa-ra-dees'*]

paragraph, Absatz, ⸗e (m) [*ap'-zats, ap'-ze-tsə*]

parallel *adj.,* parallel [*pa-ra-lehl'*]

paralyze *v.,* lähmen [*leh'-mən*]

parcel, Paket, -e (n) [*pa-keht'*]

pardon *v.,* verzeihen (irreg) [*fer-tsai'-ən*]

    Pardon me! Verzeihung! [*fer-tsai'-ung*]

pardon *n.,* Verzeihung (f) [*fer-tsai'-ung*]

parents, Eltern (pl) [*el'-tərn*]

park *n.,* Park, -s (m) [*park, parks*]

park *v.,* parken [*par'-kən*]

    No parking! Kein Parken! [*kain par'-kən*]

parking lot, Parkplatz, ⸗e (m) [*park'-plats, park'-plet-sə*]

parliament, Parlament, -e (n) [*par-la-ment'*]

parlor, Salon, -s (m) [*za-lon', za-lons'*]

parsley, Petersilie (f) [*peh-tər-zee'-li-ə*]

part [portion], Teil, -e (m) [*tail*]

part [in a play], Rolle, -n (f) [*ro'-lə*]

partially, teilweise [*tail'-vai-zə*]

participate *v.*, teil-nehmen (irreg) [*tail'-neh-mən*]

particular, besonder [*be-zon'-dər*]

partner [business], Gesellschafter, - (m) [*gə-zel'-shaf-tər*]

party [entertainment], Gesellschaft, -en (f) [*gə-zel'-shaft*]

party [political], Partei, -en (f) [*par-tai'*]

pass (by) *v.*, vorbei-gehen (irreg; *Aux:* SEIN) [*fohr-bai'-geh-ən*]

pass *n.*, Pass, ⸗e (m) [*pas, pe'-sə*]

passenger, Passagier, -e (m) [*pa-sa-zheer'*]

passenger train, Personenzug, ⸗e (m) [*per-zoh'-nən-tsook, per-zoh'-nən-tsüh-gə*]

passion, Leidenschaft, -en (f) [*lai'-dən-shaft*]

passionate, leidenschaftlich [*lai'-dən-shaft-liç*]

passive, passiv [*pa'-seef*]

passport, Pass, ⸗e (m) [*pas, pe'-sə*]

past *n.*, Vergangenheit (f) [*fer-gang'₋-ən-hait*]

past *adj.*, vergangen [*fer-gang'-ən*]

pastry, Konditoreiwaren (f, pl) [*kon-dee-to-rai'-vah-rən*]

pastry shop, Konditorei, -en (f) [*kon-dee-to-rai'*]

path, Pfad, -e (m) [*pfaht, pfah'-də*]

patience, Geduld (f) [*gə-dult'*]

patient [male] *n.*, Patient, -en (m) [*pa-tsi-ent'*]

patient [female] *n.*, Patientin, -nen (f) [*pa-tsi-en'-tin*]

patriotic, patriotisch [*pa-tri-oh'-tish*]

pattern [dress], Muster, - (n) [*mus'-tər*]

pause *n.*, Pause, -n (f) [*pou'-zə*]

pavement, Pflaster, - (n) [*pfla'-stər*]

paw, Pfote, -n (f) [*pfoh'-tə*]

pawn *v.*, verpfänden [*ver-pfen'-dən*]

pawnshop, Leihhaus, ⸗er (n) [*lai'-hous, lai'-hoi-zər*]

pay *v.*, bezahlen [*bə-tsah'-lən*]

    pay a compliment, ein Kompliment machen [*ain kom-pli-ment' ma'-khən*]

    pay a debt, eine Schuld bezahlen [*ai'-nə shult bə-tsah'-lən*]

    pay by instalments, in Raten zahlen [*in rah'-tən tsah'-lən*]

pay cash, bar zahlen [*bahr tsah'-len*]
payment, Bezahlung, -en (f) [*bə-tsah'-lung*]
pea, Erbse, -n (f) [*erp'-sə*]
pea soup, Erbsensuppe, -n (f) [*erp'-sən-zu-pə*]
peace, Frieden (m) [*free'-dən*]
 in peacetime, im Frieden [*im free'-dən*]
peaceful, friedlich [*freet'-liç*]
peach, Pfirsich, -e (m) [*pfir'-ziç*]
peak *n.,* Gipfel, - (m) [*gi'-pfəl*]
peanut, Erdnuss, ⸗e (f) [*ehrt'-nus, ehrt'-nü-sə*]
pear, Birne, -n (f) [*bir'-nə*]
pearl, Perle, -n (f) [*per'-lə*]
pearl necklace, Perlenkette, -n (f) [*per'-lən-ke-tə*]
peasant, Bauer, -n (m) [*bou'-ər*]
pebble, Kieselstein, -e (m) [*kee'-zəl-shtain*]
pedestrian *n.,* Fussgänger, - (m) [*foos'-geng-ər*]
peel [foods] *v.,* schälen [*sheh'-lən*]
pen, Feder, -n (f) [*feh'-dər*]
penalty, Strafe, -n (f) [*shtrah'-fə*]
pencil, Bleistift, -e (m) [*blai'-shtift*]
peninsula, Halbinsel, -n (f) [*halp'-in-zəl*]
penknife, Federmesser, - (n) [*feh'-dər-me-sər*]
penny, Pfennig, -e (m) [*pfe'-niç, pfe'-ni-gə*]
people, Leute (pl) [*loi'-tə*]
pepper, Pfeffer (m) [*pfe'-fər*]
peppermint, Pfefferminz (f) [*pfe-fər-mints'*]
perceive *v.,* wahr-nehmen (irreg) [*vahr'-neh-mən*]
percent, Prozent, -e (n) [*pro-tsent'*]
perfect *adj.,* vollkommen [*fol'-ko-mən*]
perfection, Vollkommenheit (f) [*fol-ko'-mən-hait*]
performance [of machine], Leistung, -en (f) [*lai'-stung*]
performance [theater], Vorstellung, -en (f) [*fohr'-shte-lung*]
perfume, Parfüm, -e (n) [*par-fühm'*]
perhaps, vielleicht [*fee-laiçt'*]
period [of time], Zeitraum, ⸗e (m) [*tsait'-roum, tsait'-roi-mə*]
period [punctuation], Punkt, -e (m) [*punkt*]
permanent, dauernd [*dou'-ərnt*]
permanent wave, Dauerwelle, -n (f) [*dou'-ər-ve-lə*]

permission, Erlaubnis (f) [er-loup'-nis]
permit v., erlauben [er-lou'-bən]
persecution, Verfolgung, -en (f) [fer-fol'-gung]
Persian adj., persisch [per'-zish]
persistence, Beharrlichkeit (f) [bə-har'-liç-kait]
person [human being], Mensch, -en (m) [mensh]
person [law], Person, -en (f) [per-zohn']
personal, persönlich [per-zöhn'-liç]
personal property, (das) bewegliche Eigentum [(das) bə-vehk'-li-çə ai'-gən-toom]
personality, Persönlichkeit, -en (f) [per-zöhn'-liç-kait]
personnel, Personal (n) [per-zo-nahl']
perspiration, Schweiss (m) [shvais]
perspire v., schwitzen [shvit'-sən]
persuade v., überreden [üh-bər-reh'-dən]
pertaining to, betreffend (plus acc) [bə-tre'-fənt]
pessimist, Pessimist, -en (m) [pe-si-mist']
pessimistic, pessimistisch [pe-si-mi'-stish]
petition, Bittschrift, -en (f) [bit'-shrift]
pharmacy, Apotheke, -n (f) [a-po-teh'-kə]
phase, Phase, -n (f) [fah'-zə]
philosopher, Philosoph, -en (m) [fi-lo-zohf']
philosophy, Philosophie, -n (f) [fi-lo-zo-fee']
phone v., telefonieren [te-le-fo-nee'-rən]
phone n., Telefon, -e (n) [te-le-fohn']
  by phone, telefonisch [te-le-foh'-nish]
photograph n., Photo, -s (n) [foh'-toh, foh'-tohs]
photograph [take a photo] v., photographieren [fo-to-gra-fee'-rən]
photographer, Photograph, -en (m) [fo-to-grahf']
physical, physisch [füh'-zish]
physician [female], Ärztin, -nen (f) [ehrt'-stin]
physician [male], Arzt, ⸗e (m) [ahrtst, ehrt'-stə]
pianist, Pianist, -en (m) [pi-a-nist']
piano, Klavier, -e (n) [kla-veer']
pick up v., auf-heben (irreg) [ouf'-heh-bən]
picture, Bild, -er (n) [bilt, bil'-dər]
picturesque, malerisch [mah'-lə-rish]

pie, Torte, -n (f) [*tor'-tə*]
piece, Stück, -e (n) [*shtük*]
pier, Pier, -e (m) [*peer*]
pig, Schwein, -e (n) [*shvain*]
pigeon, Taube, -n (f) [*tou'-bə*]
pile *n.*, Haufen, - (m) [*hou'-fən*]
pill, Pille, -n (f) [*pi'-lə*]
pillow, Kissen, - (n) [*ki'-sən*]
pilot [plane] *n.*, Pilot, -en (m) [*pi-loht'*]
pin, Nadel, -n (f) [*nah'-dəl*]
pinch *v.*, kneifen (irreg) [*knai'-fən*]
pine *n.*, Kiefer, -n (f) [*kee'-fər*]
pineapple, Ananas, - (f) [*a'-na-nas*]
pink, rosa [*roh'-za*]
pious, fromm [*from*]
pipe [smoking], Pfeife, -n (f) [*pfai'-fə*]
pipe [water], Röhre, -n (f) [*röh'-rə*]
pistol, Pistole, -n (f) [*pi-stoh'-lə*]
pitcher, Krug, ⸗e (m) [*krook, krüh'-gə*]
pity, Mitleid (n) [*mit'-lait*]
   What a pity! Wie schade! [*vee shah'-də*]
place *n.*, Platz, ⸗e (m) [*plats, ple'-tsə*]
   in place of, anstatt (plus gen) [*an-shtat'*]
   take place *v.*, statt-finden (irreg) [*shtat'-fin-dən*]
place *v.*, stellen; legen [*shte'-lən; leh'-gən*]
plain [flat] *adj.*, flach [*flakh*]
plain [simple], einfach [*ain'-fakh*]
plan *n.*, Plan, ⸗e (m) [*plahn, pleh'-nə*]
plan *v.*, planen [*plah'-nən*]
planet, Planet, -en (m) [*pla-neht'*]
plant *n.*, Pflanze, -n (f) [*pflan'-tsə*]
plant *v.*, pflanzen [*pflan'-tsən*]
plaster, Pflaster, - (n) [*pfla'-stər*]
plate [dish], Teller, - (m) [*te'-lər*]
platform [train], Bahnsteig, -e (m) [*bahn'-shtaik, bahn'-shtai-gə*]
play *v.*, spielen [*shpee'-lən*]
play [theater] *n.*, Schauspiel, -e (n) [*shou'-shpeel*]

pleasant, angenehm [*an'-ge-nehm*]
please *v.*, erfreuen [*er-froi'-ən*]
  Does it please you? Gefällt es Ihnen? [*gə-felt' es ee'-nən*]
  Please! Bitte! [*bi'-tə*]
  Pleased to meet you, Sehr angenehm [*zehr an'-gə-nehm*]
pleasure, Vergnügen (n, sing), Vergnügungen (pl) [*fer-gnüh'-gən, fer-gnüh'-gung-ən*]
  with much pleasure, mit viel Vergnügen [*mit feel fer-gnüh'-gən*]
pleasure trip, Vergnügungsreise, -n (f) [*fer-gnüh'-gungs-rai-zə*]
plenty of, viel [*feel*]
plot [intrigue], Intrige, -n (f) [*in-tree'-gə*]
plow, Pflug, ⸗e (m) [*pflook, pflüh'-gə*]
plug [electric], Stecker, - (m) [*shte'-kər*]
plum, Pflaume, -n (f) [*pflou'-mə*]
plumber, Klempner, - (m) [*klemp'-nər*]
plural [gram.], Mehrzahl (f) [*mehr'-tsahl*]
plus, plus [*plus*]
pneumonia, Lungenentzündung, -en (f) [*lung'-ən-en-tsün-dung*]
pocket, Tasche, -n (f) [*ta'-shə*]
pocketbook, Brieftasche -n (f) [*breef'-ta-shə*]
poem, Gedicht, -e (n) [*gə-diçt'*]
poet, Dichter, - (m) [*diç'-tər*]
point [land, pins, knives] *n.*, Spitze, -n (f) [*shpit'-sə*]
pointed, spitzig [*shpit'-siç*]
pointless [meaningless], sinnlos [*zin'-lohs*]
point-of-view, Gesichtspunkt, -e (m) [*gə-ziçts'-punkt*]
poison, Gift, -e (n) [*gift*]
poisonous, giftig [*gif'-tiç*]
Poland, Polen (n) [*poh'-lən*]
pole [astronomy], Pol, -e (m) [*pohl*]
pole [rod], Stange, -n (f) [*shtang'-ə*]
police, Polizei (f) [*po-li-tsai'*]
policeman, Polizist, -en (m) [*po-li-tsist'*]
police station, Polizeiwache, -n (f) [*po-li-tsai'-va-khə*]
policy [gov.], Politik (f) [*po-li-teek'*]

policy [insurance], Police, -n (f) [*po-lee'-sə*]
polish [shoes] *v.*, putzen [*pu'-tsən*]
polish [furn.] *v.*, polieren [*po-lee'-rən*]
polish [for furniture], Möbelpolitur (f) [*möh'-bəl-po-li-toor*]
Polish *adj.*, polnisch [*pol'-nish*]
polite, höflich [*höhf'-liç*]
political, politisch [*po-lee'-tish*]
politics, Politik (f) [*po-li-teek'*]
pool [swimming], Schwimmbad, ⸗er (n) [*shvim'-baht, shvim'-beh-dər*]
pool [pond], Teich, -e (m) [*taiç*]
poor, arm [*arm*]
Pope, Papst, ⸗e (m) [*pahpst, pehp'-stə*]
popular, populär [*po-pu-lehr'*]
popularity, Beliebtheit (f) [*bə-leept'-hait*]
population, Bevölkerung, -en (f) [*bə-föl'-kə-rung*]
porch, Veranda (f, sing), Veranden (pl) [*ve-ran'-da, ve-ran'-dən*]
pork, Schweinefleisch (n) [*shvai'-nə-flaish*]
port [harbor], Hafen, ⸗ (m) [*hah'-fən, heh'-fən*]
porter [baggage], Träger, - (m) [*treh'-gər*]
portrait, Porträt, -e (n) [*por-treht'*]
Portugal, Portugal (n) [*por'-tu-gal*]
Portuguese *adj.*, portugiesisch [*por-tu-gee'-zish*]
position, Stellung, -en (f) [*shte'-lung*]
positive, bestimmt [*bə-shtimt'*]
possess *v.*, besitzen (irreg) [*bə-zi'-tsən*]
possession, Besitz (m) [*bə-zits'*]
possibility, Möglichkeit, -en (f) [*möhk'-liç-kait*]
possible, möglich [*möhk'-liç*]
  as soon as possible, so bald wie möglich [*zo balt vee möhk'-liç*]
possibly, vielleicht [*fee-laiçt'*]
post [mail] *n.*, Post (f) [*post*]
post office, Postamt, ⸗er (n) [*post'-amt, post'-em-tər*]
post office box, Schliessfach, ⸗er (n) [*shlees'-fakh, shlees'-fe-çər*]
postage, Porto (n) [*por'-toh*]

postage stamp, Briefmarke, -n (f) [*breef'-mar-kə*]
postcard, Postkarte, -n (f) [*post'-kar-tə*]
postpone *v.,* auf-schieben (irreg) [*ouf'-shee-bən*]
pot [cooking], Topf, ⸚e (m) [*topf, tö'-pfə*]
potato, Kartoffel, -n (f) [*kar-to'-fəl*]
pottery, Töpferware (f) [*tö'-pfər-vah-rə*]
pound [money, weight], Pfund, -e (n) [*pfunt, pfun'-də*]
  three pounds of meat, drei Pfund Fleisch [*drai pfunt flaish*]
pour *v.,* giessen (irreg) [*gee'-sən*]
poverty, Armut (f) [*ar'-moot*]
powder, Puder (m) [*poo'-dər*]
power, Macht, ⸚e (f) [*makht, meç'-tə*]
  horsepower, PS (abbreviation) [*peh-es'*]
power of attorney, Vollmacht, -en (f) [*fol'-makht*]
powerful, mächtig [*meç'-tiç*]
practical, praktisch [*prak'-tish*]
practice [a profession] *v.,* aus-üben [*ous'-üh-bən*]
practice [repetition] *v.,* üben [*üh'-bən*]
praise *v.,* loben [*loh'-bən*]
praise *n.,* lob (n) [*lohp*]
pray *v.,* beten [*beh'-tən*]
prayer, Gebet, -e (n) [*gə-beht'*]
precaution, Vorsicht (f) [*fohr'-ziçt*]
precede *v.,* vorher-gehen (irreg; *Aux:* SEIN) [*fohr-hehr'-geh-ən*]
precious, kostbar [*kost'-bahr*]
precious stone, Edelstein, -e (m) [*eh'-dəl-shtain*]
precise, genau [*gə-nou'*]
preface, Vorwort, -e (n) [*fohr'-vort*]
prefer *v.,* vor-ziehen (irreg) [*fohr'-tsee-ən*]
preferable, besser [*be'-sər*]
preference, Vorzug (m) [*fohr'-tsook*]
pregnancy, Schwangerschaft, -en (f) [*shvang'-ər-shaft*]
pregnant, schwanger [*shvang'-ər*]
prejudice, Vorurteil, -e (n) [*fohr'-ur-tail*]
premature, vorzeitig [*fohr'-tsai-tiç*]
premonition, Vorahnung, -en (f) [*fohr'-ah-nung*]
preparation, Vorbereitung, -en (f) [*fohr'-bə-rai-tung*]

prepare v., vor-bereiten [*fohr'-bə-rai-tən*]

prescription [medical], Rezept, -e (n) [*re-tsept'*]

presence, Anwesenheit (f) [*an'-veh-zən-hait*]

present adj., anwesend [*an'-veh-zənt*]

  at present, gegenwärtig [*geh'-gən-ver-tiç*]

present [a gift] v., schenken [*shen'-kən*]

present [gift] n., Geschenk, -e (n) [*gə-shenk'*]

president, Präsident, -en (m) [*pre-zi-dent'*]

press [clothes] v., bügeln [*büh'-gəln*]

press [squeeze] v., pressen [*pre'-sən*]

pressing adj., dringend [*dring'-ənt*]

pressure, Druck (m) [*druk*]

prestige, Ansehen (n) [*an'-zeh-ən*]

pretence, Vorwand, ⸗e (m) [*fohr'-vant, fohr'-ven-də*]

pretend v., vor-geben (irreg) [*fohr'-geh-bən*]

pretentious, anspruchsvoll [*an'-shprukhs-fol*]

pretty, hübsch [*hüpsh*]

prevent v., verhindern [*fer-hin'-dərn*]

previously, früher [*früh'-ər*]

price, Preis, -e (m) [*prais, prai'-zə*]

price list, Preisliste, -n (f) [*prais'-li-stə*]

pride, Stolz (m) [*shtolts*]

priest, Priester, - (m) [*pree'-stər*]

primitive adj., primitiv [*pri-mi-teef'*]

prince, Prinz, -en (m) [*prints*]

princess, Prinzessin, -nen (f) [*prin-tse'-sin*]

principal adj., Haupt- [*houpt-*]

principally, hauptsächlich [*houpt'-zeç-liç*]

principle [moral], Prinzip, -ien (n) [*prin-tseep'*]

  on principle, aus Prinzip [*ous prin-tseep'*]

print v., drucken [*dru'-kən*]

printed matter, Drucksache, -n (f) [*druk'-za-khə*]

printer, Drucker, - (m) [*dru'-kər*]

prison, Gefängnis, -se (n) [*gə-feng'-nis*]

  put in prison v., ein-sperren [*ain'-shpe-rən*]

prisoner, Gefangene, -n (m, f) [*gə-fang'-ə-nə*]

private adj., privat [*pri-vaht'*]

privilege, Vorrecht, -e (n) [*fohr'-reçt*]

prize, Preis, -e (m) [*prais, prai'-zə*]
probable, wahrscheinlich [*vahr-shain'-liç*]
problem, Problem, -e (n) [*pro-blehm'*]
procedure, Verfahren, -(n) [*ver-fah'-rən*]
process, Verfahren, - (n) [*ver-fah'-rən*]
produce *v.,* erzeugen [*er-tsoi'-gən*]
product, Produkt, -e (n) [*pro-dukt'*]
production, Herstellung (f) [*hehr'-shte-lung*]
profession, Beruf, -e (m) [*bə-roof'*]
professor, Professor, -en (m) [*pro-fe'-sor, pro-fe-soh'-rən*]
profit *n.,* Gewinn, -e (m) [*gə-vin'*]
profit *v.,* Vorteil ziehen (irreg) aus (plus dat) [*for'-tail tsee'-ən ous*]
program, Programm, -e (n) [*pro-gram'*]
progress *n.,* Fortschritt (m) [*fort'-shrit*]
progress *v.,* Fortschritte machen [*fort'-shri-tə ma'-khən*]
progressive, fortschrittlich [*fort'-shrit-liç*]
prohibit *v.,* verbieten (irreg) [*fer-bee'-tən*]
prohibited, verboten [*fer-boh'-tən*]
project *n.,* Entwurf, ≠e (m) [*ent-vurf', ent-vür'-fə*]
prominent, hervorragend [*her-fohr'-rah-gənt*]
promise *n.,* Versprechen, - (n) [*fer-shpre'-çən*]
promise *v.,* versprechen (irreg) [*fer-shpre'-çən*]
promotion, Beförderung, -en (f) [*bə-för'-de-rung*]
prompt, schnell [*shnel*]
pronounce *v.,* aus-sprechen (irreg) [*ous'-shpre-çən*]
   How do you pronounce it? Wie sprechen Sie das aus?
   [*vee sphre'-çən zee das ous*]
pronunciation, Aussprache (f) [*ous'-shprah-khə*]
proof, Beweis, -e (m) [*bə-vais', bə-vai'-zə*]
propaganda, Propaganda (f) [*pro-pa-gan'-da*]
propeller, Propeller, - (m) [*pro-pe'-lər*]
property, Eigentum (n) [*ai'-gən-toom*]
prophecy, Prophezeiung, -en (f) [*pro-fe-tsai'-ung*]
proportion, Verhältnis, -se (n) [*fer-helt'-nis*]
proposal, Vorschlag, ≠e (m) [*fohr'-shlahk, fohr'-shleh-gə*]
propose *v.,* vor-schlagen (irreg) [*fohr'-shlah-gən*]
proprietor, Eigentümer, - (m) [*ai'-gən-tüh-mər*]

prosperity, Wohlstand (m) [*vohl'-shtant*]
prosperous, erfolgreich [*er-folk'-raiç*]
protect *v.*, schützen [*shüt'-sən*]
protection, Schutz (m) [*shuts*]
protest *v.*, protestieren [*pro-tes-tee'-rən*]
Protestant, Protestant, -en (m) [*pro-tes-tant'*]
proud, stolz [*shtolts*]
prove *v.*, beweisen (irreg) [*bə-vai'-zən*]
proverb, Sprichwort, ⸗er (n) [*shpriç'-vort, shpriç'-vör-tər*]
provided that, vorausgesetzt dass [*fo-rous'-gə-zetst das*]
province, Provinz, -en (f) [*pro-vints'*]
provincial, provinziell [*pro-vin-tsi-əl'*]
provisions, Lebensmittel (n, pl) [*leh'-bəns-mi-təl*]
prune, Backpflaume, -n (f) [*bak'-pflou-mə*]
psychiatrist, Psychiater, - (m) [*psü-çi-ah'-tər*]
psychiatry, Psychiatrie (f) [*psü-çi-ah-tree'*]
psychoanalysis, Psychoanalyse (f) [*psü-ço-a-na-lüh'-zə*]
psychological, psychologisch [*psü-ço-loh'-gish*]
public *adj.*, öffentlich [*öf'-ənt-liç*]
publicity, Werbung (f) [*ver'-bung*]
publish *v.*, veröffentlichen [*fer-öf'-ənt-li-çən*]
pull *v.*, ziehen (irreg) [*tsee'-ən*]
   pull out, heraus-ziehen (irreg) [*he-rous'-tsee-ən*]
pulse, Puls, -e (m) [*puls, pul'-zə*]
pump *n.*, Pumpe, -n (f) [*pum'-pə*]
pumpkin, Kürbis, -se (m) [*kür'-bis*]
punctual, pünktlich [*pünkt'-liç*]
punish *v.*, bestrafen [*bə-shtrah'-fən*]
punishment, Strafe, -n (f) [*shtrah'-fə*]
pupil [male], Schüler, - (m) [*shüh'-lər*]
pupil [female], Schülerin, -nen (f) [*shüh'-lə-rin*]
purchase *n.*, Kauf, ⸗e (m) [*kouf, koi'-fə*]
purchase *v.*, kaufen [*kou'-fən*]
pure, rein [*rain*]
purple, purpurn [*pur'-purn*]
purpose, Zweck, -e (m) [*tsvek*]
   on purpose, absichtlich [*ap'-ziçt-liç*]
purse, Geldtasche, -n (f) [*gelt'-ta-shə*]

pursue v., verfolgen [fer-fol'-gən]
push [a button] v., drücken; stossen (irreg) [drü'-kən; shtoh'-sən]
put v., stellen; setzen; legen [shte'-lən; ze'-tsən; leh'-gən]
   put off, auf-schieben (irreg) [ouf'-shee-bən]
   put on [a light], an-machen [an'-ma-khən]
   put on [clothes], an-ziehen (irreg) [an'-tsee-ən]
   put out [a light], aus-machen [ous'-ma-khən]
puzzled, verwirrt [fer-virt']
pyjamas, Pyjama, -s (m) [pü-dzhah'-ma, pü-dzhah'-mas]
pyramid, Pyramide, -n (f) [pü-ra-mee'-də]

Q

quality, Qualität, -en (f) [kva-li-teht']
quantity, Menge, -n (f) [meng'-ə]
quarrel, Streit (m, sing), Streitigkeiten (pl) [shtrait, shtrai'-tiç-kai-tən]
quarrelsome, streitsüchtig [shtrait'-züç-tiç]
quarter, Viertel, - (n) [fir'-təl]
quarter hour, Viertelstunde, -n (f) [fir-təl-shtun'-də]
queen, Königin, -nen (f) [köh'-ni-gin]
queer, komisch [koh'-mish]
   How queer! Wie sonderbar! [vee zon'-der-bahr]
question n., Frage, -n (f) [frah'-gə]
question mark, Fragezeichen, - (n) [frah'-gə-tsai-çən]
quick, schnell [shnel]
quiet, ruhig [roo'-iç]
   Be quiet, Seien Sie ruhig [zai'-ən zee roo'-iç]
quotation [literary], Zitat, -e (n) [tsi-taht']
quote v., zitieren [tsi-tee'-rən]

R

rabbi, Rabbiner, - (m) [*ra-bee'-nər*]
rabbit, Kaninchen, - (n) [*ka-neen'-çən*]
race [human], Rasse, -n (f) [*ra'-sə*]
race [contest] *n.,* Rennen, - (n) [*re'-nən*]
   horse race, Pferderennen, - (n) [*pfehr'-də-re-nən*]
race *v.,* rennen (irreg; *Aux:* SEIN) [*re'-nən*]
radiator [house], Heizkörper, - (m) [*haits'-kör-pər*]
radio, Radio, -s (n) [*rah'-di-oh, rah'-di-ohs*]
radio station, Sender, - (m) [*zen'-dər*]
radish, Rettich, -e (m) [*re'-tiç*]
rag, Lumpen, - (m) [*lum'-pən*]
railroad, railway, Eisenbahn, -en (f) [*ai'-zən-bahn*]
railroad car, Eisenbahnwagen, - (m) [*ai'-zən-bahn-vah-gən*]
railroad crossing, Eisenbahnkreuzung, -en (f) [*ai'-zən-bahn-
   kroi-tsung*]
railroad station, Bahnhof, ⸗e (m) [*bahn'-hohf, bahn'-höh-fə*]
rain *v.,* regnen [*rehg'-nən*]
rain *n.,* Regen (m) [*reh'-gən*]
rainbow, Regenbogen, ⸗ (m) [*reh'-gən-boh-gən, reh'-gən-
   böh-gən*]
raincoat, Regenmantel, ⸗ (m) [*reh'-gən-man-təl, reh'-gən-
   men-təl*]
rainproof, regendicht [*reh'-gən-diçt*]
raise [lift] *v.,* heben (irreg) [*heh'-bən*]
raise [prices] *v.,* erhöhen [*er-höh'-ən*]
raisin, Rosine, -n (f) [*ro-zee'-nə*]
range [extension] *n.,* Bereich, -e (m) [*bə-raiç'*]
rank *n.,* Rang, ⸗e (f) [*rang, reng'-ə*]
rapid, schnell [*shnel*]
rare [unusual], selten [*zel'-tən*]
rare [for meats], halbroh [*halp'-roh*]
raspberry, Himbeere, -n (f) [*him'-beh-rə*]

rat, Ratte, -n (f) [ra'-tə]

rate n., Rate, -n (f) [rah'-tə]

  at the rate of, zum Preise von [tsum prai'-zə fon]

rather, lieber; eher [lee'-bər; eh'-ər]

  I would rather, Ich möchte lieber [iç möç'-tə lee'-bər]

raw, roh [roh]

raw material, Rohstoff, -e (m) [roh'-shtof]

rayon, Kunstseide (f) [kunst'-zai-də]

razor, Rasiermesser, - (n) [ra-zeer'-me-sər]

  electric razor, Rasierapparat, -e (m) [ra-zeer'-a-pa-raht]

razor blade, Rasierklinge, -n (f) [ra-zeer'-kling-ə]

reach v., erreichen [er-rai'-çən]

reaction, Reaktion, -en (f) [re-ak-tsi-ohn']

read v., lesen (irreg) [leh'-zən]

reading, Lektüre (f) [lek-tüh'-rə]

ready, fertig; bereit [fer'-tiç; bə-rait']

  Are you ready? Sind Sie fertig? [zint zee fer'-tiç]

ready-made clothes, Konfektion (f) [kon-fek-tsi-ohn']

real [genuine], echt [eçt]

real [actual], wirklich [virk'-liç]

rear [children] v., erziehen (irreg) [er-tsee'-ən]

reason n., Grund, ⸗e (m) [grunt, grün'-də]

reason [about] v., vernünftig denken (irreg) über (plus acc)
  [fer-nünf'-tiç den'-kən üh'-bər]

reasonable, vernünftig [fer-nünf'-tiç]

recall v., sich erinnern an (plus acc) [ziç er-in'-ərn an]

receipt, Quittung, -en (f) [kvi'-tung]

receive v., bekommen (irreg) [bə-ko'-mən]

recent, neu [noi]

recently, neulich [noi'-liç]

reception, Empfang, ⸗e (m) [em-pfang', em-pfeng'-ə]

recipe, Rezept, -e (n) [re-tsept']

recital [music], Konzert, -e (n) [kon-tsert']

recognize v., erkennen (irreg) [er-ke'-nən]

recommend v., empfehlen (irreg) [em-pfeh'-lən]

recommendation, Empfehlung, -en (f) [em-pfeh'-lung]

reconstruction, Wiederaufbau (m) [vee-dər-ouf'-bou]

record [phonograph] n., Platte, -n (f) [pla'-tə]

record [sports] *n.*, Rekord, -e (m) [*re-kort'*, *re-kor'-də*]
record [school] *n.*, Zeugnis, -se (n) [*tsoik'-nis*]
recover [one's health] *v.*, sich erholen [*ziç er-hoh'-lən*]
recreation, Erholung (f) [*er-hoh'-lung*]
red, rot [*roht*]
Red Cross, (das) Rote Kreuz (n) [*(dahs) roh'-tə kroits*]
red tape *adj.*, bürokratisch [*bü-ro-krah'-tish*]
reduce [prices] *v.*, herab-setzen [*he-rap'-ze-tsən*]
reduce [weight] *v.*, ab-nehmen (irreg) [*ap'-neh-mən*]
reduction, Ermässigung, -en (f) [*er-meh'-si-gung*]
refer to *v.*, sich beziehen (irreg) auf (plus acc) [*ziç bə-tsee'-ən ouf*]
referee, Schiedsrichter, - (m) [*sheets'-riç-tər*]
reference, Referenz, -en (f) [*re-fe-rənts'*]
    with reference to, in Bezug auf (plus acc) [*in bə-tsook' ouf*]
refined, verfeinert [*fer-fai'-nərt*]
refinery, Raffinerie, -n (f) [*ra-fi-ne-ree'*]
reflection [light], Spieglung, -en (f) [*shpeeg'-lung*]
reform *n.*, Reform, -en (f) [*re-form'*]
refresh *v.*, erfrischen [*er-frish'-shən*]
refreshing, erfrischend [*er-frish'-ənt*]
refreshment, Erfrischung, -en (f) [*er-fri'-shung*]
refrigerator, Kühlschrank, ⸗e (m) [*kühl'-shrank, kühl'-shren-kə*]
refugee, Flüchtling, -e (m) [*flüçt'-ling*]
refund *v.*, zurück-zahlen [*tsu-rük'-tsah-lən*]
refuse *v.*, verweigern [*fer-vai'-gərn*]
regain *v.*, wieder-gewinnen (irreg) [*vee'-dər-gə-vi-nən*]
regardless of, ungeachtet (plus gen) [*un'-ge-akh-tət*]
    in regard to, bezüglich auf (plus acc) [*bə-tsühk'-liç ouf*]
regards, Grüsse (m, pl) [*grüh'-sə*]
    kind regards, beste Grüsse [*be'-stə grüh'-sə*]
regiment, Regiment, -er (n) [*re-gi-ment'*, *re-gi-mən'-tər*]
region, Gegend, -en (f) [*geh'-gənt, geh'-gən-dən*]
register *n.*, Verzeichnis, -se (n) [*fer-tsaiç'-nis*]
register [letters] *v.*, einschreiben lassen (irreg) [*ain'-shrai-bən la'-sən*]

register [for courses] v., belegen [*bə-leh′-gən*]

registered letter, Einschreibebrief, -e (m) [*ain′-shrai-bə-breef*]

regret v., bedauern [*bə-dou′-ərn*]

regular, regelmässig [*reh′-gəl-meh-siç*]

regulation, Verordnung, -en (f) [*fer-ord′-nung*]

rehearsal, Probe, -n (f) [*proh′-bə*]

reign v., regieren [*re-gee′-rən*]

rein n., Zügel, - (m) [*tsüh′-gəl*]

related: be related to, verwandt sein mit (plus dat) [*fer-vant′ zain mit*]

relative adj., relativ [*re-la-teef′*]

relationship, Verwandschaft (f) [*fer-vant′-shaft*]

relatives, (die) Verwandten (m, f, pl) [*(dee) fer-van′-tən*]

release v., frei-geben (irreg) [*frai′-geh-bən*]

reliable, zuverlässig [*tsoo′-fer-le-siç*]

relief [aid], Hilfe (f) [*hil′-fə*]

relief [from discomfort], Erleichterung, -en (f) [*er-laiç′-tə-rung*]

religion, Religion, -en (f) [*re-li-gi-ohn′*]

religious, fromm [*from*]

rely on v., sich verlassen (irreg) auf (plus acc) [*ziç fer-la′-sən ouf*]

remain v., bleiben (irreg; Aux: SEIN) [*blai′-bən*]

remainder, Rest, -e (m) [*rest*]

remark n., Bemerkung, -en (f) [*bə-mer′-kung*]

remark v., bemerken [*bə-mer′-kən*]

remarkable, bemerkenswert [*bə-mer′-kəns-vehrt*]

remedy, Arznei, -en (f) [*arts-nai′*]

remember v., sich erinnern an (plus acc) [*ziç er-in′-ərn an*]
  Do you remember him? Erinnern Sie sich an ihn? [*er-in′-ərn zee ziç an een*]

remind of v., erinnern an (plus acc) [*er-in′-ərn an*]

remittance, Überweisung, -en (f) [*üh-bər-vai′-zung*]

remote, entfernt [*ent-fernt′*]

remove v., entfernen [*ent-fer′-nən*]

renew v., erneuern [*er-noi′-ərn*]

rent v., vermieten [*fer-mee′-tən*]

rent n., Miete, -n (f) [*mee'-tə*]
  for rent, zu vermieten [*tsu fer-mee'-tən*]
repair n., Reparatur, -en (f) [*re-pa-ra-toor'*]
repair v., reparieren [*re-pa-ree'-rən*]
repeat v., wiederholen [*vee-dər-hoh'-lən*]
  Please repeat! Wiederholen Sie bitte! [*vee-dər-hoh'-lən
  zee bi'-tə*]
replace v., ersetzen [*er-ze'-tsən*]
reply n., Antwort, -en (f) [*ant'-vort*]
report (to) v., sich melden (bei) [*ziç mel'-dən (bai)*]
reporter [female], Berichterstatterin, -nen (f) [*bə-riç'-tər-
  shta-tə-rin*]
reporter [male], Berichterstatter, - (m) [*bə-riçt'-ər-shta-tər*]
represent v., vertreten (irreg) [*fer-treh'-tən*]
representative, Vertreter, - (m) [*fer-treh'-tər*]
reproduction, Reproduktion, -en (f) [*re-pro-duk-tsi-ohn'*]
republic, Republik, -en (f) [*re-pu-bleek'*]
reputation, Ruf (m) [*roof*]
request v., bitten (irreg) um (plus acc) [*bi'-tən um*]
require v., benötigen [*be-nöh'-ti-gən*]
rescue v., retten [*re'-tən*]
research, Forschung (f) [*for'-shung*]
research v., erforschen [*er-for'-shən*]
resemblance, Ähnlichkeit, -en (f) [*ehn'-liç-kait*]
resemble v., ähneln [*eh'-nəln*]
resent v., übel-nehmen (irreg) [*üh'-bəl-neh-mən*]
resentment, Ärger (m) [*er'-gər*]
reservation [hotel, plane, etc], Reservierung, -en (f) [*re-zer-
  vee'-rung*]
residence, Wohnsitz, -e (m) [*vohn'-zits*]
resident n., Bewohner, -(m) [*bə-voh'-nər*]
resign v., zurück-treten (irreg; *Aux:* SEIN) [*tsu-rük'-
  treh-tən*]
resist v., widerstehen [*vee-dər-shteh'-ən*]
resolve v., beschliessen (irreg) [*bə-shlee'-sən*]
respect n., Achtung (f) [*akh'-tung*]
respect v., achten [*akh'-tən*]
  in all respects, in jeder Hinsicht [*in yeh'-dər hin'-ziçt*]

respectable, ehrenwert [*eh'-rən-vehrt*]

respectful, achtungsvoll [*akh'-tungs-fol*]

responsibility, Verantwortung (f, sing), Verantwortlich-
keiten (pl) [*fer-ant'-vor-tung, fer-ant'-vort-liç-kai-tən*]

responsible, verantwortlich [*fer-ant'-vort-liç*]

rest [remainder] *n.,* Rest, -e (f) [*rest*]

rest *v.,* ruhen [*roo'-ən*]

restaurant, Restaurant, -s (n) [*re-sto-rant', re-sto-rants'*]

result *n.,* Resultat, -e (n) [*re-zul-taht'*]

resume *v.,* wieder-auf-nehmen (irreg) [*vee-dər-ouf'-neh-mən*]

retail trade, Einzelhandel (m) [*ain'-zəl-han-dəl*]

retain *v.,* behalten (irreg) [*bə-hal'-tən*]

retire [pension off], *v..* pensionieren [*pen-zi-o-nee'-rən*]

retire [from work] *v.,* in den Ruhestand treten (irreg;
Aux: SEIN) [*in dehn roo'-ə-shtant treh'-tən*]

retire [to bed] *v.,* schlafen gehen (irreg; *Aux:* SEIN)
[*shlah'-fən gəh'-ən*]

return *n.,* Rückkehr (f) [*rük'-kehr*]

return *v.,* zurück-kommen (irreg; *Aux:* SEIN) [*tsu-rük'-
kom-ən*]

   When will she return? Wann kommt sie zurück? [*van
komt zee tsu-rük'*]

revenge, Rache (f) [*ra'-khə*]

review [periodical], Zeitschrift, -en (f) [*tsait'-shrift*]

review [of a book], Kritik, -en (f) [*kri-teek'*]

revise *v.,* überarbeiten [*üh-bər-ar'-bai-tən*]

revolution, Revolution, -en (f) [*re-vo-lu-tsi-ohn'*]

revolver, Revolver, - (m) [*re-vol'-vər*]

reward *n.,* Belohnung, -en (f) [*bə-loh'-nung*]

reward *v.,* belohnen [*bə-loh'-nən*]

rib, Rippe, -n (f) [*ri'-pə*]

ribbon, Band, ⸗er (n) [*bant, ben'-dər*]

rice, Reis (m) [*rais*]

rich, reich [*raiç*]

rid: (get) rid of *v.,* los-werden (irreg; *Aux:* SEIN) [*lohs'-
vehr-dən*]

ride *n.,* Ritt, -e (m) ; Fahrt, -en (f) [*rit; fahrt*]

ride [in car, etc.], *v.,* fahren (irreg; *Aux:* SEIN) [*fah'-rən*]

ride [a horse] *v.*, reiten (irreg; *Aux:* SEIN) [*rai'-tən*]

ridicule *n.*, Spott (m) [*shpot*]

ridiculous, lächerlich [*le'-çər-liç*]

rifle, Gewehr, -e (n) [*gə-vehr'*]

right *n.*, Recht, -e (n) [*reçt*]
  be right *v.*, recht haben [*reçt hah'-bən*]

right [direction], rechts [*reçts*]
  all right, in Ordnung [*in ord'-nung*]
  right away, sofort [*zo-fort'*]

ring [on finger], Ring, -e (m) [*ring*]

ring *v.*, läuten [*loi'-tən*]

riot *n.*, Aufruhr (m, sing), Krawalle (pl) [*ouf'-ruhr, krava'-le*]

ripe, reif [*raif*]

rise *v.*, sich erheben (irreg) [*ziç er-heh'-bən*]

risk, Risiko (n, sing), Risiken (pl) [*ree'-zi-ko, ree'-zi-ken*]

rival, Rival, -en (m) [*ri-vahl'*]

river, Fluss, ⸗e (m) [*flus, flü'-sə*]

riverside, Flussufer, - (n) [*flus'-uh-fər*]

road, Strasse, -n (*f*) [*shtra'-sə*]

roadway, Fahrdamm, ⸗e (m) [*fahr'-dam, fahr'-de-mə*]

roast *n.*, Braten, - (m) [*brah'-tən*]

roast *v.*, braten (irreg) [*brah'-tən*]

roasted, gebraten [*gə-brah'-tən*]

rob *v.*, rauben [*rou'-bən*]

robber, Räuber, - (m) [*roi'-bər*]

robbery, Diebstahl, ⸗e (m) [*deep'-shtahl, deep'-shteh-lə*]

rock *n.*, Felsen, - (m); Stein, -e (m) [*fel'-zən; shtain*]

Roman *adj.*, römisch [*röh'-mish*]

romantic, romantisch [*ro-man'-tish*]

Rome, Rom (n) [*rohm*]

roof, Dach, ⸗er (n) [*dakh, de'-çər*]

room [house,] Zimmer, - (n) [*tsi'-mər*]

room [space], Platz, ⸗e (m) [*plats, ple'-tsə*]
  There's no room here, Es gibt keinen Platz hier [*es gibt kai'-nən plats heer*]

rooster, Hahn, ⸗e (m) [*hahn, heh'-nə*]

root, Wurzel, -n (f) [*vur'-tsəl*]

rope, Seil, -e (n) [*zail*]

rose *n.*, Rose, -n (f) [*roh'-zə*]

rotten, verfault [*fer-foult'*]

rouge, Schminke, -n (f) [*shmin'-kə*]

rough, rauh [*rou*]

round, rund [*runt*]

round trip, Rundreise, -n (f) [*runt'-rai-zə*]

route, Strecke, -n (f) [*shtre'-kə*]

routine, Routine, -n (f) [*roo-tee'-nə*]

row [line], Reihe, -n (f) [*rai'-hə*]

row *v.*, rudern [*roo'-dərn*]

royal, königlich [*köh'-nik-liç*]

rub *v.*, reiben (irreg) [*rai'-bən*]

   rub out, aus-streichen (irreg) [*ous'-shtrai-çən*]

rubber, Gummi, -s (m) [*gu'-mee, gu'-mees*]

ruby, Rubin, -e (m) [*ru-been'*]

rude, grob [*grohp*]

rudeness, Grobheit, -en (f) [*grohp'-hait*]

rug, Teppich, -e (m) [*te'-piç*]

ruin *n.*, Ruine, -n (f) [*ru-ee'-nə*]

rule *v.*, regieren [*re-gee'-rən*]

ruler [for measuring], Lineal, -e (n) [*li-ne-ahl'*]

ruler [state], Herrscher, - (m) [*her'-shər*]

rumor, Gerücht, -e (n) [*gə-rüçt'*]

run *v.*, laufen (irreg; *Aux:* SEIN) [*lou'-fən*]

   run across, zufällig treffen (irreg) [*tsoo'-fe-liç tre'-fən*]

   run after, nach-laufen (plus dat) (irreg; *Aux:* SEIN)
     [*nakh'-lou-fən*]

   run into [meet], treffen (irreg) [*tre'-fən*]

   run over, überfahren (irreg; *Aux:* SEIN) [*üh-bər-fah'-rən*]

running water, fliessendes Wasser [*flee'-sən-dəs va'-sər*]

Russia, Russland (n) [*rus'-lant*]

Russian *adj.*, russisch [*ru'-sish*]

rust, Rost (m) [*rost*]

rustic, ländlich [*lent'-liç*]

rye, Roggen (m) [*ro'-gən*]

S

sabotage n., Sabotage (f) [za-bo-tah'-zhə]
sabotage v., sabotieren [za-bo-tee'-rən]
sack n., Sack, ⁼e (m) [zak, ze'-kə]
sacred, heilig [hai'-liç]
sacrifice n., Opfer, - (n) [o'-pfər]
sad, traurig [trou'-riç]
saddle, Sattel, ⁼ (m) [za'-təl, ze'-təl]
sadness, Traurigkeit (f) [trou'-riç-kait]
safe n., Geldschrank, ⁼e (m) [gelt'-shrank, gelt-shren'-kə]
safe adj., sicher [zi'-çər]
  safe and sound, frisch und gesund [frish unt gə-zunt']
safety, Sicherheit (f) [zi'-çər-hait]
sail n., Segel, - (n) [zeh'-gəl]
sail v., segeln; fahren (irreg; Aux: SEIN) [zeh'-gəln; fah'-ren]
  When does the ship sail? Wann fährt das Schiff ab?
    [van fehrt das shif ap]
sailboat, Segelboot, -e (n) [zeh'-gəl-boht]
sailor, Seemann (m, sing), Seeleute (pl) [zeh'-man, zeh'-
    loi-tə]
saint, Heilige, -n (m, f) [hai'-li-gə]
sake: for heaven's sake, um Himmelswillen [um hi'-məls-
    vi-lən]
  for your sake, Ihretwegen [ee'-rət-veh-gən]
salad, Salat, -e (m) [za-laht']
salary, Gehalt, ⁼er (n) [gə-halt', gə-hel'-tər]
sale, Verkauf, ⁼e (m) [fer-kouf', fer-koi'-fə]
  for sale, zu verkaufen [tsu fer-kou'-fən]
salesclerk [male], Verkäufer, - (m) [fer-koi'-fər]
salesclerk [female], Verkäuferin, -nen (f) [fer-koi'-fə-rin]
salmon, Lachs, -e (m) [laks]
salt, Salz, -e (n) [zalts]
salty, salzig [zal'-tsiç]

113

salute v., grüssen [grüh'-sən]

(the) same, derselbe, dieselbe, dasselbe [dehr-zel'-bə, dee-zel'-bə, das-zel'-bə]

 It's all the same to me, Es ist mir gleich [es ist meer glaiç]

sample n., Muster, - (n) [mu'-stər]

sanatorium, Sanatorium (n, sing), Sanatorien (pl) [za-na-toh'-ri-um, za-na-toh'-ri-ən]

sand, Sand (m) [zant]

sandwich, das belegte Brot [das bə-lehk'-tə broht]

sane, geistig gesund [gai'-stiç gə-zunt']

sanitary, hygienisch [hü-gi-eh'-nish]

sapphire, Saphir, -e (m) [za'-fir, za-fee'-rə]

sarcastic, sarkastisch [zar-ka'-stish]

satire, Satire, -n (f) [za-tee'-rə]

satirical, satirisch [za-tee'-rish]

satisfactory, befriedigend [bə-free'-di-gənt]

satisfied, zufrieden [tsu-free'-dən]

satisfy v., befriedigen [bə-free'-di-gən]

Saturday, Sonnabend, -e (m); Samstag, -e (m) [zon'-ah-bənt, zon'-ah-bən-də; zams'-tahk, zams'-tah-gə]

sauce, Sosse, -n (f) [zoh'-sə]

saucer, Untertasse, -n (f) [un'-tər-ta-sə]

sausage, Wurst, ⸗e (f) [vurst, vür'-stə]

savage, wild [vilt]

save [life] v., retten [re'-tən]

save [money] v., sparen [shpah'-rən]

savings account, Sparkonto (n, sing), Sparkonten (pl) [shpahr'-kon-to, shpahr'-kon-tən]

saw [tool], Säge, -n (f) [zeh'-gə]

say v., sagen [zah'-gən]

scale [music], Tonleiter, -n (f) [tohn'-lai-tər]

scandal, Skandal, -e (m) [skan-dahl']

scar, Narbe, -n (f) [nar'-bə]

scarce, selten; knapp [zel'-tən; knap]

scarcely, kaum [koum]

scare v., erschrecken [er-shre'-kən]

scarf, Schal, -s (m) [shahl, shahls]

scarlet fever, Scharlachfieber (n) [shar'-lakh-fee-bər]

scene, Szene, -n (f) [*stseh'-nə*]

scenery [theater], Dekoration, -en (f) [*de-ko-ra-tsi-ohn'*]

scenery [nature], Landschaft, -en (f) [*lant'-shaft*]

schedule [train], Fahrplan, ≈e (m) [*fahr'-plahn, fahr'-pleh-nə*]

school, Schule, -n (f) [*shoo'-lə*]

schoolmate, Mitschüler, - (m) [*mit'-shüh-lər*]

schoolteacher [female], Lehrerin, -nen (f) [*leh'-re-rin*]

schoolteacher [male], Lehrer, - (m) [*leh'-rər*]

science, Wissenschaft, -en (f) [*vi'-sən-shaft*]

scientist, Wissenschaftler, - (m) [*vi'-sən-shaft-lər*]

scissors, Schere, -n (f) [*sheh'-rə*]

scold v., schelten (irreg) [*shel'-tən*]

Scotch adj., schottisch [*sho'-tish*]

Scotland, Schottland (n) [*shot'-lant*]

scratch [of the skin] n., Ritz, -e (m) [*rits*]

scratch v., kratzen [*kra'-tsən*]

scream n., Schrei, -e (m) [*shrai*]

scream v., schreien (irreg) [*shrai'-ən*]

screen [films] n., Leinwand, ≈e (f) [*lain'-vant, lain'-ven-də*]

screw n., Schraube, -n (f) [*shrou'-bə*]

screwdriver, Schraubenzieher, - (m) [*shrou'-bən-tsee-ər*]

sculpture n., Skulptur, -en (f) [*skulp-toor'*]

sea, Meer, -e (n) [*mehr*]

seal [animal], Seehund, -e (m) [*zeh'-hunt, zeh'-hun-də*]

seal [document] n., Siegel, - (n) [*zee'-gəl*]

seal [with sealing wax, etc.], versiegeln [*fer-zee'-gəln*]

seal [close envelope] v., zu-kleben [*tsoo'-kleh-bən*]

seam, Naht, ≈e (f) [*naht, neh'-tə*]

seaport, Seehafen, ≈ (m) [*zeh'-hah-fən, zeh'-heh-fən*]

search n., Suche (f) [*zoo'-khə*]

search v., suchen [*zoo'-khən*]

  search for, suchen nach (plus dat) [*zoo'-khən nakh*]

seaside, Strand (m, sing), Küsten (pl) [*shtrant, kü'-stən*]

season n., Jahreszeit, -en (f) [*yah'-rəs-tsait*]

seat n., Sitz, -e (m) [*zits*]

  Have a seat, please, Bitte, nehmen Sie Platz [*bi'-tə neh'-mən zee plats*]

second [time] *n.*, Sekunde, -n (f) [*ze-kun′-də*]
second *adj.*, zweit [*tsvait*]
secret, Geheimnis, -se (n) [*gə-haim′-nis*]
secretary [female], Sekretärin, -nen (f) [*zek-re-teh′-rin*]
secretary [male], Sekretär, -e (m) [*zek-re-tehr′*]
section, Abteilung, -en (f) [*ap′-tai-lung*]
secure *adj.*, sicher [*zi′-çər*]
secure [make secure] *v.*, sichern [*zi′-çərn*]
security [safety], Sicherheit (f) [*zi′-çər-hait*]
seduce *v.*, verführen [*fer-füh′-rən*]
see *v.*, sehen (irreg) [*zeh′-ən*]
   Let's see! Sehen wir! [*zeh′-ən veer*]
seed, Samen, - (m) [*zah′-mən*]
seek *v.*, suchen [*zoo′-khən*]
seem *v.*, scheinen (irreg) [*shai′-nən*]
   How does it seem to you? Was halten Sie davon?
     [*vas hal′-tən zee da-fon′*]
   It seems to me that . . . , Es scheint mir, dass . . .
     [*es shaint meer das*]
seize *v.*, ergreifen (irreg) [*er-grai′-fən*]
seldom, selten [*zel′-tən*]
select *v.*, aus-suchen [*ous′-zoo-khən*]
self, selbst [*zelpst*]
   I myself, ich selbst [*iç zelpst*]
   I wash myself, Ich wasche mich [*iç va′-shə miç*]
self-consciousness, Befangenheit (f) [*bə-fang′-ən-hait*]
selfish, egoistisch [*e-go-i′-stish*]
sell *v.*, verkaufen [*fer-kou′-fən*]
senate, Senat, -e (m) [*se-naht′*]
senator, Senator, -en (m) [*ze-nah′-tor, ze-na-toh′-rən*]
send *v.*, senden (irreg) [*zen′-dən*]
   send for, kommen lassen (irreg) [*ko′-mən la′-sən*]
sender, Absender, - (m) [*ap′-zen-dər*]
sense *n.*, Sinn, -e (m) [*zin*]
   common sense, der gesunde Menschenverstand (m) [*dehr*
     gə-zun′-də men′-shən-fer-shtant]
sensible, vernünftig [*fer-nünf′-tiç*]
sensitive, empfindlich [*emp-fint′-liç*]

sensual, sinnlich [*zin'-liç*]

sentence [grammar], Satz, ≈e (m) [*zats, zet'-sə*]

sentence [legal], Urteil, -e (n) [*ur'-tail*]

sentimental, sentimental [*zen-ti-men-tahl'*]

separate *v.,* trennen [*tre'-nən*]

separate *adj.,* getrennt [*gə-trent'*]

separation, Trennung, -en (f) [*tre'-nung*]

September, September (m) [*zep-tem'-bər*]

sergeant [army], Feldwebel, - (m) [*felt'-veh-bəl*]

series, Serie, -n (f) [*zeh'-ri-ə*]

serious, ernst [*ernst*]

sermon, Predigt, -en (f) [*preh'-diçt*]

servant [female], Dienerin, -nen (f) [*dee'-nə-rin*]

servant [male], Diener, - (m) [*dee'-nər*]

serve *v.,* dienen [*dee'-nən*]

service, Dienst, -e (m) [*deenst*]

set *n.,* Satz, ≈e (m) [*zats, zet'-sə*]

set *v.,* setzen [*zet'-sən*]

  set aside, beiseite stellen [*bai-zai'-tə shtel'-lən*]

  set a watch, eine Uhr stellen [*ai'-nə oor shte'-lən*]

  set off, hervor-heben (irreg) [*her-fohr'-heh-bən*]

settle [an account] *v.,* eine Rechnung begleichen (irreg) [*ai'-nə reç'-nung bə-glai'-çən*]

settle [a country] *v.,* sich nieder-lassen (irreg) [*ziç nee'-dər-la-sən*]

seven, sieben [*zee'-bən*]

seventeen, siebzehn [*zeep'-tsehn*]

seventh, siebent [*zee'-bənt*]

seventy, siebzig [*zeep'-tsiç*]

several, mehrere [*meh'-rə-rə*]

severe, streng [*shtreng*]

sew *v.,* nähen [*neh'-ən*]

sewing machine, Nähmaschine, -n (f) [*neh'-ma-shee-nə*]

sex, Geschlecht, -er (n) [*gə-shleçt', gə-shleç'-tər*]

sexual, geschlechtlich [*gə-shleçt'-liç*]

sexual intercourse, Geschlechtsverkehr (m) [*gə-shleçts'-fer-kehr*]

shade, shadow, Schatten, - (m) [*sha'-tən*]

shady, schattig [*sha'-tiç*]
shake v., schütteln [*shü'-təln*]
  shake hands, Hände schütteln [*hen'-də shü'-təln*]
shall [future], werden (irreg; *Aux:* SEIN) [*vehr'-dən*]
  I shall [future], ich werde [*iç vehr'-də*]
shame, Schande (f) [*shan'-də*]
shameful, schändlich [*shent'-liç*]
shameless person, unverschämter Mensch [*un-fer-shem'-tər mensh*]
shampoo, Shampoo, -s (n) [*sham-poo'*, *sham-poos'*]
shape n., Form, -en (f) [*form*]
shape v., formen [*for'-mən*]
share [part] n., Teil, -e (m) [*tail*]
share [stock] n., Aktie, -n (f) [*ak'-tsi-ə*]
share v., teilen [*tai'-lən*]
shark, Haifisch, -e (m) [*hai'-fish*]
sharp, scharf [*sharf*]
shave v., rasieren [*ra-zee'-rən*]
shaving brush, Rasierpinsel, - (m) [*ra-zeer'-pin-zəl*]
shaving cream, Rasierkrem (m) [*ra-zeer'-krem*]
shawl, Schal, -s (m) [*shahl*, *shahls*]
she, sie [*zee*]
sheet [bed], Bettuch, ̈er (n) [*bet'-tuhkh*, *bet'-tüh-çər*]
sheet [paper], Blatt, ̈er (n) [*blat*, *ble'-tər*]
shelf, Regal, -e (n) [*re-gahl'*]
shell [sea], Muschel, -n (f) [*mu'-shəl*]
shell [egg], Schale, -n (f) [*shah'-lə*]
shell [gun], Granate, -n (f) [*gra-nah'-tə*]
shelter [air attack] n., Bunker, - (m) [*bun'-kər*]
sherry, Sherry (m) [*she'-ri*]
shift v., schieben (irreg) [*shee'-bən*]
shine [sun] v., scheinen (irreg) [*shai'-nən*]
shine [glisten] v., glänzen [*glent'-sən*]
shine [shoes] v., putzen [*pu'-tsən*]
ship n., Schiff, -e (f) [*shif*]
shipwreck, Schiffbruch, ̈e (m) [*shif'-brukh*, *shif'-brü-çə*]
ship v., verladen (irreg) [*fer-lah'-dən*]
shirt, Hemd, -en (n) [*hemt*, *hem'-dən*]

shiver *v.*, zittern [*tsi'-tərn*]
shock, Schock, -s (m) [*shok, shoks*]
shoe, Schuh, -e (m) [*shoo*]
shoelace, Schnürsenkel, - (m) [*shnühr'-zen-kəl*]
shoemaker, Schuhmacher, - (m) [*shoo'-ma-khər*]
shoeshine boy, Schuhputzer, - (m) [*shoo'-put-sər*]
shoe store, Schuhgeschäft, -e (n) [*shoo'-gə-sheft*]
shoot [fire] *v.*, schiessen (irreg) [*shee'-sən*]
shoot [kill] *v.*, erschiessen (irreg) [*er-shee'-sən*]
shop *n.*, Geschäft, -e (n) [*gə-sheft'*]
shop [go shopping] *v.*, einkaufen gehen (irreg; *Aux:* SEIN)
   [*ain'-kou-fən geh'-ən*]
shopwindow, Schaufenster, - (n) [*shou'-fen-stər*]
shore, Küste, - n (f) [*kü'-stə*]
short [not long], kurz [*kurts*]
  in a short time, in kurzer Zeit [*in kur'-tsər tsait*]
short [not big or tall], klein [*klain*]
shortsighted, kurzsichtig [*kurts'-ziç-tiç*]
shortcut, Abkürzung, -en (f) [*ap'-kür-tsung*]
shot *n.*, Schuss, ⸗e (m) [*shus, shü'-sə*]
should, sollte [*zol'-tə*]
  I, he, she, it should, ich, er, sie, es sollte [*iç, ehr, zee, es*
   zol'-tə]
  we, you [formal], **they should,** wir, Sie, sie sollten [*veer, zee,*
   zee zol'-tən]
  we should go, wir sollten gehen [*veer zol'-tən geh'-ən*]
shoulder, Schulter, -n (f) [*shul'-tər*]
shout *n.*, Ruf, -e (m) [*roof*]
shovel, Schaufel, -n (f) [*shou'-fəl*]
show [theater] *n.*, Vorstellung, -en (f) [*fohr'-shte-lung*]
show [exhibition] *n.*, Ausstellung, -en (f) [*ous'-shte-lung*]
show *v.*, zeigen [*tsai'-gən*]
  Show me! Zeigen Sie mir! [*tsai'-gən zee meer*]
shower [bath] *n.*, Dusche, -n (f) [*dooh'-shə*]
shrimp, Krabbe, -n (f) [*kra'-bə*]
shrink [garment], *v.*, ein-laufen (irreg; *Aux:* SEIN) [*ain'-lou-fən*]
shudder *v.*, schaudern [*shou'-dərn*]
shut *v.*, schliessen (irreg) [*shlee'-sən*]

shut in, ein-sperren [*ain'-shpe-rən*]
shut out, aus-schliessen (irreg) [*ous'-shlee-sən*]
shutter [camera] *n.*, Verschluss, ⁼e (m) [*fer-shlus', fer-shlü'-sə*]
shy, scheu [*shoi*]
Sicilian *adj.*, sizilisch [*zi-tsee'-lish*]
Sicily, Sizilien (n) [*zi-tsee'-li-ən*]
sick, krank [*krank*]
sickness, Krankheit, -en (f) [*krank'-hait*]
side *n.*, Seite, -n (f) [*zai'-tə*]
sidewalk, Bürgersteig, -e (m) [*bür'-gər-shtaik, bür'-gər-shtai-gə*]
sideways, seitwärts [*zait'-verts*]
sight *n.*, Sicht (f) [*ziçt*]
sight [catch sight of] *v.*, erblicken [*er-bli'-kən*]
sign [symbol] *n.*, Zeichen, - (n) [*tsai'-çən*]
sign [written sign] *n.*, Schild, -er (n) [*shilt, shil'-dər*]
sign *v.*, unterschreiben (irreg) [*un-tər-shrai'-bən*]
signature, Unterschrift, -en (f) [*un'-tər-shrift*]
significance, Bedeutung (f) [*bə-doi'-tung*]
signpost [shop, traffic], Schild, -er (n) [*shilt, shil'-dər*]
silence *n.*, Stille (f) [*shti'-lə*]
silent, still [*shtil*]
silk, Seide (f) [*zai'-də*]
silly, albern [*al'-bərn*]
silver, Silber (n) [*zil'-bər*]
similar, ähnlich [*ehn'-liç*]
simple, einfach [*ain'-fakh*]
sin, Sünde, -n (f) [*zün'-də*]
since *adv.*, seitdem [*zait-dehm'*]
since *prep.*, seit (plus dat) [*zait*]
  since when? seit wann? [*zait van*]
since *conj.*, da [*dah*]
sincere, aufrichtig [*ouf'-riç-tiç*]
sincerely yours, Ihr ergebener [*eer er-geh'-bən-ər*]
sing *v.*, singen (irreg) [*zing'-ən*]
singer [female], Sängerin, -nen (f) [*zen'-gə-rin*]
singer [male], Sänger, - (m) [*zeng'-ər*]

single [not married], ledig [*leh'-diç*]
single [alone], einzeln [*ain'-tsəln*]
  not a single one, nicht ein einziger [*niçt ain ain'-tsi-gər*]
sink [go down] v., versinken (irreg; *Aux.* SEIN) [*fer-zin'-kən*]
sink [scuttle] v., versenken [*fer-zen'-kən*]
Sir [in direct address], Herr; mein Herr [*her; main her*]
sister, Schwester, -n (f) [*shve'-stər*]
sister-in-law, Schwägerin, -nen (f) [*shveh'-gə-rin*]
sit v., sitzen (irreg) [*zit'-sən*]
  sit down, sich setzen [*ziç zet'-sən*]
    Sit down, please! Setzen Sie sich, bitte! [*zet'-sən zee ziç bi'tə*]
  sit up, sich auf-richten [*ziç ouf'-riç-tən*]
situated, gelegen [*gə-leh'-gən*]
situation, Lage, -n (f) [*lah'-gə*]
six, sechs [*zeks*]
sixteen, sechzehn [*zeç'-tsehn*]
sixth, sechst [*zekst*]
sixty, sechzig [*zeç'-tsiç*]
size, Grösse, -n (f) [*gröh'-sə*]
skate v., Schlittschuh laufen (irreg; *Aux:* SEIN) [*shlit'-shoo lou'-fən*]
skater, Schlittschuhläufer, - (m) [*shlit'-shoo-loi-fər*]
skates n., Schlittschuhe (m, pl) [*shlit'-shoo-ə*]
ski n., Ski, Schi, -er (m) [*skee, shee, skee'-ər, shee'-ər*]
ski v., Ski laufen (irreg; *Aux:* SEIN) [*shee lou'-fən*]
skier, Skiläufer, - (m) [*shee'-loi-fər*]
ski lift, Skilift, -e (m) [*shee'-lift*]
skillful, geschickt [*gə-shikt'*]
skill, Geschicklichkeit, -en (f) [*gə-shik'-liç-kait*]
skin, Haut, ⸗e (f) [*hout, hoi'-tə*]
skinny, mager [*mah'-gər*]
skirt, Rock, ⸗e (f) [*rok, rö'-kə*]
sky, Himmel, - (m) [*hi'-məl*]
skylight, Oberlicht, -er (n) [*oh'-bər-liçt, oh'-bər-liç-tər*]
skyline, Silhouette, -n (f) [*zi-lu-e'-tə*]
skyscraper, Wolkenkratzer, - (m) [*vol'-kən-kra-tsər*]
slave, Sklave, -n (m) [*sklah'-və*]

slavery, Sklaverei (f) [*sklah-ve-rai'*]

sleep *n.*, Schlaf (m) [*shlahf*]

sleep, be asleep *v.*, schlafen (irreg) [*shlah'-fən*]
  be sleepy, schläfrig sein [*shlehf'-riç zain*]

sleeping car, Schlafwagen, - (m) [*shlahf'-vah-gən*]

sleeve, Ärmel, - (m) [*er'-məl*]

slender, schlank [*shlank*]

slice *n.*, Scheibe, -n (f) [*shai'-bə*]
  slice off, ab-schneiden (irreg) [*ap'-shnai-dən*]

slide *v.*, gleiten (irreg; *Aux:* SEIN) [*glai'-tən*]

slight *adj.*, gering [*gə-ring'*]

slip *v.*, aus-rutschen [*ous'-rut-shən*]

slip [false step] *n.*, Fehltritt, -e (m) [*fehl'-trit*]

slip [garment] *n.*, Unterkleid, -er (n) [*un'-tər-klait, un'-tər-klai-dər*]

slippers, Hausschuhe (m, pl) [*hous'-shoo-ə*]

slippery, schlüpfrig [*shlüpf'-riç*]

slow, langsam [*lang'-zam*]

small, klein [*klain*]

small change, Kleingeld (n) [*klain'-gelt*]

smallpox, Pocken (f, pl) [*po'-kən*]

smart [clever], gescheit [*gə-shait'*]

smart [stylish], elegant [*e-le-gant'*]

smash *v.*, zerschmettern [*tser-shme'-tərn*]

smell *n.*, Geruch, ⸗e (f) [*gə-rukh', gə-rü'-çə*]

smell *v.*, riechen (irreg) [*ree'-çen*]

smile *v.*, lächeln [*le'-çəln*]

smoke *n.*, Rauch (m) [*roukh*]

smoke *v.*, rauchen [*rou'-khən*]

smooth, glatt [*glat*]

smug, selbstzufrieden [*zelpst'-tsu-free-dən*]

snail, Schnecke, -n (f) [*shne'-kə*]

snake, Schlange, -n (f) [*shlang'-ə*]

sneeze *v.*, niesen [*nee'-zən*]

snore *v.*, schnarchen [*shnar'-çən*]

snow *n.*, Schnee (m) [*shneh*]

snow *v.*, schneien [*shnai'-ən*]

snowflake, Schneeflocke, -n (f) [*shneh'-flo-kə*]

snowstorm, Schneesturm, ⸗e (m) [*shneh'-shturm, shneh'-shtür-mə*]

so, so [*zoh*]

    I don't think so, Ich glaube nicht [*iç glou'-bə niçt*]

    I hope so! Hoffentlich! [*ho'-fənt-liç*]

    Is that so? Wirklich? [*virk'-liç*]

    so far [time], bis jetzt [*bis yetst*]

    So far as I know, Soviel ich weiss [*zo-feel' iç vais*]

    So far as I am concerned, Was mich betrifft [*vas miç bə-trift'*]

    and so forth, und so weiter [*unt zoh vai'-tər*]

    so that, sodass [*zo-das'*]

soap, Seife, -n (f) [*zai'-fə*]

sober, nüchtern [*nüç'-tərn*]

social, sozial [*zo-tsi-ahl'*]

socialist, Sozialist, -en (m) [*zo-tsi-a-list'*]

society, Gesellschaft, -en (f) [*gə-zel'-shaft*]

sock *n.,* Socke, -n (f) [*zo'-kə*]

soda water, Mineralwasser, ⸗ (n) [*mi-ne-rahl'-va-sər, mi-ne-rahl'-ve-sər*]

sofa, Sofa, -s (n) [*zoh'-fah, zoh'-fahs*]

soft, weich [*vaiç*]

softness, Weichheit (f) [*vaiç'-hait*]

soiled, beschmutzt [*bə-shmutst'*]

soldier, Soldat, -en (m) [*zol-daht'*]

sole [of shoe], Sohle, -n (f) [*zoh'-lə*]

sole [fish], Scholle, -n (f) [*sho'-lə*]

sole *adj.,* einzig [*ain'-tsiç*]

solid, fest; solid [*fest;* zo-leet'*]

solitary, einsam [*ain'-zam*]

solution, Lösung, -en (f) [*löh'-zung*]

solve *v.,* lösen [*löh'-zən*]

some *adj.,* irgendein; etwas [*ir'-gənt-ain, et'-vas*]

some *adv.,* etwas [*et'-vas*]

somebody, someone, jemand [*yeh'-mant*]

something, etwas [*et'-vas*]

sometimes, manchmal [*mançh'-mal*]

somewhere, irgendwo [*ir-gənt-voh'*]

somewhere else, irgendwo anders; anderswo [*ir-gǝnt-voh' an'-dǝrs*; *an'-dǝrs-woh*]

son, Sohn, ⸗e (m) [*zohn, zöh'-nǝ*]

son-in-law, Schwiegersohn, ⸗e (m) [*shvee'-gǝr-zohn, shvee'-gǝr-zöh-nǝ*]

song, Lied, -er (n) [*leet, lee'-dǝr*]

soon, bald [*balt*]

  as soon as, sobald wie [*zo-balt' vee*]

  How soon? Wie bald? [*vee balt*]

sooner, früher; eher [*früh'-ǝr*; *eh'-ǝr*]

  sooner or later, früher oder später [*früh'-ǝr oh'-dǝr shpeh'-tǝr*]

sore *n.,* Wunde, -n (f) [*vun'-dǝ*]

sore *adj.,* wund [*vunt*]

sore throat, Halsschmerzen (m, pl) [*hals'-shmer-tsǝn*]

sorrow, Kummer (m) [*ku'-mǝr*]

sorrowful, kummervoll [*ku'-mǝr-fol*]

sorry: be sorry *v.,* bedauern [*bǝ-dou'-ǝrn*]

  I am very sorry, Es tut mir sehr leid [*es toot meer zehr lait*]

sort *n.,* Art, -en (f); Sorte, -n (f) [*art*; *zor'-tǝ*]

soul, Seele, -n (f) [*zeh'-lǝ*]

sound [noise] *n.,* Geräusch, -e (n) [*gǝ-roish'*]

sound [tone] *n.,* Laut, -e (m) [*lout*]

sound *v.,* klingen (irreg) [*kling'-ǝn*]

soundproof *adj.,* schalldicht [*shal'-diçt*]

soup, Suppe, -n (f) [*zu'-pǝ*]

sour, sauer [*zou'-ǝr*]

south, Süden (m) [*züh'-dǝn*]

South America, Südamerika [*züht'-a-meh-ri-kah*]

South American *adj.,* südamerikanisch [*züht'-a-me-ri-kah-nish*]

souvenir, Andenken, - (n) [*an'-den-kǝn*]

space *n.,* Raum, ⸗e (m) [*roum, roi'-mǝ*]

space suit, Raumanzug, ⸗e (m) [*roum'-an-tsook, roum'-an-tsüh-gǝ*]

spacious, geräumig [*gǝ-roi'-miç*]

Spain, Spanien (n) [*shpah'-ni-ǝn*]

Spaniard [female], Spanierin, -nen (f) [*shpah'-ni-ǝ-rin*]

Spaniard [male], Spanier, - (m) [*shpah'-ni-ər*]
Spanish, spanisch [*shpah'-nish*]
spare parts, Ersatzteile (m, pl) [*er-zats'-tai-lə*]
spare tire, Ersatzreifen, - (m) [*er-zats'-rai-fən*]
spark *n.*, Funke, -n (m) [*fun'-kə*]
spark plug, Zündkerze, -n (f) [*tsünt'-ker-tsə*]
sparrow, Sperling, -e (m) [*shper'-ling*]
speak *v.*, sprechen (irreg) [*shpre'-çən*]
  Do you speak English? Sprechen Sie englisch? [*shpre'-çən zee eng'-lish*]
special *adj.*, besonder [*bə-zon'-dər*]
specialist, Spezialist, -en (m) [*shpe-tsi-a-list'*]
specialty, Spezialität, -en (f) [*shpe-tsi-a-li-teht'*]
spectacle, Schauspiel, -e (n) [*shou'-shpeel*]
spectator, Zuschauer, - (m) [*tsoo'-shou-ər*]
speech, Rede, -n (f) [*reh'-də*]
speed *n.*, Geschwindigkeit, -en (f) [*gə-shvin'-diç-kait*]
  Full speed ahead! Volle Fahrt voraus! [*fo'-lə fahrt fo-rous'*]
speed limit, Höchstgeschwindigkeit, -en (f) [*höhçst'-gə-shvin-diç-kait*]
speed *v.*, rasen (*Aux:* SEIN) [*rah'-zən*]
speedy, schnell [*shnel*]
spell [words] *v.*, buchstabieren [*bookh-shta-bee'-rən*]
  How is it spelled? Wie wird es geschrieben? [*vee virt es gə-shree'-bən*]
spend [money] *v.*, aus-geben (irreg) [*ous'-geh-bən*]
spend [time] *v.*, verbringen (irreg) [*fer-bring'-ən*]
spice *n.*, Würze, -n (f) [*vür'-tsə*]
spider, Spinne, -n (f) [*shpi'-nə*]
spinach, Spinat (m) [*shpi-naht'*]
spine, Rückgrat, -e (n) [*rük'-graht*]
spiral *n.*, Spirale, -n (f) [*shpi-rah'-lə*]
spirit, Geist, -er (m) [*gaist, gai'-stər*]
spiritual *adj.*, geistig [*gai'-stiç*]
spit *v.*, spucken [*shpu'-kən*]
spite: (in) spite of, trotz (plus gen) [*trots*]
splendid, ausgezeichnet [*ous'-gə-tsaiç-nət*]

split *v.*, spalten [*shpal'-tən*]

spoil [go bad] *v.*, verderben (irreg; *Aux:* SEIN) [*fer-der'-bən*]

spoil [ruin] *v.*, verderben (irreg; *Aux:* HABEN) [*fer-der'-bən*]

spoil [a child] *v.*, verwöhnen [*fer-vöh'-nən*]

sponge, Schwamm, ≈e (m) [*shvam, shve'-mə*]

spoon, Löffel, - (m) [*lö'-fəl*]
   teaspoon, Teelöffel, - (m) [*teh'-lö-fəl*]

sport, Sport (m, sing), Sportarten (pl) [*shport, shport'-ahr-tən*]

spot [stain] *n.*, Fleck, -en (f) [*flek*]

spotless, fleckenlos [*fle'-kən-lohs*]

spouse [female], Gattin, -nen (f) [*ga'-tin*]

spouse [male], Gatte, -n (m) [*ga'-tə*]

sprain *v.*, verrenken [*fer-ren'-kən*]

spray *v.*, zerstäuben [*tser-shtoi'-bən*]

spread *v.*, streuen [*shtroi'-ən*]

spring [season], Frühling, -e (m) [*früh'-ling*]

spring [of water], Quelle, -n (f) [*kve'-lə*]

spring [of a machine], Feder, -n (f) [*feh'-dər*]

spring *v.*, springen (irreg; *Aux:* SEIN) [*shpring'-ən*]

sprinkle *v.*, besprengen [*bə-shpreng'-ən*]

spy *n.*, Spion, -e (m) [*shpi-ohn'*]

spy *v.*, spähen [*shpeh'-ən*]

square *adj.*, quadratisch [*kva-drah'-tish*]

square [of a city], Platz, ≈e (m) [*plats, ple'-tsə*]

squeeze [fruit] *v.*, pressen [*pre'-sən*]

squirrel, Eichhörnchen, - (n) [*aiç'-hörn-çən*]

stab *v.*, erstechen (irreg) [*er-shte'-çən*]

stable *n.*, Stall, ≈e (m) [*shtal, shte'-lə*]

stadium, Stadion (n, sing), Stadien (pl) [*shtah'-di-on, shtah'-di-ən*]

stage *n.*, Bühne, -n (f) [*büh'-nə*]

stain *n.*, Fleck, -en (m) [*flek*]

stairs, staircase, Treppe, -n (f) [*tre'-pə*]

stale, abgestanden [*ab'-gə-shtan-dən*]

stamp [postage] *n.*, Briefmarke, -n (f) [*breef'-mar-kə*]

stamp [letters] *v.*, stempeln [*shtem'-pəln*]

stand *v.*, stehen (irreg) [*shteh'-ən*]

stand up, auf-stehen (irreg; *Aux:* SEIN) [*ouf'-shteh-ən*]
standard, Norm, -en (f) [*norm*]
standpoint, Standpunkt, -e (m) [*shtant'-punkt*]
star, Stern, -e (m) [*shtern*]
starch, Stärke (f) [*shter'-kə*]
start *v.,* an-fangen (irreg) [*an'-fan-gən*]
start *n.,* Start, -e (m) [*shtahrt*]
starter [of car], Anlasser, - (m) [*an'-la-sər*]
starve *v.,* hungern [*hung'-ərn*]
state *v.,* an-geben (irreg) [*an'-geh-bən*]
state *n.,* Staat, -en [*shtaht*]
statement [of account], Rechnungsauszug, =e (m) [*reç'-nungs-ous-tsook, reç'-nungs-ous-tsüh-gə*]
stateroom, Kabine, -n (f) [*ka-bee'-nə*]
statesman, Staatsmann, =er (m) [*shtahts'-man, shtahts'-men-ər*]
station, Haltestelle, -n (f) [*hal'-tə-shte-lə*]
  railway station, Bahnhof, =e (m) [*bahn'-hohf, bahn'-höh-fə*]
stationery, Schreibwaren (f, pl) [*shraip'-vah-rən*]
statue, Statue, -n (f) [*shtah'-tu-ə*]
stay *v.,* bleiben (irreg; *Aux:* SEIN) [*blai'-bən*]
  At what hotel are you staying? In welchem Hotel wohnen Sie? [*in vel'-çəm ho-tel' voh'-nən zee*]
  Stay here! Bleiben Sie hier! [*blai'-bən zee heer*]
steadfast, fest [*fest*]
steady, beständig [*bə-shten'-diç*]
steak, Steak, -s (n) [*stehk, stehks*]
steal *v.,* stehlen (irreg) [*shteh'-lən*]
steam, Dampf, =e (m) [*dampf, dem'-pfə*]
steamship line, Schiffahrtslinie, -n (f) [*shif'-fahrts-lee-ni-ə*]
steel, Stahl, =e (m) [*shtahl, shteh'-lə*]
steep, steil [*shtail*]
steering wheel, Steuerrad, =er (n) [*shtoi'-ər-raht, shtoi'-ər-reh-der*]
stenographer, Stenograph, -en (m) [*shte-no-grahf'*]
step [walk] *v.,* treten (irreg; *Aux:* SEIN) [*treh'-tən*]
  step on, treten (irreg; *Aux:* HABEN) [*treh'-tən*]

step on the gas, Gas geben (irreg) [*gahs geh'-bən*]
step *n.,* Schritt, -e (m) [*shrit*]
  step by step, Schritt für Schritt [*shrit führ shrit*]
stepfather, Stiefvater, ⸗ (m) [*shteef'-fah-tər, shteef'-feh-tər*]
stepmother, Stiefmutter, ⸗ (f) [*shteef'-mu-tər, shteef'-mü-tər*]
sterilized, sterilisiert [*shte-ri-li-zeert'*]
stern [boat], Heck, -e (n) [*hek*]
stern *adj.,* streng [*shtreng*]
steward, Steward, -s (m) [*styoo'-ərt, styoo'-ərts*]
stewardness, Stewardess, -en (f) [*styoo'-ər-des*]
stick *n.,* Stock, ⸗e (m) [*shtok, shtö'-kə*]
stick *v.,* kleben [*kleh'-bən*]
stiff, steif [*shtaif*]
still *adj.,* ruhig [*roo'-iç*]
still *adv.,* noch immer [*nokh i'-mər*]
still [however], doch; dennoch [*dokh; den'-nokh*]
stimulant, Reizmittel, - (n) [*raits'-mit-təl*]
sting *v.,* stechen (irreg) [*shte'-çən*]
stir *v.,* rühren [*rüh'-rən*]
stitch *v.,* nähen [*neh'-ən*]
stock [share], Aktie, -n (f) [*ak'-tsi-ə*]
stockbroker, Börsenmakler, - (m) [*bör'-zən-mahk-lər*]
stock exchange, Börse, -n (f) [*bör'-zə*]
stocking, Strumpf, ⸗e (m) [*shtrumpf, shtrüm'-pfə*]
stomach, Magen, ⸗ (m) [*mah'-gən, meh'-gən*]
stomach ache, Leibschmerzen (m, pl) [*laip'-shmer-tsən*]
stone, Stein, -e (m) [*shtain*]
stop *n.,* Haltestelle, -n (f) [*hal'-tə-shte-lə*]
stop *v.,* halten (irreg) [*hal'-tən*]
  Stop! Halt! [*halt*]
  Stop here! Halten Sie hier! [*hal'-tən zee heer*]
  Stop that! Lassen Sie das! [*la'-sən zee das*]
stoplight, Stopplicht, -er (n) [*shtop'-liçt, shtop'-liç-tər*]
stopwatch, Stoppuhr, -en (f) [*shtop'-oor*]
storage, Aufbewahrung (f) [*ouf'-bə-vah-rung*]
store, Laden, ⸗ (m) [*lah'-dən, leh'-dən*]
  department store, Warenhaus, ⸗er (n) [*vah'-rən-hous,
  vah'-rən-hoi-zər*]

storm, Sturm, ≈e (m) [*shturm, shtür'-mə*]

story [tale], Geschichte, -n (f) [*gə-shiç'-tə*]

story [floor], Etage, -n (f) [*e-tah'-zhə*]

stove, Ofen, ≈ (m) [*oh'-fən, öh'-fən*]

straight, gerade [*gə-rah'-də*]

straight ahead, geradeaus [*gə-rah-də-ous'*]

strain *n.*, Anstrengung, -en (f) [*an'-shtreng-ung*]

strange, fremd; sonderbar [*fremt*; *zon'-dər-bahr*]

stranger, Fremde, -n (m, f) [*frem'-də*]

strap *n.*, Riemen, - (m) [*ree'-mən*]

straw, Stroh (n) [*shtroh*]

strawberry, Erdbeere, -n (f) [*ehrt'-beh-rə*]

stream, Wasserlauf, ≈e (m) [*va'-sər-louf, va'-sər-loi-fə*]

street, Strasse, -n (f) [*shtra'-sə*]

strength, Stärke (f) [*shter'-kə*]

strengthen *v.*, stärken [*shter'-kən*]

stress [emphasis] *n.*, Betonung, -en (f) [*be-toh'-nung*]

strict, streng [*shtreng*]

strike [hit] *v.*, schlagen (irreg) [*shlah'-gən*]

strike [walk out] *v.*, streiken [*shtrai'-kən*]

strike [walk-out] *n.*, Streik, -s (m) [*shtraik, shtraiks*]

string, Schnur, ≈e (f) [*shnoor, shnüh'-rə*]

stroll *n.*, Bummel, - (m) [*bu'-məl*]

strong, stark [*shtark*]

structure, Struktur, -en (f) [*shtruk-toor'*]

struggle *n.*, Kampf, ≈e (m) [*kampf, kem'-pfə*]

struggle *v.*, kämpfen [*kem'-pfən*]

stubborn, hartnäckig [*hart'-ne-kiç*]

student [college, female], Studentin, -nen (f) [*shtu-dən'-tin*]

student [college, male], Student, -en (m) [*shtu-dənt'*]

student [grade & high school, female], Schülerin, -nen (f) [*shüh'-lər-in*]

student [grade & high school, male], Schüler, - (m) [*shüh'-lər*]

study [room], Studierstube, -n (f) [*shtu-deer'-shtoo-bə*]

study *v.*, studieren [*shtu-dee'-rən*]

stuff, Zeug (n) [*ɪsoik*]

stupid, dumm [*dum*]

style [art], Stil, -e (m) [*shteel*]
style [fashion], Mode, -n (f); Schnitt, -e (m) [*moh'-də; shnit*]
subject [grammar], Subjekt, -e (n) [*zup-yekt'*]
subject [theme], Gegenstand, ⸗e (m) [*geh'-gən-shtant, geh'-gən-shten-də*]
submarine *n.*, Unterseeboot, -e (n) [*un'-tər-zeh-boht*]
submit [plans] *v.*, vor-legen [*fohr'-leh-gən*]
subsequently, nachher [*nakh-hehr'*]
substantial, wesentlich [*veh'-zənt-liç*]
substitute, Ersatz (m) [*er-zats'*]
substitution, Vertretung, -en (f) [*fer-treh'-tung*]
subtle, subtil [*zup-teel'*]
suburb, Vorort, -e (m) [*fohr'-ort*]
subway, Untergrundbahn, -en (f) [*un'-tər-grunt-bahn*]
succeed (in) *v.*, gelingen (plus dat) (irreg; *Aux:* SEIN) [*gə-ling'-ən*]
  He succeeded in fleeing, Es ist ihm gelungen zu fliehen; die flucht gelang ihm [*es ist eem gə-lung'-ən tsu flee'-ən; dee Flukht gə-lang' eem*]
success, Erfolg, -e (m) [*er-folk', er-fol'-gə*]
successively, nacheinander [*nakh-ai-nan'-dər*]
such, solch; solcher, solche, solches [*zolç; zol'-çər, zol'-çə, zol'-çəs*]
  no such thing, nichts Derartiges [*niçts dehr'-ahr-ti-gəs*]
  Such is life! So ist das Leben! [*zoh ist das leh'-bən*]
suddenly, plötzlich [*plöts'-liç*]
suffer *v.*, leiden (irreg), [*lai'-dən*]
sufficient, genügend [*gə-nüh'-gənt*]
sugar, Zucker (m) [*tsu'-kər*]
sugar bowl, Zuckerdose, -n (f) [*tsu'-kər-doh-zə*]
suggest *v.*, vor-schlagen (irreg) [*fohr'-shlah-gən*]
suggestion, Vorschlag, ⸗e (m) [*fohr'-shlahk, fohr'-shleh-gə*]
suicide, Selbstmord, -e (m) [*zelpst'-mort, zelpst'-mor-də*]
suit [clothes], Anzug, ⸗e (m) [*an'-tsook, an'-tsüh-gə*]
suit [in court], Prozess, -e (m) [*pro-tses'*]
suit *v.*, passen (plus dat) [*pa'-sən*]
suitable, passend [*pa'-sənt*]
suitcase, Koffer, - (m) [*ko'-fər*]

sullen, mürrisch [*mü'-rish*]
sum, Summe, -n (f) [*zu'-mə*]
summary, Zusammenfassung, -en (f) [*tsu-za'-mən-fa-sung*]
summer, Sommer, - (m) [*zo'-mər*]
summons, Vorladung, -en (f) [*fohr'-lah-dung*]
sun, Sonne, -n (f) [*zo'-nə*]
sunburn, Sonnenbrand (m) [*zo'-nən-brant*]
sunburned, sonnenverbrannt [*zo'-nən-fer-brant*]
Sunday, Sonntag, -e (m) [*zon'-tahk, zon'-tah-gə*]
sunglasses, Sonnenbrille, -n (f) [*zo'-nən-bri-lə*]
sunrise, Sonnenaufgang, ⸗e (m) [*zo'-nən-ouf-gang, zo'-nən-ouf-geng-ə*]
sunset, Sonnenuntergang, ⸗e (m) [*zo'-nən-un-tər-gang, zo'-nən-un-tər-geng-ə*]
superb, herrlich [*her'-liç*]
superficial, oberflächlich [*oh'-bər-fleç-liç*]
superfluous, überflüssig [*üh'-bər-flü-siç*]
superior, besser [*be'-sər*]
superiority, Überlegenheit (f) [*üh-bər-leh'-gən-hait*]
superstitous, abergläubisch [*ah'-bər-gloi-bish*]
supper, Abendessen (n) [*ah'-bənt-e-sən*]
   have supper v., zu Abend essen [*tsu ah'-bənt e'-sən*]
supply n., Vorrat, ⸗e (m) [*fohr'-raht, fohr'-reh-tə*]
supply v., versorgen [*fer-zor'-gən*]
support v., unterstützen [*un-tər-shtü'-tsən*]
suppose v., an-nehmen (irreg) [*an'-neh-mən*]
supreme, höchst; Ober- [*höçst; oh'-bər-*]
sure, sicher [*zi'-çər*]
   Are you sure? Sind Sie sicher? [*zint zee zi'-çər*]
surely, sicherlich [*zi'-çər-liç*]
surf, Brandung (f) [*bran'-dung*]
surface n., Oberfläche, -n (f) [*oh'-bər-fle-çə*]
surgeon, Chirurg, -en (m) [*çi-rurk', çi-rur'-gən*]
surgery, Chirurgie (f) [*çi-rur-gee'*]
surprise v., überraschen [*üh-bər-rash'-ən*]
   be surprised, überrascht sein [*üh-bər-rasht' zain*]
surprise n., Überraschung, -en (f) [*üh-bər-ra'-shung*]
surprising, überraschend [*üh-bər-ra'-shənt*]

surrender v., sich ergeben (irreg) [ziç er-geh'-bən]
surround v., umgeben (irreg) [um-geh'-bən]
surroundings, Umgebung (f) [um-geh'-bung]
survive v., überleben [üh-bər-leh'-bən]
survivor, Überlebende, -n (m, f) [üh-bər-leh'-bən-də]
suspect v., im Verdacht haben [im fer-dakht' hah'-bən]
suspicion, Verdacht (m, sing), Verdächtigungen (pl) [fer-
    dakht', fer- deç'- ti-gung-ən]
swallow [bird] n., Schwalbe, -n (f) [shval'-bə]
swallow v., schlucken [shlu'-kən]
swear v., schwören [shvöh'-rən]
Sweden, Schweden (n) [shveh'-dən]
Swedish, schwedisch [shveh'-dish]
sweep v., fegen [feh'-gən]
sweet, süss [zühs]
sweetheart, Schatz, ≈e (m) [shats, shet'-sə]
swell v., schwellen (irreg; Aux: SEIN) [shve'-lən]
swim v., schwimmen (irreg; Aux: SEIN) [shvi'-mən]
swimmer [female], Schwimmerin, -nen (f) [shvim'-mə-rin]
swimmer [male], Schwimmer, - (m) [shvi'-mər]
swimming pool, Schwimmbad, ≈er (n) [shvim'-baht, shvim'-
    beh-dər]
swimming suit, Badeanzug, ≈e (m) [bah'-də-an-tsook,
    bah'-də-an-tsüh-gə]
Swiss adj., schweizerisch [shvai'-tsə-rish]
switch [electric], Schalter, - (m) [shal'-tər]
Switzerland, die Schweiz (f) [dee shvaits]
  in Switzerland, in der Schweiz [in der shvaits]
sword, Schwert, ≈er (n) [shvehrt, shvehr'-tər]
sympathy, Mitgefühl (n) [mit'-gə-fühl]
  my deepest sympathy, mein herzlichstes Beileid
    [main herts'-liç-stəs bai'-lait]
symphony, Symphonie, -n (f) [züm-fo-nee']
symptom, Symptom, -e (n) [zümp-tohm']
synthetic, synthetisch [zün-teh-'tish]
system, System, -e (n) [züs-tehm']
systematic, systematisch [züs-te-mah'-tish]

T

table, Tisch, -e (m) [*tish*]
   set the table *v.*, den Tisch decken [*dehn tish de'-kən*]
tablespoon, Esslöffel, - (m) [*es'-lö-fəl*]
tablet, Tablette, -n (f) [*ta-ble'-tə*]
tact, Takt (m) [*takt*]
tactless, taktlos [*takt'-lohs*]
tail, Schwanz, ̈e (m) [*shvants, shven'-tsə*]
tailor, Schneider, - (m) [*shnai'-dər*]
take *v.*, nehmen (irreg) [*neh'-mən*]
   take advantage of, aus-nützen (plus acc) [*ous'-nü-tsən*]
   take a walk, einen Spaziergang machen [*ai'-nən shpa-tseer'-gang ma'-khən*]
   take away, weg-nehmen (irreg) [*vek'-neh-mən*]
   take care of, sorgen für (plus acc) [*zor'-gən führ*]
   take leave, sich verabschieden [*ziç fer-ap'-shee-dən*]
   take off [hat], ab-nehmen (irreg) [*ap'-neh-mən*]
   take the opportunity, die Gelegenheit wahr-nehmen (irreg) [*dee gə-leh'-gən-hait vahr'-neh-mən*]
tale, Erzählung, -en (f) [*er-tseh'-lung*]
talent, Gabe, -n (f) [*gah'-bə*]
talented, begabt [*bə-gahpt'*]
talk *n.*, Gespräch, -e (n) [*gə-shprehç'*]
talk *v.*, sprechen (irreg) [*shpre'-çən*]
tall, gross; hoch [*grohs; hohkh*]
tame *adj.*, zahm [*tsahm*]
tapestry, Wandteppich, -e (m) [*vant'-te-piç*]
tardy, langsam [*lang'-zam*]
tariff, Tarif, -e (m) [*ta-reef'*]
task, Aufgabe, -n (f) [*ouf'-gah-bə*]
taste *n.*, Geschmack (m) [*gə-shmak'*]
taste *v.*, schmecken [*shme'-kən*]
   This tastes good, Das schmeckt gut [*das shmekt goot*]

tax *n.*, Steuer, -n (f) [*shtoi'-ər*]
tax-free, steuerfrei [*shtoi'-ər-frai*]
taxi, Taxi, -s (n) [*tak'-see, tak'-sees*]
tea, Tee, -s (m) [*teh, tehs*]
teach *v.*, lehren [*leh'-rən*]
teacher [female], Lehrerin, -nen (f) [*leh'-rə-rin*]
teacher [male], Lehrer, - (m) [*leh'-rər*]
teacup, Teetasse, -n (f) [*teh'-ta-sə*]
team, Mannschaft, -en (f) [*man'-shaft*]
tear [teardrop] *n.*, Träne, -n (f) [*treh'-nə*]
tear [rend] *v.*, zerreissen (irreg) [*tser-rai'-sən*]
teaspoon, Teelöffel, - (m) [*teh'-lö-fəl*]
technical, technisch [*teç'-nish*]
teeth, Zähne (m, pl) [*tseh'-nə*]
telegram, Telegramm, -e (n) [*te-le-gram'*]
telephone *v.*, telephonieren [*te-le-fo-nee'-rən*]
telephone *n.*, Telephon, -e (n) [*te-le-fohn'*]
  answer the telephone *v.*, ans Telephon gehen (irreg; *Aux:*
  SEIN) [*ans te-le-fohn' geh'-ən*]
  on the telephone, am Telephon [*am te-le-fohn'*]
telephone booth, Telephonzelle, -n (f) [*te-le-fohn'-tse-lə*]
telephone call, Anruf, -e (m) [*an'-roof*]
telephone operator [female], Telephonistin, -nen (f)
  [*te-le-fo-nis'-tin*]
telephone operator [male], Telephonist, -en (m) [*te-le-fo-nist'*]
television, Fernsehen (n) [*fern'-zeh-ən*]
television set, Fernsehapparat, -e (m) [*fern'-zeh-ap-pa-raht*]
tell *v.*, sagen [*zah'-gən*]
  Tell me! Sagen Sie mir! [*zah'-gən zee meer*]
  Tell us (her, him)! Sagen Sie uns (ihr, ihm)! [*zah'-gən
  zee uns (eer, eem)*]
temperature, Temperatur, -en (f) [*tem-pe-ra-toor'*]
temple, Tempel, - (m) [*tem'-pəl*]
ten, zehn [*tsehn*]
tenant, Mieter, - (m) [*mee'-tər*]
tender, zart [*tsahrt*]
tenth, zehnt [*tsehnt*]
terrible, schrecklich [*shrek'-liç*]

territory, Gebiet, -e (n) [*gə-beet'*]

terror, Schrecken, - (m) [*shre'-kən*]

test *n.*, Probe, -n (f) [*proh'-bə*]

test *v.*, prüfen [*prüh'-fən*]

text, Text, -e (m) [*tekst*]

than, als [*als*]

thank *v.*, danken (plus dat) [*dan'-kən*]

    Thank you! Danke schön! [*dan'-kə shöhn*]

    Thank you very much! Besten Dank! [*be'-stən dank*]

thankful, dankbar [*dank'-bahr*]

that *conj.*, dass [*das*]

that *dem. adj.*, dieser, diese, dieses [*dee'-zər, dee'-zə, dee'-zəs*]

that *rel. pron.*, der, die, das; welcher, welche, welches [*dehr, dee, das; vel'- çər, vel'-çə, vel'-çəs*]

the, der, die, das [*dehr, dee, das*]

theater, Theater, - (n) [*te-ah'-tər*]

theft, Diebstahl, ⸗e (m) [*deep'-shtahl, deep'-shteh-lə*]

their, ihr, ihre (pl) [*eer, ee'-rə*]

theirs, der (die, das) ihre [*dehr (dee, das) ee'-rə*]

them, sie (acc); ihnen (dat) [*zee; ee'-nən*]

themselves, sie selbst, sich selbst [*zee zelpst; ziç zelpst*]

    They dress themselves, Sie ziehen sich selbst an [*zee tsee'-ən ziç zelpst an*]

then, dann [*dan*]

    now and then, dann und wann [*dan unt van*]

there, da; dort [*dah; dort*]

    there is; there are, es gibt [*es gipt*]

thermometer, Thermometer, - (n) [*ter-mo-meh'-tər*]

these, diese [*dee'-zə*]

they, sie [*zee*]

they [impersonal: one, people], man [*man*]

    They say, Man sagt; Sie sagen [*man zahkt; zee zah'-gən*]

thick, dick [*dik*]

thief, Dieb, -e (m) [*deep, dee'-bə*]

thin, dünn [*dün*]

thing, Ding, -e (n) [*ding*]

think *v.*, denken (irreg) [*den'-kən*]

think of, denken an (plus acc) [*den'-kən an*]
third, dritt [*drit'*]
thirst *n.,* Durst (m) [*durst*]
   be thirsty *v.,* Durst haben (irreg) [*durst hah'-bən*]
thirteen, dreizehn [*drai'-tsehn*]
thirty, dreissig [*drai'-siç*]
this, dieser, diese, dieses [*dee'-zər, dee'-zə, dee'-zəs*]
thorn, Dorn, -en (m) [*dorn*]
thoroughly, gründlich [*grünt'-liç*]
those *adj. & pron.,* jene; die, solche [*yeh'-nə; dee, zol'-çə*]
though *conj.,* obwohl [*op-vohl'*]
thought, Gedanke, -n (f) [*gə-dan'-kə*]
thoughtless, gedankenlos [*gə-dan'-kən-lohs*]
thousand, tausend [*tou'-zənt*]
thread, Faden, = (m) [*fah'-dən, feh'-dən*]
threat, Drohung, -en (f) [*droh'-ung*]
threaten *v.,* drohen [*droh'-ən*]
three, drei [*drai*]
thrifty, sparsam [*shpar'-zam*]
thrilling, aufregend [*ouf'-reh-gənt*]
throat, Kehle, -n (f) [*keh'-lə*]
   have a sore throat *v.,* Halsschmerzen haben [*hals'-shmer-tsən hah'-bən*]
throne, Thron, -e (m) [*trohn*]
through *prep.,* durch (plus acc) [*durç*]
through [finished], fertig [*fer'-tiç*]
throughout, durchaus [*durç-ous'*]
throw *v.,* werfen (irreg) [*ver'-fən*]
thumb, Daumen, - (m) [*dou'-mən*]
thunder, Donner (m) [*don'-nər*]
thunderstorm, Gewitter, - (n) [*gə-vi'-tər*]
Thursday, Donnerstag, -e (m) [*do'-nərs-tahk, do'-nərs-tah-gə*]
thus, so [*zoh*]
ticket [for trains, shows], Fahrkarte, Karte, -n (f) [*fahr'-kar-tə, kar'-tə*]
ticket window, Kartenschalter, - (m) [*kar'-tən-shal-tər*]
   round-trip ticket, Rückfahrkarte, -n (f) [*rük'-fahr-kar-tə*]

tie [necktie], Krawatte, -n (f) [*kra-va'-tə*]
tie [bond], Band, -e (n) [*bant, ban'-də*]
tie v., binden (irreg) [*bin'-dən*]
tight, dicht; fest [*diçt; fest*]
tighten v., enger machen [*eng'-ər ma'-khən*]
till [until], bis [*bis*]
time [instance], Mal, -e (n) [*mahl*]
time [duration], Zeit, -en (f) [*tsait*]
   at times, manchmal [*manç'-mal*]
   At what time? Um wieviel Uhr? [*um vee'-feel oor*]
   Have a good time! Viel Vergnügen! [*feel fer-gnüh'-gən*]
   What time is it? Wie spät ist es? [*vee shpeht ist es*]
timetable, Fahrplan, ⸗e (m) [*fahr'-plan, fahr'-pleh-nə*]
timid, scheu [*shoi*]
tin [metal], Zinn (n) [*tsin*]
tinfoil, Stanniol (n) [*shta-ni-ohl'*]
tiny, winzig [*vin'-tsiç*]
tip [end], Spitze, -n (f) [*shpi'-tsə*]
tip [money], Trinkgeld (n) [*trink'-gelt*]
tire [for car], Reifen, - (m) [*rai'-fən*]
tired, müde [*müh'-də*]
tiresome, ermüdend [*er-müh'-dənt*]
tissue paper, Seidenpapier (n) [*zai'-dən-pa-peer*]
title, Titel, - (m) [*tee'-təl*]
to, zu; gegen, nach, an, in, auf; bis zu; um zu [*tsu; geh'-gən, nakh, an, in, ouf; bis tsu; um tsu*]
toast [breakfast], Toast, -e (m) [*tohst*]
toast [to one's health], Trinkspruch, ⸗e (m) [*trink'-shprukh, trink'-shprü-çə*]
toaster, Röster, - (m) [*rö'-stər*]
tobacco, Tabak, -e (m) [*tah'-bak*]
today, heute [*hoi'-tə*]
   from today on, von heute an [*fon hoi'-tə an*]
toe, Zehe, -n (f) [*tseh'-ə*]
together, zusammen [*tsu-za'-mən*]
toilet, Toilette, -n (f) [*to-a-le'-tə*]
toilet paper, Toilettenpapier (n) [*to-a-le'-tən-pa-peer*]
tolerate v., dulden [*dul'-dən*]

toll *n.*, Zoll, ⸗e (m) [*tsol, tsö'-lə*]
tomato, Tomate, -n (f) [*to-mah'-tə*]
tomato juice, Tomatensaft (m) [*to-mah'-tən-zaft*]
tomb, Grab, ⸗er (n) [*grahp, greh'-bər*]
tombstone, Grabstein, -e (m) [*grahp'-shtain*]
tomorrow, morgen [*mor'-gən*]
  tomorrow morning, morgen früh [*mor'-gən früh*]
ton, Tonne, -n (f) [*to'-nə*]
tone, Ton, -e (m) [*tohn, töh'-nə*]
tongue, Zunge, -n (f) [*tsung'-ə*]
tonight, heute abend [*hoi'-tə ah'-bənt*]
tonsils, Mandeln (f, pl) [*man'-dəln*]
too [too much], zu [*tsoo*]
too [also], auch [*oukh*]
tool, Werkzeug, -e (n) [*verk'-tsoik, verk'-tsoi-gə*]
tooth, Zahn, ⸗e (m) [*tsahn, tseh'-nə*]
toothache, Zahnschmerzen (m, pl) [*tsahn'-shmer-tsən*]
toothbrush, Zahnbürste, -n (f) [*tsahn'-bür-stə*]
toothpaste, Zahnpasta (f) [*tsahn'-pas-tah*]
top [cover] *n.*, Deckel, - (m) [*de'-kəl*]
top [high point], Gipfel, - (m) [*gi'-pfəl*]
  on top of, oben auf (plus dat; acc for motion) [*oh'-bən ouf*]
topic, Thema (n, sing), Themen (pl) [*teh'-mah, teh'-mən*]
torture *v.*, quälen [*kveh'-lən*]
toss [fling] *v.*, werfen (irreg) [*ver'-fən*]
total, gesamt [*gə-zamt'*]
touch *v.*, berühren [*bə-rüh'-rən*]
touching, rührend [*rüh'-rənt*]
touchy, empfindlich [*emp-fint'-liç*]
tough, hart; zäh [*hart; tseh*]
tour *n.*, Rundreise, -n (f) [*runt'-rai-zə*]
tourist [female], Touristin, -nen (f) [*tu-rist'-in*]
tourist [male], Tourist, -en (m) [*tu-rist'*]
tournament, Turnier, -e (m) [*tur-neer'*]
toward, zu; zum (m), zur (f); gegen, nach, auf [*tsu; tsum, tsur; geh'-gən, nakh, ouf*]
towel, Handtuch, ⸗er (n) [*hant'-tukh, hant'-tüh-çər*]

tower, Turm, ⸗e (m) [*turm, tür'-mə*]

town, Stadt, ⸗e (f) [*shtat, shte'-tə*]

town hall, Rathaus, ⸗er (n) [*raht'-hous, raht'-hoi-zər*]

toy, Spielzeug (n, sing), Spielsachen (pl) [*shpeel'-tsoik, shpeel'-za-khən*]

trace *n.,* Spur, -en (f) [*shpoor*]

trace *v.,* auf-spüren [*ouf'-shpüh-rən*]

tracks [railroad], Geleise (n, pl) [*gə-lai'-zə*]

trade *n.,* Handel (m) [*han'-dəl*]

trade *v.,* handeln [*han'-dəln*]

trademark, Warenzeichen, - (n) [*vah'-rən-tsai-çən*]

tradesman, Ladeninhaber, - (m) [*lah'-dən-in-hah-bər*]

tradition, Tradition, -en (f) [*tra-di-tsi-ohn'*]

traditional, traditionell [*tra-di-tsi-o-nel'*]

traffic, Verkehr (m) [*fer-kehr'*]

tragedy, Tragödie, -n (f) [*tra-göh'-di-ə*]

tragic, tragisch [*trah'-gish*]

trail *n.,* Pfad, -e (m) [*pfaht, pfah'-də*]

train *n.,* Zug, ⸗e (m) [*tsook, tsüh'-gə*]

train [rear] *v.,* erziehen (irreg) [*er-tsee'-ən*]

train [for occupation] *v.,* aus-bilden [*ous'-bil-dən*]

trait, Charakterzug, ⸗e (f) [*ka-rak'-tər-tsook, ka-rak'-tər-tsüh-gə*]

traitor, Verräter, - (m) [*fer-reh'-tər*]

tranquil, ruhig [*roo'-iç*]

transfer *v.,* versetzen [*fer-ze'-tsən*]

transform (into) *v.,* um-wandeln (in, plus acc) [*um'-van-dəln*]

transient *adj.,* flüchtig [*flüç'-tiç*]

translate *v.,* übersetzen [*üh-bər-zet'-sən*]

translation, Übersetzung, -en (f) [*üh-bər-zet'-sung*]

translator, Übersetzer, - (m) [*üh-bər-zet'-sər*]

transmission, Übertragung, -en (f) [*üh-bər-trah'-gung*]

transportation, Beförderung (f) [*be-för'-də-rung*]

trap *n.,* Falle, -n (f) [*fa'-lə*]

trap *v.,* fangen (irreg) [*fang'-ən*]

   set a trap *v.,* eine Falle stellen [*ai'-nə fa'-lə shte'-lən*]

travel *n.,* Reise, -n (f) [*rai'-zə*]

travel *v.*, reisen (*Aux:* SEIN) [*rai'-zən*]

travel agency, Reisebüro, -s (n) [*rai'-zə-bü-roh, rai'-zə-bü-rohs*]

traveler, Reisende, -n (m, f) [*rai'-zen-də*]

traveler's check, Reisescheck, -s (m) [*rai'-zə-shek, rai'-zə-sheks*]

tray, Tablett, -e (n) [*ta-blet'*]

treachery, Verrat (m) [*fer-raht'*]

treason, Verrat (m) [*fer-raht'*]

treasure, Schatz, ⸗e (m) [*shats, shet'-sə*]

treasurer, Schatzmeister, - (m) [*shats'-mai-stər*]

treasury, Schatzamt, ⸗er (n) [*shats'-amt, shats'-em-tər*]

treat [of food] *n.*, Schmaus, ⸗e (m) [*shmous, shmoi'-zə*]

treat *v.*, behandeln [*bə-han'-dəln*]

treatment, Behandlung, -en (f) [*bə-hand'-lung*]

treaty, Vertrag, ⸗e (m) [*fer-trahk', fer-treh'-gə*]

tree, Baum, ⸗e (m) [*boum, boi'-mə*]

tremble *v.*, zittern [*tsi'-tərn*]

trial [legal], Prozess, -e (m) [*pro-tses'*]

trial [test], Probe, -n (f) [*proh'-bə*]

tribe, Stamm, ⸗e (m) [*shtam, shte'-mə*]

tribute, Tribut, -e (m) [*tri-boot'*]

trick, Trick, -s (f) [*trik, triks*]

trip *n.*, Reise, -n (f) [*rai'-zə*]

trip (over) *v.*, stolpern (über, plus acc) (*Aux:* SEIN) [*shtol'-pərn (üh'-bər)*]

triumphant, siegreich [*zeek'-raiç*]

trivial, alltäglich [*al-tehk'-liç*]

trolley car, Strassenbahn, -en (f) [*shtra'-sən-bahn*]

troop *n.*, Schar, -en (f) [*shahr*]

tropical, tropisch [*troh'-pish*]

trouble *n.*, Mühe, -n (f); Not, ⸗e (f) [*müh'-ə; noht, nöh'-tə*]

   Don't trouble yourself! Machen Sie sich keine Mühe! [*ma'-khən zee ziç kai'-nə müh'-ə*]

   It's no trouble! Es macht nichts aus! [*es makht niçts ous*]

trousers, Hose, -n (f) [*hoh'-zə*]

trout, Forelle, -n (f) [*fo-re'-lə*]

truck, Lastwagen, - (m) [*last'-vah-gən*]

true, wahr [*vahr*]
  Is it true? Ist es wahr? [*ist es vahr*]
trunk, Koffer, - (m) [*ko'-fər*]
trust *n.,* Vertrauen (n) [*fer-trou'-ən*]
truth, Wahrheit, -en (f) [*vahr'-hait*]
try *v.,* versuchen [*fer-zoo'-khən*]
  try on, an-probieren [*an'-pro-bee-rən*]
tub, Badewanne, -n (f) [*bah'-də-va-nə*]
tuberculosis, Tuberkulose (f) [*tu-ber-ku-loh'-zə*]
Tuesday, Dienstag, -e (m) [*deens'-tahk, deens'-tah-gə*]
tune, Melodie, -n (f) [*me-lo-dee'*]
tunnel, Tunnel, -s (m) [*tu'-nəl, tu'-nəls*]
turkey [hen], Pute, -n (f) [*poo'-tə*]
Turkey, die Türkei (f) [*dee tür-kai'*]
Turkish, türkisch [*tür'-kish*]
turn *n.,* Drehung, -en (f) [*dreh'-ung*]
turn *v.,* drehen [*dreh'-ən*]
  turn around, sich um-drehen [*ziç um'-dreh-ən*]
  turn away, weg-wenden (irreg) [*vek'-ven-dən*]
  turn back, zurück-kehren (*Aux:* SEIN) [*tsu-rük'-keh-rən*]
  turn down, ab-lehnen [*ap'-leh-nən*]
  turn off [light], aus-schalten [*ous'-shal-tən*]
  turn on [light], ein-schalten [*ain'-shal-tən*]
turnip, Kohlrübe, -n (f) [*kohl'-rüh-bə*]
twelfth, zwölft [*tsvölft*]
twelve, zwölf [*tsvölf*]
twenty, zwanzig [*tsvan'-tsiç*]
twice, zweimal; doppelt [*tsvai'-mahl; do'-pəlt*]
twilight, Zwielicht (n) [*tsvee'-liçt*]
twin, Zwilling, -e (m) [*tsvi'-ling*]
twist *v.,* zusammen-drehen [*tsu-za'-mən-dreh-ən*]
two, zwei [*tsvai*]
type [kind] *n.,* Typ, -en (m) [*tühp*]
typewriter, Schreibmaschine, -n (f) [*shraip'-ma-shee-nə*]
typical, typisch [*tüh'-pish*]
typist [shorthand], Stenotypistin, -nen (f) [*shte-no-tü-pi'-stin*]
tyranny, Tyrannei (f) [*tü-ra-nai'*]
tyrant, Tyrann, -en (m) [*tü-ran'*]

U

ugly, hässlich [*hes'-liç*]
umbrella, Regenschirm, -e (m) [*reh'-gən-shirm*]
unable, unfähig [*un'-feh-iç*]
  be unable *v.*, nicht können (irreg) [*niçt kö'-nən*]
unabridged, ungekürzt [*un'-gə-kürtst*]
unanimous, einstimmig [*ain'-shti-miç*]
uncertain, unsicher [*un'-zi-çər*]
uncle, Onkel, - (m) [*on'-kəl*]
uncomfortable, unbequem [*un'-bə-kvehm*]
unconscious, unbewusst [*un'-bə-vust*]
uncover *v.*, auf-decken [*ouf'-de-kən*]
under *prep.*, unter (plus dat; acc for motion) [*un'-tər*]
underground, unterirdisch [*un'-tər-ir-dish*]
understand *v.*, verstehen (irreg) [*fer-shteh'-ən*]
  Do you understand? Verstehen Sie? [*fer-shteh'-ən zee*]
  It is understood, Es versteht sich [*es fer-shteht' ziç*]
understatement, Untertreibung, -en (f) [*un-tər-trai'-bung*]
undertake *v.*, unternehmen (irreg) [*un-tər-neh'-mən*]
undertaking, Verpflichtung, -en (f) [*fer-pfliç'-tung*]
underwear, Leibwäsche (f) [*laip'-ve-shə*]
underworld, Unterwelt (f) [*un'-tər-velt*]
undo [a button] *v.*, auf-machen [*ouf'-ma-khən*]
undo [ruin] *v.*, vernichten [*fer-niç'-tən*]
undress *v.*, aus-ziehen (irreg) [*ous'-tsee-ən*]
uneasy, unruhig [*un-roo'-iç*]
unemployed, arbeitslos [*ar'-baits-lohs*]
unequal, ungleich [*un'-glaiç*]
unexpected, unerwartet [*un'-er-var-tət*]
unfair, unfair [*un'-fehr*]
unfaithful, untreu [*un'-troi*]
unfavorable, ungünstig [*un'-gün-stiç*]
unfit, untauglich [*un'-touk-liç*]

142

unforseen, unvorhergesehen [*un'-fohr-hehr-gə-zeh-ən*]
unforgettable, unvergesslich [*un-fer-ges'-liç*]
unforgiving, unversöhnlich [*un'-fer-zöhn-liç*]
unfortunate, unglücklich; bedauernswert [*un'-glük-liç; bə-dou'-ərns-vehrt*]
unfortunately, leider [*lai'-dər*]
ungrateful, undankbar [*un'-dank-bar*]
unhappy, unglücklich [*un'-glük-liç*]
unharmed, unversehrt [*un'-fer-zehrt*]
unhealthy, ungesund [*un'-gə-zunt*]
uniform *adj.,* einheitlich [*ain'-hait-liç*]
uniform *n.,* Uniform, -en (f) [*u-ni-form'*]
unimaginable, undenkbar [*un'-denk-bar*]
unimportant, unwichtig [*un'-viç-tiç*]
unintelligible, unverständlich [*un'-fer-shtent-liç*]
uninteresting, uninteressant [*un'-in-tə-re-sant*]
union, Verbindung, -en (f) [*fer-bin'-dung*]
unit, Einheit, -en (f) [*ain'-hait*]
unite *v.,* vereinigen [*fer-ai'-ni-gən*]
united, vereinigt [*fer-ai'-niçt*]
United Nations, die Vereinten Nationen [*dee fer-ain'-tən na-tsi-oh'-nən*]
United States, die Vereinigten Staaten (pl) [*dee fer-ai'-niç-tən shtah'-tən*]
unity, Einigkeit (f) [*ai'-niç-kait*]
universal, allgemein [*al-gə-main'*]
universe, Weltall (n) [*velt'-al*]
university, Universität, -en (f) [*u-ni-ver-zi-teht'*]
unjust, ungerecht [*un'-gə-reçt*]
unkind, unfreundlich (*un'-froint-liç*)
unknown, unbekannt [*un'-bə-kant*]
unlawful, rechtswidrig [*reçts'-vee-driç*]
unless, wenn nicht; ausser wenn [*ven niçt; ou'-sər ven*]
unlike, unähnlich [*un'-ehn-liç*]
unload *v.,* entladen (irreg) [*ent-lah'-dən*]
unlock, auf-schliessen (irreg) [*ouf'-shlee-sən*]
unlucky, unglücklich [*un'-glük-liç*]
unoccupied, unbesetzt; frei [*un'-bə-zetst; frai*]

unpack, v., aus-packen [*ous'-pa-kən*]
unpleasant, unangenehm [*un'-an-gə-nehm*]
unprepared (for), unvorbereitet (auf, plus acc) [*un'-fohr-bə-rai-tət (ouf)*]
unquestionable, unzweifelhaft [*un-tsvai'-fəl-haft*]
unsafe, gefährlich [*gə-fehr'-liç*]
unselfish, selbstlos [*zelpst'-lohs*]
unspeakable, unsäglich [*un-zehk'-liç*]
until, bis [*bis*]
untimely, unzeitig [*un'-tsai-tiç*]
untruthful, unwahr [*un'-vahr*]
unusual, ungewöhnlich [*un'-gə-vöhn-liç*]
unwelcome, unwillkommen [*un'-vil-ko-mən*]
unwilling, unwillig [*un'-vi-liç*]
up, auf; hinauf, herauf [*ouf; hi-nouf', he-rouf'*]
   up and down, auf und ab [*ouf unt ap*]
   What's up? [slang], Was ist los? [*vas ist lohs*]
up-to-date, modern [*mo-dern'*]
upbringing, Erziehung (f) [*er-tsee'-ung*]
uphill, bergauf [*berk-ouf'*]
upper, ober [*oh'-bər*]
upper floor, das obere Stockwerk [*das oh'-be-rə shtok'-verk*]
uppermost, höchst [*höhçst*]
uproar, Tumult, -e (m) [*tu-mult'*]
ups and downs, das Auf und Ab [*das ouf unt ap*]
upstairs, oben [*oh'-bən*]
upwards adv., aufwärts [*ouf'-verts*]
urban städtisch [*shte'-tish*]
urgent, dringend [*dring'-ənt*]
us, uns [*uns*]
use n., Gebrauch (m) [*gə-broukh'*]
use v., gebrauchen [*gə-brou'-khən*]
useful, nützlich [*nüts'-liç*]
useless, nutzlos [*nuts'-lohs*]
usual, üblich [*ühp'-liç*]
usually, gewöhnlich [*gə-vöhn'-liç*]
utility, Nützlichkeit (f) [*nüts'-liç-kait*]
utmost, äusserst [*oi'-serst*]

V

vacant, frei [*frai*]
vacate, *v.*, räumen [*roi'-mən*]
vacation, Ferien (pl) [*feh'-ri-ən*]
vaccination, Impfung, -en (f) [*im'-pfung*]
vacuum cleaner, Staubsauger, - (m) [*shtoup'-zou-gər*]
vagabond, Landstreicher, - (m) [*lant'-strai-çər*]
vague, unbestimmt [*un'-bə-shtimt*]
vain, eitel [*ai'-təl*]
  in vain, vergeblich [*fer-gehp'-liç*]
valid, gültig [*gül'-tiç*]
valley, Tal, ⸗er (n) [*tahl, teh'-lər*]
valuable, wertvoll [*vehrt'-fol*]
value *n.*, Wert, -e (m) [*vehrt*]
value *v.*, schätzen [*shet'-sən*]
valve, Klappe, -n (f) [*kla'-pə*]
vanish, verschwinden (irreg; Aux: SEIN) [*fer-shvin'-dən*]
vanity, Eitelkeit, -en (f) [*ai'-təl-kait*]
variety, Mannigfaltigkeit (f) [*ma'-niç-fal-tiç-kait*]
various, mannigfaltig [*ma'-niç-fal-tiç*]
vast, riesig [*ree'-ziç*]
vault, Gewölbe, - (n) [*gə-völ'-bə*]
veal, Kalbfleisch (n) [*kalp'-flaish*]
vegetable, Gemüse, - (n) [*gə-müh'-zə*]
veil *n.*, Schleier, - (m) [*shlai'-ər*]
vein, Ader (f) [*ah'-dər*]
velvet, Samt (m) [*zamt*]
vengeance, Rache (f) [*ra'-khə*]
verb, Verb, -en (n) [*verp, ver'-bən*]
verdict, Urteilsspruch, ⸗e (m) [*ur'-tails-shprukh, ur'-tails-shprü-çe*]
verify *v.*, bestätigen [*bə-shteh'-ti-gən*]
versatile, vielseitig [*feel'-zai-tiç*]

verse, Vers, -e (m) [*vers, ver'-zə*]
vertical, senkrecht [*zenk'-reçt*]
very, sehr [*zehr*]
  very much, sehr [*zehr*]
veteran, Kriegsteilnehmer, - (m) [*kreeks'-tail-neh-mər*]
veterinary, Tierarzt, ⸗e (m) [*teer'-ahrtst, teer'-ehrts-tə*]
vex *v.*, ärgern [*er'-gərn*]
vice, Laster, - (n) [*la'-stər*]
vicinity, Nähe (f) [*neh'-ə*]
vicious, bösartig [*böhz'-ahr-tiç*]
victim, Opfer, - (n) [*o'-pfər*]
victory, Sieg, -e (m) [*zeek, zee'-gə*]
view *n.*, Blick, -e (m) [*blik*]
viewfinder, Sucher, - (m) [*zoo'-khər*]
viewpoint, Gesichtspunkt, -e (m) [*gə-ziçts'-punkt*]
vigorous, kräftig [*kref'-tiç*]
villa, Villa (f, sing), Villen (pl) [*vi'-la, vi'-lən*]
village, Dorf, ⸗er (n) [*dorf, dör'-fər*]
villain, Bösewicht, -e (m) [*böh'-zə-viçt*]
vine, Weinstock, ⸗e (m) [*vain'-shtok, vain'-shtö-kə*]
vinegar, Essig (m) [*e'-siç*]
vineyard, Weinberg, -e (m) [*vain'-berk, vain'-ber-gə*]
violate *v.*, verletzen [*fer-le'-tsən*]
violence, Gewaltsamkeit (f) [*gə-valt'-zam-kait*]
violin, Geige, -n (f) [*gai'-gə*]
virgin, Jungfrau, -en (f) [*yung'-frou*]
virtue, Tugend, -en (f) [*too'-gənt, too'-gən-dən*]
virtuous, tugendhaft [*too'-gənt-haft*]
Visa, Visum (n, sing), Visen (pl) [*vee'-zum, vee'-zən*]
visible, sichtbar [*ziçt'-bahr*]
vision, Vision, -en (f) [*vi-zi-ohn'*]
visionary, visionär [*vi-zi-o-nehr'*]
visit *v.*, besuchen [*bə-zoo'-khən*]
visit *n.*, Besuch, -e (m) [*bə-zookh'*]
visiting card, Visitenkarte, -n (f) [*vi-zee'-tən-kar-tə*]
visitor, Besucher, - (m) [*bə-zoo'-khər*]
vivid, lebhaft [*lehp'-haft*]
vocalist [female], Sängerin, -nen (f) [*zeng'-ə-rin*]

vocalist [male], Sänger, - (m) [*zeng'-ər*]
vocation, Beruf, -e (m) [*bə-roof'*]
vocational, beruflich [*bə-roof'-liç*]
voice, Stimme, -n (f) [*shti'-mə*]
volcano, Vulkan, -e (m) [*vul-kahn'*]
volume, Band, ⁼e (m) [*bant, ben'-də*]
voluntary, freiwillig [*frai'-vil-iç*]
volunteer *n.*, Freiwillige, -n (m, f) [*frai'-vi-li-gə*]
vomit *v.*, aus-brechen (irreg) [*ous'-bre-çən*]
vote *n.*, Wahlstimme, -n (f) [*vahl'-shti-mə*]
vote for *v.*, wählen [*veh'-lən*]
vow *v.*, schwören (irreg) [*shvöh'-rən*]
vow *n.*, Gelübde, - (n) [*gə-lüp'-də*]
vowel, Vokal, -e (m) [*vo-kahl'*]
voyage, Seereise, -n (f) [*zeh'-rai-zə*]
vulgar, vulgär; ordinär [*vul-gehr', or-di-nehr'*]
vulnerable, verwundbar [*fer-vunt'-bahr*]

W

wade *v.*, waten (*Aux:* SEIN) [*vah'-tən*]
wagon, Wagen, - (m) [*vah'-gən*]
waist, Taille, -n (f) [*tal'-yə*]
wait *v.*, warten [*var'-tən*]
  Wait a moment! Warten Sie einen Augenblick! [*var'-tən zee ai'-nən ou'-gən-blik*]
  Wait for me! Warten Sie auf mich! [*var'-tən zee ouf miç*]
waiter, Kellner, - (m) [*kel'-nər*]
waiting room, Wartezimmer, - (n) [*var'-tə-tsi-mər*]
waitress, Kellnerin, -nen (f) [*kel'-nə-rin*]
wake *v.*, auf-wachen (*Aux:* SEIN) [*ouf'-va-khən*]
walk *n.*, Spaziergang, ⁼e (m) [*shpa-tseer'-gang, shpa-tseer'-gen-gə*]
  take a walk *v.*, spazieren gehen (irreg; *Aux:* SEIN) [*shpa-tsee'-rən geh'-ən*]

walk v., (zu Fuss) gehen (irreg; *Aux:* SEIN) [(*tsu foos*) geh'-ən]

  walk in, hinein-gehen (irreg); herein-kommen (*Aux:* SEIN) [*hi-nain'-geh-ən; he-rain'-ko-mən*]

  walk out, hinaus-gehen (irreg; *Aux:* SEIN) [*hi-nous'-geh-ən*]

  walk up, hinauf-gehen (irreg; *Aux:* SEIN) [*hi-nouf'-geh-ən*]

wall, Wand, ⸗e (f); Mauer, -n (f) [*vant, ven'-də; mou'-ər*]

wallet, Brieftasche, -n (f) [*breef'-ta-shə*]

wallpaper, Tapete, -n (f) [*ta-peh'-tə*]

walnut, Walnuss, ⸗e (f) [*val'-nus, val'-nii-sə*]

waltz n., Walzer, - (m) [*valt'-sər*]

wander v., wandern (*Aux:* SEIN) [*van'-dərn*]

want v., brauchen; wollen (irreg) [*brou'-khən; vo'-lən*]

war, Krieg, -e (m) [*kreek, kree'-gə*]

wardrobe, Kleiderschrank, ⸗e (m) [*klai'-dər-shrank, klai'-dər-shren-kə*]

warehouse, Lagerhaus, ⸗er (n) [*lah'-gər-hous, lah'-gər-hoi-zər*]

warm adj., warm [*varm*]

warm v., wärmen [*ver'-mən*]

  warm up, auf-wärmen [*ouf'-ver-mən*]

warmhearted, warmherzig [*varm'-her-tsiç*]

warmth, Wärme (f) [*ver'-mə*]

warn v., warnen [*var'-nən*]

warning n., Warnung, -en (f) [*var'-nung*]

warrant, Bürgschaft (f); Befehl, -e (m) [*bürk'-shaft; bə-fehl'*]

warship, Kriegsschiff, -e (n) [*kreeks'-shif*]

was, war [*vahr*]

  there was, es war; es gab [*es vahr; es gahp*]

wash v., waschen (irreg) [*va'-shən*]

washbasin, Waschbecken, - (n) [*vash'-be-kən*]

washing machine, Waschmaschine, -n (f) [*vash'-ma-shee-nə*]

wasp, Wespe, -n (f) [*ves'-pə*]

waste v., verschwenden [*fer-shven'-dən*]

wastebasket, Papierkorb, ⸗e (m) [*pa-peer'-korp, pa-peer'-kör-bə*]

wasteful, verschwenderisch [*fer-shven'-də-rish*]

watch v., auf-passen [*ouf'-pa-sən*]

  Watch out! Passen Sie auf! [*pa'-sən zee ouf*]

watch n., Uhr, -en (f) [*oor*]
  pocket watch, Taschenuhr, -en (f) [*ta'-shən-oor*]
  wrist watch, Armbanduhr, -en (f) [*arm'-bant-oor*]
watchful, wachsam [*vakh'-zam*]
watchmaker, Uhrmacher, - (m) [*oor'-ma-khər*]
watchman, Wächter, - (m) [*veç'-tər*]
watchword, Losung, -en (f) [*loh'-zung*]
water, Wasser (n, sing), Wässer, Gewässer (pl) [*va'-sər, veh'-sər, gə-veh'-sər*]
  fresh water, Süsswasser (n) [*zühs'-va-sər*]
  mineral water, Mineralwasser, ‑ (n) [*mi-ne-rahl'-va-sər, mi-ne-rahl'-ve-sər*]
  running water, fliessendes Wasser [*flee'-sen-dəs va'-sər*]
water bottle, Wasserflasche, -n (f) [*va'-sər-fla-shə*]
waterfall, Wasserfall, ‑e (m) [*va'-sər-fal, va'-sər-fe-lə*]
waterfront, Hafengebiet, -e (n) [*hah'-fən-gə-beet*]
watermelon, Wassermelone, -n (f) [*va'-sər-me-loh-nə*]
waterproof, wasserdicht [*va'-sər-diçt*]
wave n., Welle, -n (f) [*ve'-lə*]
  permanent wave, Dauerwelle, -n (f) [*dou'-ər-ve-lə*]
wave v., winken [*vin'-kən*]
wax n., Wachs, -e (n) [*vaks*]
way [manner], Art, -en (f) [*ahrt*]
way [road], Weg, -e (m); Strasse, -n (f) [*vehk, veh'-gə; shtra'-sə*]
  by the way, übrigens [*übh'-ri-gəns*]
  in this way, auf diese Art [*ouf dee'-zə ahrt*]
wayside, Strassenrand, ‑er (m) [*shtra'-sən-rant, shtra'-sən-ren-dər*]
wayward, launisch [*lou'-nish*]
we, wir [*veer*]
weak, schwach [*shvakh*]
weakness, Schwäche, -n (f) [*shve'-çə*]
wealth, Wohlstand (m) [*vohl'-shtant*]
wealthy, reich [*raiç*]
weapon, Waffe, -n (f) [*va'-fə*]
wear v., tragen (irreg); an-haben (irreg) [*trah'-gən; an'-hah-bən*]

wear out, sich ab-tragen (irreg) [*ziç ap'-trah-gən*]
weary, müde [*müh'-də*]
weather, Wetter (n) [*ve'-tər*]
 How is the weather? Wie ist das Wetter? [*vee ist das ve'-tər*]
weave v., weben [*veh'-bən*]
weaver, Weber, - (m) [*veh'-bər*]
web, Gewebe, - (n) [*gə-veh'-bə*]
wedding, Hochzeit, -en (f) [*hokh'-tsait*]
wedding cake, Hochzeitskuchen, - (m) [*hokh'-tsaits-koo-khən*]
wedding ring, Trauring, -e (m) [*trou'-ring*]
Wednesday, Mittwoch (m) [*mit'-vokh*]
weed, Unkraut, ⸗er (n) [*un'-krout, un'-kroi-tər*]
week, Woche, -n (f) [*vo'-khə*]
weekend, Wochenende, -n (n) [*vo'-khən-en-də*]
weekly, wöchentlich [*vö'-çənt-liç*]
weep v., weinen [*vai'-nən*]
weigh v., wiegen (irreg) [*vee'-gən*]
weight, Gewicht, -e (n) [*gə-viçt'*]
welcome adj., willkommen [*vil-ko'-mən*]
 You are welcome! Bitte schön! [*bi'-tə shöhn*]
welcome v., willkommen heissen [*vil-ko'-mən hai'-sən*]
welfare, Wohlfahrt (f) [*vohl'-fahrt*]
well n., Brunnen, - (m) [*bru'-nən*]
well adv., gut [*goot*]
 be well v., gesund sein [*gə-zunt' zain*]
 Very well! Sehr gut! [*zehr goot*]
well [in hesitation], Na; Nun; Also [*nah; noon; al'-zoh*]
well interj., Gut!, Ei!, [*goot, ai*]
well-bred, wohlerzogen [*vohl'-er-tsoh-gən*]
well-known, wohlbekannt [*vohl'-bə-kant*]
well-off, wohlhabend [*vohl'-hah-bənt*]
were, waren; wäre [*vah'-rən; veh'-rə*]
 there were, es gab [*es gahp*]
west, Westen (m) [*ve'-stən*]
western, westlich [*vest'-liç*]
wet adj., nass [*nas*]

get wet v., nass werden (irreg; *Aux:* SEIN) [*nas vehr'-dən*]
whale, Wal, -e (m) [*vahl*]
wharf, Kai, -s (m) [*kai, kais*]
what, was; wie [*vas; vee*]
  What a pity! Wie schade! [*vee shah'-də*]
  What for? Wozu? [*voh-tsoo'*]
  What is the matter? Was ist los? [*vas ist lohs*]
  What next? Was sonst noch? [*vas zonst nokh*]
  What's the time? Wie spät ist es? [*vee shpeht ist es*]
whatever, was auch (immer) [*vas oukh (i'-mər)*]
wheat, Weizen (m) [*vai'-tsən*]
wheel, Rad, ⸗er (n) [*raht, reh'-dər*]
  steering wheel, Steuerrad, ⸗er (n) [*shtoi'-ər-raht, shtoi'-ər-reh-dər*]
wheelbarrow, Schubkarre, -n (f) [*shoop'-ka-rə*]
when, wann; als, wenn [*van; als, ven*]
  since when, seit wann [*zait van*]
  When do we go? Wann gehen wir? [*van geh'-ən veer*]
whenever, jedesmal wenn [*yeh'-dəs-mahl ven*]
where, wo; wohin [*voh; voh-hin'*]
  Where did you get that? Woher haben Sie das? [*voh-hehr' hah'-bən zee das*]
wherever, wo auch immer [*voh oukh i'-mər*]
whether, ob [*op*]
which, der, die, das; welcher, welche, welches; was [*dehr, dee, das; vel'-çər, vel'-çə, vel'-çəs; vas*]
while *conj.*, während [*veh'-rənt*]
whipped cream, Schlagsahne (f) [*shlahk'-zah-nə*]
whisper *n.*, Geflüster (n) [*gə-flü'-stər*]
whisper *v.*, flüstern [*flü'-stərn*]
whistle [sound] *n.*, Pfiff, -e (m) [*pfif*]
whistle *v.*, pfeifen (irreg) [*pfai'-fən*]
white, weiss [*vais*]
who, wer; der, die, das; welcher, welche, welches [*vehr; dehr, dee, das; vel'-çər, vel'-çə, vel'-çəs*]
whoever, wer auch immer [*vehr oukh i'-mər*]
whole, ganz, vollkommen [*gants, fol'-ko-mən*]
wholehearted, rückhaltlos [*rük'-halt-lohs*]

wholesale, im grossen [*im groh'-sən*]

whom, wen; den, die, das; welchen, welche, welches [*vehn; dehn, dee, das; vel'-çən, vel'-çə, vel'-çəs*]

whose, wessen (interrogative); dessen, deren (relative); deren (pl) [*ve'-sən; de'-sən, deh'-rən; deh'-rən*]

why, warum; weshalb [*va-rum'; ves-halp'*]
  Why not? Warum nicht? [*var-rum' niçt*]

wicked, böse [*böh'-zə*]

wide, weit; breit [*vait; brait*]

wide-awake, schlau [*schlou*]

widespread, weitverbreitet [*vait'-fer-brai-tət*]

widow, Witwe, -n (f) [*vit'-və*]

widower, Witwer, - (m) [*vit'-vər*]

width, Weite (f); Breite (f) [*vai'-tə; brai'-tə*]

wife, Frau, -en (f); Ehefrau, -en (f) [*frou, eh'-ə-frou*]

wig, Perücke, -n (f) [*pe-rü'-kə*]

wild, wild [*vilt*]

will [intent] *n.,* Wille (m) [*vi'-lə*]

will [testament] *n.,* Testament, -e (n) [*tes-ta-ment'*]

will [future] *v.,* werden (irreg; *Aux;* SEIN), wollen (mod aux, irreg) [*vehr'-dən, vol'-ən*]
  he, she, it will [future], er, sie, es wird [*er, zee, es virt*]
  you, we, they will [future], Sie, wir, sie werden [*zee, veer, zee vehr'-dən*]
  She will go, Sie wird gehen [*zee virt geh'-ən*]

willing, willig [*vi'-liç*]

willingly, gern [*gern*]

willpower, Willenskraft (f) [*vi'-ləns-kraft*]

win *v.,* gewinnen (irreg) [*gə-vi'-nən*]

wind *n.,* Wind, -e (m) [*vint, vin'-də*]

wind *v.,* winden (irreg) [*vin'-dən*]
  wind a watch, eine Taschenuhr auf-ziehen (irreg) [*ai'-nə ta'-shən-oor ouf'-tsee-ən*]

windmill, Windmühle, -n (f) [*vint'-müh-lə*]

window, Fenster, - (n) [*fen'-stər*]

windowpane, Fensterscheibe, -n (f) [*fen'-stər-shai-bə*]

window shade, Rouleau, -s (n) [*ru-loh', ru-lohs'*]

windy, windig [*vin'-diç*]

wine, Wein, -e (m) [*vain*]
  red wine, Rotwein (m) [*roht'-vain*]
  white wine, Weisswein (m) [*vais'-vain*]
wing, Flügel, - (m) [*flüh'-gəl*]
winner, Sieger, - (m) [*zee'-gər*]
winter, Winter, - (m) [*vin'-tər*]
  in winter, im Winter [*im vin'-tər*]
wipe *v.,* ab-wischen [*ap'-vi-shən*]
wire *n.,* Telegramm, -e (n) [*te-le-gram'*]
wisdom, Weisheit (f) [*vais'-hait*]
wise, weise [*vai'-zə*]
wish *n.,* Wunsch, =e (m) [*vunsh, vün'-shə*]
wish *v.,* wünschen [*vün'-shən*]
  Do you wish something? Wünschen Sie etwas? [*vün'-shən
    zee et'-vas*]
wit, Verstand (m) [*fer-shtant'*]
witch, Hexe, -n (f) [*hek'-sə*]
with, mit (plus dat) [*mit*]
withdraw *v.,* zurück-ziehen (irreg) [*tsu-rük'-tsee-ən*]
withhold *v.,* zurück-halten (irreg) [*tsu-rük'-hal-tən*]
within, innerhalb; drinnen; zu Hause [*i'-nər-halp; dri'-nən;
    tsu hou'-zə*]
without, ohne (plus acc) [*oh'-nə*]
witness [female], Zeugin, -nen (f) [*tsoi'-gin*]
witness [male], Zeuge, -n (m) [*tsoi'-gə*]
witty, witzig [*vi'-tsiç*]
wolf, Wolf, =e (m) [*volf, völ'-fə*]
woman, Frau, -en (f) [*frou*]
wonder *n.,* Wunder, - (n) [*vun'-dər*]
wonder *v.,* sich wundern [*ziç vun'-dərn*]
wonderful, wunderbar [*vun'-dər-bahr*]
wood [timber], Holz, =er (n) [*holts, höl'-tsər*]
wood [forest], Wald, =er (m) [*valt, vel'-dər*]
wooden [fig.], steif [*shtaif*]
wool, Wolle (f) [*vo'-lə*]
woolen, wollen [*vo'-lən*]
word, Wort, -e, =er (n) [*vort, vor'tə, vör'-tər*]
wordy, wortreich [*vort'-raiç*]

work n., Arbeit, -en (f) [ar'-bait]
  work of art, Kunstwerk, -e (n) [kunst'-verk]
work v., arbeiten [ar'-bai-tən]
  Where does she work? Wo arbeitet sie? [voh ar'-bai-tət
  zee]
  This isn't working, Das geht nicht [das geht niçt]
workday, Werktag, -e (m) [verk'-tahk, verk'-tah-gə]
worker [female], Arbeiterin, -nen (f) [ar'-bai-tə-rin]
worker [male], Arbeiter, - (m) [ar'-bai-tər]
workshop, Werkstatt, ⸗e (f) [verk'-shtat, verk'-shte-tə]
world, Welt, -en (f) [velt]
worldliness, Weltlichkeit (f) [velt'-liç-kait]
world war, Weltkrieg, -e (m) [velt'-kreek, velt'-kree-gə]
  the Second World War, der zweite Weltkrieg [dehr
  tsvai'-tə velt'-kreek]
worldwide, weitverbreitet [vait'-fer-brai-tət]
worm, Wurm, ⸗er (m) [vurm, vür'-mər]
worn-out [clothes], abgetragen; [person], ermüdet [ap'-gə-trah-
  gən; er-müh'-dət]
worried adj., besorgt [bə-zorkt']
worry n., Sorge, -n (f) [zor'-gə]
worry v., sich beunruhigen [ziç bə-un'-roo-i-gən]
  Don't worry! Machen Sie sich keine Sorgen! [ma'-khən
  zee ziç kai'-nə zor'-gən]
worse, schlimmer; schlechter [shli'-mər; shleç'-tər]
worship n., Verehrung (f) [fer-eh'-rung]
worship v., an-beten [an'-beh-tən]
worst adv., am schlechtesten; am schlimmsten [am shleç'-
  tə-stən; am shlim'-stən]
worth n., Wert (m) [vehrt]
  How much is that worth? Wieviel ist das wert? [vee-feel'
  ist das vehrt]
worthy, würdig [vür'-diç]
would mod. aux., wollte; würde [vol'-tə; vür'-də]
wound n., Wunde, -n (f) [vun'-də]
wounded, verwundet [fer-vun'-dət]
wrap up v., ein-packen [ain'-pa-kən]
wrench [tool], Schraubenschlüssel, - (m) [shrou'-bən-

shlü-səl]
wrestling *n.*, Ringkampf, ⸗e (m) [*ring'-kampf, ring'-kem-pfə*]
wrinkle *v.*, runzeln [*run'-tsəln*]
wrist, Handgelenk, -e (n) [*hant'-gə-lenk*]
write *v.*, schreiben (irreg) [*shrai'-bən*]
writer [female], Autorin, -nen (f) [*ou-toh'-rin*]
writer [male], Schriftsteller, - (m) [*shrift'-shte-lər*]
writing [composition], Schriftstück, -e (n) [*shrift'-shtük*]
  in writing, schriftlich [*shrift'-liç*]
writing paper, Schreibpapier (n) [*shraip'-pa-peer*]
wrong *adj.*, falsch; unrecht [*falsh; un'-reçt*]
wrong *n.*, Unrecht (n) [*un'-reçt*]
  be wrong *v.*, unrecht haben (irreg) [*un'-reçt hah'-bən*]

X

x rays, Röntgenstrahlen (m, pl) [*rönt'-gən-shtrah-lən*]
Xerox *v.*, vervielfältigen [*fər-feel'-fel-ti-gən*]

Y

yacht, Jacht, -en (f) [*yakht*]
yard, Hof, ⸗e (m) [*hohf, höh'-fə*]
yarn [filament], Garn, -e (n) [*garn*]
yawn *n.*, Gähnen (n) [*geh'-nən*]
yawn *v.*, gähnen [*geh'-nən*]
year, Jahr, -e (n) [*yahr*]
  last year, letztes Jahr [*lets'-təs yahr*]
  next year, nächstes Jahr [*nehç'-stəs yahr*]
yearly, jährlich [*yehr'-liç*]
yell *v.*, schreien (irreg) [*shrai'-ən*]
yellow, gelb [*gelp*]

yes, ja [*yah*]

yesterday, gestern [*ge'-stərn*]

yet *adv.*, noch [*nokh*]

yield *v.*, ein-bringen (irreg) [*ain'-brin-gən*]

you, Sie (formal, sing & pl); du (informal, sing); ihr (informal, pl) [*zee; doo; eer*]

young, jung [*yung*]

young man, junger Mann [*yung'-ər man*]

young woman, junge Frau [*yung'-ə frou*]

your [*familiar form*], dein, deiner, dein (sing), deine (pl) [*dain, dai'-nər, dain, dai'-nə*]

your [*formal and polite form*], Ihr; Ihre [*eer; ee'-rə*]

yours, der (die, das) Ihre (formal); der (die, das) deine (informal) [*dehr (dee, das) ee'-rə; dehr (dee, das) dai'-nə*]

　Very truly yours, Ihr sehr ergebener [*eer zehr er-geh'-bə-nər*]

youth, Jugend (f) [*yoo'-gənt*]

youthful, jugendlich [*yoo'-gənt-liç*]

Z

zero, Null, -en (f) [*nul*]

zinc, Zink (n) [*tsink*]

zipper, Reissverschluss, ⸗e (m) [*rais'-fer-shlus, rais'-fer-shlü-sə*]

zone, Zone, -n (f) [*tsoh'-nə*]

zoo, Zoo, -s (m) [*tsoh, tsohs*]

German/English

A

ab [*ap*] off, down, away from
   ab und zu [*ap unt tsoo*] now and then
ab-bestellen *v.* [*ap'-bə-shte-lən*] cancel
Abbildung, -en *f.* [*ap'-bil-dung*] picture
abbürsten *v.* [*ap'-bür-stən*] brush off
Abend, -e *m.* [*ah'-bənt, ah'-bən-də*] evening
   am Abend [*am ah'-bənt*] in the evening
   morgen abend [*mor'-gən ah'-bənt*] tomorrow evening
   gestern abend [*ge'-stərn ah'-bənt*] yesterday evening
   Guten Abend! [*goo'-tən ah'-bənt*] Good evening!
Abendessen *n.* [*ah'-bənt-e-sən*] supper, dinner
Abendkleid, -er *n.* [*ah'-bənt-klait, ah'-bənt-klai-dər*] evening
   dress
Abenteuer, - *n.* [*ah'-bən-toi-ər*] adventure
aber [*ah'-bər*] but, however
abergläubisch [*ah'-ber-gloi-bish*] superstitious
ab-fahren *v. irreg. (Aux: SEIN)* [*ap'-fah-rən*] leave, depart
Abfall, ⁼e *m.* [*ap'-fal, ap'-fe-lə*] garbage
ab-fertigen *v.* [*ap'-fer-ti-gən*] dispatch
ab-geben *v. irreg.* [*ap'-geh-bən*] give, check
Abgeordnete, -n *m., f.* [*ap'-gə-ord-nə-tə*] deputy
abgesehen von [*ap'-gə-zeh-ən fon*] apart from
ab-hängen (von) *v. irreg.* [*ap'-heng-ən (fon)*] depend (on)
   Das hängt davon ab [*das hengt da-fon' ap*] That depends
abhängig (von) [*ap'-heng-iç (fon)*] dependent (on)
ab-heben *v. irreg.* [*ap'-heh-ben*] withdraw [money]
ab-holen *v.* [*ap'-hoh-lən*] call for, come for
ab-kürzen *v.* [*ap'-kür-tsən*] shorten; abbreviate [word, story]
Abkürzung, -en *f.* [*ap'-kür-tsung*] shortcut
ab-laden *v. irreg.* [*ap'-lah-dən*] unload
ab-lehnen *v.* [*ap'-leh-nən*] decline, turn down
ab-liefern *v.* [*ap'-lee-fərn*] deliver

ab-machen v. [*ap'-ma-khən*] remove, settle, arrange
  Abgemacht! [*ap'-gə-makht*] It's a deal!
ab-nehmen v. *irreg.* [*ap'-neh-mən*] take off, remove, lose
  weight
Abneigung, -en f. [*ap'-nai-gung*] dislike
Abreise, -n f. [*ap'-rai-zə*] departure
ab-sagen v. [*ap'-zah-gən*] cancel
Absatz, ⸗e m. [*ap'-zats, ap'-ze-tsə*] heel [of shoe]; paragraph
Abscheu m. [*ap'-shoi*] aversion, loathing
ab-schicken v. [*ap'-shi-kən*] send, send off
Abschied, -e m. [*ap'-sheet, ap'-shee-də*] farewell
ab-schliessen v. *irreg.* [*ap'-shlee-sən*] lock; wind up
ab-schneiden v. *irreg.* [*ap'-shnai-dən*] slice off, cut off
Absender, - m. [*ap'-zen-der*] sender
Absicht, -en f. [*ap'-siçt*] intention, purpose
absichtlich [*ap'-ziçt-liç*] intentional, on purpose
absolut [*ap-zo-loot'*] absolute
Abstand, ⸗e m. [*ap'-shtant, ap'-shten-də*] distance, interval
ab-steigen v. *irreg.* [*ap'-shtai-gən*] descend, get off
abstrahieren v. [*ap-stra-hee'-rən*] abstract
abstrakt [*ap-strakt'*] abstract
Abstraktion, -en f. [*ap-strak-tsi-ohn'*] abstraction
Absturz, ⸗e m. [*ap'-shturts, ap'-shtür-tsə*] fall, crash
Abteil, -e n. [*ap'-tail*] compartment [of railway carriage]
Abteilung, -en f. [*ap'-tai-lung*] compartment, department,
  division
ab-trocknen v. [*ap'-trok-nən*] dry
ab-warten v. [*ap'-var-tən*] wait for
abwärts [*ap'-verts*] downward
abwesend [*ap'-veh-zənt*] absent
Abwesenheit, -en f. [*ap'-veh-zən-hait*] absence
ab-zahlen v. [*ap'-tsah-lən*] pay in installments
Abzeichen, - n. [*ap'-tsai-çən*] badge
ach! [*akh*] ah!, alas!
Achse, -n f. [*ak'-sə*] axle
acht [*akht*] eight, eighth
achten v. [*akh'-tən*] respect
Achtung f. [*akh'-tung*] respect

Achtung, Gefahr! [*akh'-tung, gə-fahr'*] Danger!
achtzehn [*akht'-tsehn*] eighteen
achtzig [*akht'-tsiç*] eighty
Acker, = *m.* [*a'-kər, e'-kər*] acre
Adel *m.* [*ah'-dəl*] nobility
Ader, -n *f.* [*ah'-dər*] vein
Adjektiv, -e *n.* [*at'-yek-teef, at'-yek-tee-və*] adjective
Adler, - *m.* [*ahd'-lər*] eagle
Admiral, -e *m.* [*at-mi-rahl'*] admiral
Adresse, -n *f.* [*a-dre'-sə*] address [place]
adressieren *v.* [*a-dre-see'-rən*] address [a letter]
Affe, -n *m.* [*a'-fə*] monkey, ape
affektiert [*a-fek-teert'*] affected
Afrika *n.* [*a'-fri-kah*] Africa
Agent, -en *m.* [*a-gent'*] agent
Agentur, -en *f.* [*a-gen-toor'*] agency
Ägypten *n.* [*e-güp'-tən*] Egypt
ägyptisch [*e-güp'-tish*] Egyptian
ähnlich (plus dat.) [*ehn'-liç*] similar to, like
Ähnlichkeit, -en *f.* [*ehn'-liç-kait*] resemblance
Akademie, -n *f.* [*a-ka-de-mee', a-ka-de-mee'-ən*] academy
Akt, -e *m.* [*akt*] act [of a play]
Aktie, -n *f.* [*ak'-tsi-ə*] share [stock]
aktiv [*ak-teef'*] active
Akzent, -e *m.* [*ak-tsent'*] accent
Alarm, -e *m.* [*a-larm'*] alarm
albern [*al'-bərn*] silly; foolish
Alkohol, -e *m.* [*al'-ko-hol*] alcohol
Alkoholismus *m.* [*al-ko-ho-lis'-mus*] alcoholism
alle [*a'-lə*] all
Allee, -n *f.* [*a-leh', a-leh'-ən*] avenue
allein [*a-lain'*] alone
alles [*a'-ləs*] everything, all
allgemein [*al-gə-main'*] general
Alliierten *m., pl.* [*a-li-eer'-tən*] Allies
alltäglich [*al-tehk'-liç*] trivial
Alpdrücken *n.* [*alp'-drü-kən*] nightmare
als [*als*] when, than, as

als ob, als wenn [*als op, als ven*] as if, as though

also [*al'-zoh*] so, thus, well [interjection]

alt [*alt*] old

    Wie alt sind Sie? [*vee alt zint zee*] How old are you?

Altar, ⸗e *m.* [*al-tahr', al-teh'-rə*] altar

Alter *n.* [*al'-tər*] age [person]

    Sie ist in meinem Alter [*zee ist in mai'-nəm al'-tər*]
        She's my age.

älter [*el'-tər*] elder, older

altern *v.* [*al'-tərn*] age

Altertum, ⸗er *n.* [*al'-tər-toom*] antiquity

altmodisch [*alt'-moh-dish*] old-fashioned

am: an dem [*am*] at the, to the, by the, near the

    am meisten [*am mai'-stən*] most

Ameise, -n *f.* [*ah'-mai-zə*] ant

Amerika *n.* [*a-meh'-ri-ka*] America

Amerikaner, - *m.* [*a-me-ri-kah'-nər*] American [male]

Amerikanerin, -nen *f.* [*a-me-ri-kah'-nə-rin*] American [female]

amerikanisch *adj.* [*a-me-ri-kah'-nish*] American

Amt, ⸗er *n.* [*amt, em'-tər*] office

amüsieren *v.* [*a-mü-zee'-rən*] amuse

    Amüsieren Sie sich! [*a-mü-zee'-rən zee ziç*] Enjoy
        yourself!, Have a good time!

an (plus dat. or acc.) [*an*] at, to, by, near

    an Bord [*an bort*] aboard

Analyse, -n *f.* [*a-na-lüh'-zə*] analysis

Ananas, - *f.* [*a'-na-nas*] pineapple

Anarchie, -n *f.* [*a-nar-çee'*] anarchy

anbeten *v.* [*an'-beh-tən*] adore, worship

an-bieten *v. irreg.* [*an'-bee-tən*] offer

an-binden *v. irreg.* [*an'-bin-dən*] tie on

Anblick, -e *m.* [*an'-blik*] view, sight

Andenken, - *n.* [*an'-den-kən*] souvenir, remembrance

ander [*an'-dər*] other, next

ändern *v.* [*en'-dərn*] alter

anders [*an'-dərs*] otherwise, else

anderseits [*an'-dər-zaits*] on the other hand

anderthalb [*an'-dərt-halp*] one and a half

aneinander [*an'-ai-nan-dər*] against one another, to one
  another
Anekdote, -n *f.* [*a-nek-doh'-tə*] anecdote
an-erkennen *v. irreg.* [*an'-er-ke-nən*] acknowledge, appreciate
Anfall, ⸗e *m.* [*an'-fal, an'-fe-lə*] attack, fit
Anfang, ⸗e *m.* [*an'-fang, an'-feng-ə*] beginning
an-fangen *v. irreg.* [*an'-fang-ən*] begin, start
  Fangen Sie wieder an! [*fang'-ən zee vee'-dər an*] Begin
    again!
anfangs [*an'-fangs*] in the beginning
Anfrage, -n *f.* [*an'-frah-gə*] inquiry
an-fragen *v.* [*an'-frah-gən*] inquire
Angabe, -n *f.* [*an'-gah-bə*] declaration
an-geben *v. irreg.* [*an'-geh-ben*] state, give [name]
Angebot, -e *n.* [*an'-gə-boht*] offer
angefüllt mit [*an'-gə-fült mit*] crowded with, full of
Angelegenheit, -en *f.* [*an'-gə-leh-gən-hait*] affair
angeln *v.* [*ang'-əln*] fish
  Angeln verboten [*ang'-əln fer-boh'-tən*] No fishing
angenehm [*an'-gə-nehm*] pleasant
  Sehr angenehm! [*zehr an'-gə-nehm*] How do you do!
an-greifen *v. irreg.* [*an'-grai-fən*] attack, denounce
Angriff, -e *m.* [*an'-grif*] attack, assault
Angst, ⸗e *f.* [*angst*] anguish, fear
  Angst haben vor (plus dat.) *v.,* [*angst hah'-bən for*] be
    afraid of
ängstlich [*engst'-liç*] anxious
an-halten *v. irreg.* [*an'-hal-tən*] stop, pull up
an-hängen *v.* [*an'-heng-ən*] hang on
Anker, - *m.* [*an'-kər*] anchor
an-klagen *v.* [*an'-klah-gən*] accuse
Ankläger, - *m.* [*an'-kleh-gər*] accuser
an-kleben *v.* [*an'-kleh-bən*] stick on
an-kleiden *v.* [*an'-klai-dən*] put on clothes
an-klopfen *v.* [*an'-klo-pfən*] knock
an-kommen *v. irreg.* [*an'-ko-mən*] arrive
an-kündigen *v.* [*an'-kün-di-gən*] announce
Ankunft, ⸗e *f.* [*an'-kunft, an'-künf-tə*] arrival

Anlasser, - *m.* [*an'-la-sər*] starter [of car]

an-legen *v.* [*an'-leh-gən*] invest [money], lay out, put on [clothes]

(sich) anlehnen *v.* [(ziç) *an'-leh-nən*] lean against

an-machen *v.* [*an'-ma-khən*] put on [a light]

Anmut *f.* [*an'-moot*] grace

an-nageln *v.* [*an'-nah-gəln*] nail (on)

an-nähen *v.* [*an'-neh-ən*] sew on

Annahme, -n *f.* [*an'-nah-mə*] assumption, acceptance

an-nehmen *v. irreg.* [*an'-neh-mən*] assume, suppose, accept

anonym [*a-no-nühm'*] anonymous

an-probieren *v.* [*an'-pro-bee-rən*] try on [clothes]

an-reden *v.* [*an'-reh-dən*] address

Anrichte, -n *f.* [*an'-riç-tə*] dresser

Anruf, -e *m.* [*an'-roof*] telephone call

an-rufen *v. irreg.* [*an'-roo-fən*] call

an-rühren *v.* [*an'-rüh-rən*] touch

an-sagen *v.* [*an'-zah-gən*] announce

an-schauen *v.* [*an'-shou-en*] look at

Anschrift, -en *f.* [*an'-shrift*] address

an-sehen *v. irreg.* [*an'-zeh-ən*] look at, view

Ansehen *n.* [*an'-zeh-ən*] prestige

Ansicht, -en *f.* [*an'-ziçt*] view, opinion

Ansichtskarte, -n *f.* [*an'-ziçts-kar-tə*] picture postcard

Ansprache, -n *f.* [*an'-shprah-khə*] address, speech

an-sprechen *v. irreg.* [*an'-shpre-çən*] address

Anspruch, ⸗e *m.* [*an'-shprukh, an'-shprü-çə*] claim

anspruchsvoll [*an'-shprukhs-fol*] prententious

Anstalt, -en *f.* [*an'-shtalt*] institution

anständig [*an'-shten-diç*] decent, respectable

anstatt *prep.* (plus gen.) [*an-shtat'*] instead of

an-stecken *v.* [*an'-shte-kən*] infect, pin on

ansteckend [*an'-shte-kənt*] contagious

an-stellen *v.* [*an'-shte-lən*] employ, make [experiments], turn on [machine]

Anstellung, -en *f.* [*an'-shte-lung*] employment

an-streichen *v. irreg.* [*an'-shtrai-çən*] paint

an-strengen *v.* [*an'-shtreng-ən*] strain, exert

Anstrengung, -en *f.* [*an'-shtreng-ung*] strain, effort
antik [*an-teek'*] antique
Antiquität, -en *f.* [*an-tik-vi-teht'*] ancient relic
Antrag, ≃e *m.* [*an'-trahk, an'-treh-gə*] application
Antwort, -en *f.* [*ant'-vort*] answer, reply
antworten (plus dat.) *v.* [*ant'-vor-tən*] answer
Anwalt, ≃e *m.* [*an'-valt, an'-vel-tə*] attorney, lawyer [male]
an-wenden *v.* [*an'-ven-dən*] make use of, apply
Anzahl *f.* [*an'-tsahl*] number
Anzahlung, -en *f.* [*an'-tsah-lung*] down payment
Anzeige, -n *f.* [*an'-tsai-gə*] advertisement
an-ziehen *v. irreg.* [*an'-tsee-en*] put on [clothes]; pull, attract
anziehend [*an'-tsee-ənt*] attractive
Anziehungskraft, ≃e *f.* [*an'-tsee-ungs-kraft*] attraction
Anzug, ≃e *m.* [*an'-tsook, an'-tsüh-gə*] suit [clothes]
an-zünden *v.* [*an'-tsün-dən*] light, ignite
Apfel, ≃ *m.* [*a'-pfəl, e'-pfəl*] apple
Apfelbaum, ≃e *m.* [*a'-pfəl-boum, a'-pfəl-boi-mə*] apple tree
Apfelpastete, -n *f.* [*a'-pfəl-pa-steh-tə*] apple pie
Apfelsine, -n *f.* [*ap-fəl-zee'-nə*] orange
Apfelwein *m.* [*a'-pfəl-vain*] cider
Apotheke, -n *f.* [*a-po-teh'-kə*] pharmacy, drugstore
Apotheker, - *m.* [*a-po-teh'-kər*] druggist
Apparat, -e *m.* [*a-pa-raht'*] apparatus
Appetit, -e *m.* [*a-pe-teet'*] appetite
Aprikose, -n *f.* [*a-pri-koh'-zə*] apricot
April *m.* [*a-pril'*] April
Äquivalent, -e *n.* [*e-kvi-va-lent'*] equivalent
Araber, - *m.* [*ah'-ra-bər*] Arab [male]
Araberin, -nen *f.* [*ah'-ra-bə-rin*] Arab [female]
arabisch [*a-rah'-bish*] Arabic
Arbeit, -en *f.* [*ar'-bait*] work, labor, job
arbeiten *v.* [*ar'-bai-ten*] work, labor
Arbeiter, - *m.* [*ar'-bai-tər*] laborer, worker
Arbeitgeber, - *m.* [*ar'-bait-geh-bər*] employer [male]
Arbeitgeberin, -nen *f.* [*ar'-bait-geh-be-rin*] employer [female]
arbeitslos [*ar'-baits-lohs*] unemployed
Architekt, -en *m.* [*ar-çi-tekt'*] architect

Architektur, -en f. [ar-çi-tek-toor'] architecture
Ärger m. [er'-gər] resentment
ärgern v. [er'-gərn] annoy, vex
argwöhnisch [ark'-vöh-nish] suspicious, distrustful
Aristokrat, -n m. [a-ri-sto-kraht'] aristocrat
aristokratisch [a-ri-sto-krah'-tish] aristocratic
arm [arm] poor
Arm, -e m. [arm] arm [anat.]
Armband, ⸗er n. [arm'-bant, arm'-ben-dər] bracelet
Armbanduhr, -en f. [arm'-bant-oor] wristwatch
Armee, -n f. [ar-meh', ar-mehn'] army
Ärmel, - m. [er'-məl] sleeve
Armut f. [ar'-moot] poverty
Art, -en f. [ahrt] kind, sort; way; manners
Arterie, -n f. [ar-teh'-ri-ə] artery
Artikel, - m. [ar-tee'-kəl] article, item
Arznei, -en f. [arts-nai'] remedy, medicine
Arzt, ⸗e m. [ahrtst, ehrt'-stə] physician [male]
    Rufen Sie den Arzt! [roo'-fən zee den ahrtst] Call the
      doctor!
Ärztin, -nen f. [ehrt'-stin] physician [female]
Asche, -n f. [a'-shə] ash
Aschenbecher, - m. [a'-shən-be-çər] ashtray
Asien n. [ah'-zi-ən] Asia
Astronomie f. [a-stro-no-mee'] astronomy
atemlos [ah'-tem-lohs] breathless
Atemzug, ⸗e m. [ah'-təm-tsook, ah'-təm-tsüh-gə] breath
atletisch [at-leh'-tish] athletic
atmen v. [aht'-mən] breathe
Atmosphäre, -n f. [at-mo-sfeh'-rə] atmosphere
auch [oukh] also, too
auf prep. (plus dat. or acc.) [ouf] on, in, at, of, by, to
auf adv. [ouf] up, open
    auf und ab [ouf unt ap] up and down
    auf immer [ouf i'-mər] forever
Aufbewahrung, -en f. [ouf'-bə-vah-rung] storage, keeping
auf-bringen v. irreg. [ouf'-bring-ən] bring up [a topic]; enrage
auf-decken v. [ouf'-de-kən] uncover, disclose

aufeinanderfolgend [*ouf-ai-nan'-dər-fol-gənt*] successive

Aufenthalt, -e *m.* [*ouf'-ent-halt*] stay, residence

auffallend [*ouf'-fa-lənt*] conspicuous, striking

Aufgabe, -n *f.* [*ouf'-gah-bə*] task, problem, homework, challenge

auf-geben *v. irreg.* [*ouf'-geh-bən*] abandon, give up

aufgeregt [*ouf'-gə-rehkt*] excited, upset

auf-halten *v. irreg.* [*ouf'-halt-ən*] keep open; detain

auf-heben *v. irreg.* [*ouf'-heh-bən*] pick up, lift; break off [engagement]; keep

auf-hören *v.* [*ouf'-höh-rən*] discontinue, stop

auf-lösen *v.* [*ouf'-löh-zən*] undo, dissolve [business, marriage]

auf-machen *v.* [*ouf'-ma-khən*] open; undo [a dress]

aufmerksam [*ouf'-merk-sam*] thoughtful, kind, attentive

Aufnahme, -n *f.* [*ouf'-nah-mə*] snapshot; reception

auf-passen *v.* [*ouf'-pa-sən*] pay attention

auf-räumen *v.* [*ouf'-roi-mən*] put in order

auf-regen *v.* [*ouf'-reh-gən*] excite

   Regen Sie sich nicht auf! [*reh'-gən zee ziç niçt ouf*] Don't get excited!

aufregend [*ouf'-reh-gənt*] thrilling

Aufruhr, -e *m.* [*ouf'-roor*] riot, turmoil

auf-schieben *v. irreg.* [*ouf'-shee-bən*] postpone, put off

auf-schliessen *v. irreg.* [*ouf'-shlee-sən*] unlock

Aufschnitt, -e *m.* [*ouf'-shnit*] cold cuts

auf-stehen *v. irreg.* (*Aux:* SEIN) [*ouf'-shteh-ən*] stand up, rise, revolt, get up

auf-stellen *v.* [*ouf'-shte-lən*] set up, erect; make [assertion]

Aufstieg, -e *m.* [*ouf'-shteek, ouf'-shtee-gə*] ascent

Auftrag, ⸗e *m.* [*ouf'-trahk, ouf'-treh-gə*] commission, order

aufwärts [*ouf'-verts*] upwards

Aufzug, ⸗e *m.* [*ouf'-tsook, ouf'-tsüh-gə*] elevator

Auge, -n *n.* [*ou'-gə*] eye

Augenarzt, ⸗e *m.* [*ou'-gən-ahrtst, ou'-gən-ehrt-stə*] oculist

Augenblick, -e *m.* [*ou'-gən-blik*] moment

Augenbraue, -n *f.* [*ou'-gən-brou-ə*] eyebrow

Augenlid, -er *n.* [*ou'-gən-leet, ou'-gən-lee-dər*] eyelid

August *m.* [*ou-gust'*] August

aus *prep.* (plus dat.) [*ous*] out of, from, of, by, for, on,
    upon, in
aus *adv.* [*ous*] over
    Das Spiel ist aus [*das shpeel ist ous*] The game is over
    Der Tee ist aus [*dehr teh ist ous*] We are out of tea
aus-arbeiten *v.* [*ous'-ar-bai-tən*] work out, elaborate
aus-bessern *v.* [*ous'-be-sərn*] mend, repair
aus-bilden *v.* [*ous'-bil-dən*] educate, train [for occupation]
Ausbildung, -en *f.* [*ous'-bil-dung*] education, training
aus-brechen *v. irreg.* [*ous'-bre-çən*] break out; vomit
aus-dehnen *v.* [*ous'-deh-nən*] stretch, extend
aus-drücken *v.* [*ous'-drü-kən*] express; press, squeeze
Ausflug, ᵋe *m.* [*ous'-flook, ous'-flüh-gə*] excursion, outing
Ausgabe, -n *f.* [*ous'-gah-bə*] expense; edition [of book]
Ausgang, ᵋe *m.* [*ous'-gang, ous'-geng-ə*] exit
aus-geben *v. irreg.* [*ous'-geh-bən*] spend [money]
aus-gehen *v. irreg.* [*ous'-geh-ən*] go out
ausgezeichnet [*ous-gə-tsaiç'-nət*] excellent, splendid
aus-halten *v. irreg.* [*ous'-hal-tən*] bear, endure, stand
Ausland *n.* [*ous'-lant*] foreign country, foreign parts
Ausländer, - *m.* [*ous'-len-dər*] foreigner [male]
Ausländerin, -nen *f.* [*ous'-len-də-rin*] foreigner [female]
ausländisch [*ous'-len-dish*] foreign
aus-löschen *v.* [*ous'-lö-shən*] extinguish
aus-machen *v.* [*ous'-ma-khen*] put out [light]; make up
    [sum]; settle [dispute]
Ausnahme, -n *f.* [*ous'-nah-mə*] exception
aus-nützen *v.* [*ous'-nü-tsən*] take advantage of
aus-packen *v.* [*ous'-pa-kən*] unpack
Ausrede, -n *f.* [*ous'-reh-də*] excuse; pretense
Ausrüstung, -en *f.* [*ous'-rü-stung*] equipment
aus-rutschen *v.* [*ous'-rut-shən*] slip
aus-schalten *v.* [*ous'-shal-tən*] turn off [light]
aus-schliessen *v. irreg.* [*ous'-shlee-sen*] exclude, expel
aus-sehen *v. irreg.* [*ous'-seh-ən*] look [like], appear
    Er sieht gut aus [*ehr zeet goot ous*] He looks well
Aussenpolitik *f.* [*ou'-sən-po-li-teek*] foreign policy
ausser *prep.* (plus dat.) [*ou'-sər*] except

ausserdem [*ou'-sər-dehm*] besides

ausser wenn *conj.* [*ou'-sər ven*] unless

Äussere, -n *n.* [*oi'-sə-rə*] exterior

ausserhalb *prep.* (plus gen.) [*ou'-sər-halp*] outside

äusserst [*oi'-sərst*] extreme

Aussicht, -en *f.* [*ous'-ziçt*] view, prospect

Aussprache, -n *f.* [*ous'-shprah-khə*] pronunciation

aus-sprechen *v. irreg.* [*ous'-shpre-çən*] pronounce

   Wie sprechen Sie das aus? [*vee shpre'-çən zee das ous*]
     How do you pronounce it?

aus-spülen *v.* [*ous'-shpüh-lən*] flush, wash away

Ausstattung, -en *f.* [*ous'-shta-tung*] outfit; dowry

aus-steigen *v. irreg.* [*ous'-shtai-gən*] get off

aus-stellen *v.* [*ous'-shte-lən*] display, exhibit

Ausstellung, -en *f.* [*ous'-shte-lung*] show, exhibition

aus-suchen *v.* [*ous'-zoo-khən*] select, choose

aus-tauschen *v.* [*ous'-tou-shən*] exchange

Auster, -n *f.* [*ou'-stər*] oyster

aus-üben *v.* [*ous'-üh-bən*] exercise, practice [profession]

Ausverkauf, ⁼e *m.* [*ous'-fer-kouf, ous'-fer-koi-fə*] clearance
   sale

Auswahl, -en *f.* [*ous'-vahl*] assortment

aus-wählen *v.* [*ous'-veh-lən*] choose

Auswanderer, - *m.* [*ous'-van-de-rər*] emigrant

Ausweiskarte, -n *f.* [*ous'-vais-kar-tə*] identification card

auswendig [*ous'-ven-diç*] by heart

aus-ziehen *v. irreg.* [*ous'-tsee-ən*] take out, extract; take off
   [garment]

authentisch [*ou-ten'-tish*] authentic

Auto, -s *n.* [*ou'-toh, ou'-tohs*] car, auto

Autobahn, -en *f.* [*ou'-to-bahn*] superhighway

Autofahrer, - *m.* [*ou'-toh-fah-rər*] motorist

automatisch [*ou-to-mah'-tish*] automatic

Autor, -en *m.* [*ou'-tor, ou-toh'-rən*] author

Axt, ⁼e *f.* [*akst, ek'-stə*] axe

B

Baby, Babies *n.* [*beh'-bi, beh'-bis*] baby
Bach, ⸗e *m.* [*bakh, be'-çe*] brook
Backe, -n *f.* [*ba'-kə*] cheek
backen *v. irreg.* [*ba'-kən*] bake
Bäcker, - *m.* [*be'-kər*] baker
Bäckerei, -en *f.* [*be-kə-rai'*] bakery
Bad, ⸗er *n.* [*baht, beh'-der*] bath, bathroom
  ein Bad nehmen *v.* [*ain baht neh'-mən*] take a bath
Badeanzug, ⸗e *m.* [*bah'-də-an-tsook, bah'-də-an-tsüh-gə*]
    bathing suit
baden *v.* [*bah'-dən*] bathe
Badewanne, -en *f.* [*bah'-də-va-nə*] bathtub
Badezimmer, - *n.* [*bah'-də-tsi-mər*] bathroom
Bahn, -en *f.* [*bahn*] course; railway; rink [skating]
Bahnhof, ⸗e *m.* [*bahn'-hohf, bahn'-höh-fə*] railroad station
Bahnsteig, -e *m.* [*bahn'-shtaik, bahn'-shtai-gə*]
    platform [train]
bald [*balt*] soon, by and by
  sobald wie [*zo-balt' vee*] as soon as
  Wie bald? [*vee balt*] How soon?
Balkon, -e *m.* [*bal-kon'*] balcony
Ball ⸗e *m.* [*bal, be'-lə*] ball; dance
Ballett, -e *n.* [*ba-let'*] ballet
Banane, -n *f.* [*ba-nah'-ne*] banana
Band, ⸗er *n.* [*bant, ben'-dər*] ribbon
Band, -e *n.* [*bant, ban'-də*] bond [tie]
Band, -e *m.* [*bant, ben-'də*] volume, book
Bank, - ⸗e *f.* [*bangk, beng'-kə*] bench
Bank, -en *f.* [*bangk, bang'-kən*] bank
Bankkonto, -s *n.* [*bank'-kon-toh, bank'-kon-tohs*]
    checking account
Banknote, -n *f.* [*bank'-noh-tə*] bank note

Bar, -s *f.* [*bahr, bahrs*] bar
Bär, -en *m.* [*behr*] bear
barfuss [*bahr'-foos*] barefoot
Bargeld *n.* [*bahr'-gelt*] cash
barhäuptig [*bahr'-hoip-tiç*] bareheaded
Barock *m.* [*ba-rok'*] baroque
Baron, -e *m.* [*ba-rohn'*] baron
Barrikade, -n *f.* [*ba-ri-kah'-də*] barricade
Bart, ⸗e *m.* [*bahrt, behr'-tə*] beard
bartlos [*bahrt'-lohs*] beardless
Basis *f. sing.* **Basen** *pl.* [*bah'-zis, bah'-zən*] base
Batterie, -n *f.* [*ba-tə-ree'*] battery
Bau, -ten *m.* [*bou, bou'-tən*] construction, building
Bauch, ⸗e *m.* [*boukh, boi'-çə*] belly
bauen *v.* [*bou'-ən*] build
Bauer, -n *m.* [*bou'-ər*] farmer, peasant
Bäuerin, -nen *f.* [*boi'-ə-rin*] farmer's wife
Bauernhof, ⸗e *m.* [*bou'-ərn-hohf, bou'-ərn-höh-fə*] farm
Baum, ⸗e *m.* [*boum, boi'-mə*] tree
Baumwolle, -n *f.* [*boum'-vo-lə*] cotton
beabsichtigen *v.* [*bə-ap'-ziç-ti-gən*] intend, mean
Beamte, -n *m., f.* [*bə-am'-tə*] official, civil servant
Becher, - *m.* [*be'-çər*] cup, goblet, mug
Becken, - *n.* [*be'-kən*] basin; pelvis
bedauern *v.* [*bə-dou'-ərn*] be sorry for, pity [someone];
     regret [something]
bedecken *v.* [*bə-de'-kən*] cover
bedeuten *v.* [*bə-doi'-tən*] mean
     Was bedeutet das? [*vas bə-doi'-tət das*] What does it mean?
Bedeutung, -en *f.* [*be-doi'-tung*] significance, meaning
bedienen *v.* [*be-dee'-nən*] serve, wait on
Bedingungen *f. pl.* [*bə-ding'-ung-ən*] terms
Beefsteak, -s *n.* [*beef'-stehk, beef'-stehks*] beefsteak
beeinflussen *v.* [*bə-ain'-flu-sən*] influence
beenden *v.* [*bə-en'-dən*] finish, end
Beere, -n *f.* [*beh'-rə*] berry
Befangenheit, -en *f.* [*bə-fang'-ən-hait*] self-consciousness
Befehl, -e *m.* [*bə-fehl'*] order, command

befehlen *v. irreg.* [*bə-feh'-lən*] command
befestigen *v.* [*bə-fe'-sti-gən*] fasten, fortify
Beförderung, -en *f.* [*bə-för'-də-rung*] promotion
befreien *v.* [*bə-frai'-ən*] free
befriedigen *v.* [*bə-free'-di-gən*] satisfy
begabt [*bə-gahpt'*] talented, gifted
begegnen *v.* (*Aux:* SEIN) [*bə-gehg'-nən*] meet [by accident]
begehen *v. irreg.* [*bə-geh'-ən*] commit
   Selbstmord begehen [*zelpst'-mort bə-geh'-ən*]
     commit suicide
beginnen *v. irreg.* [*bə-gi'-nən*] begin
begleiten *v.* [*bə-glai'-tən*] accompany
Begleiter, - *m.* [*bə-glai'-tər*] escort, attendant,
   accompanist [music]
begraben *v. irreg.* [*bə-grah'-bən*] bury
Begräbnis, -se *n.* [*bə-grehp'-nis, bə-grehp'-ni-sə*] burial,
   funeral
begreifen *v. irreg.* [*bə-grai'-fən*] comprehend
Begriff, -e *m.* [*bə-grif'*] concept, idea
behalten *v. irreg.* [*bə-hal'-tən*] retain, keep
Behälter, - *m.* [*bə-hel'-tər*] container, box
behandeln *v.* [*bə-han'-dəln*] treat, deal with [a topic]
Behandlung, -en *f.* [*bə-hand'-lung*] treatment
behaupten *v.* [*bə-houp'-tən*] maintain
behilflich [*bə-hilf'-liç*] helpful
bei *prep.* (plus dat.) [*bai*] near, at, by
Beichte, -n *f.* [*baiç'-tə*] confession
beide [*bai'-də*] both
Beifall *m.* [*bai'-fal*] applause
Beifallsruf, -e *m.* [*bai'-fals-roof*] cheer [of applause]
Beileid *n.* [*bai'-lait*] sympathy, condolence
   mein herzlichstes Beileid [*main herts'-liç-stəs bai'-lait*]
     my deepest sympathy
beim: bei dem [*baim*] near the, at the, by the
Bein, -e *n.* [*bain*] leg
beinahe [*bai'-na-hə*] almost, nearly
beiseite [*bai-zai'-tə*] aside
Beispiel, -e *n.* [*bai'-shpeel*] example

zum Beispiel [*tsum bai'-shpeel*] for instance, for example
beissen *v. irreg.* [*bai'-sən*] bite
Beistand, ⸗e *m.* [*bai'-shtant, bai'-shten-də*] assistance
bei-wohnen (plus dat.) *v.* [*bai'-voh-nən*] attend
bejahen *v.* [*bə-yah'-ən*] affirm
bejahrt [*bə-yahrt'*] elderly
bekannt [*bə-kant'*] familiar, known
bekannt machen *v.* [*bə-kant' ma'-khən*] acquaint, introduce
bekehren *v.* [*bə-keh'-rən*] convert
Bekehrte, -n *m., f.* [*bə-kehr'-tə*] convert
beklagen *v.* [*bə-klah'-gən*] lament, deplore
  sich beklagen [*ziç bə-klah'-gən*] complain
bekommen *v. irreg.* [*bə-ko'-mən*] get, receive
belasten *v.* [*bə-la'-stən*] burden
beleben *v.* [*bə-leh'-bən*] animate
belegen *v.* [*bə-leh'-gən*] register [for course of lectures]; verify
beleidigen *v.* [*bə-lai'-di-gən*] offend, insult
Beleidigung, -en *f.* [*bə-lai'-di-gung*] offense, insult
beleidigend [*bə-lai'-di-gənt*] offensive
Belgien *n.* [*bel'-gi-ən*] Belgium
belgisch [*bel'-gish*] Belgian
Beliebtheit *f.* [*bə-leept'-hait*] popularity
belohnen *v.* [*bə-loh'-nən*] reward
Belohnung, -en *f.* [*bə-loh'-nung*] reward
bemerken *v.* [*bə-mer'-kən*] notice, remark
bemerkenswert [*bə-mer'-kəns-vehrt*] remarkable
Bemerkung, -en *f.* [*bə-mer'-kung*] remark
(sich) bemühen *v.* [(*ziç*) *bə-müh'-ən*] trouble; give trouble
  Bemühen Sie sich nicht! [*bə-müh'-ən zee ziç niçt*]
    Don't bother!
Benehmen *n.* [*bə-neh'-mən*] conduct, behavior
(sich) benehmen *v. irreg.* [(*ziç*) *bə-neh'-mən*] behave
beneiden *v.* [*bə-nai'-dən*] envy
benötigen *v.* [*bə-nöh'-ti-gən*] need, require
benutzen *v.* [*bə-nu'-tsən*] use
  die Gelegenheit benutzen [*dee gə-leh'-gən-hait*
    bə-nu'-tsən] take the opportunity
Benzin *n.* [*ben-tseen'*] gasoline

beobachten v. [bə-ohb'-akh-tən] observe

bequem [be-kvehm'] comfortable
  Machen Sie sich bequem! [ma'-khən zee ziç bə-kvehm'] Make yourself comfortable!

beraten v. irreg. [bə-rah'-tən] advise, deliberate

Beratung, -en f. [bə-rah'-tung] debate, conference

berechnen v. [bə-reç'-nən] calculate

Bereich, -e m. [bə-raiç'] range, reach

bereit [bə-rait'] ready, prepared, willing

bereuen v. [bə-roi'-ən] repent, regret

Berg, -e m. [berk, ber'-gə] mountain

bergauf [berk-ouf'] uphill

Bergmann m. sing. **Bergleute** pl. [berk'-man, berk'-loi-tə] miner

Bergwerk, -e n. [berk'-verk] mine

Bericht, -e m. [bə-riçt'] report

Berichterstatter, - m. [bə-riçt'-er-shta-tər] reporter [male]

Berichterstatterin, -nen f. [bə-riçt'-er-shta-tə-rin] reporter [female]

berichtigen v. [bə-riç'-ti-gən] rectify

bersten v. irreg. (Aux: SEIN) [ber'-stən] burst

Beruf, -e m. [bə-roof'] profession, vocation

beruflich [bə-roof'-liç] vocational, professional

(sich) beruhigen v. [(ziç) be-roo'-i-gən] calm down

berühmt [bə-rühmt'] famous

berühren v. [bə-rüh'-rən] touch

Berührung, -en f. [bə-rüh'-rung] touch, contact
  in Berührung kommen mit v., [in bə-rüh'-rung ko'-mən mit] come into contact with

beschädigt [bə-sheh'-diçt] damaged

beschäftigt [bə-shef'-tiçt] busy, employed

Beschäftigung, -en f. [bə-shef'-ti-gung] employment, occupation

beschämen v. [bə-sheh'-mən] shame

beschämt [be-shehmt'] ashamed

bescheiden [bə-shai'-dən] modest, unassuming

Bescheidenheit f. [bə-shai'-dən-hait] modesty

beschliessen v. irreg. [bə-shlee'-sən] end, resolve

beschmutzt [bə-shmutst'] soiled

beschreiben v. irreg. [bə-shrai'-ben] describe

Beschreibung, -en f. [bə-shrai'-bung] description

beschuldigen v. [bə-shul'-di-gən] accuse

Besen, - m. [beh'-zən] broom

besetzen v. [bə-ze'-tsən] occupy

besetzt [bə-zetst'] occupied [seat, country]

besichtigen v. [bə-ziç'-ti-gən] inspect

besiegen v. [bə-zee'-gən] conquer, defeat

Besitz m. sing. **Besitztümer** pl. [bə-zits', bə-zits'-tüh-mər]
    possession, property

besitzen v. irreg. [bə-zi'-tsən] own, possess

Besitzer, - m. [bə-zi'-tsər] owner

besonder [bə-zon'-dər] special, peculiar

besprechen v. irreg. [bə-shpre'-çən] discuss; review [book]

besprengen v. [bə-shpreng'-ən] sprinkle

besser [be'-sər] better, superior

besser machen v., [be'-sər ma'-khən] mend [matters]

best [best] best

beständig [bə-shten'-diç] constant, lasting

bestätigen v. [bə-shteh'-ti-gən] confirm, verify

bestechen v. irreg. [bə-shte'-çən] bribe, corrupt

Bestechungsgeld, -er n. [bə-shte'-çungz-gəlt, bə-shte'-
    çungz-gel-dər] bribe

bestehen v. irreg. [bə-shteh'-ən] stand; pass [test]; exist
  bestehen auf (plus dat.) [bə-shteh'-ən ouf] insist on
  bestehen aus (plus dat.) [bə-shteh'-ən ous] consist of

besteigen v. irreg. [bə-shtai'-gən] climb up [mountain];
    board [bus, train]

bestellen v. [bə-shte'-lən] order [something]
  Ist etwas zu bestellen? [ist et'-vas tsu be-shte'-len]
    Are there any messages?

besteuern v. [bə-shtoi'-ərn] tax

bestimmen v. [bə-shti'-mən] determine, appoint [time, place]

bestimmt [bə-shtimt'] determined, positive, definite

bestrafen v. [bə-shtrah'-fən] punish

Besuch, -e m. [bə-zookh'] visit, visitor

besuchen v. [be-zoo'-khən] visit, attend

Besucher, - *m.* [bə-zoo'-khər] visitor

Besuchszeit *f.* [bə-zookhs'-tsait] visiting hours

beten *v.* [beh'-tən] pray

betonen *v.* [bə-toh'-nən] accent, emphasize

Betonung, -en *f.* [bə-toh'-nung] stress, emphasis

betreffend [bə-tre'-fənd] pertaining to

betreten *v. irreg.* [bə-treh'-tən] set foot on/in; enter

    Betreten des Rasens verboten [bə-treh'-tən des rah'-zəns fer-boh'-tən] Keep off the grass

Betrug, ⸚ereien *m.* [bə-trook', bə-troog-ə-rai'-ən] deception, fraud

betrügen *v. irreg.* [bə-trüh'-gən] cheat, defraud

Bett, -en *n.* [bet] bed

Bettdecke, -n *f.* [bet'-de-kə] bed cover

Bettler, - *m.* [bet'-lər] beggar

Bettuch, ⸚er *n.* [bet'-tookh, bet'-tüh-çər] sheet [bed]

beunruhigen *v.* [bə-un'-ruh-i-gən] alarm

Beutel, - *m.* [boi'-təl] bag, purse

Bevölkerung, -en *f.* [bə-föl'-kə-rung] population

bevor *conj.* [bə-fohr]' before

bewaffnen *v.* [bə-vaf'-nən] arm

Bewässerung, -en *f.* [bə-ve'-sə-rung] irrigation

bewegen *v.* [bə-veh'-gən] move, stir

Bewegung, -en *f.* [bə-veh'-gung] movement, motion, exercise

Beweis, -e *m.* [bə-vais', bə-vai'-zə] proof, evidence

beweisen *v. irreg.* [bə-vai'-zən] prove, show [interest]

Bewerbung, -en *f.* [bə-ver'-bung] application

Bewohner, - *m.* [bə-voh'-nər] resident

bewundern *v.* [bə-vun'-dərn] admire

bewundernswert [bə-vun'-dərns-vehrt] admirable

bewusst [be-vust'] conscious, aware, deliberate

bezahlen *v.* [be-tsah'-lən] pay

    Was habe ich zu bezahlen? [vas hah'-bə iç tsu bə-tsah'-lən] What is the fare?

Bezahlung, -en *f.* [bə-tsah'-lung] payment

bezaubern *v.* [bə-tsou'-bərn] fascinate

bezaubernd [bə-tsou'-bərnt] fascinating, enchanting

bezeichnen (als) *v.* [bə-tsaiç'-nən (als)] describe (as)

Why We Make This Generous Offer

There are three important reasons why the Cortina Institute of Languages is pleased to make this special Free Cassette and Sample Lesson offer:

First, never before have there been so many fascinating opportunities open to those who speak foreign languages fluently. Besides the cultural and travel benefits, there are many practical dollars-and-cents advantages—and an ever-increasing number of interesting, well-paying jobs.

The Natural Method

Second, our long experience in the language field has convinced us that the "learn-by-listening" method is the fastest, most convenient and most effective one. It enables you to learn *naturally*—the way you learned English as a child. You acquire a perfect accent and perfect grammar—because that's all you hear.

Just Listen—and Learn

Finally, our professional standing in the field of languages has enabled us to make these generous arrangements with one of the foremost language schools—the inventors of the "learn-by-listening" method. And we are pleased to provide this service for those of our students who want to speak and understand a foreign language "like a native."

There is no obligation and *no salesman will call.* Just mail the card TODAY for your FREE Cassette and Sample Lesson.

--- **What Others Say:** ---

Bob Hope says... "I am studying the course in French... I think it's a great way to study a language."

Enjoyed by Children "It is surprising how much our two children have absorbed by listening."
—Mrs. C.M.J.

"A Good Investment" "Just returned from Mexico ... Course good investment!"
—Phillips B. Iden

CORTINA INSTITUTE OF LANGUAGES
19 Newtown Turnpike, Westport, CT 06880

You may call us toll-free at 1-800-245-2145. To receive your FREE Cassette and Lesson, be sure to ask for Department HHTD.

CORTINA INSTITUTE OF LANGUAGES
Dept. HHTD, 19 Newtown Turnpike
Westport, CT 06880

Please have the originators of the famous "learn-by-listening" method send me, FREE, the Sample Record and Lesson in the one language checked below—also information which describes fully the complete course anc method.

▲ **Please check FREE Language Recording and Lesson you wish:**

☐ Spanish ☐ French ☐ German ☐ Italian ☐ Brazilian-Portuguese
☐ Russian ☐ Japanese ☐ Modern Greek ☐ English (for Spanish-or
☐ Arabic   Portuguese-speaking people)

Name _____

Address _____

City _____ State _____ Zip Code _____

Phone (_____) _____
        Area

This offer limited to USA and Canada
due to foreign customs regulations.

HHTD/893/70M

(sich) beziehen auf (plus acc.) *v. irreg.* [(ziç) bə-tsee'-ən ouf]
  refer to
beziehen *v.* [bə-tsee'-ən] draw [salary]; subscribe to
Bezirk, -e *m.* [bə-tsirk'] district
Bezug, ⸚e *m.* [bə-tsook', bə-tsüh'-gə] cover, subscription
  in Bezug auf (plus acc.) [in bə-tsook' ouf] with reference to
Bibel, -n *f.* [bee'-bəl] bible
Bibliothek, -en *f.* [bib-li-o-tehk'] library
(sich) biegen *v. irreg.* [(ziç) bee'-gən] bend
Biene, -n *f.* [bee'-nə] bee
Bier, -e *n.* [beer] beer
Bilanz, -en *f.* [bi-lants'] balance
Bild, -er *n.* [bilt, bil'-dər] picture
bilden *v.* [bil'-den] form, educate
billig [bi'-liç] cheap
billigen *v.* [bi'-li-gən] approve
Billigung, -en *f.* [bi'-li-gung] approval
Binde, -n *f.* [bin'-də] bandage
binden *v. irreg.* [bin'-dən] tie
Birne, -n *f.* [bir'-nə] pear
bis *conj.* [bis] till; until
bis *prep.* (an plus acc.; auf plus acc.; zu plus dat.) [bis]
  till; to; as far as
  bis vier zählen [bis feer tseh'-lən] count up to four
  Alle blieben bis auf drei [a'-lə blee'-ben bis auf drai]
    All stayed except three
Bischof, ⸚e *m.* [bi'-shohf, bi'-shöh-fə] bishop
Bitte, -n *f.* [bi'-tə] request
bitten (um plus acc.) *v. irreg.* [bi'-tən (um)] request, ask
  Bitte! [bi'-tə] Please!
  Bitte schön [bi'-tə shöhn] You are welcome
bitter [bi'-tər] bitter
Bittschrift, -en *f.* [bit'-shrift] petition
blank [blank] blank; shining
Blase, -n *f.* [blah'-zə] blister; bladder
blasen *v. irreg.* [blah'-zən] blow
Blatt, ⸚er *n.* [blat, ble'-tər] sheet [of paper], leaf
  [of plant or book]; (news)paper

blau [*blou*] blue

Blei *n.* [*blai*] lead [metal]

bleiben *v. irreg. (Aux:* SEIN) [*blai'-bən*] stay, remain
  Bleiben Sie draussen! [*blai'-bən zee drou'-sən*] Keep out!
  Bleiben Sie hier! [*blai'-bən zee heer*] Stay here!

bleich [*blaiç*] pale

Bleistift, -e *m.* [*blai'-shtift*] pencil

Blick, -e *m.* [*blik*] view, glance

blind [*blint*] blind

Blinddarmentzündung, -en *f.* [*blint'-darm-ent-tsün-dung*]
    appendicitis

Blindheit *f.* [*blint'-hait*] blindness

Blitz, -e *m.* [*blits*] lightning

blond [*blont*] blond, fair

bloss [*blohs*] merely

blühen *v.* [*blüh'-ən*] blossom

Blume, -n *f.* [*bloo'-mə*] flower

Blumengeschäft, -e *n.* [*bloo'-mən-gə-sheft*] flower shop

Bluse, -n *f.* [*bloo'-zə*] blouse

Blut *n.* [*bloot*] blood

Blüte, -n *f.* [*blüh'-tə*] blossom

bluten *v.* [*bloo'-tən*] bleed

Boden, ⁼ *m.* [*boh'-dən, böh'-dən*] ground, bottom; loft
    [of house]

Bogen, ⁼ *m.* [*boh'-gən, böh'-gən*] arch; bow [archery];
    sheet [paper]

Bohne, -n *f.* [*boh'-nə*] bean
  grüne Bohnen [*grüh'-nə boh'-nən*] string beans

bohren *v.* [*boh'-rən*] bore, drill

Bombe, -n *f.* [*bom'-bə*] bomb

Bonbons *n. pl.* [*bon-bons'*] hard candy

Boot, -e *n.* [*boht*] boat

Börse, -n *f.* [*bör'-zə*] stock exchange; purse

Börsenmakler, - *m.* [*bör'-zən-mahk-lər*] stockbroker

böse [*böh'-zə*] evil, wicked, spiteful; angry

Bösewicht, -e *m.* [*böh'-ze-viçt*] villain

Boss, -e *m.* [*bos*] boss

Bote, -n *m.* [*boh'-tə*] messenger

Botengang, ⸗e *m.* [*boh'-tən-gang, boh'-tən-geng-ə*] errand
Botschaft, -en *f.* [*boht'-shaft*] embassy; message
Boxen *n.* [*bok'-sən*] boxing [sport]
Brand, ⸗e *m.* [*brant, bren'-də*] fire, conflagration
Brandung *f.* [*bran'-dung*] surf, breakers
Brandwunde, -n *f.* [*brant'-vun-də*] burn
Brasilien *n.* [*bra-zee'-li-ən*] Brazil
brasilisch [*bra-zee'-lish*] Brazilian
braten *v.* [*brah'-tən*] roast, fry
Braten, - *m.* [*brah'-ten*] roast
Bratpfanne, -n *f.* [*braht'-pfa-nə*] frying pan
brauchen *v.* [*brou'-khən*] need, use
braun [*broun*] brown
Bräune *f.* [*broi'-nə*] tan
Brause, -n *f.* [*brou'-zə*] shower
Braut, ⸗e *f.* [*brout, broi'-tə*] fiancee
Bräutigam, -e *m.* [*broi'-ti-gam*] bridegroom
Brautjungfer, -n *f.* [*brout'-yung-fər*] bridesmaid
brav [*brahf*] honest, good
brechen *v. irreg.* [*bre'-çən*] break
breit [*brait*] broad
Bremse, -n *f.* [*brem'-ze*] brake
bremsen *v.* [*brem'-zən*] brake
brennen *v. irreg.* [*bre'-nən*] burn
Brennpunkt, -e *m.* [*bren'-punkt*] focus
Brett, -er *n.* [*bret, bre'-tər*] board
Brief, -e *m.* [*breef*] letter [mail]
Briefkasten, ⸗ *m.* [*breef'-ka-stən, breef'-ke-stən*] mailbox
Briefmarke, -n *f.* [*breef'-mar-kə*] stamp [postage]
Briefmarkensammler, - *m.* [*breef'-mar-kən-zam-lər*]
   stamp collector
Brieftasche, -n *f.* [*breef'-ta-shə*] pocketbook, wallet
Briefträger, - *m.* [*breef'-treh-gər*] mailman
Briefwechsel, - *m.* [*breef'-ve-ksəl*] correspondence
Brille, -n *f.* [*bri'-lə*] eyeglasses
bringen *v. irreg.* [*bring'-ən*] bring
Brise, -n *f.* [*bree'-zə*] breeze
Britannien *n.* [*bri-ta'-ni-ən*] Britain

britisch [*bri'-tish*] British

Bronze, -n *f.* [*bron'-sə*] bronze

Brot, -e *n.* [*broht*] bread

Brötchen, - *n.* [*bröht'-çən*] roll

Bruch, ≠e *m.* [*brukh, brü'-çə*] fracture; fraction; violation

Brücke, -n *f.* [*brü'-kə*] bridge

    eine Brücke schlagen über (plus acc.) *v. irreg.* [*ai'-nə brü'-kə shlah'-gən üh'-bər*] bridge

Bruder, ≠ *m.* [*broo'-dər, brüh'-dər*] brother

Brühe, -n *f.* [*brüh'-ə*] broth

Brünette, -n *f.* [*brü-ne'-tə*] brunette

Brunnen, - *m.* [*bru'-nən*] spring, well, fountain

Brust, ≠e *f.* [*brust, brü'-stə*] breast, chest [anat.]

Buch, ≠er *n.* [*bookh, büh'-çər*] book

Bücherregal, -e *n.* [*büh'-çər-re-gahl*] bookshelf

Bücherschrank, ≠e *m.* [*büh'-çər-shrank, büh'-çər-shren-kə*] bookcase

Buchhalter, - *m.* [*bookh'-hal-tər*] bookkeeper

Buchhandlung, -en *f.* [*bookh'-hand-lung*] bookstore

Büchse, -n *f.* [*bük'-sə*] can; rifle

Buchstabe, -n *m.* [*bookh'-shtah-bə*] letter [of alphabet]

buchstabieren *v.* [*bookh-shta-bee'-rən*] spell out [words]

Bügeleisen, - *n.* [*büh'-gəl-ai-zən*] flatiron

bügeln *v.* [*büh'-geln*] iron, press [clothes]

Bühne, -n *f.* [*büh'-nə*] stage

Bulgarien *n.* [*bul-gah'-ri-en*] Bulgaria

bulgarisch [*bul-gah'-rish*] Bulgarian

Bummel, - *m.* [*bu'-mel*] stroll

bummeln *v.* [*bu'-məln*] loaf

Bündel, - *n.* [*bün'-dəl*] bundle

Bundesrepublik *f.* [*bun'-dəs-re-pub-leek*] Federal Republic [West Germany]

Bunker, - *m.* [*bun'-kər*] shelter [air attack]

Burg, -en *f.* [*burk, bur'-gən*] castle

Bürger, - *m.* [*bür'-gər*] citizen [male]

Bürgerin, -nen *f.* [*bür'-gə-rin*] citizen [female]

Bürgermeister, - *m.* [*bür'-gər-mai-stər*] mayor

Bürgerrecht *n.* [*bür'-gər-reçt*] citizenship; civil rights

Bürgersteig, -e *m.* [*bür'-gər-shtaik, bür'-gər-shtai-gə*] sidewalk

Büro, -s *n.* [*bü-roh', bü-rohs'*] office

bürokratisch [*bü-ro-krah'-tish*] red tape

Bursch, -en *m.* [*bursh*] young man, youth, lad

Bürste, -n *f.* [*bür'-stə*] brush

bürsten *v.* [*bür'-stən*] brush

Busen, - *m.* [*boo'-zən*] bosom

Büstenhalter, - *m.* [*bü'-stən-hal-tər*] brassiere

Butter *f.* [*bu'-tər*] butter

Butterbrot, -e *n.* [*bu'-tər-broht*] slice of bread and butter
  belegtes Butterbrot [*be-lehk'-təs bu'-tər-broht*] sandwich

C

Café, -s *n.* [*ka-feh', ka-fehs'*] cafe

Champagner *m.* [*sham-pan'-yar*] champagne

Charakter, -e *m.* [*ka-rak'-tər, ka-rak-teh'-rə*] character

Charakterzug, ⸗e *f.* [*ka-rak'-tər-tsook, ka-rak'-tər-tsüh-gə*] trait

Chauffeur, -e *m.* [*sho-föhr'*] chauffeur

Chemie *f.* [*çe-mee'*] chemistry

Chemiker, - *m.* [*çeh'-mi-kər*] chemist

chemisch reinigen *v.* [*çeh'-mish rai'-ni-gən*] dry-clean

Chile *n.* [*çi'-leh*] Chile

chilenisch [*çi-leh'-nish*] Chilean

China *n.* [*çee'-nah*] China

chinesisch [*çi-neh'-zish*] Chinese

Chirurg, -en *m.* [*çi-rurk', çi-rur'-gən*] surgeon

Chirurgie *f.* [*çi-rur-gee'*] surgery

Chor, ⸗e *m.* [*kohr, köh'-rə*] choir

christlich [*krist'-liç*] Christian

College, -s *n.* [*ko'-lidzh, ko'-li-dzhəs*] college

Couch, -es *f.* [*kouch, kou'-chəs*] couch

D

da *adv.* [*dah*] there
da *conj.* [*dah*] as, when, while, since
dabei [*da-bai'*] besides, nevertheless
Dach, ⸗er *n.* [*dakh, de'-çər*] roof
Dachstube, -n *f.* [*dakh'-shtuh-bə*] attic
dadurch [*da-durç'*] through it; thereby
dafür [*da-führ'*] for it
dagegen [*da-geh'-gən*] against it, on the other hand
daheim [*da-haim'*] at home
daher [*da-hehr'*] therefore, from there
dahinten *adv.* [*da-hin'-tən*] behind, behind there
Dame, -n *f.* [*dah'-mə*] lady
Damensalon, -s *m.* [*dah'-mən-sa-lohn, dah'-mən-sa-lohns*]
    beauty parlor
Damentoilette, -n *f.* [*dah'-mən-to-a-le-tə*] ladies' room
damit *adv.* [*da-mit'*] with it, by it
damit *conj.* [*da-mit'*] so that, in order that
Damm, ⸗e *m.* [*dam, de'-mə*] dam
Dämmerung, -en *f.* [*de'-mə-rung*] dusk, dawn
Dampf, ⸗e *m.* [*dampf, dem'-pfə*] steam, vapor
danach [*da-nahkh'*] afterwards, after that
daneben [*da-neh'-bən*] near it, next to it, beside
Dänemark *n.* [*deh'-nə-mark*] Denmark
dänisch [*deh'-nish*] Danish
Dank *m.* [*dank*] thanks, gratitude
    Besten Dank! [*bə'-stən dank*] Thank you very much!
dankbar [*dank'-bar*] thankful
danken (plus dat.) *v.* [*dan'-kən*] thank
    Danke schön! [*dan'-kə shöhn*] Thank you very much!
    Gott sei Dank! [*got zai dank*] Thank God!
dann [*dan*] then
    dann und wann [*dan unt van*] now and then

182

daran [*da-ran'*] on it, on that; at it, at that; to it, to that

daraus [*da-rous'*] from there, from this

darf *1st & 3d pers. sing. of* DÜRFEN [*darf*] is allowed to; may
Darf ich eintreten? [*darf iç ain'-treh-tən*] May I come in?

darin [*da-rin'*] in it, therein

Darm, ⸗e *m.* [*darm, der'-mə*] intestine

Darsteller, - *m.* [*dar'-shte-lər*] actor

darüber [*da-rüh'-bər*] over it, above it, about it

darum [*dah-rum'*; emphatic: *da-rum'*] therefore, for it

darunter [*da-run'-tər*] underneath, under it

das *n., def. art.* [*das*] the

das *n., dem. pron.* [*das*] it; that one, that, this, this one
Was ist das? [*vas ist das*] What is this?

das *n., rel. pron.* [*das*] who, whom, which, that

Dasein *n.* [*dah'-zain*] existence, life

dass *conj.* [*das*] that, so that

Dattel, -n *f.* [*da'-təl*] date [fruit]

Datum *n. sing.* **Daten** *pl.* [*dah'-tum, dah'-ten*] date
    [day of month]

Dauer *f.* [*dou'-ər*] duration

dauerhaft [*dou'-ər-haft*] durable, lasting

dauern *v.* [*dou'-ərn*] last

Dauerwelle, -n *f.* [*dou'-er-ve-lə*] permanent wave

Daumen, - *m.* [*dou'-mən*] thumb

davon [*da-fon'*] from it, that; from there

davor [*da-fohr'*] in front of it, before it

dazu [*da-tsoo'*, emphatic: *dah-tsoo'*] to it, to that

dazwischen [*da-tsvi'-shən*] in between

Deck, -e *n.* [*dek*] deck [of ship]

Decke, -n *f.* [*de'-kə*] cover, blanket, ceiling

Deckel, - *m.* [*de'-kəl*] cover [of box, top]; lid [of piano]

decken *v.* [*de'-kən*] cover
    den Tisch decken [*den tish de'-kən*] set the table

Definition, -en *f.* [*de-fi-ni-tsi-ohn'*] definition

dein *poss. pron.* [*dain*] your, yours

Dekoration, -en *f.* [*de-ko-ra-tsi-ohn'*] decoration

dem *dat. sing. of* DAS & DER [*dehm*] to the; to this;
    to that

Demokratie, -n *f.* [*de-mo-kra-tee′*, *de-mo-kra-tee′-ən*] democracy

demokratisch [*de-mo-krah′-tish*] democratic

Demonstration, -en *f.* [*de-mon-stra-tsi-ohn′*] demonstration

Demut *f.* [*deh′-moot*] humility

demütig [*deh′-müh-tiç*] humble

den *acc. sing. of* DER; *dat. pl. of* DIE, *pl.* [*dehn*] the; this, that; to these, to those

denken *v. irreg.* [*den′-kən*] think

denken an (plus acc.) [*den′-kən an*] think of

Denkmal, ⸗er *n.* [*denk′-mal*, *denk′-meh-lər*] monument

denn [*den*] for, because

dennoch [*den′-nokh*] nevertheless, just the same

Depesche, -n *f.* [*de-pe′-shə*] telegram

der *m.* **die** *f.* **das** *n.*, *def. art.* [*dehr*, *dee*, *das*] the

der *m.* **die** *f.* **das** *n.*, *demon. pron.* [*dehr*, *dee*, *das*] he, this one, that one, this, that

der *m.* **die** *f.* **das** *n.*, *rel. pron.* [*dehr*, *dee*, *das*] who, whom, which

der *gen. & dat. sing. of* DIE, *sing.* [*dehr*, *der*] of the, to the

der *gen. pl. of* DIE, *pl.* [*dehr*, *der*] of the

deren *gen. sing. & pl. of* DIE, *sing. & pl.* [*deh′-rən*] whose; of which, of whom

derjenige *m.* **diejenige** *f.* **dasjenige** *n.* **diejenigen** *pl.* [*dehr′-yeh-ni-gə*, *dee′-yeh-ni-gə*, *das′-yeh-ni-gə*, *dee′-yeh-ni-gən*] he, she, it; that one; those, they

derselbe *m.* **dieselbe** *f.* **dasselbe** *n.* **dieselben** *pl.* [*dehr-zel′-bə*, *dee-zel′-bə*, *das-zel′-bə*, *dee-zel′-bən*] (the) same

des *gen. sing. of* DER & DAS [*des*] of the

deshalb [*des′-halp*] therefore, for this reason

dessen *pron.* [*de′-sən*] whose, of which; of it

Detektiv, -e *m.* [*de-tek-teef′*, *de-tek-tee′-və*] detective

deutsch [*doich*] German

Deutsche, -n *m.*, *f.* [*doi′-chə*] German [male, female]

Deutsche Mark (DM), - *f.* [*doi′-chə mark*] German mark

Deutschland *n.* [*doich′-lant*] Germany

Dezember *m.* [*de-tsem′-bər*] December

Dezimalsystem *n.* [*de-tsi-mahl′-süs-tehm*] metric system

Diagnose, -n *f.* [*di-ag-noh'-zə*] diagnosis

Dialekt, -e *m.* [*di-a-lekt'*] dialect

Dialog, -e *m.* [*di-a-lohk', di-a-loh'-gə*] dialogue

Diamant, -en *m.* [*di-a-mant'*] diamond

Diät *f.* [*di-eht'*] diet

 diät leben *v.,* [*di-eht' leh'-bən*] be on a diet

dicht [*diçt*] dense, thick

Dichter, - *m.* [*diç'-tər*] poet

Dichtheit, -en *f.* [*diçt'-hait*] density

dick [*dik*] thick, fat

die *f., def. art.* [*dee*] the

die *f., dem. pron.* [*dee*] she, it, that one that, this, this one

die *f., rel. pron.* [*dee*] who, whom, which, that

die *nom. & acc. pl. of* DER, DIE, DAS [*dee*] the, these, those, who, whom, which

Dieb, -e *f.* [*deep, dee'-bə*] thief

Diebstahl, ‌ꝫe *m.* [*deep'-shtahl, deep'-shteh-lə*] robbery, theft

Diele, -n *f.* [*dee'-lə*] hall

dienen *v.* [*dee'-nən*] serve

 Womit kann ich Ihnen dienen? [*vo-mit' kan iç ee'-nən dee'-nən*] What can I do for you?

Diener, - *m.* [*dee'-nər*] servant [male]

Dienerin, -nen *f.* [*dee'-nə-rin*] servant [female]

Dienst, -e *m.* [*deenst*] service, duty, employment

 Dienst haben *v.,* [*deenst hah'-bən*] be on duty

Dienstag, -e *m.* [*deens'-tahk, deens'-tah-gə*] Tuesday

dieser *m.* **diese** *f.* **dieses** *n.* [*dee'-zər, dee'-zə, dee'-zəs*] this, that, the latter

diesmal [*deez'-mal*] this time

Diktat, -e *n.* [*dik-taht'*] dictation

diktieren *v.* [*dik-tee'-rən*] dictate

Ding, -e *n.* [*ding*] thing

Diplom, -e *n.* [*di-plohm'*] diploma

Diplomat, -en *m.* [*di-plo-maht'*] diplomat

diplomatisch [*di-plo-mah'-tish*] diplomatic

dir *dat. of* DU [*deer*] to you, you

direkt [*di-rekt'*] direct

Direktor, -en *m.* [*di-rek'-tor, di-rek-toh'-rən*] director

Dirigent, -en *m.* [*di-ri-gent'*] director
Diskussion, -en *f.* [*dis-ku-si-ohn'*] discussion
Disziplin, -en *f.* [*dis-tsi-pleen'*] discipline
Division, -en *f.* [*di-vi-zi-ohn'*] division [mil.]
doch [*dokh*] but, however; yes, yes, indeed [in answer to a
    negative question]
Dock, -s *n.* [*dok, doks*] dock
docken *v.* [*do'-kən*] dock
Doktor, -en *m.* [*dok'-tor, dok-toh'-rən*] doctor
Dokument, -e *n.* [*do-ku-ment'*] document
Dolch, -e *m.* [*dolç*] dagger
Dollar, -s *m.* [*do'-lar, do'-lars*] dollar
Dolmetscher, - *m.* [*dol'-me-chər*] interpreter
Dom, -e *m.* [*dohm*] cathedral
Donner, - *m.* [*do'-nər*] thunder
Donnerstag, -e *m.* [*do'-ners-tahk, do'-nərs-tah-gə*] Thursday
Donnerwetter! *interj.* [*do'-nər-ve-tər*] Confound it!, Hang it
    all!, Wow!, I'll be damned!
doppelt [*do'-pelt*] double
Dorf, ⸗er *n.* [*dorf, dör'-fər*] village
Dorn, -en *m.* [*dorn*] thorn
dort [*dort*] there, over there
dorthin [*dort'-hin*] to that place; that way
Dose, -n *f.* [*doh'-zə*] can
Dosenöffner, - *m.* [*doh'-zən-öf-nər*] can opener
Dosis *f. sing.* **Dosen** *pl.* [*doh'-zis, doh'-zən*] dose
Draht, ⸗e *m.* [*draht, dreh'-tə*] wire
Drama *n. sing.* **Dramen** *pl.* [*drah'-ma, drah'-mən*] drama
dramatisch [*dra-mah'-tish*] dramatic
drängen *v.* [*dreng'-ən*] push
drängend [*dreng'-ənt*] pressing
draussen [*drou'-sen*] outside, outdoors
drehen *v.* [*dreh'-ən*] turn
    (sich) drehen [(*ziç*) *dreh'-ən*] turn
    Die Frage dreht sich um [*dee frah'-gə dreht ziç um*]
        The question hinges on
Drehung, -en *f.* [*dreh'-ung*] turn
drei [*drai*] three

dreissig [*drai'-siç*] thirty
dreizehn [*drai'-tsehn*] thirteen
dringend [*dring'-ənt*] urgent
drinnen [*dri'-nən*] inside, indoors
dritt [*drit*] third
Droge, -n *f.* [*droh'-gə*] drug [medicine]
Drogerie, -n *f.* [*droh'-gə-ree*] drugstore [not pharmacy]
drohen *v.* [*droh'-ən*] threaten
Drohung, -en *f.* [*droh'-ung*] threat
drüben [*drüh'-bən*] over there, yonder
Druck, ⸗e *m.* [*druk*] pressure; strain
drucken *v.* [*dru'-kən*] print
drücken *v.* [*drü'-kən*] squeeze [hand]; push [button]
Drucker, - *m.* [*dru'-kər*] printer
Druchsache, -n *f.* [*druk'-za-khə*] printed matter
du *pers. pron.* (familiar form) [*doo*] you
Duft, ⸗e *m.* [*duft, düf'-tə*] fragrance
dulden *v.* [*dul'-dən*] tolerate, endure [*pain, grief*]
dumm [*dum*] dumb, stupid
Dummheit, -en *f.* [*dum'-hait*] stupidity
Dummkopf, ⸗e *m.* [*dum'-kopf, dum'-kö-pfə*] fool
Dünger *m.* [*düng'-ər*] fertilizer, dung
dunkel [*dun'-kəl*] dark
Dunkelheit *f.* [*dun'-kəl-hait*] darkness
dünn [*dün*] thin
durch *prep.* (plus acc.) [*durç*] through, by
durch *adv.* [*durç*] throughout
durchaus [*durç-ous'*] throughout, by all means, altogether
   durchaus nicht [*durç-ous' niçt*] not at all
durcheinander [*durç-ai-nan'-dər*] in disorder, confused
Durchfahrt, -en *f.* [*durç'-fahrt*] thoroughfare
   Keine Durchfahrt! [*kai'-nə durç'-fahrt*] No thoroughfare!
durch-fallen *v. irreg.* [*durç'-fa-lən*] fall through; fail [exam]
durch-führen *v.* [*durç'-füh-rən*] carry through
Durchgang, ⸗e *m.* [*durç'-gang, durç'-geng-ə*] passageway
Durchmesser, - *m.* [*durç'-me-sər*] diameter
Durchschnitt, -e *m.* [*durç'-shnit*] average
   im Durchschnitt [*im durç'-shnit*] on the average

durch-sehen v. irreg. [durç'-zeh-ən] see through,
   look through; revise
durch-setzen v. [durç'-ze-tsən] carry out forcefully
Durchzug, ⸗e m. [durç'-tsook, durç'-tsiih-gə] draft [air]
dürfen mod. aux. [dür'-fən] may, can, be allowed to
Dürre, -n f. [dü'-rə] drought
Durst m. [durst] thirst
   Durst haben v. [durst hah'-bən] be thirsty
durstig [dur'-stiç] thirsty
Dusche, -n f. [doo'-shə] shower [bath]
duschen v. [doo'-shən] take a shower
düster [düh'-stər] gloomy
Dutzend, -e n. [du'-tsənt, du'-tsen-də] dozen
Dynamit n. [dü-na-meet'] dynamite

E

Ebbe f. [eh'-bə] low tide
eben adj. [eh'-bən] even, level, smooth
eben adv. [eh'-bən] exactly, just
Ebene, -n f. [eh'-bə-nə] plain
ebenso [eh'-bən-zoh] likewise
Echo, -s n. [e'-çoh, e'-çohs] echo
echt [eçt] genuine, true
Ecke, -n f. [e'-kə] corner, angle
edel [eh'-dəl] noble
Edelstein, -e m. [eh'-dəl-shtain] precious stone, gem
egal [e-gahl'] equal, alike
   Das ist mir egal [das ist meer e-gahl'] That's all the same
   to me
egoistisch [e-go-i'-stish] selfish
Ehe, -n f. [eh'-e] marriage, wedlock
eher [eh'-ər] sooner, rather
   Je eher, je besser [yeh eh'-ər, yeh be'-sər] The sooner
   the better

Ehre, -n *f.* [*eh'-rə*] honor
  Ich habe die Ehre [*iç hah'-bə dee eh'-rə*] I have the honor
    [Means "Hello" or "Goodbye" in southern Germany]
ehren *v.* [*eh'-rən*] honor
ehrenwert [*eh'-rən-vehrt*] respectable, honorable
Ehrenwort, -e *n.* [*eh'-rən-vort*] word of honor
Ehrgeiz *m.* [*ehr'-gaits*] ambition
ehrgeizig [*ehr'-gai-tsiç*] ambitious
ehrlich [*ehr'-liç*] honest
Ei, -er *n.* [*ai, ai'-ər*] egg
  hart gekochte Eier [*hart gə-kokh'-tə ai'-ər*] hard-boiled
    eggs
  weich gekochte Eier [*vaiç gə-kokh'-tə ai'-ər*] soft-boiled
    eggs
  Rührei *n.* [*rühr'-ai*] scrambled eggs
  Spiegeleier *n. pl.* [*shpee'-gəl-ai-ər*] fried eggs
Eiche, -n *f.* [*ai'-çə*] oak
Eichhörnchen, - *n.* [*aiç'-hörn-çən*] squirrel
Eid, -e *m.* [*ait, ai'-də*] oath
eifersüchtig [*ai'-fər-züç-tiç*] jealous
eifrig [*aif'-riç*] eager
eigen [*ai'-gən*] own, one's own; odd, peculiar
Eigentum, -er *n.* [*ai'-gən-toom, ai'-gən-tüh-mər*] property
Eigentümer, - *m.* [*ai'-gən-tüh-mər*] proprietor
Eile *f.* [*ai'-lə*] haste
  Durch Eilboten [*durç ail'-boh-tən*] By special delivery
eilen *v.* [*ai'-lən*] hurry
  es eilig haben *v. irreg.* [*es al'-liç hah'-bən*] (be) in a hurry
Eilzug, ∺e *m.* [*ail'-tsook, ail'-tsüh-gə*] fast train, express
Eimer, - *m.* [*ai'-mər*] pail, bucket
ein *m.* **eine** *f.* **ein** *n., indef. art.* [*ain, ai'-nə, ain*] a, an
ein *adj.* [*ain*] one
einander [*ai-nan'-dər*] each other, one another
Einbahnstrasse, -n *f.* [*ain'-bahn-shtrah-sə*] one-way street
Einberufung, -en *f.* [*ain'-be-roo-fung*] draft [army]
Einbildung, -en *f.* [*ain'-bil-dung*] conceit, imagination
Einbrecher, - *m.* [*ain'-breç-ər*] burglar
Einbruch, ∺e *m.* [*ain'-brukh, ain'-brü-çə*] burglary

Einbruch der Nacht [*ain'-brukh dehr nakht*] nightfall

Eindruck, ⸚e *m.* [*ain'-druk, ain'-drü-kə*] impression

einfach [*ain'-fakh*] simple, plain; frugal [meal]

Einfluss, ⸚e *m.* [*ain'-flus, ain'-flü-sə*] influence

Eingang, ⸚e *m.* [*ain'-gang, ain'-geng-ə*] entrance

eingebildet [*ain'-gə-bil-dət*] conceited

Eingebung, -en *f.* [*ain'-geh-bung*] inspiration

einheimisch [*ain'-hai-mish*] native, domestic

Einheit, -en *f.* [*ain'-hait*] unity, oneness; unit

einheitlich [*ain'-hait-liç*] uniform

ein-holen *v.* [*ain'-hoh-lən*] catch up with

Einigkeit *f.* [*ai'-niç-kait*] unity, concord

einkaufen gehen *v. irreg. (Aux:* SEIN*)* [*ain'-kou-fən geh'-ən*] go shopping

Einkommen, - *n.* [*ain'-ko-mən*] income

Einkommensteuer *f.* [*ain'-ko-mən-shtoi-ər*] income tax

ein-laden *v. irreg.* [*ain'-lah-dən*] invite; load

Einladung, -en *f.* [*ain'-lah-dung*] invitation

Einleitung, -en *f.* [*ain'-lai-tung*] introduction

einmal [*ain'-mahl*] once

noch einmal [*nokh ain'-mahl*] once more, once again

ein-packen *v.* [*ain'-pa-kən*] wrap up

ein-richten *v.* [*ain'-riç-tən*] establish, set up [shop]; furnish [room]

eins [*ains*] one [number]; agreed

einsam [*ain'-zam*] lonely, solitary

ein-schalten *v.* [*ain'-shal-tən*] turn on [light]

ein-schenken *v.* [*ain'-shen-kən*] pour in; pour out

ein-schlafen *v. irreg.* [*ain'-shlah-fən*] fall asleep

ein-schliessen *v. irreg.* [*ain'-shlee-sən*] enclose, include, lock in

ein-schreiben lassen *v. irreg.* [*ain'-shrai-bən la'-sən*] register [letters]

Einschreibebrief, -e *m.* [*ain'-shrai-bə-breef*] registered letter

ein-schrumpfen *v. (Aux:* SEIN*)* [*ain'-shrum-pfən*] shrink

ein-sperren *v.* [*ain'-shpe-rən*] put in prison, shut in

ein-steigen (plus acc.) *v. irreg. (Aux:* SEIN*)* [*ain'-shtai-gən*] board, get in, get on

Einsteigen! [*ain'-shtai-gən*] Take your seats!, All aboard!

einstimmig [*ain'-shti-miç*] unanimous

ein-treten *v. irreg. (Aux:* SEIN*)* [*ain'-treh-tən*] enter

Eintritt, -e *m.* [*ain'-trit*] entrance, admission

    Eintritt verboten! [*ain'-trit fər-boh'-tən*] Do not enter!
    No admission.

Eintrittsgeld, -er *n.* [*ain'-trits-gelt, ain'-trits-gel-der*] admission
    [fee]

Einwand, ⸗e *m.* [*ain'-vant, ain'-ven-də*] objection

Einwanderung, -en *f.* [*ain'-van-də-rung*] immigration

ein-wechseln *v.* [*ain'-vek-səln*] cash

ein-willigen (in plus acc.**)** *v.* [*ain'-vi-li-gən (in)*] consent (to);
    agree

Einwohner, - *m.* [*ain'-voh-nər*] inhabitant, resident

Einzahl, -en *f.* [*ain'-tsahl*] singular

ein-zahlen *v.* [*ain'-tsah-lən*] deposit, pay in

Einzahlung, -en *f.* [*ain'-tsah-lung*] deposit

Einzelheit, -en *f.* [*ain'-tsel-hait*] detail

einzeln [*ain'-tseln*] single, individual

einzig [*ain'-tsiç*] only, single, unique

Eis *n.* [*ais*] ice, ice-cream

Eisbein *n.* [*ais'-bain*] pig's knuckles

Eisen, - *n.* [*ai'-zən*] iron [metal]

Eisenbahn, -en *f.* [*ai'-zən-bahn*] railroad, railway

Eisenbahnkreuzung, -en *f.* [*ai'-zən-bahn-kroi-tsung*]
    railroad crossing

Eisenbahnwagen, - *m.* [*ai'-zən-bahn-vah-gən*] railroad car

eitel [*ai'-təl*] vain

Eitelkeit, -en *f.* [*ai'-təl-kait*] vanity

ekelhaft [*eh'-kəl-haft*] disgusting

Elefant, -en *m.* [*e-le-fant'*] elephant

elegant [*e-le-gant'*] elegant, smart

Eleganz *f.* [*e-le-gants'*] elegance

elektrisch [*e-lek'-trish*] electric

Elektrizität *f.* [*e-lek-tri-tsi-teht'*] electricity

Element, -e *n.* [*e-le-ment'*] element

elementar [*e-le-men-tahr'*] elementary

elend [*eh'-lənt*] miserable, needy

Elend *n.* [*eh'-lənt*] misery

elf [*elf*] eleven

Elfenbein *n.* [*el'-fən-bain*] ivory

elfte [*elf'-tə*] eleventh

Ellbogen, - *m.* [*el'-boh-gən*] elbow

Eltern *pl.* [*el'-tərn*] parents

Empfang, =e *m.* [*em-pfang'*, *em-pfeng'-ə*] reception

Empfänger, - *m.* [*em-pfeng'-ər*] recipient, addressee

empfehlen *v. irreg.* [*em-pfeh'-lən*] recommend

empfindlich [*em-pfint'-liç*] sensitive, touchy

Ende, -n *n.* [*en'-də*] end

enden *v.* [*en'-dən*] end, come to an end

endgültig [*ent'-gül-tiç*] final

endlich [*ent'-liç*] at last

endlos [*ent'-lohs*] endless

Energie, -n *f.* [*e-ner-gee'*] energy

eng [*eng*] narrow; tight [clothes]

Engel, - *m.* [*eng'-əl*] angel

England *n.* [*eng'-lant*] England

englisch [*eng'-lish*] English

Enkel, - *m.* [*en'-kəl*] grandson

Enkelkind, -er *n.* [*en'-kəl-kint*, *en'-kəl-kin-dər*] grandchild

Enkelin, -nen *f.* [*en'-kə-lin*] granddaughter

entdecken *v.* [*ent-de'-kən*] discover

Entdeckung, -en *f.* [*ent-de'-kung*] discovery

Ente, -n *f.* [*en'-tə*] duck

entfernen *v.* [*ent-fer'-nən*] remove

entfernt [*ent-fernt'*] distant, remote

Entfernung, -en *f.* [*ent-fer'-nung*] distance

entfliehen (plus dat.) *v. irreg. (Aux:* SEIN) [*ent-flee'-ən*] escape

entführen *v.* [*ent-füh'-rən*] kidnap, highjack

enthalten *v. irreg.* [*ent-hal'-tən*] contain

entladen *v. irreg.* [*ent-lah'-dən*] unload, discharge

entlang *prep.* (plus acc.) [*ent-lang'*] along

entlassen *v. irreg.* [*ent-la'-sən*] dismiss

entmutigen *v.* [*ent-moo'-ti-gən*] discourage

entscheiden *v. irreg.* [*ent-shai'-dən*] decide

entschuldigen *v.* [*ent-shul'-di-gən*] excuse

Entschuldigung, -en *f.* *[ent-shul'-di-gung]* apology, excuse
   Entschuldigung! *[ent-shul'-di-gung]* Excuse me!
enttäuschen *v.* *[ent-toi'-shən]* disappoint [a person]
enttäuscht *[ent-toisht']* disappointed
entwässern *v.* *[ent-ve'-sərn]* drain
entweder . . . oder *[ent-veh'-dər . . . oh'-dər]* either . . . or
entwickeln *v.* *[ent-vi'-kəln]* develop
Entwicklung, -en *f.* *[ent-vik'-lung]* development
Entwurf, ⸗e *m.* *[ent-vurf', ent-vür'-fə]* project; draft, outline
entzückend *[ent-tsü'-kənt]* delightful
Entzündung, -en *f.* *[ent-tsün'-dung]* infection
er *pers. pron.* *[ehr, er]* he
Erbe, -n *m.* *[er'-bə]* heir
erben *v.* *[er'-bən]* inherit
Erbin, -nen *f.* *[er'-bin]* heiress
erblicken *v.* *[er-bli'-kən]* catch sight of
Erbschaft, -en *f.* *[erp'-shaft]* inheritance
Erbse, -n *f.* *[erp'-sə]* pea
Erbsensuppe, -n *f.* *[erp'-sən-zu-pə]* pea soup
Erdbeben, - *n.* *[ehrd'-beh-bən]* earthquake
Erdbeere, -n *f.* *[ehrd'-beh-rə]* strawberry
Erde, -n *f.* *[ehr'-də]* earth
Erdgeschoss, -e *n.* *[ehrd'-gə-shos]* ground floor
Erdnuss, ⸗e *f.* *[ehrd'-nus, ehrd'-nü-sə]* peanut
Ereignis, -se *n.* *[e-raik'-nis]* event, occurrence
erfahren *v. irreg.* *[er-fah'-rən]* learn, experience
Erfahrung, -en *f.* *[er-fah'-rung]* experience
   aus Erfahrung *[ous er-fah'-rung]* by experience
erfinden *v. irreg.* *[er-fin'-dən]* invent
Erfinder, - *m.* *[er-fin'-dər]* inventor
Erfindung, -en *f.* *[er-fin'-dung]* invention
Erfolg, -e *m.* *[er-folk', er-fol'-gə]* success
erfolgreich *[er-folk'-raiç]* successful
erforschen *v.* *[er-for'-shən]* investigate, explore, research
erfreuen *v.* *[er-froi'-ən]* please, delight
   Sehr erfreut! *[zehr er-froit']* How do you do?
     [in introductions]
Erfrischung, -en *f.* *[er-fri'-shung]* refreshment

ergeben (plus dat.) *adj.* [*er-geh'-bən*] devoted to
ergreifen *v. irreg.* [*er-grai'-fən*] seize, grasp, apprehend
erhalten *v. irreg.* [*er-hal'-tən*] get, obtain, maintain
erhängen *v.* [*er-heng'-ən*] hang [a person]
(sich) erheben *v. irreg.* [(*ziç*) *er-heh'-bən*] arise
erhob *past tense of* ERHEBEN [*er-hohp'*] rose
erhoben *past part. of* ERHEBEN [*er-hoh'-bən*] risen
(sich) erholen *v.* [(*ziç*) *er-hoh'-lən*] recover [one's health]
(sich) erinnern an (plus acc.) *v.* [(*ziç*) *er-in'-ərn an*] remember;
    recall
  Erinnern Sie sich an ihn? [*er-in'-ərn zee ziç an een*]
    Do you remember him?
(sich) erkälten *v.* [(*ziç*) *er-kel'-tən*] catch a cold
erkennen *v. irreg.* [*er-ke'-nən*] recognize
erklären *v.* [*er-kleh'-rən*] explain, declare
  Erklären Sie es bitte [*er-kleh'-rən zee es bi'-tə*] Please
    explain
Erklärung, -en *f.* [*er-kleh'-rung*] explanation, declaration
erlauben *v.* [*er-lou'-bən*] allow, permit
Erlaubnis *f.* [*er-loup'-nis*] permission
Erläuterung, -en *f.* [*er-loi'-tə-rung*] comment, explanation
Ermässigung, -en *f.* [*er-meh'-si-gung*] reduction
ermorden *v.* [*er-mor'-dən*] murder
ermutigen *v.* [*er-moo'-ti-gən*] encourage
Ernährung *f.* [*er-neh'-rung*] nutrition
ernennen *v. irreg.* [*er-ne'-nən*] appoint, nominate
erneuern *v.* [*er-noi'-ərn*] renew
ernst [*ernst*] serious, earnest
Ernte, -n *f.* [*ern'-tə*] harvest, crop
erobern *v.* [*er-oh'-bərn*] conquer
erraten *v. irreg.* [*er-rah'-tən*] guess
Erregung *f.* [*er-reh'-gung*] excitement
erreichen *v.* [*er-rai'-çən*] reach; catch [train]; attain
Ersatz *m.* [*er-zats'*] substitute, compensation
Ersatzreifen, - *m.* [*er-zats'-rai-fən*] spare tire
erscheinen *v. irreg.* (*Aux:* SEIN) [*er-shai'-nən*] appear
Erscheinung, -en *f.* [*er-shai'-nung*] appearance
erschiessen *v. irreg.* [*er-shee'-sən*] shoot [dead]

erschöpft [*er-shöpft'*] exhausted
erschrecken *v. irreg. (Aux: SEIN)* [*er-shre'-kən*] be frightened
erschrecken *v. (Aux: HABEN)* [*er-shre'-kən*] frighten
ersetzen *v.* [*er-ze'-tsən*] replace
erst [*ehrst*] first, only
erstaunlich [*er-shtoun'-liç*] astonishing
erstechen *v. irreg.* [*er-shte'-çən*] stab [to death]
erster [*ehr'-stər*] first
erstklassig [*ehrst'-kla-siç*] first class
ertrinken *v. irreg. (Aux: SEIN)* [*er-trin'-kən*] drown
erwachen *v. (Aux: SEIN)* [*er-va'-khən*] awake
erwachsen [*er-vak'-sən*] grown-up
erwähnen *v.* [*er-veh'-nən*] mention
erwarten *v.* [*er-var'-tən*] expect, wait for
erwerben *v. irreg.* [*er-ver'-bən*] acquire
Erz, -e *n.* [*erts*] ore
erzählen *v.* [*er-tseh'-lən*] narrate
Erzählung, -en *f.* [*er-tseh'-lung*] tale, story
erzeugen *v.* [*er-tsoi'-gən*] produce, make
erziehen *v. irreg.* [*er-tsee'-ən*] train; rear [children]
Erziehung *f.* [*er-tsee'-ung*] upbringing, education
es *pers. pron.* [*es*] it
Esel, - *m.* [*eh'-zəl*] donkey, ass
essbar [*es'-bahr*] edible
essen *v. irreg.* [*e'-sən*] eat
Essig *m.* [*e'-siç*] vinegar
Esslöffel, - *m.* [*es'-lö-fəl*] tablespoon
Esszimmer, - *n.* [*es'-tsi-mər*] dining room
Etage, -n *f.* [*e-tah'-zhə*] story [floor]
etwas *indef. pron.* [*et'-vas*] something, anything
etwas *adj.* [*et'-vas*] some, any
euch *pers. pron.* (familiar form) [*oiç*] you; to you; yourselves;
     each other
euer *poss. pron.* (familiar form) [*oi'-ər*] your
Eule, -n *f.* [*oi'-lə*] owl
Europa *n.* [*oi-roh'-pa*] Europe
europäisch [*oi-ro-peh'-ish*] European
evangelisch [*e-vang-geh'-lish*] Protestant

ewig [*eh'-viç*] eternal
Ewigkeit, -en *f.* [*eh'-viç-kait*] eternity
Existenz, -en *f.* [*ek-si-stents'*] existence
Expedition, -en *f.* [*eks-pe-di-tsi-ohn'*] expedition
Experiment, -e *n.* [*eks-pe-ri-ment'*] experiment
exportieren *v.* [*eks-por-tee'-rən*] export
extra [*eks'-tra*] extra

F

Fabel, -n *f.* [*fah'-bəl*] fable, tale
fabelhaft [*fah'-bəl-haft*] fabulous
Fabrik, -en *f.* [*fa-breek'*] factory
Fabrikant, -en *m.* [*fa-bri-kant'*] manufacturer
Fachmann *m. sing.* **Fachleute** *pl.* [*fakh'-man, fakh'-loi-tə*]
    expert
**Faden, = ** *m.* [*fah'-dən, feh'-dən*] thread
fähig [*feh'-iç*] capable, able
Fähigkeit, -en *f.* [*feh'-iç-kait*] ability
Fahne, -n *f.* [*fah'-nə*] flag
Fährboot, -e *n.* [*fehr'-boht*] ferryboat
fahren *v. irreg.* (*Aux:* SEIN) [*fah'-rən*] go; travel; drive
    per Anhalter fahren [*per an'-hal-tər fah'-rən*] hitchhike
fahren *v. irreg.* (*Aux:* HABEN) [*fah'-rən*] ride, drive, steer
    [a car, wagon, etc.]
Fahrer, - *m.* [*fah'-rər*] driver
Fahrgeld *n.* [*fahr'-gəlt*] fare
Fahrkarte, -n *f.* [*fahr'-kar-tə*] ticket
Fahrplan, =e *m.* [*fahr'-plahn, fahr'-pleh-nə*] schedule [train],
    timetable
Fahrpreis, -e *m.* [*fahr'-prais, fahr'-prai-zə*] fare [travel]
Fahrrad, =er *n.* [*fahr'-raht, fahr'-reh-dər*] bicycle
Fahrstuhl, =e *m.* [*fahr'-stool, fahr'-stüh-lə*] elevator
Fakultät, -en *f.* [*fa-kul-teht'*] faculty [university]
Fall, =e *m.* [*fal, fe'-lə*] case
    im Falle, dass [*im fa'-lə das*] in the event that

auf jeden Fall [*ouf yeh'-dən fal*] in any case
auf keinen Fall [*ouf kai'-nən fal*] by no means
Falle, -n *f.* [*fa'-lə*] trap, pitfall
  eine Falle stellen *v.* [*ai'-nə fa'-lə shte'-lən*] set a trap
fallen *v. irreg. (Aux:* SEIN*)* [*fa'-lən*] fall
fallen lassen *v. irreg.* [*fa'-lən la'-sən*] drop
fällig [*fe'-liç*] due, payable
  fällig werden *v. irreg. (Aux:* SEIN*)* [*fe'-liç ver'-dən*]
    fall due
falls [*fals*] in the event, if
Fallschirm, -e *m.* [*fal'-shirm*] parachute
falsch [*falsh*] false, wrong
fälschen *v.* [*fel'-shən*] falsify, forge
Falschheit, -en *f.* [*falsh'-hait*] falsehood
Falte, -n *f.* [*fal'-tə*] fold, wrinkle
falten *v.* [*fal'-tən*] fold
familiär [*fa-mi-li-ehr'*] familiar, informal
Familie, -n *f.* [*fa-mee'-li-ə*] family
Familienname, -n *m.* [*fa-mee'-li-ən-nah-mə*] last name
fangen *v. irreg.* [*fang'-ən*] catch, trap
Farbe, -n *f.* [*far'-bə*] color, paint, dye
färben *v.* [*fer'-bən*] dye, stain, tint
farbig [*far'-biç*] colored
Färbung, -en *f.* [*fer'-bung*] coloring, hue
Fasching *m.* [*fa'-shing*] carnival
Fass, ⸗er *n.* [*fas, fe'-sər*] barrel
fassen *v.* [*fa'-sən*] grasp, seize, hold
Fassung, -en *f.* [*fa'-sung*] composure; version, mounting
  die Fassung verlieren *v.* [*dee fa'-sung fər-lee'-rən*] lose
    control
fast [*fast*] almost, nearly
fasten *v.* [*fa'-stən*] fast
faul [*foul*] lazy; foul
Faust, ⸗e *f.* [*foust, foi'-stə*] fist
Februar *m.* [*feh'-bru-ahr*] February
Fechten *n.* [*feç'-tən*] fencing
Feder, -n *f.* [*feh'-dər*] pen; feather; spring [of a machine]
Federmesser, - *n.* [*feh'-dər-me-sər*] penknife

fegen v. [*feh'-gən*] sweep

fehlen v. [*feh'-len*] (be) missing, lacking, absent

Fehler, - m. [*feh'-lər*] fault, mistake, error

    Wer machte den Fehler? [*vehr makh'-tə dehn feh'-lər*]
      Who made the mistake?

    Das ist mein Fehler [*das ist main feh'-lər*] It's my fault

Fehlschlag, ⸗e m. [*fehl'-shlahk, fehl'-shleh-gə*] failure

fehl-schlagen v. irreg. (*Aux:* SEIN) [*fehl'-shlah-gən*] fail

Fehltritt, -e m. [*fehl'-trit*] slip, false step

Feier, -n f. [*fai'-ər*] celebration

feiern v. [*fai'-ərn*] celebrate

Feiertag, -e m. [*fai'-ər-tahk, fai'-ər-tah-gə*] holiday

Feige, -n f. [*fai'-gə*] fig

Feigling, -e m. [*faik'-ling*] coward

Feile, -n f. [*fai'-lə*] file [tool]

fein [*fain*] fine, choice; delicate; distinguished

Feind, -e m. [*faint, fain'-də*] foe, enemy

feindlich [*faint'-liç*] hostile

Feinschmecker, - m. [*fain'-shme-kər*] gourmet

Feld, -er n. [*felt, fel'-dər*] field

Feldwebel, - m. [*felt'-veh-bəl*] sergeant [army]

Fell, -e n. [*fel*] fur; skin, hide

Felsen, - m. [*fel'-zən*] rock

Fenster, - n. [*fen'-stər*] window

Ferien pl. [*feh'-ri-ən*] vacation

fern [*fern*] far, distant, remote

Fernglas, ⸗er n. [*fern'-glahs, fern'-gleh-zər*] telescope

Fernsehapparat, -e m. [*fern'-zeh-a-pa-raht*] television set

Fernsehen n. [*fern'-zeh-ən*] television

Fernsprecher, - m. [*fern'-shpre-çər*] telephone

Ferse, -n f. [*fer'-zə*] heel [foot]

fertig [*fer'-tiç*] ready; through, finished

    Sind Sie fertig? [*zint zee fer'-tiç*] Are you ready?

    sich fertig machen v. [*ziç fer'-tiç ma'-khən*] make ready

fertige Kleidungsstücke n. pl. [*fer'-ti-gə klai'-dungs-shtü-kə*]
    ready-made clothes

fest [*fest*] firm, fixed

    (der) feste Preis [(*dehr*) *fe'-stə prais*] (the) fixed price

Fest, -e *n.* [*fest*] festival

festlich [*fest'-liç*] solemn, festive

fest-machen *v.* [*fest'-ma-khən*] fasten, fix

Feststellung, -en *f.* [*fest'-shte-lung*] statement [of fact]

Festung, -en *f.* [*fe'-stung*] fort

Fett, -e *n.* [*fet*] grease, fat

feucht [*foiçt*] humid, damp

Feuer, - *n.* [*foi'-ər*] fire

   Feuer geben *v.* [*foi'-ər geh'-bən*] give a light

feuerfest [*foi'-ər-fest*] fireproof

Feuerzeug, -e *n.* [*foi'-ər-tsoik, foi'-ər-tsoi-gə*] lighter

Fieber *n.* [*fee'-bər*] fever

fieberisch [*fee'-bə-rish*] feverish

Fiebermesser, - *m.* [*fee'-bər-me-sər*] thermometer

Figur, -en *f.* [*fi-goor'*] figure

Fiktion, -en *f.* [*fik-tsi-ohn'*] fiction

Film, -e *m.* [*film*] film

Filter, - *m.* [*fil'-tər*] filter

Finanzen *f. pl.* [*fi-nan'-tsən*] finances

finanziell [*fi-nan-tsi-el'*] financial(ly)

Finanzministerium *n. sing.* **Finanzministerien** *pl.* [*fi-nants'-mi-ni-ste-ri-um, fi-nants'-mi-ni-ste-ri-ən*] Treasury Department

finden *v. irreg.* [*fin'-dən*] find

Finger, - *m.* [*fing'-ər*] finger

finster [*fin'-stər*] dark, obscure

Firma *f. sing.* **Firmen** *pl.* [*fir'-mah, fir'-mən*] firm, company

Fisch, -e *m.* [*fish*] fish

fischen *v.* [*fi'-shən*] fish

Fischen *n.* [*fi'-shən*] fishing

Fischer, - *m.* [*fi'-shər*] fisherman

Fischerboot, -e *n.* [*fi'-shər-boht*] fishing boat

flach [*flakh*] plain, flat

Fläche, -n *f.* [*fle'-çə*] plane, surface

Flamme, -n *f.* [*fla'-mə*] flame

Flasche, -n *f.* [*fla'-shə*] flask, bottle

Flaschenöffner, - *m.* [*fla'-shən-öf-nər*] bottle-opener

Fleck, -e *m.* [*flek*] stain [of wine]; spot [of grease]

fleckenlos [*fle'-kən-lohs*] spotless

Fleisch *n.* [*flaish*] flesh, meat

Fleischbrühe, -n *f.* [*flaish'-brüh-ə*] broth

Fleiss *m.* [*flais*] diligence

fleissig [*flai'-siç*] diligent, industrious

Fliege, -n *f.* [*flee'-gə*] fly

fliegen *v. irreg.* (*Aux:* SEIN) [*flee'-gən*] fly

fliehen *v. irreg.* (*Aux:* SEIN) [*flee'-ən*] flee

fliessen *v. irreg.* (*Aux:* SEIN) [*flee'-sən*] flow

fliessend [*flee'-sənt*] fluent(ly)

   fliessendes Wasser [*flee'-sən-dəs va'-sər*] running water

Flitterwochen *f. pl.* [*fli'-tər-vo-khən*] honeymoon

Floh, ⸗e *m.* [*floh, flöh'-ə*] flea

Flöte, -n *f.* [*flöh'-tə*] flute

Flotte, -n *f.* [*flo'-tə*] navy, fleet

Fluch, ⸗e *m.* [*flookh, flüh'-çə*] curse

fluchen *v.* [*floo'- khən*] curse

Flucht *f.* [*flukht*] flight [fleeing], escape

flüchtig [*flüç'-tiç*] transient, fleeting, volatile

Flüchtling, -e *m.* [*flüçt'-ling*] refugee

Flug, ⸗e *m.* [*flook, flüh'-gə*] flight [flying]

Fluggesellschaft, -en *f.* [*flook'-gə-sel-shaft*] airline

Flughafen, ⸗ *m.* [*flook'-hah-fən, flook'-heh-fən*] airport

Flugzeug, -e *n.* [*flook'-tsoik, flook'-tsoi-gə*] airplane

Flur, -e *m.* [*floor*] hall, entrance

Fluss, ⸗e *m.* [*flus, flü'-sə*] river

flüssig [*flü'-siç*] liquid

Flussufer, - *n.* [*flus'-oo-fər*] riverside

flüstern *v.* [*flü'-stərn*] whisper

Flut, -en *f.* [*floot*] high tide, flood

föderalistisch [*fö-də-ra-li'-stish*] federal

Folge, -n *f.* [*fol'-gə*] consequence, result

folgen (plus dat.) *v.* (*Aux:* SEIN) [*fol'-gən*] follow

   Folgen Sie mir! [*fol'-gən zee meer*] Follow me!

folgend (auf plus acc.) [*fol'-gənt* (*ouf*)] consequent (on)

Folter, -n *f.* [*fol'-tər*] torture

fordern *v.* [*for'-dern*] claim, demand, ask

Forelle, -n *f.* [*fo-re'-lə*] trout

Form, -en *f.* [*form*] form, shape
Formalität, -en *f.* [*for-ma-li-teht'*] formality
Formel, -n *f.* [*for'-mel*] formula
formell [*for-mel'*] formal
Forschung, -en *f.* [*for'-shung*] research, exploration
fort [*fort*] away, gone
fort-fahren *v. irreg.* [*fort'-fah-rən*] continue, keep on
fort-gehen *v. irreg.* (*Aux:* SEIN) [*fort'-geh-ən*] go away
Fortschritt, -e *m.* [*fort'-shrit*] advancement, progress
Fortschritte machen *v.* [*fort'-shri-tə ma'-khən*] progress
fortschrittlich [*fort'-shrit-liç*] progressive
Forum *n. sing.* **Foren** *pl.* [*foh'-rum, foh'-rən*] forum
Fracht *f.* [*frakht*] freight
Frage, -n *f.* [*frah'-gə*] question
fragen *v.* [*frah'-gən*] ask
Fragezeichen, - *n.* [*frah'-gə-tsai-çən*] question mark
Frankreich *n.* [*frank'-raiç*] France
Franzose, -n *m.* [*fran-tsoh'-zə*] Frenchman
Französin, -nen *f.* [*fran-tsöh'-zin*] Frenchwoman
französisch [*fran-tsöh'-zish*] French
Frau, -en *f.* [*frou*] woman, wife; Mrs., madam
Fräulein, - *n.* [*froi'-lain*] Miss
Fräulein vom Amt [*froi'-lain fom amt*] operator [telephone girl]
frei [*frai*] free, vacant
frei-geben *v. irreg.* [*frai'-geh-bən*] release
freigebig [*frai'-geh-biç*] generous, liberal
Freiheit, -en *f.* [*frai'-hait*] freedom, liberty
frei-sprechen *v. irreg.* [*frai'-shpre-çən*] acquit
Freitag, -e *m.* [*frai'-tahk, frai'-tah-gə*] Friday
freiwillig [*frai'-vi-liç*] voluntary
Freiwillige, -n *m., f.* [*frai'-vi-li-gə*] volunteer
fremd [*fremt*] strange, foreign
Fremde, -n *m., f.* [*frem'-də*] stranger
Fremdenführer, - *m.* [*frem'-dən-füh-rər*] tourist guide
Fremdsprache, -n *f.* [*fremt'-shprah-khə*] foreign language
fressen *v. irreg.* [*fre'-sən*] eat [of animals]
Freude, -n *f.* [*froi'-də*] joy

freudig [*froi'-diç*] joyful

sich freuen *v.* [*ziç froi'-ən*] be glad
   Es freut mich sehr [*es froit miç zehr*] I'm very glad
   Ich freue mich auf (plus acc.) [*iç froi'-ə miç ouf*]
     I'm looking forward to

Freund, -e *m.* [*froint, froin'-də*] boy-friend, friend

freundlich [*froint'-liç*] friendly, kind

Freundschaft, -en *f.* [*froint'-shaft*] friendship

Friede, -n *m.* [*free'-də*] peace
   im Frieden [*im free'-dən*] in peacetime

Friedhof, ⸗e *m.* [*freet'-hohf, freet'-höh-fə*] cemetery

friedlich [*freet'-liç*] peaceful

frieren *v. irreg.* (*Aux:* SEIN) [*free'-rən*] freeze [turn to ice]

frieren *v. irreg.* (*Aux:* HABEN) [*free'-rən*] freeze [feel cold]

frisch [*frish*] fresh
   frisch und gesund [*frish unt gə-zunt'*] safe and sound
   Frisch gestrichen! [*frish gə-shtri'-çən*] Wet paint!

Friseur, -e *m.* [*fri-zöhr'*] hairdresser, barber

froh [*froh*] joyful, glad

fröhlich [*fröh'-liç*] gay, happy

fromm [*from*] pious, religious

Front, -en *f.* [*front*] front

fror *past tense of* FRIEREN [*frohr*] froze

Frosch, ⸗e *m.* [*frosh, frö'-shə*] frog

Frost, ⸗e *m.* [*frost, frö'-stə*] frost

Frucht, ⸗e *f.* [*frukht, früç'-tə*] fruit

fruchtbar [*frukht'-bahr*] fertile

Fruchtsaft, ⸗e *m.* [*frukht'-zaft, frukht'-zef-tə*] fruit juice

früh *adv.* [*früh*] in the morning, early
   in der Frühe [*in der früh'-ə*] early in the morning

früher [*früh'-ər*] earlier, formerly, sooner

Frühling, -e *f.* [*früh'-ling*] spring [season]

Frühstück, -e *n.* [*früh'-shtük*] breakfast

frühstücken *v.* [*früh'-shtü-kən*] have breakfast

frühzeitig [*früh'-tsai-tiç*] premature, early

Fuchs, ⸗e *m.* [*fuks, fük'-sə*] fox

fühlen *v.* [*füh'-lən*] feel
   Fühlen Sie sich wie zu Hause! [*füh'-lən zee ziç vee tsu*

hou'-zə] Make yourself at home!

fuhr *past tense of* FAHREN [*foor*] rode, drove, went

führen *v.* [*füh'-rən*] lead, guide, conduct [a campaign, etc.];
    deal in [goods]; lead [life]

führend [*füh'-rənt*] leading

Führer, - *m.* [*füh'-rər*] leader, conductor, guide

füllen *v.* [*fü'-lən*] fill

Füllfeder, -n *f.* [*fül'-feh-dər*] fountain pen

fünf [*fünf*] five

fünft [*fünft*] fifth

fünfzehn [*fünf'-tsehn*] fifteen

fünfzig [*fünf'-tsiç*] fifty

Funke, -n *m.* [*fun'-kə*] spark

Funktion, -en *f.* [*funk-tsi-ohn'*] function

für *prep.* (plus acc.) [*führ, für*] for; in return for
   für mich, für Sie [*für miç, für zee*] for me, for you

Furcht *f.* [*furçt*] fear

furchtbar [*furçt'-bahr*] awful, terrible

fürchten *v.* [*fürç'-tən*] fear, be afraid of

furchtlos [*furçt'-los*] fearless

Fuss, ⸗e *m.* [*foos, füh'-sə*] foot
   zu Fuss [*tsu foos*] on foot

Fussball, ⸗e *m.* [*foos'-bal, foos'-be-lə*] football

Fussballspieler, - *m.* [*foos'-bal-shpee-lər*] football player

Fussboden, ⸗ *m.* [*foos'-boh-dən, foos'-böh-dən*] floor

Fussgänger, - *m.* [*foos'-geng-ər*] pedestrian

Fussknöchel, - *m.* [*foos'-knö-çəl*] ankle

füttern *v.* [*fü'-tərn*] feed [cattle]

G

gab *past tense of* GEBEN [*gahp*] gave

Gabe, -n *f.* [*gah'-bə*] talent, gift

Gabel, -n *f.* [*gah'-bəl*] fork

Gang, ⸗e *m.* [*gang, geng'-ə*] gear [motor]; corridor, stroll

erster (zweiter) Gang [*ehr'-stər (tsvai'-tər) gang*]
    first (second) gear
Gans, ⸗e *f.* [*gans, gen'-zə*] goose
ganz [*gants*] all, whole, complete
    Ganz richtig! [*gants riç'-tiç*] Exactly!
    im ganzen [*im gan'-tsen*] on the whole
gänzlich [*gents'-liç*] entirely
gar (usually in combination with other words) [*gahr*]
    quite, entirely, very, even, at all
    gar nicht [*gahr niçt*] not at all
    gar nichts [*gahr niçts*] nothing at all
Garage, -n *f.* [*ga-rah'-zhə*] garage
Garantie, -n *f.* [*ga-ran-tee'*] guarantee
Garderobe, -n *f.* [*gar-de-roh'-bə*] wardrobe
Gardine, -n *f.* [*gar-dee'-nə*] curtain
Garn, -e *n.* [*garn*] yarn
Garten, ⸗ *m.* [*gar'-tən, ger'-tən*] garden
Gärtner, - *m.* [*gert'-nər*] gardener
Gas, -e *n.* [*gahs, gah'-zə*] gas
Gasse, -n *f.* [*ga'-sə*] alley, lane
Gast, ⸗e *m.* [*gast, ge'-stə*] guest
Gastfreundschaft *f.* [*gast'-froint-shaft*] hospitality
Gastgeber, - *m.* [*gast'-geh-bər*] host
Gastgeberin, -nen *f.* [*gast'-geh-bə-rin*] hostess
Gasthaus, ⸗er *n.* [*gast'-hous, gast'-hoi-zər*] inn, restaurant
Gatte, -n *m.* [*ga'-tə*] husband, spouse [male]
Gattin, -nen *f.* [*ga'-tin*] wife, spouse [female]
Gauner, - *m.* [*gou'-nər*] crook
Gebäck *n.* [*gə-bek'*] pastry
gebären *v. irreg.* [*gə-beh'-rən*] bear, give birth
Gebäude, - *m.* [*gə-boi'-də*] building
geben *v. irreg.* [*geh'-bən*] give
    (Karten) geben [*(kar'-tən) geh'-bən*] deal (cards)
    es gibt [*es geept*] there is, there are
Gebet, -e *n.* [*gə-beht'*] prayer
Gebiet, -e *n.* [*gə-beet'*] territory, region, district
gebildet [*ge-bil'-det*] educated
Gebirge, - *n.* [*gə-bir'-gə*] mountains, mountain chain

Gebirgskette, -n *f.* [*gə-birks'-ke-tə*] mountain range

geboren *past part. of* GEBÄREN [*gə-boh'-rən*] born

Gebot, -e *n.* [*gə-boht'*] order, command, offer

  die zehn Gebote *pl.* [*dee tsehn ge-boh'-tə*]
  the Ten Commandements

gebraten *past part. of* BRATEN [*gə-brah'-tən*] roasted; fried

Gebrauch, ⸗e *m.* [*gə-broukh', gə-broi'-çə*] use, custom

gebrauchen *v.* [*gə-brou'-khən*] use

Gebühr, -en *f.* [*gə-bühr'*] fee, dues

Geburt, -en *f.* [*gə-boort'*] birth

Geburtsschein, -e *f.* [*gə-boorts'-shain*] birth certificate

Geburtstag, -e *f.* [*gə-burts'-tahk, gə-burts'-tah-gə*] birthday

  Herzlichen Glückwunsch zum Geburtstag! [*herts'-li-çən
  glük'-vunsh tsum gə-burts'-tahk*] Happy Birthday!

Gebüsch, -e *n.* [*gə-büsh'*] bushes

Gedächtnis, -se *n.* [*gə-deçt'-nis*] memory

Gedanke, -n *m.* [*gə-dan'-kə*] thought

gedankenlos [*gə-dan'-kən-los*] thoughtless

Gedicht, -e *n.* [*gə-diçt'*] poem

gedruckt [*gə-drukt'*] printed

Geduld *f.* [*gə-dult'*] patience

geduldig [*gə-dul'-diç*] patient

Gefahr, -en *f.* [*gə-fahr'*] danger

  ausser Gefahr [*ou'-sər gə-fahr'*] out of danger

gefahren *past part. of* FAHREN [*gə-fah'-rən*] gone;
  traveled; driven, ridden

gefährlich [*gə-fehr'-liç*] dangerous

  Gefährliche Kurve [*gə-fehr'-li-çə kur'-və*] Dangerous curve

Gefährte, -n *m.* [*gə-fehr'-tə*] companion [male]

Gefährtin, -nen *f.* [*gə-fehr'-tin*] companion [female]

Gefallen *m.* [*gə-fa'-lən*] favor

  Tun Sie mir den Gefallen [*toon zee meer dehn gə-fa'-lən*]
  Do me the favor

gefallen *v. irreg.* [*gə-fa'-lən*] to please, to suit

  Gefällt es Ihnen? [*gə-felt' es ee'-nən*] Does it please you?,
  Do you like it?

Gefangene, -n *m., f.* [*gə-fang'-ə-nə*] prisoner

Gefängnis, -se *n.* [*gə-feng'-nis*] prison, jail

Geflügel *n.* [*gǝ-flüh'-gǝl*] poultry
gefroren *past part. of* FRIEREN [*gǝ-froh'-rǝn*] frozen
Gefühl, -e *n.* [*gǝ-fühl'*] feeling
gegen *prep.* (plus acc.) [*geh'-gǝn*] against; around, about; opposed to; somewhere near
  gegen Mittag [*geh'-gǝn mi'-tahk*] around noon
  gegen zehn Uhr [*gǝh'-gǝn tsehn oor*] around 10 o'clock
Gegend, -en *f.* [*geh'-gǝnt, geh'-gǝn-dǝn*] region
Gegengift, -e *n.* [*geh'-gǝn-gift*] antidote
Gegensatz, ⸗e *m.* [*geh'-gǝn-zats, geh'-gǝn-ze-tsǝ*] contrast
gegenseitig [*geh'-gǝn-zai-tiç*] mutual
Gegenstand, ⸗e *m.* [*geh'-gǝn-shtant, geh'-gǝn-shten-dǝ*] subject [general]; object
Gegenteil *n.* [*geh'-gǝn-tail*] contrary
  im Gegenteil [*im geh'-gǝn-tail*] on the contrary
gegenüber [*geh-gǝn-üh'-bǝr*] vis-à-vis, opposite, across
Gegenwart *f.* [*geh'-gǝn-vart*] present, presence
gegenwärtig *adv.* [*geh-gǝn-ver'-tiç*] at present
Gegner, - *m.* [*gehg'-nǝr*] adversary
gehabt *past part. of* HABEN [*gǝ-hapt'*] had
Gehalt, ⸗er *n.* [*gǝ-halt', gǝ-hel'-tǝr*] salary
gehalten *past part. of* HALTEN [*gǝ-hal'-tǝn*] held
geheim [*gǝ-haim'*] secret
Geheimnis, -se *n.* [*gǝ-haim'-nis*] secret, mystery
geheimnisvoll [*gǝ-haim'-nis-fol*] mysterious
gehen *v. irreg.* (*Aux:* SEIN) [*geh'-ǝn*] go
  Gehen Sie zurück! [*geh'-ǝn zee tsu-rük'*] Go back!
Gehirn, -e *n.* [*gǝ-hirn'*] brain
Gehör *n.* [*gǝ-hohr'*] hearing, ear
gehorchen *v.* [*gǝ-hor'-çǝn*] obey
gehören (plus dat.) *v.* [*gǝ-höh'-rǝn*] belong (to)
gehorsam [*gǝ-hohr'-zahm*] obedient
Geige, -n *f.* [*gai'-gǝ*] violin
Geist, -er *m.* [*gaist, gai'-stǝr*] spirit
geisteskrank [*gai'-stǝs-krank*] mentally ill, insane
geistig [*gai'-stiç*] spiritual, intellectual, mental
  geistig gesund [*gai'-stiç gǝ-zunt'*] sane
Geistliche, -n *m.* [*gaist'-li-çǝ*] minister [church]

Geistlichkeit *f.* [*gaist'-liç-kait*] clergy
geizig [*gai'-tsiç*] stingy
gekannt *past part. of* KENNEN [*gə-kant'*] known
gekonnt *past part. of* KÖNNEN [*gə-kont'*] known
Gelächter *n.* [*gə-leç'-tər*] laughter
gelähmt [*gə-lehmt'*] paralyzed
gelassen [*gə-la'-sən*] calm
gelaufen *past part. of* LAUFEN [*gə-lou'-fən*] run
gelaunt [*gə-lount'*] disposed
   gut gelaunt [*goot gə-lount'*] in a good mood
   schlecht gelaunt [*shleçt gə-lount'*] in a bad mood
gelb [*gelp*] yellow
Geld, -er *n.* [*gelt, gel'-dər*] money
Geld aus-geben *v. irreg.* [*gelt ous'-geh-bən*] spend money
Geldmittel *n. pl.* [*gelt'-mi-təl*] funds
Geldschrank, ⸚e *m.* [*gelt'-shrank, gelt'-shren-kə*] safe
Geldtasche, -n *f.* [*gelt'-ta-shə*] purse
Gelee, -s *n.* [*zhe-leh', zhe-lehs'*] jelly
gelegen *past part. of* LIEGEN [*gə-leh'-gən*] located, situated
gelesen *past part. of* LESEN [*gə-leh'-zən*] read
Gelegenheit, -en *f.* [*gə-leh'-gən-hait*] opportunity
gelegentlich [*gə-leh'-gənt-liç*] occasionally
Gelehrsamkeit *f.* [*gə-lehr'-sam-kait*] learning
gelehrt *adj.* [*gə-lehrt'*] learned
Gelehrte, -n *m., f.* [*gə-lehr'-tə*] scholar
Geleise, - *n.* [*gə-lai'-zə*] tracks [of railroad]
Gelenk, -e *n.* [*gə-lenk'*] joint
geliehen *past part. of* LEIHEN [*gə-lee'-ən*] lent
gelingen (plus dat.) *v. irreg.* (*Aux:* SEIN) [*gə-ling'-ən*]
   succeed in
gelten *v.* [*gel'-tən*] matter, be valid
  Das gilt nicht [*das gilt niçt*] That does not count
Gelübde, - *n.* [*gə-liip'-də*] vow
Gemahl, -e *m.* [*gə-mahl'*] husband
Gemahlin, -nen *f.* [*gə-mah'-lin*] wife
Gemälde, - *n.* [*gə-mehl'-də*] painting
gemein [*gə-main'*] common; low, vulgar, mean
Gemeinde, -n *f.* [*gə-main'-də*] community; congregation

Gemeinheit, -en *f.* [*gə-main'-hait*] vulgarity, mean trick

Gemeinschaft, -en *f.* [*gə-main'-shaft*] community

gemischt [*gə-misht'*] mixed

Gemüse, - *n.* [*gə-müh'-zə*] vegetable

gemütlich [*gə-müht'-liç*] comfortable, cosy

Gemütlichkeit *f.* [*gə-müht'-liç-kait*] cosiness; good nature; comfort

genau [*gə-nou'*] exact, precise

Genauigkeit *f.* [*gə-nou'-iç-kait*] accuracy

General, -e *m.* [*ge-ne-rahl'*] general

Generation, -en *f.* [*ge-nə-ra-tsi-ohn'*] generation

Genesung *f.* [*gə-neh'-zung*] convalescence

Genick, -e *n.* [*gə-nik'*] neck

Genie, -s *n.* [*zhe-nee', zhe-nees'*] genius

geniessen *v. irreg.* [*gə-nee'-sən*] enjoy

genug [*gə-nook'*] enough

   mehr als genug [*mehr als gə-nook'*] more than enough

   Das ist genug [*das ist gə-nook'*] That's enough

genügend [*gə-nüh'-gənt*] sufficient

Genugtuung, -en *f.* [*gə-nook'-too-ung*] satisfaction

Genuss, ⸗e *m.* [*gə-nus', gə-nü'-sə*] enjoyment

geöffnet [*gə-öf'-net*] open

Geographie *f.* [*ge-o-gra-fee'*] geography

Gepäck *n.* [*gə-pek'*] baggage, luggage

Gepäckschein, -e *m.* [*gə-pek'-shain*] baggage check

Gepäckträger, - *m.* [*gə-pek'-treh-gər*] porter

Geplauder *n.* [*gə-plou'-dər*] chat

gerade [*gə-rah'-də*] straight, erect, even

   gerade wie [*gə-rah'-də vee*] just as

   gerade Zahl [*ge-rah'-də tsahl*] even number

geradeaus [*gə-rah'-də-ous*] straight ahead

Gerät, -e *n.* [*gə-reht'*] implement, tool; household stuff

geräumig [*ge-roi'-miç*] spacious

Geräusch, -e *n.* [*gə-roish'*] noise

gerecht [*gə-reçt'*] just, fair

Gerechtigkeit *f.* [*gə-reç'-tiç-kait*] justice

Gericht, -e *n.* [*gə-riçt'*] court of justice; dish, course

gering [*gə-ring'*] slight

geringst [gə-ringst'] least
gern [gern] with pleasure, willingly
  Gern geschehen! [gern gə-sheh'-ən] Don't mention it!
  Trinken Sie gern Bier? [trin'-kən zee gern beer] Do you
    like beer?
  gern haben v. irreg. [gern hah'-bən] like
Geruch, ⸗e m. [gə-rukh', gə-rü'-çə] smell, odor
Gerücht, -e n. [gə-riiçt'] rumor
gesamt [gə-zamt'] total
Gesandte, -n m. [gə-zan'-tə] ambassador
Gesandtin, -nen f. [gə-zan'-tin] ambassadress
Gesang, ⸗e m. [gə-zang', gə-zeng'-ə] song, singing
Geschäft, -e n. [gə-sheft'] business; shop, store; affair
Geschäftsman m. sing. **Geschäftsleute** pl. [gə-shefts'-man,
  gə-shefts'-loi-tə] businessman
geschehen v. irreg. (Aux: SEIN) [gə-sheh'-ən] happen
  Wann ist das geschehen? [van ist das gə-sheh'-ən]
    When did it happen?
gescheit [gə-shait'] smart, clever
Geschenk, -e n. [gə-shenk'] present, gift
Geschichte, -n f. [gə-shiç'-tə] story, tale, history
geschickt [ge-shikt'] skillful, clever
Geschicklichkeit, -en f. [gə-shik'-liç-kait] skill
Geschirr n. [gə-shir'] dishes
geschlafen past part. of SCHLAFEN [gə-shlah'-fən] slept
geschlagen past part. of SCHLAGEN [gə-shlah'-gən] struck, hit
Geschlecht, -er n. [gə-shleçt', gə-shleç'-tər] sex, gender
geschlechtlich [gə-shleçt'-liç] sexual
Geschlechtsverkehr m. [gə-shleçts'-fer-kehr] sexual intercourse
geschlossen past part. of SCHLIESSEN [gə-shlo'-sən] shut,
  closed
Geschmack, ⸗e m. [gə-shmak', ge-shme'-kə] taste, flavor
Geschöpf, -e n. [gə-shöpf'] creature
Geschrei n. [gə-shrai'] screams, shouting
Geschütz, -e n. [gə-shüts'] gun, cannon
Geschwindigkeit, -en f. [gə-shvin'-diç-kait] velocity, speed
Geschwindigkeitsgrenze, -n f. [gə-shvin'-diç-kaits-gren-tsə]
  speed limit

Geschworenen *pl.* [gə-shvoh'-re-nən] jury

gesehen *past part. of* SEHEN [gə-zeh'-ən] seen

Gesellschaft, -en *f.* [gə-zel'-shaft] society, company; party

Gesellschafter, - *m.* [gə-zel'-shaf-tər] partner [business]

gesessen *past part. of* SITZEN [gə-ze'-sən] sat

Gesetz, -e *n.* [gə-zets'] law

gesetzlich [gə-zets'-liç] legal

gesetzwidrig [gə-zets'-veed-riç] illegal, against the law

Gesicht, -er *n.* [gə-ziçt', ge-ziç'-tər] face

Gesichtspunkt, -e *m.* [gə-ziçts'-punkt] viewpoint

Gesichtszug, ⸗e *m.* [gə-ziçts'-tsook, gə-ziçts'-tsüh-gə]
    feature [face]

Gespenst, -er *n.* [gə-shpenst', gə-shpen'-stər] ghost

Gespräch, -e *n.* [gə-shpreḥç'] talk, conversation

gesprochen *past part. of* SPRECHEN [gə-shpro'-khən] spoken

gesprungen *past part. of* SPRINGEN [gə-shprung'-ən] sprung

Gestalt, -en *f.* [gə-shtalt'] form, shape, figure

gestalten *v.* [gə-shtal'-tən] form

gestanden *past part. of* STEHEN [gə-shtan'-dən] stood

Geständnis, -se *n.* [gə-shtent'-nis] confession

gestehen *v. irreg.* [gə-shteh'-ən] confess

gestern [ge'-stərn] yesterday

    gestern abend [ge'-stərn ah'-bənt] last night

gestohlen *past part. of* STEHLEN [gə-shtoh'-lən] stolen

gesund [gə-zunt'] healthy

    der gesunde Menschenverstand *m.* [dehr gə-zun'-də men'-
    shən-fer-shtant] common sense

Gesundheit *f.* [gə-zunt'-hait] health

    bei guter Gesundheit sein *v.,* [bai goo'-tər gə-zunt'-hait zain]
    be in good health

    Gesundheit! [gə-zunt'-hait] God bless you!

gesunken *past part. of* SINKEN [gə-zun'-kən] sunk

Getränk, -e *n.* [gə-trenk'] drink, beverage

Getreide, - *n.* [gə-trai'-də] corn, grain

getrennt *adj.* [gə-trent'] separate

getroffen *past part. of* TREFFEN [gə-tro'-fən] met
    [definite appointment]

gewachsen *past part. of* WACHSEN [gə-vak'-sən] grown

gewähren *v.* [*gə-veh'-rən*] award

Gewalt, -en *f.* [*gə-valt'*] force, power, violence

Gewaltsamkeit *f.* [*gə-valt'-zam-kait*] violence

gewalttätig [*gə-valt'-teh-tiç*] violent

Gewand, ⸗er *n.* [*gə-vant'*, *gə-ven'-dər*] garment

Gewebe, - *n.* [*gə-veh'-bə*] tissue, fabric

Gewehr, -e *n.* [*gə-vehr'*] gun, rifle

Gewicht, -e *n.* [*gə-viçt'*] weight

Gewinn, -e *m.* [*gə-vin'*] gain, gains, profit

gewinnen *v. irreg.* [*gə-vi'-nən*] win, gain

gewiss [*gə-vis'*] certain(ly)

Gewissen *n.* [*gə-vi'-sən*] conscience

gewissenhaft [*gə-vi'-sən-haft*] conscientious

Gewitter, - *n.* [*gə-vi'-tər*] thunderstorm

(sich) gewöhnen *v.* [(*ziç*) *gə-vöh'-nən*] become accustomed to

Gewohnheit, -en *f.* [*gə-vohn'-hait*] habit, routine

gewöhnlich [*gə-vöhn'-liç*] common, usual, vulgar

Gewölbe, - *n.* [*gə-völ'-bə*] vault

Gewürz, -e *n.* [*gə-vürts'*] spice

gewusst *past part. of* WISSEN [*gə-vust'*] known

giessen *v. irreg.* [*gee'-sən*] pour

Gift, -e *n.* [*gift*] poison

giftig [*gif'-tiç*] poisonous

Gipfel, - *m.* [*gi'-pfəl*] top, summit

Gitarre, -n *f.* [*gi-ta'-rə*] guitar

glänzen *v.* [*glent'-sən*] glitter, shine

glänzend [*glent'-sənt*] brilliant

Glas, ⸗er *n.* [*glahs*, *gleh'-zər*] glass

Gläschen, - *n.* [*glehs'-çən*] little glass

glatt [*glat*] smooth

Glatze, -n *f.* [*gla'-tsə*] bald head

Glaube(n) *m.* [*glou'-bə(n)*] faith, belief

glauben *v.* [*glou'-bən*] believe, trust

glaubhaft [*gloup'-haft*] credible

Gläubiger, - *m.* [*gloi'-bi-gər*] creditor

gleich [*glaiç*] even, equal, like

   Es ist mir gleich [*es ist meer glaiç*] It's all the same to me

Gleichberechtigung *f.* [*glaiç'-bə-reç-ti-gung*] equality of rights

gleichen *v. irreg.* [*glai'-çən*] resemble; equal
Gleichfalls! [*glaiç'-fals*] Likewise!
gleichgültig [*glaiç'-gül-tiç*] indifferent
Gleichheit, -en *f.* [*glaiç'-hait*] equality
gleichzeitig [*glaiç'-tsai-tiç*] simultaneous(ly)
Gletscher, - *m.* [*gle'-chər*] glacier
Glied, -er *n.* [*gleet, glee'-dər*] limb
Glocke, -n *f.* [*glo'-kə*] bell
Glück *n.* [*glük*] happiness; good luck
   Glück haben *v.* [*glük hah'-bən*] be lucky
   Viel Glück! [*feel glük*] Good luck!
glücklich [*glük'-liç*] happy, fortunate
glücklicherweise [*glük'-li-çər-vai-zə*] fortunately
Glückwunsche *m. pl.* [*glük'-vun-shə*] congratulations
Glühbirne, -n *f.* [*glüh'-bir-nə*] bulb [light]
glühen *v.* [*glüh'-ən*] glow
Glut, -en *f.* [*gloot*] glow; fire
Gnade, -n *f.* [*gnah'-də*] favor; mercy, grace, clemency
gnädig [*gneh'-diç*] gracious, kind, merciful
   Gnädige Frau *f.* [*gneh'-di-gə frou*] Madam
   [form of address]
Gold *n.* [*golt*] gold
   aus Gold [*ous golt*] (of) gold
golden [*gol'-dən*] golden
Golf *n.* [*golf*] golf
Gotik *f.* [*goh'-tik*] Gothic
gotisch [*goh'-tish*] Gothic
Gott, ⸗er *m.* [*got, gö'-tər*] God
   Gott steht uns bei! [*got shteht uns bai*] God help us!
   Mein Gott! [*main got*] Good heavens!
göttlich [*göt'-liç*] divine
Grab, ⸗er *n.* [*grahp, greh'-bər*] tomb, grave
Graben, ⸗ *m.* [*grah'-bən, greh'-bən*] ditch, trench
graben *v. irreg.* [*grah'-bən*] dig
Grabstein, -e *m.* [*grahp'-shtain, grahp'-shtai-nə*] tombstone
Grad, -e *m.* [*graht, grah'-də*] degree, grade
Graf, -en *m.* [*grahf, graf'-en*] count
Gräfin, -nen *f.* [*greh'-fin*] countess

Grammatik, -en *f.* [*gra-ma'-tik*] grammar

Granate, -n *f.* [*gra-nah'-tə*] shell [gun]

Gras, ⸗er *n.* [*grahs, greh'-sər*] grass

gratis [*grah'-tis*] gratis

gratulieren (plus dat.) *v.* [*gra-tu-lee'-rən*] congratulate

grau [*grou*] grey

grausam [*grou'-zam*] cruel

Grausamkeit, -en *f.* [*grou'-zam-kait*] cruelty

greifen *v. irreg.* [*grai'-fən*] grasp

Greis, -e *m.* [*grais*] old man

Greisin, -nen *f.* [*grai'-zin*] old woman

Grenze, -n *f.* [*grent'-sə*] limit, border, boundary

grenzen (an plus acc.) *v.* [*grent'-sən*] verge (on)

Griechenland *n.* [*gree'-çən-lant*] Greece

griechisch [*gree'-çish*] Greek

Griff, -e *m.* [*grif*] grip, handle

grob [*grohp*] rude, coarse

Grobheit, -en *f.* [*grohp'-hait*] rudeness

gross [*grohs*] tall, big, large, great

   die Grossen *pl.* [*dee groh'-sən*] the grown-ups

grossartig [*grohs'-ar-tiç*] great, first-rate

Grossbritannien *n.* [*grohs'-bri-ta-ni-ən*] Great Britain

Grösse, -n *f.* [*gröh'-sə*] size, greatness

Grosseltern *pl.* [*grohs'-el-tərn*] grandparents

Grossmutter, ⸗ *f.* [*grohs'-mu-tər, grohs'-mü-tər*] grandmother

Grossvater, ⸗ *m.* [*grohs'-fah-tər, grohs'-feh-tər*] grandfather

Grube, -n *f.* [*groo'-bə*] ditch, hole, mine

grün [*grühn*] green

Grund, ⸗e *m.* [*grunt, grün'-də*] reason

gründen *v.* [*grün'-dən*] establish, found

grundlegend [*grunt'-leh-gənt*] basic

gründlich [*grünt'-liç*] thorough(ly)

Grundsatz, ⸗e *m.* [*grunt'-zats, grunt'-ze-tsə*] principle

Grundstück, -e *n.* [*grunt'-shtük*] property, lot, realty

Gründung, -en *f.* [*grün'-dung*] foundation

Gruppe, -n *f.* [*gru'-pə*] group

Grüsse *m. pl.* [*grüh'-sə*] greetings

   beste Grüsse [*be'-stə grüh'-sə*] kind regards

grüssen v. [grüh'-sən] greet, salute
    Grüssen Sie ihn von mir [grüh'-sən zee een fon meer]
      Remember me to him
gültig [gül'-tiç] valid
Gummi n. [gu'-mee] rubber
Gummi, -s m. [gu'-mee, gu'-mees] eraser
günstig [gün'-stiç] favorable
Günstling, -e m. [günst'-ling] favorite
Gurke, -n f. [gur'-kə] cucumber
Gürtel, - m. [gür'-təl] girdle, belt
Gut, ⸗er n. [goot, güh'-tər] estate, farm; blessing
gut [goot] good
    Guten Abend! [goo'-tən ah'-bənt] Good evening!
    Guten Morgen! [goo'-tən mor'-gən] Good morning!
    Gute Nacht! [goo'-tə nakht] Good night!
    Guten Tag! [goo'-tən tahk] Good day!
    Guten Tag! Wie geht es Ihnen? [goo'-tən tahk vee geht
      es ee'-nən] How do you do? [at introductions]
gut aussehend [goot ous'-zeh-ənt] goodlooking
Güte f. [güh'-tə] goodness
Guthaben, - n. [goot'-hah-bən] credit
gütig [güh'-tiç] good, kind
Gutschein, -e m. [goot'-shain] coupon
Gymnastik f. [giim-na'-stik] gymnastics

H

Haar, -e n. [hahr] hair
    Ich liess mir gestern die Haare schneiden [iç lees meer
      ge'-stərn dee hah'-rə shnai-dən] I had a hair-cut
      yesterday
Haarbürste, -n f. [hahr'-bür-stə] hairbrush
Haarnetz, -e n. [hahr'-nets] hairnet
Haarschnitt, -e m. [hahr'-shnit] haircut
Haarwasser, ⸗ n. [hahr'-va-sər, hahr'-veh-sər] hair tonic

haben *v. irreg.* [*hah'-bən*] have

Hafen, ⸗ *m.* [*hah'-fən, heh'-fən*] port, harbor

Hafenstadt, ⸗e *f.* [*hah'-fən-shtat, hah-fen-shte'-tə*] seaport

Hafer, - *m.* [*hah'-fər*] oats

Haft *f.* [*haft*] detention, custody

Hagel *m.* [*hah'-gəl*] hail

Hahn, ⸗e *m.* [*hahn, heh'-nə*] faucet, rooster

Haifisch, -e *m.* [*hai'-fish*] shark

Haken, - *m.* [*hah'-kən*] hook

halb [*halp*] half

 halb acht [*halp akht*] half-past seven

 halb zwei [*halp tsvai*] half-past one

Halbinsel, -n *f.* [*halp'-in-zəl*] peninsula

halbwegs [*halp'-vehks*] halfway

Hälfte, -n *f.* [*helf'-tə*] half

Hallo! [*ha-loh'*] Hello!

Hals, ⸗e *m.* [*hals, hel'-zə*] neck, throat

Hals- und Beinbruch! [*hals- unt bain'-brukh*] Good luck! [Am. theatrical equiv.: Break a leg!]

Halskette, -n *f.* [*hals'-ke-tə*] necklace

Halsschmerzen *m. pl.* [*hals'-shmer-tsən*] sore throat

 Halsschmerzen haben *v.* [*hals'-shmer-tsən hah'-bən*] have a sore throat

Halstuch, ⸗er *n.* [*hals'-tookh, hals'-tü-çər*] scarf

halten *v. irreg.* [*hal'-tən*] hold, maintain; keep [a promise]; make [a speech]

 Halt! [*halt*] Stop!

 Halten Sie hier! [*hal'-tən zee heer*] Stop here!

 Ich halte viel von ihr [*iç hal'-tə feel fon eer*] I think highly of her

 Was halten Sie davon? [*vas hal'-tən zee da-fon'*] How does it seem to you?

Haltestelle, -n *f.* [*hal'-tə-shte-lə*] (bus)stop

Hammelfleisch *n.* [*ha'-məl-flaish*] mutton

Hammer, ⸗ *m.* [*ha'-mər, he'-mər*] hammer

Hand, ⸗e *f.* [*hant, hen'-də*] hand

Handarbeit, -en *f.* [*hant'-ar-bait*] handmade; needlework

Handel *m.* [*han'-dəl*] trade, business, transaction

handeln v. [han'-dəln] trade, deal in goods; bargain; act
  sich handeln um [ziç han'-dəln um] be about; be a
    question of
  Das Buch handelt von . . . [das bookh han'-dəlt fon]
    The book deals with . . .
Handelsgesellschaft, -en f. [han'-dəls-gə-zel-shaft]
    company [business]
handgenäht [hant'-gə-neht] handsewn
Handgriff, -e m. [hant'-grif] handle
handhaben v. [hant'-hah-bən] handle; manage, manipulate
Händler, - m. [hend'-lər] dealer
Handlung, -en f. [hand'-lung] action, deed; shop
Handschuh, -e m. [hant'-shoo] glove
Handtasche, -n f. [hant'-ta-shə] handbag
Handtuch, ⸗er n. [hant'-tookh, hand'-tüh-çər] towel
Handwerk, -e n. [hant'-verk] handicraft, trade
Handwerker, - m. [hant'-ver-kər] craftsman, artisan
hängen v, irreg. [heng'-ən] hang [an object]
hängen v. irreg. [heng'-ən] hang [be suspended]
Harfe, -n f. [har'-fə] harp
hart [hart] hard
hartherzig [hart'-her-tsiç] hardhearted
hartnäckig [hart'-ne-kiç] stubborn
Hase, -n m. [hah'-zə] hare
Hass m. [has] hate, hatred
hassen v. [ha'-sən] hate
hässlich [hes'-liç] ugly
Hast f. [hast] haste, hurry
hat 3d. pers. sing. pres. tense of HABEN [hat] has
hatte past tense of HABEN [ha'-tə] had
hätte ich pres. subj. of HABEN [he'-tə iç] if I had; had I
Hau ab! [hou ap] Beat it!
Haufen, - m. [hou'-fən] pile, heap
häufig [hoi'-fiç] frequently
Haupt- prefix [houpt] principal, chief, main
Hauptbahnhof, ⸗e m. [houpt'-bahn-hohf, houpt-bahn-höh'-fə]
    central railway station
Hauptpostamt, ⸗er n. [houpt'-post-amt, houpt'-post-em-tər]

general post-office

Hauptquartier, -e *n.* [*houpt'-kvar-teer*] headquarters [army]

Hauptsache, -n *f.* [*houpt'-za-khə*] main thing, main point

hauptsächlich *adv.* [*houpt-zeç'-liç*] essentially, mainly

Hauptstadt, =e *f.* [*houpt'-shtat, houpt'-shte-tə*] capital [city]

Hauptstrasse, -n *f.* [*houpt'-shtrah-sə, -shtrah-sən*] main street

Hauptwort, =er *n.* [*houpt'-vort, houpt'-vör-tər*] noun

Haus, =er *n.* [*hous, hoi'-zər*] house

  im Hause [*im hou'-zə*] indoors

  zu Hause [*tsu hou'-zə*] at home

Hausfrau, -en *f.* [*hous'-frou*] housewife

Haushalt, -e *m.* [*hous'-halt*] household

Haushaltsplan, =e *m.* [*hous'-halts-plahn, hous'-halts-pleh-nə*] budget

Haushälterin, -nen *f.* [*hous'-hel-tə-rin*] housekeeper

Hausschuhe *m. pl.* [*hous'-shoo-ə*] slippers

Haustier, -e *n.* [*hous'-teer*] domestic animal

Haut, =e *f.* [*hout, hoi'-tə*] skin

heben *v. irreg.* [*heh'-bən*] raise, lift

hebräisch [*he-breh'-ish*] Hebrew

Heer, -e *n.* [*hehr*] army

Hefe, -n *f.* [*heh'-fə*] yeast

Heft, -e *n.* [*heft*] notebook; issue [of periodical]; handle [of knife]

heften *v.* [*hef'-tən*] fasten, pin; stitch, baste; staple

heftig [*hef'-tiç*] violent

heilen *v.* [*hai'-lən*] cure

heilig [*hai'-liç*] sacred, holy

Heilige, -n *m., f.* [*hai'-li-gə*] saint

Heilung, -en *f.* [*hai'-lung*] cure

Heim, -e *n.* [*haim*] home

Heimatland, -er *n.* [*hai'-mat-lant, hai'-mat-len-dər*] native land

heimlich [*haim'-liç*] secret, clandestine

Heimweh *n.* [*haim'-veh*] homesickness, nostalgia

  Heimweh haben *v.* [*haim'-veh hah'-bən*] be homesick

Heirat, -en *f.* [*hai'- raht*] marriage

heiraten *v.* [*hai'-rah-tən*] marry

heiser [*hai'-zər*] hoarse

heiss [*hais*] hot

heissen *v. irreg.* [*hai'-sən*] be called

   Wie heissen Sie? Ich heisse . . . [*vee hai'-sən zee? iç hai'-sə*]
     What is your name? My name is . . .

heiter [*hai'-tər*] cheerful, serene

Heiterkeit *f.* [*hai'-tər-kait*] gaiety, serenity

heizen *v.* [*hait'-sən*] heat

Heizkörper, - *m.* [*haits'-kör-pər*] radiator

Heizung, -en *f.* [*hait'-sung*] heating

Held, -en *m.* [*helt, hel'-dən*] hero

helfen *v. irreg.* [*hel'-fən*] help

hell [*hel*] clear, bright

Hemd, -en *n.* [*hemt, hem'-dən*] shirt

hemmen *v.* [*he'-mən*] check, inhibit

Henne, -n *f.* [*he'-nə*] hen

her [*hehr*] here, this way

   Kommen Sie her! [*ko'-mən zee hehr*] Come here!

herab-setzen *v.* [*he-rap'-ze-tsən*] reduce [prices]

herauf [*he-rouf'*] upwards; from below [toward the speaker]

heraus [*he-rous'*] out

heraus-fordern *v.* [*he-rous'-for-dərn*] challenge

Herausforderung, -en *f.* [*he-rous'-for-də-rung*] challenge

heraus-kommen *v. irreg.* (*Aux:* SEIN) [*he-rous'-ko-mən*]
   come out, be published

heraus-ziehen *v. irreg.* [*he-rous'-tsee-ən*] pull out

Herbst, -e *m.* [*herpst*] autumn, fall

Herd, -e *m.* [*hehrt, hehr'-də*] hearth; oven

Herde, -n *f.* [*hehr'-də*] flock, herd

Herein! [*he-rain'*] Come in!

Hering, -e *m.* [*heh'-ring*] herring

herein-bringen *v. irreg.* [*he-rain'-bring-ən*] bring in

herein-rufen *v. irreg.* [*he-rain'-roo-fən*] call in

her-kommen *v. irreg.* (*Aux:* SEIN) [*her'-ko-mən*] come from,
   arise from

Herr, -en *m.* [*her*] Mr. [followed by proper name],
   gentleman; lord, master

   Herr, mein Herr [*her, main her*] Sir [in direct address]

   der Herr [*dehr her*] the Lord [God]

Herren *pl.* [*he'-rən*] Gentlemen

herrlich [*her'-liç*] superb

Herrscher, - *m.* [*her'-shər*] ruler [male]

Herrscherin, -nen *f.* [*her'-shə-rin*] ruler [female]

her-stellen *v.* [*her'-shte-lən*] manufacture; establish

Herstellung *f.* [*her'-shte-lung*] production

herum [*he-rum'*] around, about

herunter [*he-run'-tər*] down, downward

herunter-kommen *v. irreg.* (*Aux:* SEIN) [*he-run'-tər-ko-mən*] descend, come down(stairs); come down in the world

hervor-heben *v. irreg.* [*her-fohr'-heh-bən*] emphasize, give prominence to

hervorragend [*her-fohr'-rah-gənt*] outstanding, first-rate, conspicuous

Herz, -en *n.* [*herts*] heart

Herzkrankheit, -en *f.* [*herts'-krank-hait*] heart disease

herzlich [*herts'-liç*] cordial, affectionate

Herzog, ⸗e *m.* [*her'-tsohk, her'-tsöh-gə*] duke

Herzogin, -nen *f.* [*her'-tso-gin*] duchess

Heu *n.* [*hoi*] hay

heuer [*hoi'-ər*] (in) this year

heute [*hoi'-tə*] today

    von heute an [*fon hoi'-tə an*] from today on

    heute nachmittag [*hoi'-tə nakh'-mi-tahk*] this afternoon

    heute abend [*hoi'-tə ah'-bənt*] this evening, tonight

heutzutage [*hoit'-tsu-tah-gə*] nowadays

hielt *past tense of* HALTEN [*heelt*] held; maintained; kept [a promise]; made [a speech]

hier [*heer*] here

    Hier ist es [*heer ist es*] Here it is

hiermit [*heer'-mit*] herewith

Hilfe, -n *f.* [*hil'-fə*] relief, help

    Hilfe! [*hil'-fə*] Help!

hilflos [*hilf'-los*] helpless

Himbeere, -n *f.* [*him'-beh-rə*] raspberry

Himmel, - *m.* [*hi'-mel*] heaven, sky

    Lieber Himmel! [*lee'-bər hi'-məl*] Heavens!

    um Himmelswillen [*um hi'-məls-vi-lən*] for heaven's sake

hin [*hin*] to, toward
   hin und wieder [*hin unt vee'-der*] now and then
   Wo gehen Sie hin? [*voh geh'-ən zee hin*] Where are you
     going to?
hinab [*hi-nap'*] down, downward [away from the speaker]
hinauf [*hi-nouf'*] up, upward
hinauf-steigen auf (plus acc.) *v. irreg.* (*Aux:* SEIN)
   [*hi-nouf'-shtai-gən ouf*] climb
hinaus [*hi-nous'*] out
hinaus-gehen *v. irreg.* (*Aux:* SEIN) [*hi-nous'-geh-ən*] go out
hindern *v.* [*hin'-dərn*] prevent
hinein *adv.* [*hi-nain'*] in, into
hinein-gehen *v. irreg.* (*Aux:* SEIN) [*hi-nain'-geh-ən*] go in
(sich) hin-legen *v.* [(*ziç*) *hin'-leh-gən*] lie down
(sich) hin-setzen *v.* [(*ziç*) *hin'-ze-tsən*] sit down
Hinsicht *f.* [*hin'-ziçt*] regard, respect
   in jeder Hinsicht [*in yeh'-dər hin'-ziçt*] in all respects
hinten *adv.* [*hin'-tən*] behind, at the back
hinter *prep.* (plus dat.; acc. for motion) [*hin'-tər*] behind,
   back of
Hinterstube, -n *f.* [*hin'-tər-shtoo-bə*] back room
hinunter *adv.* [*hi-nun'-tər*] down, downstairs
hin-weisen auf (plus acc.) *v. irreg.* [*hin'-vai-sən ouf*] indicate,
   point out
hinzu-fügen *v.* [*hin-tsoo'-füh-gən*] add
Hirsch, -e *m.* [*hirsh*] stag, deer
Hitze *f.* [*hit'-sə*] heat
hoch [*hohkh*] high, tall
   Wie hoch ist dieses Gebäude? [*vee hohkh ist dee'-ses
     gə-boi'-də*] How tall is this building?
Hochachtungsvoll! [*hohkh'-akh-tungs-fol*] Very truly yours
   [close of a letter]
Hochschule, -n *f.* [*hohkh'-shoo-lə*] university, college
Hochspannung! [*hohkh'-shpa-nung*] High tension wires!
höchst *adv.* [*höhçst*] highest, supreme, highly
höchstens *adv.* [*höhç'-stəns*] at best, at most
Höchstgeschwindigkeit, -en *f.* [*höhçst'-gə-shvin-diç-kait*]
   speed limit

Hochzeit, -en *f.* [*hokh'-tsait*] wedding
Hochzeitsreise, -n *f.* [*hokh'-tsaits-rai-zə*] honeymoon trip
Hof, ⸗e *m.* [*hohf, höh'-fə*] court, courtyard, farm(stead), farmyard
hoffen *v.* [*ho'-fən*] hope
hoffentlich [*ho'-fənt-liç*] I hope so; with any luck
Hoffnung, -en *f.* [*hof'-nung*] hope
hoffnungslos [*hof'-nungs-lohs*] hopeless
hoffnungsvoll [*hof'-nungs-fol*] hopeful
höflich [*höhf'-liç*] polite, courteous, respectful
Höhe, -n *f.* [*höh'-ə*] altitude, height
   auf der Höhe sein *v.* [*ouf dehr höh'-ə zain*] be up to the mark
höher [*höh'-ər*] higher
höhere Schule, -n *f.* [*höh'-ə-rə shoo'-lə*] high school
hohl [*hohl*] hollow
Höhle, -n *f.* [*höh'-lə*] cave
Hohn *m.* [*hohn*] scorn, disdain
holen *v.* [*hoh'-lən*] fetch
   holen lassen *v. irreg.* [*hoh'-lən la'-sən*] send for
Holland *n.* [*ho'-lant*] Holland
holländisch [*ho'-len-dish*] Dutch
Hölle, -n *f.* [*hö'-lə*] hell
Holz, ⸗er *n.* [*holts, höl'-tsər*] wood
Honig *m.* [*hoh'-niç*] honey [from bees]
horchen *v.* [*hor'-çən*] listen; eavesdrop
hören *v.* [*höh'-rən*] hear
Horizont, -e *m.* [*ho-ri-tsont'*] horizon
Horn, ⸗er *n.* [*horn, hör'-nər*] horn [of animal]
Hose, -n *f.* [*hoh'-zə*] trousers, pants
Hotel, -s *n.* [*ho-tel', ho-tels'*] hotel
Hotelpage, -n *m.* [*ho-tel'-pah-zhə*] bellboy
Hotelzimmer, - *n.* [*ho-tel'-tsi-mər*] hotel room
hübsch [*hüpsh*] pretty
Hüfte, -n *f.* [*hüf'-tə*] hip
Hügel, - *m.* [*hüh'-gəl*] hill
Huhn, ⸗er *n.* [*hoon, hüh'-nər*] chicken
   Brathuhn, Huhn gebraten [*braht'-hoon, hoon gə-braht'-tən*] roast chicken

Hühnchen, - *n.* [*hühn'-çən*] chicken
Hülle, -n *f.* [*hü'-lə*] wrapping, cover
Humanität *f.* [*hu-ma-ni-teht'*] humanity
Hummer, - *m.* [*hu'-mər*] lobster
Humor *m.* [*hu-mohr'*] humor
humoristisch [*hu-mo-ri'-stish*] humorous
Hund, -e *m.* [*hunt, hun'-də*] dog
hundert [*hun'-dərt*] hundred
Hunger *m.* [*hung'-ər*] hunger
   Ich habe Hunger [*iç hah'-bə hung'-ər*] I'm hungry
hungern *v.* [*hung'-ərn*] starve
hungrig [*hung'-riç*] hungry
Hupe, -n *f.* [*hoo'-pə*] horn [on auto]
Husten *m.* [*hoo'-stən*] cough
husten *v.* [*hoo'-sten*] cough
Hut, ⸗e *m.* [*hoot, hüh'-tə*] hat
(sich) hüten vor (plus dat.) *v.* [(*ziç*) *hüh'-tən fohr*] beware (of), guard against
Hüter, - *m.* [*hüh'-tər*] guardian
Hütte, -n *f.* [*hü'-tə*] cottage, cabin
hygienisch [*hü-gi-eh'-nish*] sanitary
hysterisch [*hü-steh'-rish*] hysterical
Hypothek, -en *f.* [*hü-po-tehk'*] mortgage

I

ich [*iç*] I
ich selbst [*iç zelpst*] I myself
ideal [*i-de-ahl'*] ideal
Idee, -n *f.* [*i-deh'*] idea
identifizieren *v.* [*i-den-ti-fi-tsee'-rən*] identify
identisch [*i-den'-tish*] identical
Idiot, -en *m.* [*id-i-oht'*] idiot
ihm *dat. sing. of* ER [*eem*] (to, for) him, (to, for) it
ihn *acc. sing. of* ER [*een*] him, it

ihnen *dat. pl. of* SIE, *pl.* [*ee'-nən*] (to, for) them

Ihnen *dat. pl. of* SIE [*polite*] *sing. & pl.* [*ee'-nən*] (to, for) you

ihr *dat. sing. of* SIE, *sing.* [*eer*] to her, to it; her, its, their; you [pl., informal]

Ihr *poss. pron.* (polite form) [*eer*] your

ihr *m.* **ihrer** *m.* **ihre** *f.* **ihres** *n., poss. pron.* [*eer, ee'-rər, ee'-rə, ee'-res*] hers, its, theirs

Ihretwegen *adv.* [*ee'-ret-veh-gən*] for your sake [formal]

ihretwegen *adv.* [*ee'-ret-veh-gən*] for her (their) sake

illustriert [*i-lu-streert'*] illustrated

im: in dem [*im*] in the

immer [*i'-mər*] always

    wie immer [*vee i'-mər*] as ever

impfen *v.* [*im'-pfən*] inoculate, vaccinate

Import, -e *m.* [*im-port'*] importation

importieren *v.* [*im-por-tee'-rən*] import

importiert [*im-por-teert'*] imported

imstande [*im-shtan'-də*] capable (of)

in *prep.* (plus dat.; acc. for motion) [*in*] in, at, into, to, within

    In Ordnung! [*in ord'-nung*] All right!

indem *conj.* [*in-dehm'*] while, on, by

Index *m. sing.* **Indices** *pl.* [*in'-deks, in'-di-tses*] index

Indien *n.* [*in'-di-ən*] India

indirekt [*in'-di-rekt*] indirect

indisch [*in'-dish*] Indian

indiskret [*in'-dis-kreht*] indiscreet

individuell [*in-di-vi-du-el'*] individual

Individuum *n. sing.* **Individuen** *pl.* [*in-di-vee'-du-um, in-di-vee'-du-ən*] individual

indossieren *v.* [*in-do-see'-rən*] endorse

Industrie, -en *f.* [*in-du-stree'*] industry

industriell [*in-du-stri-el'*] industrial

Infanterie, -n *f.* [*in-fan-tə-ree'*] infantry

Infinitiv, -e *m.* [*in'-fi-ni-teef, in'-fi-ni-tee-və*] infinitive

infolge *prep.* (plus gen.) [*in-fol'-gə*] on account of, as a result of

Ingenieur, -e *m.* [*in-zhe-ni-öhr'*] engineer

Inhalt, -e *m.* [*in'-halt*] contents
Inland *n.* [*in'-lant*] inland, home (country)
    Inlandsmärkte und Auslandsmärkte *m. pl.*
        [*in'-lants-merk-tə unt ous'-lants-merk-tə*] domestic
        markets and foreign markets
    im Inland und im Ausland [*im in'-lant unt im ous'-lant*]
        at home and abroad
inländisch [*in'-len-dish*] domestic
inner [*i'-nər*] interior, inner, internal; domestic
Innere *n.* [*i'-nə-rə*] interior
innerhalb [*i'-nər-halp*] within
ins: in das [*ins*] into the, to the
    Ich gehe ins Restaurant [*iç geh'-ə ins re-sto-rahnt'*]
        I'm going to the restaurant
insbesondere [*ins'-bə-zon-də-rə*] particularly
Inschrift, -en *f.* [*in'-shrift*] inscription
Insekt, -en *n.* [*in-zekt'*] insect, bug
Insel, -n *f.* [*in'-zəl*] island
insgesamt [*ins-gə-zamt'*] altogether
insofern [*in-zoh-fern'*] inasmuch
Inspektor, -en *m.* [*in-shpek'-tor*] inspector
Instinkt, -e *m.* [*in-stinkt'*] instinct
Institut, -e *n.* [*in-sti-toot'*] institution
Instrument, -e *n.* [*in-stru-ment'*] instrument, tool
intellektuell [*in-te-lek-tu-el'*] intellectual
intelligent [*in-te-li-gent'*] intelligent
intensiv [*in-ten-zeef'*] intense, intensive
interessant [*in-te-re-sant'*] interesting
Interesse, -n *n.* [*in-te-re'-sə*] interest
(sich) interessieren für *v.* [(*ziç*) *in-te-re-see'-rən für*] take an
    interest in
international [*in-tər-na-tsi-o-nahl'*] international
Interview, -s *n.* [*in-tər-vyoo', in-tər-vyoos'*] interview
intim [*in-teem'*] intimate
Invasion, -en *f.* [*in-va-zi-ohn'*] invasion
investieren *v.* [*in-ves-tee'-rən*] invest
inzwischen [*in-tsvi'-shən*] in the meantime
irgend [*ir'-gənt*] some, any

irgendein, irgendeine, irgendeiner; irgendjemand [ir'-gənt-ain, ir'-gənt-ai-nə, ir'-gənt-ai-nər; ir'-gənt-yeh-mant] someone, anyone

irgendetwas [ir'-gənt-et-vas] something, anything

irgendwie [ir'-gənt-vee] somehow, anyhow

irgendwo [ir'-gənt-voh] somewhere, anywhere

irgendwo anders [ir'-gənt-voh an'-dərs] somewhere else

irgendwohin [ir'-gənt-voh-hin] anywhere; [to] somewhere [or other]

irisch [ee'-rish] Irish

Irland n. [ir'-lant] Ireland

irrational [i-ra-tsi-o-nahl'] irrational

(sich) irren (in plus dat.) v. [(ziç) i'-ren (in)] be mistaken (in)

Irrsinn m. [ir'-zin] insanity, madness

Irrtum, ‑er m. [ir'-toom, ir'-tüh-mər] error

ist 3d pers. sing. pres. tense of SEIN [ist] is

Italien n. [i-tah'-li-ən] Italy

italienisch [i-ta-li-eh'-nish] Italian

J

ja [yah] yes

Jacke, -n f. [ya'-ke] jacket

Jagd, -en f. [yahkt] hunt

jagen v. [yah'-gən] chase, hunt

Jäger, - m. [yeh'-gər] hunter

Jahr, -e n. [yahr] year

   im Jahre des Herrn [im yah'-rə des hern] in the year of our Lord

Jahrestag, -e m. [yah'-res-tahk, yah'-rəs-tah-gə] anniversary

Jahreszeit, -en f. [yah'-res-tsait] season

Jahrhundert, -e n. [yahr-hun'-dərt] century

jährlich [yehr'-liç] annual

Jahrzehnt, -e n. [yahr-tsehnt'] decade

Jammer m. [ya'-mər] lamentation, misery

Januar *m.* [*ya-nu-ahr'*] January
Japan *n.* [*yah'-pan*] Japan
japanisch [*ya-pah'-nish*] Japanese
Jawohl! [*ya-vohl'*] Yes, indeed
Jazz *m.* [*dzhahz*] jazz
je [*yeh*] ever
jedenfalls [*yeh'-dən-fals*] in any case, at all events
jeden Nachmittag [*yeh'-dən nakh'-mi-tahk*] every afternoon
jeder, jede, jedes [*yeh'-dər, yeh'-də, yeh'-dəs*] each, every, any
jedermann [*yeh'-dər-man*] everybody, anybody
jederzeit [*yeh'-dər-tsait*] at any time
jedesmal [*yeh'-dəs-mahl*] every time, each time
jedoch [*ye-dokh'*] however
jemals [*yeh'-mahls*] ever
jemand [*yeh'-mant*] someone, somebody, anybody
   jemand anders [*yeh'-mant an'-ders*] someone else
jene *pl.* [*yeh'-nə*] those
jener, jene, jenes [*yeh'-nər, yeh'-nə, yeh'-nəs*] that (one)
jenseits *prep.* (plus gen.) [*yen'-zaits*] beyond
jetzig [*ye'-tsiç*] present, now existing
jetzt [*yetst*] now
   bis jetzt [*bis yetst*] until now
   von jetzt an [*fon yetst an*] from now on
Jod *n.* [*yoht*] iodine
Journal, -e *n.* [*zhur-nahl'*] journal
Journalist, -en *m.* [*zhur-na-list'*] journalist
jucken *v.* [*yu'-kən*] itch
Jude, -n *m.* [*yoo'-də*] Jew
Jüdin, -nen *f.* [*yüh'-din*] Jewess
jüdisch [*yüh'-dish*] Jewish
Jugend *f.* [*yoo'-gent*] youth
Juli *m.* [*yoo'-lee*] July
jung [*yung*] young
Junge, -n *m.* [*yung'-ə*] boy, youngster, fellow
Jungfrau, -en *f.* [*yung'-frou*] virgin, maiden
Junggeselle, -n *m.* [*yung'-gə-ze-lə*] bachelor
Jüngling, -e *m.* [*yüng'-ling*] young man
Juni *m.* [*yoo'-nee*] June

Jurist, -en *m.* [*yu-rist'*] lawyer; law student
Juwel, -en *n.* [*yu-vehl'*] jewel, gem
Juwelier, -e *m.* [*yu-ve-leer'*] jeweler

K

Kabel, - *n.* [*kah'-bəl*] cable
Kabine, -n *f.* [*ka-bee'-nə*] stateroom
Kachel, -n *f.* [*ka'-khəl*] tile
Kaffee, -s *m.* [*ka-feh', ka-fehs'*] coffee
   Ist noch Kaffee übrig? [*ist nokh ka-feh' üh'-briç*] Any
   coffee left?
Kaffeehaus, ⸗er *n.* [*ka-feh'-hous, ka-feh'-hoi-zər*] coffeehouse,
   café
Käfig, -e *m.* [*keh'-fiç, keh'-fi-gə*] cage
kahl [*kahl*] bald
Kai, -s *m.* [*kai, kais*] pier, wharf
Kaiser, - *m.* [*kai'-zər*] emperor
Kakao *m.* [*ka-kah'-o*] cocoa
Kalb, ⸗er *n.* [*kalp, kel'-bər*] calf
Kalbfleisch *n.* [*kalp'-flaish*] veal
Kalbskeule, -n *f.* [*kalps'-koi-lə*] leg of veal
Kalbsschnitzel, - *n.* [*kalps'-shni-tsəl*] veal cutlet
Kalender, - *m.* [*ka-len'-dər*] calendar
kalt [*kalt*] cold
   Mir ist kalt [*meer ist kalt*] I'm cold
Kälte *f.* [*kel'-tə*] cold
Kamel, -e *n.* [*ka-mehl'*] camel
Kamera, -s *f.* [*kah'-mə-rah, kah'-mə-rahs*] camera
Kamerad, -en *m.* [*ka-mə-raht', ka-mə-rah'-dən*] comrade
Kamin, -e *m.* [*ka-meen'*] fireplace
Kamm, ⸗e *m.* [*kam, ke'-mə*] comb; crest [of bird]; ridge
   [of hill]
kämmen *v.* [*ke'-mən*] comb [hair]
Kammerdiener, - *m.* [*ka'-mər-dee-nər*] valet

Kampf, ⸗e *m.* [*kampf, kem'-pfə*] fight, battle

kämpfen *v.* [*kem'-pfən*] fight, struggle

Kanada *n.* [*ka'-na-da*] Canada

kanadisch [*ka-nah'-dish*] Canadian

Kanal, ⸗e *m.* [*ka-nahl', ka-neh'-lə*] canal

Kandidat, -en *m.* [*kan-di-daht'*] candidate

Kaninchen, - *n.* [*ka-neen'-çən*] rabbit

kann *3d pers. sing. pres. tense of* KÖNNEN [*kan*] can; am [is] able to; may; know [knows] [something thoroughly]

Kanone, -n *f.* [*ka-noh'-nə*] cannon, gun

Kante, -n *f.* [*kan'-tə*] edge

Kapital *n. sing.* **Kapitalien** *pl.* [*ka-pi-tahl', ka-pi-tah'-li-ən*] capital [money]

Kapitalismus *m.* [*ka-pi-ta-lis'-mus*] capitalism

Kapitän, -e *m.* [*ka-pi-tehn'*] captain

Kapitel, - *n.* [*ka-pi'-təl*] chapter

kaputt [*ka-put'*] broken, in pieces, out of order

Karneval, -e *m.* [*kar'-nə-val*] carnival

Karotte, -n *f.* [*ka-ro'-tə*] carrot

Karriere, -n *f.* [*ka-ri-eh'-rə*] career

Karte, -n *f.* [*kar'-te*] ticket [for trains, shows]; postcard; menu; map

Kartenschalter, - *m.* [*kar'-tən-shal-tər*] ticket window

Kartenspiel, -e *n.* [*kar'-tən-shpeel*] card game

Kartoffel, -n *f.* [*kar-to'-fəl*] potato

Karton, -s *m.* [*kar-tohn', kar-tohns'*] cardboard

Käse, - *m.* [*keh'-zə*] cheese

Kaserne, -n *f.* [*ka-zer'-nə*] barracks

Kasse, -n *f.* [*ka'-sə*] cash box; box office

   Zahlen Sie an der Kasse [*tsah'-lən zee an dehr ka'-sə*] Pay the cashier

kassieren *v.* [*ka-see'-rən*] cash

Kassierer, - *m.* [*ka-see'-rər*] cashier

Kastanie, -n *f.* [*ka-stah'-ni-ə*] chestnut

Kasten, ⸗ *m.* [*ka'-stən, ke'-stən*] box, chest

Katalog, -e *m.* [*ka-ta-lohk', ka-ta-loh'-gə*] catalogue

Katastrophe, -n *f.* [*ka-ta-stroh'-fə*] catastrophe, disaster

Kathedrale, -n *f.* [*ka-te-drah'-lə*] cathedral

katholisch [*ka-toh'-lish*] Catholic

Katze, -n *f.* [*ka'-tsə*] cat

kauen *v.* [*kou'-en*] chew

Kauf, ⸗e *m.* [*kouf, koi'-fə*] purchase, bargain

kaufen *v.* [*kou'-fən*] buy

Käufer, - *m.* [*koi'-fər*] buyer, purchaser

Kaufhaus, ⸗er *n.* [*kouf'-hous, kouf'-hoi-zər*] department store

Kaufmann *m. sing.* **Kaufleute** *pl.* [*kouf'-man, kouf'-loi-tə*] merchant, businessman

kaum [*koum*] scarcely, hardly

kegeln *v.* [*keh'-gəln*] bowl

Kehle, -n *f.* [*keh'-lə*] throat

kehren *v.* [*keh'-rən*] sweep

Keim, -e *m.* [*kaim*] germ [bot.]

kein [*kain*] no, not any

keiner, keine, keines [*kai'-nər, kai'-nə, kai'-nəs*] none

keineswegs [*kai'-nəs-vehks*] by no means

Keller, - *m.* [*ke'-lər*] cellar

Kellergeschoss, -e *n.* [*ke'-lər-gə-shos*] basement

Kellner, - *m.* [*kel'-nər*] waiter

Kellnerin, -nen *f.* [*kel'-nə-rin*] waitress

kennen *v. irreg.* [*ke'-nən*] know; be acquainted with

   Kennen Sie diesen Film? [*ke'-nən zee dee'-zən film*] Do you know this film?

kennen-lernen *v.* [*ke'-nen-ler-nen*] meet [become acquainted with]

   Es freut mich, Sie kennenzulernen [*es froit miç, zee ke'-nən-tsu-ler-nən*] Delighted to meet you!

Kenner, - *m.* [*ke'-nər*] connoisseur

Kenntnis, -se *f.* [*kent'-nis*] knowledge, skill

Kennzeichen, - *n.* [*ken'-tsai-çən*] characteristic

Kern, -e *m.* [*kern*] kernel, stone, pit, core

Kerze, -n *f.* [*ker'-tsə*] candle

Kessel, - *m.* [*ke'-səl*] kettle

Kette, -n *f.* [*ke'-tə*] chain; necklace

Keule, -n *f.* [*koi'-lə*] club, leg

Kiefer, - *m.* [*kee'-fər*] jaw

Kiefer, -n *f.* [*kee'-fər*] pine

Kieselstein, -e *m.* [*kee-səl'-shtain*] pebble
Kilogramm, -e *n.* [*ki-lo-gram'*] kilogram [2.2 lbs.]
Kilometer, *m.* [*ki-lo-meh'-tər*] kilometer [0.6 mile]
Kind, -er *n.* [*kint, kin'-dər*] child
Kindermädchen, - *m.* [*kin'-dər-meht-çən*] nursemaid
Kinderzimmer, - *n.* [*kin'-dər-tsi-mər*] nursery
Kindheit *f.* [*kint'-hait*] childhood
kindisch [*kin'-dish*] childish
Kinn, -e *n.* [*kin*] chin
Kinnbacken, - *m.* [*kin'-ba-kən*] jaw
Kino, -s *n.* [*kee'-no, kee'-nos*] movie house
Kirche, -n *f.* [*kir'-çə*] church
Kirchturm, ⸗e *m.* [*kirç'-turm, kirç'-tür-mə*] steeple
Kirsche, -n *f.* [*kir'-shə*] cherry
Kissen, - *n.* [*ki'-sən*] pillow, cushion
Kiste, -n *f.* [*ki'-stə*] box, chest
Klage, -n *f.* [*klah'-gə*] complaint, lament; suit [legal]
klagen *v.* [*klah'-gən*] complain, lament; take legal action
Kläger, - *m.* [*kleh'-gər*] plaintiff
Klang, ⸗e *m.* [*klang, kleng'-ə*] sound
Klappe, -n *f.* [*kla'-pə*] valve
klar [*klahr*] clear, pure, distinct, obvious
klar-machen *v.* [*klahr'-ma-khən*] point out, explain
Klasse, -n *f.* [*kla'-sə*] class
Klassenzimmer, - *n.* [*kla'-sən-tsi-mər*] classroom
klassisch [*kla'-sish*] classic
Klatsch *m.* [*klatch*] gossip
klatschen *v.* [*kla'-chən*] applaud; gossip
Klavier, -e *n.* [*kla-veer'*] piano
kleben *v.* [*kleh'-bən*] stick
Kleid, -er *n.* [*klait, klai'-dər*] dress
kleiden *v.* [*klai'-dən*] dress
Kleider *n. pl.* [*klai'-dər*] clothes
Kleiderschrank, ⸗e *m.* [*klai'-dər-shrank, klai'-dər-shren-kə*] wardrobe
Kleidung *f.* [*klai'-dung*] clothes, attire
klein [*klain*] little, small, petty
kleiner [*klai'-nər*] smaller

Kleingeld *n.* [*klain'-gəlt*] small change
Kleinigkeit, -en *f.* [*klai'-niç-kait*] trifle, small matter
Klempner, - *m.* [*klemp'-nər*] plumber
klettern *v.* (*Aux:* SEIN) [*kle'-tərn*] climb
Klient, -en *m.* [*kli-ent'*] client [male]
Klientin, -nen *f.* [*kli-en'-tin*] client [female]
Klima, -te *n.* [*klee'-mah, klee-mah'-tə*] climate
Klimaanlage, -n *f.* [*klee'-mah-an-lah-gə*] air-conditioning
Klinge, -n *f.* [*kling'-ə*] blade
Klingel, -n *f.* [*kling'-əl*] bell
klingeln *v.* [*kling'-əln*] ring
   Es klingelt [*es kling'-əlt*] The doorbell is ringing
klingen *v. irreg.* [*kling'-ən*] sound [bell]; ring, clink
Klinik, -en *f.* [*klee'-nik*] clinical hospital; nursing home
klopfen *v.* [*klo'-pfən*] knock [at door]
Klosett, -s *n.* [*klo-zet', klo-zets'*] water closet, toilet
Kloster, ⁼ *n.* [*kloh'-stər, klöh'-stər*] convent, monastery
Klub, -s *m.* [*klup, klups*] club
klug [*klook*] clever
Knabe, -n *m.* [*knah'-bə*] boy, lad
knapp [*knap*] concise; tight [clothes]; scarce
kneifen *v. irreg.* [*knai'-fən*] pinch
Knie, - *n.* [*knee, knee'-ə*] knee
knien *v.* [*knee'-ən*] kneel
Knoblauch *m.* [*knohp'-loukh*] garlic
Knochen, - *m.* [*kno'-khən*] bone
Knochenbruch, ⁼e *m.* [*kno'-khən-brukh, kno'-khən-brü-çə*] fracture [of bone]
Knopf, ⁼e *m.* [*knopf, knö'-pfə*] button
Knospe, -n *f.* [*knos'-pə*] bud
Knoten, - *m.* [*knoh'-tən*] knot
knurren *v.* [*knu'-rən*] growl, snarl
knusprig [*knu'-spriç*] crisp
Koch, ⁼e *m.* [*kokh, kö'-çə*] cook [male]
kochen *v.* [*ko'-khən*] cook, boil
Köchin, -nen *f.* [*kö'-çin*] cook [female]
Koffer, - *m.* [*ko'-fər*] suitcase, trunk
Kognak, -s *m.* [*kon'-yak, kon'-yaks*] brandy

Kohl, -e *m.* [*kohl*] cabbage

Kohle, -n *f.* [*koh'-lə*] coal

Kohlenbergwerk, -e *n.* [*koh'-lən-berk-verk*] coal mine

Kokosnuss, ⸗e *f.* [*koh'-kos-nus, koh'-kos-nü-sə*] coconut

Kollege, -n *f.* [*ko-leh'-gə*] colleague

**Kolonialwarenhändler, - ** *m.* [*ko-lo-ni-ahl'-vah-rən-hend-lər*] grocer

Kolonialwarengeschäft, -e *n.* [*ko-lo-ni-ahl'-vah-rən-gə-sheft*] grocery

Kolonie, -n *f.* [*ko-lo-nee'*] colony

komisch [*koh'-mish*] funny, queer

Wie komisch! [*vee koh'-mish*] How queer!

Komma, -s *n.* [*ko'-mah, ko'-mahs*] comma

Kommandant, -en *m.* [*ko-man-dant'*] commander

kommen *v. irreg.* (*Aux:* SEIN) [*ko'-mən*] come, arrive

Kommen Sie her! [*ko'-mən zee hehr*] Come here!

kommen lassen *v. irreg.* [*ko'-mən la'-sən*] send for

Ich darf kommen [*iç darf ko'-mən*] I can [may] come.

Ich kann nicht kommen [*iç kan niçt ko'-mən*] I can't come

Wann kommen Sie? [*van ko'-mən zee*] When are you coming?

kommerziell [*ko-mer-tsi-el'*] commercial

Kommode, -n *f.* [*ko-moh'-də*] chest of drawers

Kommunist, -en *m.* [*ko-mu-nist'*] communist

Komödiant, -en *m.* [*ko-mö-di-ant'*] comedian

Komödie, -n *f.* [*ko-möh'-di-ə*] comedy

Kompanie, -n *f.* [*kom-pa-nee'*] company [mil.]

Kompliment, -e *n.* [*kom-pli-ment'*] compliment

ein Kompliment machen *v.* [*ain kom-pli-ment' ma'-khən*] pay a compliment

komponieren *v.* [*kom-po-nee'-rən*] compose [music]

Komponist, -en *m.* [*kom-po-nist'*] composer [male]

Komponistin, -nen *f.* [*kom-po-ni'-stin*] composer [female]

kompromittieren *v.* [*kom-pro-mi-tee'-rən*] compromise

Konditorei, -en *f.* [*kon-di-to-rai'*] pastry shop, candy store

Konditorwaren *f.*, *pl.* [*kon-dee'-tor-vah-rən*] pastry

Konferenz, -en *f.* [*kon-fe-rents'*] conference

Konflikt, -e *m.* [*kon-flikt'*] conflict

Kongress, -e *m.* [*kon-gres'*] congress
König, -e *m.* [*köh'-niç, köh'-ni-gə*] king
königlich [*köh'-nik-liç*] royal
Königin, -nen *f.* [*köh'-ni-gin*] queen
Königreich, -e *n.* [*köh'-nik-raiç*] kingdom
Konkurrenz, -en *f.* [*kon-ku-rents'*] competition
können *mod. aux.* [*kö'-nən*] can; know [something thoroughly]
   Ich kann Englisch [*iç kan eng'-lish*] I know English
   Ich kann nicht [*iç kan niçt*] I can't
   Es kann sein [*es kan zain*] It may be
konnte [*kon'-tə*] could, was able to
   Ich konnte gehen [*iç kon'-tə geh'-ən*] I could go
   Ich konnte nicht gehen [*iç kon'-tə niçt geh'-ən*] I couldn't go
Konserven *f. pl.* [*kon-zer'-vən*] canned food
Konsul, -n *m.* [*kon'-zul*] consul
Konsulat, -e *n.* [*kon-zu-laht'*] consulate
Kontinent, -e *m.* [*kon-ti-nent'*] continent
Kontrolle, -n *f.* [*kon-tro'-lə*] control
kontrollieren *v.* [*kon-tro-lee'-rən*] control, check
konzentrieren *v.* [*kon-tsen-tree'-rən*] concentrate, focus [attention]
Konzert, -e *m.* [*kon-tsert'*] recital, concert
Kopf, ⸗e *m.* [*kopf, kö'-pfə*] head [anat.]
Kopfkissen, - *n.* [*kopf'-ki-sən*] pillow
Kopfsalat, -e *m.* [*kopf'-za-laht*] lettuce
Kopfschmerzen *m. pl.* [*kopf'-shmer-tsən*] headache
Kopie, -n *f.* [*ko-pee'*] copy
Korb, ⸗e *m.* [*korp, kör'-bə*] basket
Kork, -e *m.* [*kork*] cork
Korkzieher, - *m.* [*kork'-tsee-ər*] corkscrew
Korn, ⸗er *n.* [*korn, kör'-nər*] grain, seed
Körper, - *m.* [*kör'-pər*] body
Körperschaft, -en *f.* [*kör'-pər-shaft*] corporation
Korrespondenz, -en *f.* [*ko-re-spon-dents'*] correspondence
Korridor, -e *m.* [*ko'-ri-dohr*] corridor
korrigieren *v.* [*ko-ri-gee'-rən*] correct
kostbar [*kost'-bahr*] precious
kosten *v.* [*ko'-stən*] cost; require [time]; taste, sample

Kosten *f. pl.* [*ko'-stən*] costs

köstlich [*köst'-liç*] delicious

Kostüm, -e *n.* [*kos-tühm'*] costume, suit

Kotelett, -s *n.* [*ko-tə-let', ko-tə-lets'*] chop

Kotflügel, - *m.* [*koht'-flüh-gəl*] fender

Krabbe, -n *f.* [*kra'-bə*] shrimp, crab

Krach, -e *m.* [*krakh*] noise, crash, quarrel

krachen *v.* [*kra'-khən*] crash

Kraft, ≈e *f.* [*kraft, kref'-tə*] strength, power

kräftig [*kref'-tiç*] strong; nutritious

Kraftwagen, - *m.* [*kraft'-vah-gən, kraft'-veh-gən*] motor vehicle

Kragen, - *m.* [*krah'-gən*] collar [of a dress]

Krämer, - *m.* [*kreh'-mər*] tradesman

krank [*krank*] sick, ill

Kranke, -n *m., f.* [*kran'-kə*] invalid, patient

Krankenhaus, ≈er *n.* [*kran'-kən-hous, kran'-kən-hoi-zər*] hospital

Krankenschwester, -n *f.* [*kran'-kən-shve-stər*] nurse

Krankenwagen *m.* [*kran'-kən-vah-gən*] ambulance

Krankheit, -en *f.* [*krank'-hait*] illness, disease

Kranz, ≈e *m.* [*krants, kren'-tsə*] wreath, garland

kratzen *v.* [*kra'-tsən*] scratch

kräuseln *v.* [*kroi'-zəln*] curl

Kraut, ≈er *n.* [*krout, kroi'-tər*] cabbage; weed; herb

Kravatte, -n *f.* [*kra-va'-tə*] necktie

Krebs, -e *m.* [*krehps*] crayfish; cancer

Kredit, -e *m.* [*kre-deet'*] credit

Kreide, -n *f.* [*krai'-də*] chalk

Kreis, -e *m.* [*krais, krai'-zə*] circle; district

Kreuz, -e *n.* [*kroits*] cross

kreuzen *v.* [*kroi'-tsən*] crisscross, cross

Kreuzer, - *m.* [*kroi'-tsər*] cruiser

Kreuzweg, -e *m.* [*kroits'-vehk, kroits'-veh-gə*] crossroads

kriechen *v. irreg.* (*Aux:* SEIN) [*kree'-çən*] crawl

Krieg, -e *m.* [*kreek, kree'-gə*] war

kriegen *v.* [*kree'-gən*] obtain, gain, get

Kriegsbeschädigte, -n *m.* [*kreeks'-bə-sheh-diç-tə*] disabled soldier

Krippe, -n *f.* [*kri'-pə*] crib, manger
Krise, -n *f.* [*kree'-zə*] crisis
Kristall, -e *m.* [*kri-stal'*] crystal
Kritik, -en *f.* [*kri-teek'*] review, critique, criticism
kritisch [*kree'-tish*] critical
kritisieren *v.* [*kri-ti-zee'-rən*] criticize
Krone, -n *f.* [*kroh'-nə*] crown
Krug, ⸗e *m.* [*krook, krüh'-gə*] pitcher, jug, jar
Krume, -n *f.* [*kroo'-mə*] crumb
krumm [*krum*] crooked, bent
krümmen *v.* [*krü'-mən*] bend
Krümmung, -en *f.* [*krü'-mung*] curve
Küche, -n *f.* [*kü'-çə*] kitchen
Kuchen, - *m.* [*koo'-khən*] cake
Kugel, -n *f.* [*koo'-gəl*] ball, globe, bullet
Kuh, ⸗e *f.* [*koo, küh'-ə*] cow
kühl [*kühl*] cool
Kühler, - *m.* [*küh'-lər*] radiator
Kühlschrank, ⸗e *m.* [*kühl'-shrank, kühl'-shren-kə*] refrigerator
kühn [*kühn*] bold
Kühnheit *f.* [*kühn'-hait*] daring
Kultur, -en *f.* [*kul-toor'*] culture
Kummer *m.* [*ku'-mər*] sorrow, grief
kummervoll [*ku'-mər-fol*] sorrowful
Kunde, -n *m.* [*kun'-də*] customer [male]
Kundin, -nen *f.* [*kun'-din*] customer [female]
Kunst, ⸗e *f.* [*kunst, kün'-stə*] art
Kunsthändler, - *m.* [*kunst'-hend-lər*] art dealer
Künstler, - *m.* [*künst'-lər*] artist
künstlerisch [*künst'-lə-rish*] artistic
künstlich [*künst'-liç*] artificial
Kunstmaler, - *m.* [*kunst'-mah-lər*] painter
Kunstseide *f.* [*kunst'-zai-də*] rayon
Kunststück, -e *n.* [*kunst'-shtük*] trick
Kupfer *n.* [*ku'-pfər*] copper
Kuppel, -n *f.* [*ku'-pəl*] dome
Kur, -en *f.* [*koor*] cure
Kürbis, -se *m.* [*kür'-bis*] pumpkin

Kurort, -e *m.* [*koor'-ort*] health resort
Kurve, -n *f.* [*kur'-və*] curve
   Gefährliche Kurve! [*gə-fehr'-li-çə kur'-və*] Dangerous curve!
kurz [*kurts*] short [not long], brief, concise
   in kurzer Zeit [*in kur'-tsər tsait*] in a short time
Kürze *f.* [*kür'-tsə*] shortness
kürzlich [*kürts'-liç*] lately, recently
Kurzschrift *f.* [*kurts'-shrift*] shorthand
kurzsichtig [*kurts'-ziç-tiç*] shortsighted
Kusine, -n *f.* [*ku-zee'-nə*] cousin [female]
Kuss, ⸗e *m.* [*kus, kü'-sə*] kiss
küssen *v.* [*kü'-sən*] kiss
Küste, -n *f.* [*kü'-stə*] coast, shore

L

Laboratorium *n. sing.* **Laboratorien** *pl.* [*la-bo-ra-toh'-ri-um,*
   la-bo-ra-toh'-ri-ən] laboratory
lächeln *v.* [*le'-çəln*] smile
Lächeln *n.* [*le'-çəln*] smile
lachen *v.* [*la'-khən*] laugh
lächerlich [*le'-çər-liç*] ridiculous
Lachs, -e *m.* [*laks*] salmon
Laden, ⸗ *m.* [*lah'-dən, leh'-dən*] store
Ladentisch, -e *m.* [*lah'-dən-tish*] counter
Ladung, -en *f.* [*lah'-dung*] cargo
Lage, -n *f.* [*lah'-gə*] situation, location, condition
Lager, - *n.* [*lah'-gər*] camp
lahm [*lahm*] lame
lähmen *v.* [*leh'-mən*] paralyze, lame
Laken, - *n.* [*lah'-kən*] sheet [bed]
Lamm, ⸗er *n.* [*lam, le'-mər*] lamb
Lammfleisch *n.* [*lam'-flaish*] lamb [food]
Lampe, -n *f.* [*lam'-pə*] lamp
Land, ⸗er *n.* [*lant, len'-dər*] land, country

landen *v.* (*Aux:* SEIN) [*lan'-dən*] land, disembark

Landhaus, ⁼er *n.* [*lant'-hous, lant'-hoi-zər*] country house

ländlich [*lent'-liç*] rustic

Landmarke, -n *f.* [*lant'-mar-kə*] landmark

Landschaft, -en *f.* [*lant'-shaft*] scenery, landscape

Landsmann *m. sing.* **Landsleute** *pl.* [*lants'-man, lants'-loi-tə*] countryman, compatriot

Landstrasse, -n *f.* [*lant'-shtra-sə*] highway, roadway

Landstreicher, - *m.* [*lant'-shtrai-çər*] vagabond, hobo

Landung, -en *f.* [*lan'-dung*] landing, disembarkation

Landwirtschaft *f.* [*lant'-virt-shaft*] agriculture

lang [*lang*] long, tall

  Wie lange? [*vee lang'-ə*] How long?

lange her [*lang'-ə hehr*] long ago

Länge, -n *f.* [*leng'-ə*] length

länger [*leng'-ər*] longer

langsam [*lang'-zam*] slow, tardy

  Langsam fahren! [*lang'-zam fah'-rən*] Slow down!

längst [*lengst*] long ago; by far

(sich) langweilen *v.* [(*ziç*) *lang'-vai-lən*] be bored

langweilig [*lang'-vai-liç*] boring, dull

langweiliger Mensch [*lang'-vai-li-gər mensh*] bore [person]

Lärm *m.* [*lerm*] Loud noise

las *past tense of* LESEN [*lahs*] read

lassen *v. irreg.* [*la'-sən*] let, leave, permit

  Lassen Sie das! [*la'-sən zee das*] Stop that!

  warten lassen [*var'-tən la'-sən*] keep waiting

Last, -en *f.* [*last*] burden

Laster, - *n.* [*la'-stər*] vice

lasterhaft [*la'-stər-haft*] vicious, wicked

lästig [*le'-stiç*] annoying

Lastwagen, - *m.* [*last'-vah-gən*] truck

Latein *n.* [*la-tain'*] Latin

lateinisch *adj.* [*la-tai'-nish*] Latin

Laterne, -n *f.* [*la-ter'-nə*] lantern

Laufbrücke, -n *f.* [*louf'-brü-kə*] gangway

laufen *v. irreg.* (*Aux:* SEIN) [*lou'-fən*] run; walk [go on foot]

  nach-laufen (plus dat.) *v. irreg.* (*Aux:* SEIN) [*nahkh'-lou-fən*] run

Laune, -n *f.* [*lou'-nə*] mood, temper

   Sie ist bei guter Laune [*zee ist bai goo'-tər lou'-nə*]
     She's in a good mood

   Er ist bei schlechter Laune [*er ist bai shleç'-tər lou'-nə*]
     He's in a bad mood

launisch [*lou'-nish*] moody, capricious

Laut, -e *m.* [*lout*] sound, tone

laut [*lout*] noisy, loud, aloud

lauten *v.* [*lou'-tən*] sound

läuten *v.* [*loi'-tən*] ring

Lautsprecher, - *m.* [*lout'-shpre-çər*] loudspeaker

Lawine, -n *f.* [*la-vee'-nə*] avalanche

Leben *n. sing.* **Menschenleben** *pl.* [*leh'-bən, men'-shen-leh-bən*]
   life

leben *v.* [*leh'-bən*] live

   So ist das Leben! [*zo ist das leh'-bən*] Such is life!

lebendig [*le-ben'-diç*] alive, lively

Lebensgefahr! [*leh'-bəns-gə-fahr*] Danger!

Lebenslauf, ⸗e *m.* [*leh'-bəns-louf, leh'-bəns-loi-fə*] course of
   life; curriculum vitae

Lebensmittel *n. pl.* [*leh'-bəns-mi-təl*] provisions, food

Lebensversicherung, -en *f.* [*leh'-bəns-fer-zi-çə-rung*] life
   insurance

Leber, -n *f.* [*leh'-bər*] liver

Lebewohl! [*leh'-bə-vohl*] Farewell!, Good-by!

lebhaft [*lehp'-haft*] lively, vivid

lecken *v.* [*le'-kən*] lick

lecker [*le'-kər*] dainty, delicious

Leder, - *n.* [*leh'-dər*] leather

ledig [*leh'-diç*] unmarried, single

leer [*lehr*] empty, vacant

   leer machen *v.* [*lehr ma'-khən*] vacate

leeren *v.* [*leh'-rən*] empty

legen *v.* [*leh'-gən*] put, place, lay

lehnen *v.* [*leh'-nən*] lean

Lehnstuhl, ⸗e *m.* [*lehn'-shtool, lehn'-shtüh-lə*] armchair

lehren *v.* [*leh'-rən*] teach

Lehrer, - *m.* [*leh'-rər*] instructor [male]
Lehrerin, -nen *f.* [*leh'-rə-rin*] instructor [female]
Lehrling, -e *m.* [*lehr'-ling*] apprentice
lehrreich [*lehr'-raiç*] instructive
Leib, -er *m.* [*laip, lai'-bər*] body
Leibschmerzen *m. pl.* [*laip'-shmer-tsən*] stomachache
Leibwäsche *f.* [*laip'-ve-shə*] underwear
leicht [*laiçt*] light, easy, mild
   Das ist sehr leicht! [*das ist zehr laiçt*] That's very easy!
leichtsinnig [*laiçt'-zi-niç*] thoughtless, frivolous
Leid *n.* [*lait*] injury, wrong, sorrow
   Es tut mir sehr leid [*es toot meer zehr lait*] I am very sorry
leiden *v. irreg.* [*lai'-dən*] suffer
Leidenschaft, -en *f.* [*lai'-dən-shaft*] passion
leidenschaftlich [*lai'-dən-shaft-liç*] passionate
leider [*lai'-dər*] unfortunately
leihen *v. irreg.* [*lai'-ən*] lend
Leihhaus, ⁼er *n.* [*lai'-hous, lai'-hoi-zər*] pawnshop
Leinen *n.* [*lai'-nən*] linen
Leinwand *f.* [*lain'-vant*] linen; screen [films]; canvas
   [painting]
leisten *v.* [*lai'-stən*] accomplish, perform
   Ich kann es mir nicht leisten [*iç kan es meer niçt lai'-stən*]
   I can't afford it
Leistung, -en *f.* [*lai'-stung*] performance [of machine];
   accomplishment
leiten *v.* [*lai'-tən*] lead, guide, manage, conduct
Leiter, - *m.* [*lai'-tər*] manager
Leiter, -n *f.* [*lai'-tər*] ladder
Leitung, -en *f.* [*lai'-tung*] leadership, direction
Lektion, -en *f.* [*lek-tsi-ohn'*] lesson
lenken *v.* [*len'-kən*] steer
lernen *v.* [*ler'-nən*] learn, study
lesen *v. irreg.* [*leh'-zən*] read
Lesen *n.* [*leh'-zən*] reading
letzt [*letst*] last
   der letzte [*dehr lets'-tə*] the last one
Leuchter, - *m.* [*loiç'-tər*] candlestick

leugnen *v.* [*loig'-nən*] deny

Leute *pl.* [*loi'-tə*] people

Leutnant, -s *m.* [*loit'-nant, loit'-nants*] lieutenant

liberal [*li-bə-rahl'*] liberal

Licht, -er *n.* [*liçt, liç'-tər*] light

lieb [*leep*] dear, beloved

Liebchen, - *n.* [*leep'-çən*] darling, sweetheart

Liebe *f.* [*lee'-bə*] love

lieben *v.* [*lee'-bən*] love

liebenswürdig [*lee'-bəns-vür-diç*] kind, amiable
   Das ist sehr liebenswürdig von Ihnen [*das ist zehr lee'-bəns-vür-diç fon ee'-nən*] That is very kind of you

Liebenswürdigkeit ,-en *f.* [*lee'-bəns-vür-diç-kait*] kindness

lieber *adv.* [*lee'-bər*] rather
   Ich möchte lieber . . . [*iç möç'-tə lee'-bər*] I would rather . . .
   lieber haben *v. irreg.* [*lee'-bər hah'-bən*] prefer, like better

liebevoll [*lee'-bə-fol*] affectionate

Liebhaber, - *m.* [*leep'-hah-bər*] lover [male]; amateur; leading man [theatre]

Liebhaberin, -nen *f.* [*leep'-hah-bə-rin*] lover [female]; amateur; leading lady [theatre]

lieblich [*leep'-liç*] lovely, sweet

Liebling, -e *m.* [*leep'-ling*] darling, favorite

Lieblingsgericht, -e *n.* [*leep'-lings-gə-riçt*] favorite dish

Lied, -er *n.* [*leet, lee'-dər*] song

liefern *v.* [*lee'-fərn*] deliver

Lieferung, -en *f.* [*lee'-fə-rung*] delivery

liegen *v. irreg.* [*lee'-gən*] lie, be situated

lieh *past tense of* LEIHEN [*leeh*] lent

Likör, -e [*li-köhr'*] cordial [beverage]

Lilie, -n *f.* [*lee'-li-ə*] lily

Limonade, -n *f.* [*li-mo-nah'-də*] lemonade

Lineal, -e *n.* [*li-ne-ahl'*] ruler [measure]

Linie, -n *f.* [*lee'-ni-ə*] line

links [*links*] on the left; left
   die linke Hand [*dee lin'-kə hant*] the left hand
   zur Linken [*tsur lin'-kən*] to the left

Linse, -n *f.* [*lin'-zə*] lens

Lippe, -n *f.* [*li'-pə*] lip
Lippenstift, -e *m.* [*li'-pən-shtift*] lipstick
Liste, -n *f.* [*li'-stə*] list
Liter, - *m., n.* [*lee'-tər*] liter
Literatur, -en *f.* [*li-tə-ra-toor'*] literature
Lizenz, -en *f.* [*li-tsents'*] license
Lob *n.* [*lohp*] praise
loben *v.* [*loh'-bən*] praise
Loch, ⸗er *n.* [*lokh, lö'-çər*] hole
Locke, -n *f.* [*lo'-kə*] curl
Lockung, -en *f.* [*lo'-kung*] bait; allurement
Löffel, - *m.* [*lö'-fəl*] spoon
Loge, -n *f.* [*loh'-zhə*] private box [in theatre]; lodge [society]
logisch [*loh'-gish*] logical
Lohn, ⸗e *m.* [*lohn, löh'-nə*] wage; reward, recompense
Lokomotive, -n *f.* [*lo-ko-mo-tee'-və*] locomotive
los [*lohs*] loose, free
    Bald geht es los [*balt geht es lohs*] Things will start soon
    Was ist los? [*vas ist lohs*] What's the matter?
    Was ist mit Ihnen los? [*vas ist mit ee'-nən lohs*] What's
    the matter with you?
Los! *interj.* [*lohs*] Go!
löschen *v.* [*lö'-shən*] extinguish, quench
lose [*loh'-zə*] loose, wanton
lösen *v.* [*löh'-zən*] loosen; buy [a ticket]; annul [agreement];
    solve
los-machen *v.* [*lohs'-ma-khən*] loosen
Lösung, -en *f.* [*löh'-zung*] solution
los-werden *v. irreg.* (*Aux:* SEIN) [*lohs'-vehr-dən*] get rid of
Löwe, -n *m.* [*löh'-və*] lion
Luft, ⸗e *f.* [*luft, lüf'-tə*] air
Luftpost *f.* [*luft'-post*] airmail
    mit Luftpost [*mit luft'-post*] by airmail
Lüge, -n *f.* [*lüh'-gə*] falsehood, lie
lügen *v.* [*lüh'-gən*] [tell a] lie
Lügner, - *m.* [*lühg'-nər*] liar
Lumpen, - *m.* [*lum'-pən*] rag
Lunge, -n *f.* [*lung'-ə*] lung

Lungenentzündung, -en *f.* [*lung'-ən-ent-tsün-dung*] pneumonia

Lust, "e *f.* [*lust*] delight, pleasure

lustig [*lu'-stiç*] merry

    sich lustig machen über (plus acc.) *v.* [*ziç lu'-stiç ma'-khən üh'-bər*] make fun of

Lustspiel, -e *n.* [*lust'-shpeel*] comedy

Luxemburg *n.* [*luk'-səm-burk*] Luxembourg

luxuriös [*luk-su-ri-öhs'*] luxurious

M

machen *v.* [*ma'-khən*] make, do

    Das macht nichts aus [*das makht niçts ous*] It doesn't matter

    Macht nichts! [*makht niçts*] Never mind!

    Was macht das aus? [*vas makht das ous*] What difference does it make?

Macht, "e *f.* [*makht, meç'-tə*] power, force, strength

mächtig [*meç'-tiç*] powerful

Mädchen, - *n.* [*meht'-çən*] girl, maid

mag *3d pers. sing. pres. tense of* MÖGEN [*mahk*] may; like

Magen, " *m.* [*mah'-gən, meh'-gən*] stomach

mager [*mah'-gər*] skinny, lean

Mahagoni *n.* [*ma-ha-goh'-ni*] mahogany

Mahl, -er *n.* [*mahl, meh'-lər*] meal

Mahlzeit, -en *f.* [*mahl'-tsait*] meal

mahnen *v.* [*mah'-nən*] remind, admonish

Mahnung, -en *f.* [*mah'-nung*] reminder

Mai *m.* [*mai*] May

Mais, -e *m.* [*mais*] maize, corn [Indian]

Majestät, -en *f.* [*ma-ye-steht'*] majesty

Major, -e *m.* [*ma-yohr'*] major

mal *adv.* [*mahl*] times

    Drei mal fünf ist fünfzehn [*drai mahl fünf ist fünf'-tsehn*] Three times five is fifteen

Mal, -e *n.* [*mahl*] time, occasion, instance
  das erste Mal [*das ehr'-stə mahl*] the first time
  das nächste Mal [*das nehç'-stə mahl*] the next time
malen *v.* [*mah'-lən*] paint
Maler, - *m.* [*mah'-lər*] painter [male]
Malerei, -en *f.* [*mah-lə-rai'*] painting
Malerin, -nen *f.* [*mah'-lə-rin*] painter [female]
malerisch [*mah'-lə-rish*] picturesque
man *indef. pron.* [*man*] one, you, we, they, people
  man sagt [*man zahgt*] they say
mancher [*man'-çər*] many a
manchmal [*manç'-mahl*] at times; sometimes
Mandeln *f. pl.* [*man'-dəln*] tonsils; almonds
Manieren *f. pl.* [*ma-nee'-rən*] manners
Mann, ̈er *m.* [*man, me'-nər*] man, husband
mannigfaltig [*ma'-niç-fal-tiç*] manifold, various
Mannigfaltigkeit *f.* [*ma'-niç-fal-tiç-kait*] variety, diversity
männlich [*men'-liç*] male, manly
Mannschaft, -en *f.* [*man'-shaft*] crew, team
Mantel, ̈ *m.* [*man'-təl, men'-təl*] coat, overcoat
Manuskript, -e *n.* [*ma-nu-skript'*] manuscript
Märchen, - *n.* [*mehr'-çən*] fairy-tale
Marine, -n *f.* [*ma-ree'-nə*] navy
Mark, - *f.* [*mark*] mark [currency]
Marke, -n *f.* [*mar'-kə*] brand
Markt, ̈e *m.* [*markt, merk'-tə*] market
Marmelade, -n *f.* [*mar-mə-lah'-də*] jam
Marmor, -e *m.* [*mar'-mor*] marble [stone]
Marsch, ̈e *m.* [*marsh, mer'-shə*] march
marschieren *v.* [*mar-shee'-rən*] march
März *m.* [*merts*] March [month]
Maschine, -n *f.* [*ma-shee'-nə*] machine, engine
Maschinen *f. pl.* [*ma-shee'-nən*] machinery
Masern *pl.* [*mah'-zərn*] measles
Maske, -n *f.* [*mas'-kə*] mask
Mass, -e *n.* [*mahs*] measure
  Mass nehmen *v. irreg.* [*mahs neh'-mən*] take the
    measurement of

Massage, -n *f.* [*ma-sah'-zhə*] massage

Masse, -n *f.* [*ma'-sə*] mass [quantity], multitude

Massenproduktion, -en *f.* [*ma'-sən-pro-duk-tsi-ohn*] mass production

Mast, -e *m.* [*mast*] mast

Material, -ien *n.* [*ma-te-ri-ahl', ma-te-ri-ah'-li-ən*] material

Mathematik *f.* [*ma-te-ma-teek'*] mathematics

Matratze, -n *f.* [*ma-tra'-tsə*] mattress

Matrose, -n *m.* [*ma-troh'-zə*] sailor

Mauer, -n *f.* [*mou'-ər*] wall

Maulesel, - *m.* [*moul'-eh-zəl*] mule

Maus, ⸗e *f.* [*mous, moi'-zə*] mouse

Mechaniker, - *m.* [*me-çah'-ni-kər*] mechanic

mechanisch [*me-çah'-nish*] mechanical

Medizin, -en *f.* [*me-di-tseen'*] medicine

medizinisch [*me-di-tsee'-nish*] medical

Meer, -e *n.* [*mehr*] sea, ocean

Meeresküste, -n *f.* [*meh'-rəs-kü-stə*] seaside

Mehl, -e *n.* [*mehl*] flour

mehr [*mehr*] more

   immer mehr [*i'-mər mehr*] more and more

   mehr oder weniger [*mehr oh'-dər veh'-ni-gər*] more or less

mehrere [*meh'-re-rə*] several

Mehrzahl *f.* [*mehr'-tsahl*] plural [number]; majority

Meile, -n *f.* [*mai'-lə*] mile

meinen *v.* [*mai'-nən*] mean; assume

   Was meinen Sie? [*vas mai'-nən zee*] What do you mean?

meiner *m.* **meine** *f.* **meines** *n., poss. pron.* [*mai'-nər, mai'-nə, mai'-nəs*] my, mine

   Das ist mein Buch [*das ist main bookh*] This book is mine, This is my book

   Welches ist das meine? [*vel'-çes ist das mai'-nə*] Which is mine?

meinerseits [*mai'-nər-zaits*] on my part

Meinung, -en *f.* [*mai'-nung*] opinion

meist *adj.* [*maist*] most

meist, meistens *adv.* [*maist, mai'-stəns*] usually, mostly

Meister, - *m.* [*mai'-stər*] master

Meisterwerk, -e *n.* [*mai'-stər-verk*] masterpiece
melden *v.* [*mel'-dən*] announce; inform, report
  sich melden bei (plus dat.) *v.* [*ziç mel'-dən bai*] report to
Melodie, -n *f.* [*me-lo-dee'*] tune, melody
Melone, -n *f.* [*me-loh'-nə*] melon
Menge, -n *f.* [*meng'-ə*] quantity; crowd
Mensch, -en *m.* [*mensh*] person, human being
menschlich [*mensh'-liç*] human, humane
merken *v.* [*mer'-kən*] observe, notice, perceive
merkwürdig [*merk'-vür-diç*] remarkable, peculiar
Messe, -n *f.* [*me'-sə*] fair; mass [church]
messen *v. irreg.* [*me'-sən*] measure
Messer, - *n.* [*me'-sər*] knife
Messing *n.* [*me'-sing*] brass
Metall, -e *n.* [*me-tal'*] metal
Meter, - *m.* [*meh'-tər*] meter
Methode, -n *f.* [*me-toh'-də*] method
Metzger, - *m.* [*mets'-gər*] butcher
Metzgerei, -en *f.* [*mets-gə-rai'*] butcher shop
mexikanisch [*me-ksi-kah'-nish*] Mexican
Mexiko *n.* [*me'-ksi-ko*] Mexico
mich [*miç*] me
Miete, -n *f.* [*mee'-tə*] rent
mieten *v.* [*mee'-tən*] hire, rent
Mieter, - *m.* [*mee'-tər*] tenant
Mietvertrag, ⸗e *m.* [*meet-fər-trahk'*, *meet'-fər-treh-gə*] lease
Mikrofon, -e *n.* [*mi-kro-fohn'*] microphone
Mikroskop, -e *n.* [*mi-kro-skohp'*] microscope
Milch *f.* [*milç*] milk
mild [*milt*] mild
Militärdienst *m.* [*mi-li-tehr'-deenst*] military service
militärisch [*mi-li-teh'-rish*] military
Million, -en *f.* [*mi-li-ohn'*] million
Millionär, -e *m.* [*mi-li-o-nehr'*] millionaire
minderjährig [*min'-dər-yeh-riç*] minor [age]
minderwertig [*min'-dər-vehr-tiç*] inferior
mindestens [*min'-də-stəns*] at least
Mine, -n *f.* [*mee'-nə*] mine

mineralisch [*mi-nə-rah'-lish*] mineral

Mineralwasser, ≈ *n.* [*mi-nə-rahl'-va-sər, mi-nə-rahl'-ve-sər*]
  soda water

Minimum *n. sing.* **Minima** *pl.* [*mee'-ni-mum, mee'-ni-ma*]
  minimum

Minister, - *m.* [*mi-ni'-stər*] minister [government]

Ministerium *n. sing.* **Ministerien** *pl.* [*mi-ni-steh'-ri-um,
  mi-ni-steh'-ri-ən*] ministry; department

Ministerpräsident, -en *m.* [*mi-ni'-stər-preh-zi-dent*] prime
  minister

Minute, -n *f.* [*mi-noo'-tə*] minute

mir [*meer*] to me

mischen *v.* [*mi'-shən*] mix, blend

missachten *v.* [*mis-akh'-tən*] disobey

missbilligen *v.* [*mis-bi'-li-gən*] disapprove

missbrauchen *v.* [*mis-brou'-khən*] abuse, misuse

Mission, -en *f.* [*mis-i-ohn'*] mission

Missionar, -e *m.* [*mi-si-o-nahr'*] missionary

misstrauen *v.* [*mis-trou'-ən*] mistrust, distrust

Misstrauen *n.* [*mis'-trou-ən*] distrust, mistrust

misstrauisch [*mis'-trou-ish*] suspicious, distrustful

Missverständnis, -e *n.* [*mis'-fer-shtent-nis*] misunderstanding

mit *adv.* [*mit*] along

mit *prep.* (plus dat.) [*mit*] with
  mit mir [*mit meer*] with me
  mit dem Auto [*mit dehm ou'-toh*] by car
  mit dem Flugzeug [*mit dehm flook'-tsoik*] by airplane

Mitgefühl *n.* [*mit'-gə-fühl*] sympathy

Mitglied, -er *n.* [*mit'-gleet, mit'-glee-dər*] member

Mitleid *n.* [*mit'-lait*] pity, sympathy

mit-machen *v.* [*mit'-ma-khən*] take part in, join, endure

mit-nehmen *v. irreg.* [*mit'-neh-mən*] take along

Mitreisende, -n *m., f.* [*mit'-rai-zən-də*] shipmate, fellow
  traveler

Mitschüler, - *m.* [*mit'-shüh-lər*] classmate

Mittag, -e *m.* [*mi'-tahk*] noon
  zu Mittag essen *v. irreg.* [*tsu mi'-tahk e'-sən*] have lunch

Mittagessen *n.* [*mi'-tahk-e-sən*] lunch, dinner

Mitte f. [mi'-tə] middle
mit-teilen v. [mit'-tai-lən] communicate, impart
Mitteilung, -en f. [mit'-tai-lung] communication
Mittel, - n. [mi'-təl] remedy; average; means
Mittel f. pl. [mi'-təl] means; funds
Mittelalter n. [mi'-təl-al-tər] Middle Ages
Mitteleuropa n. [mi'-təl-oi-roh-pa] Central Europe
mittelmässig [mi'-təl-meh-siç] mediocre, middling
Mittelmeer n. [mi'-təl-mehr] Mediterranean
Mittelpunkt, -e m. [mi'-təl-punkt] center
mittels prep. (plus gen.) [mi'-təls] by means of
mitten in (plus dat.; acc. for motion) [mi'-tən in] in the
middle of
Mitternacht f. [mi'-tər-nakht] midnight
Mittwoch m. [mit'-vokh] Wednesday
Möbel n. pl. [möh'-bəl] furniture
Möbelpolitur, -en f. [möh'-bəl-po-li-toor] [furniture] polish
möchte [möç'-tə] would like
   Ich möchte . . . [iç möç'-tə] I'd like . . .
   Möchten Sie . . . [möç'-tən zee] Would you like . .
Mode, -n f. [moh'-də] style, fashion, fad
Modell, -e n. [mo-del'] model
modern [mo-dern'] fashionable, modern
mögen mod. aux. [möh'-gən] like, may
möglich [möhk'-liç] possible
Möglichkeit, -en f. [möhk'-liç-kait] possibility
möglichst viel [möhk'-liçst feel] as much as possible
Möhre, -n f. [möh'-rə] carrot
Molkerei, -en f. [mol-kə-rai'] dairy
Moment, -e m. [mo-ment'] moment
   Warten Sie einen Moment! [var'-tən zee ai'-nən mo-ment']
   Wait a minute!
Monarchie, -n f. [mo-nar-çee'] monarchy
Monat, -e m. [moh'-nat] month
monatlich [moh'-nat-liç] monthly
Mönch, -e m. [mönç] monk
Mond, -e m. [mohnt, mohn'-də] moon
Mondschein m. [mohnt'-shain] moonlight

monoton [*mo-no-tohn'*] monotonous

Montag, -e *m.* [*mohn'-tahk, mohn'-tah-gə*] Monday

Moral, -en *f.* [*mo-rahl'*] moral, morale

moralisch [*mo-rah'-lish*] moral

Mord, -e *m.* [*mort, mor'-də*] murder

morden *v.* [*mor'-dən*] murder

Mörder, - *m.* [*mör'-dər*] murderer

Morgen, - *m.* [*mor'-gən*] morning

   Guten Morgen! [*goo'-tən mor'-gən*] Good morning!

morgen [*mor'-gən*] tomorrow

   morgen früh [*mor'-gən früh*] tomorrow morning

morgens [*mor'-gəns*] in the morning

Motor, -en *m.* [*moh'-tor, mo-toh'-rən*] motor

Motorrad, ⸗er *n.* [*moh'-tor-raht, moh'-tor-reh-dər*] motorcycle

Mücke, -n *f.* [*mü'-kə*] mosquito, gnat

müde [*müh'-də*] tired

Mühe, -n *f.* [*müh'-ə*] trouble, toil

   Machen Sie sich keine Mühe! [*ma'-khən zee ziç kai'-nə müh'-ə*] Don't trouble yourself!

München *n.* [*mün'-çən*] Munich

Mund, ⸗er *m.* [*munt, mün'-dər*] mouth

Munition, -en *f.* [*mu-ni-tsi-ohn'*] ammunition

Münze, -n *f.* [*mün'-tsə*] coin

mürrisch [*mü'-rish*] sullen

Muschel, -n *f.* [*mu'-shəl*] mussel; shell [sea]

Museum *n. sing.* **Museen** *pl.* [*mu-zeh'-um, mu-zeh'-ən*] museum

Musik *f.* [*mu-zeek'*] music

musikalisch [*mu-zi-kah'-lish*] musical

Musiker, - *m.* [*moo'-zi-kər*] musician

Muskel, -n *m.* [*mus'-kəl*] muscle

muss *3d pers. sing. pres. tense of* MÜSSEN [*mus*] must

Musse *f.* [*moo'-sə*] leisure

müssen *v.* [*mü'-sən*] have to, must, be obliged to

müssig [*müh'-siç*] idle

Muster, - *n.* [*mu'-stər*] pattern, model, design

Mut *m.* [*moot*] courage

mutig [*moo'-tiç*] courageous

Mutter, ⸗ *f.* [*mu'-tər, mü'-tər*] mother
Mutterschaft *f.* [*mu'-tər-shaft*] maternity, motherhood
mütterlich [*mü'-tər-liç*] maternal, motherly
Muttersprache, -n *f.* [*mu'-tər-shprah-khə*] mother tongue
Mütze, -n *f.* [*mü'-tsə*] cap
mystisch [*mü'-stish*] mystic

N

Na! [*na*] Well! Come now!
  Na also! [*na al'-zoh*] Well, after all!
nach *prep.* (plus dat.) [*nahkh*] after
  nach und nach [*nahkh unt nahkh*] little by little
  Nach Ihnen! [*nakh ee'-nən*] After you!
nach-ahmen *v.* [*nahkh'-ah-mən*] imitate
Nachahmung, -en *f.* [*nahkh'-ah-mung*] imitation
Nachbar, -n *m.* [*nakh'-bahr*] neighbor [male]
Nachbarin, -nen *f.* [*nakh'-bah-rin*] neighbor [female]
Nachbarschaft, -en *f.* [*nakh'-bar-shaft*] neighborhood
nachdem *conj.* [*nakh-dehm'*] after
nach-denken *v. irreg.* [*nahkh'-den-kən*] think, reflect
nachdenklich [*nahkh'-denk-liç*] thoughtful
nacheinander [*nahkh-ai-nan'-dər*] successively
nachher [*nakh-hehr'*] subsequently, after
nachlässig [*nahkh'-le-siç*] negligent
nach-laufen *v. irreg.* (*Aux:* SEIN) [*nahkh'-lou-fən*] run after
nach-machen *v.* [*nahkh'-ma-khən*] imitate, copy
Nachmittag, -e *m.* [*nakh'-mi-tahk, nakh'-mi-tah-gə*] afternoon
Nachnahme, -n *f.* [*nahkh'-nah-mə*] cash on delivery
Nachricht, -en *f.* [*nahkh'-riçt*] news
nach-sehen *v. irreg.* [*nahkh'-zeh-ən*] look up, check
nächst [*nehçst*] next
  nächste Woche [*nehç'-stə vo'-khə*] next week
  nächsten Monat [*nehç'-stən moh'-nat*] next month
Nacht, ⸗**e** *f.* [*nakht, neç'-tə*] night

Gute Nacht! [*goo'-tə nakht*] Good night!

vorige Nacht [*foh'-ri-gə nakht*] last night

die Nacht über [*dee nakht üh'-bər*] overnight

Nachteil, -e *m.* [*nahkh'-tail*] disadvantage

Nachthemd, -en *n.* [*nakht'-hemt, nakht'-hem-dən*] nightgown

Nachtigall, -en *f.* [*nakh'-ti-gal*] nightingale

Nachtisch *m.* [*nahkh-tish*] dessert

Nachtlokal, -e *n.* [*nakht'-lo-kahl*] nightclub

nachträglich [*nahkh'-trehk-liç*] subsequent, later; additional

Nacken, - *m.* [*na'-kən*] nape of the neck

nackt [*nakt*] bare, naked

Nadel, -n *f.* [*nah'-dəl*] needle, pin

Nagel, ¤ *m.* [*nah'-gəl, neh'-gel*] nail

nagelneu [*nah'-gəl-noi*] brand-new

nah, nahe [*nah, nah'-ə*] near, close

Was ist näher? [*vas ist neh'-ər*] Which is nearer?

Nähe *f.* [*neh'-ə*] vicinity

nähen *v.* [*neh'-ən*] sew, stitch

Näherin, -nen *f.* [*neh'-ə-rin*] seamstress

(sich) nähern *v.* [(*ziç*) *neh'-ərn*] approach

Nähmaschine, -n *f.* [*neh'-ma-shee-nə*] sewing machine

Naht, ¤e *f.* [*naht, neh'-tə*] seam

naiv [*na-eef'*] naive

Name, -n *m.* [*nah'-mə*] name

Vorname, -n *m.* [*fohr'-nah-mə*] first name

Zuname, -n *m.* [*tsoo'-nah-mə*] last name

nämlich [*nehm'-liç*] namely, to wit

Narbe, -n *f.* [*nar'-bə*] scar

Narkose, -n *f.* [*nar-koh'-zə*] anesthesia

Narr, -en *m.* [*nar*] fool

Nase, -n *f.* [*nah'-zə*] nose

nass [*nas*] wet, moist

nass werden *v. irreg.* (*Aux:* SEIN) [*nas vehr'-dən*] get wet

Nation, -en *f.* [*na-tsi-ohn'*] nation

national [*na-tsi-o-nahl'*] national

Nationalität, -en *f.* [*na-tsi-o-na-li-teht'*] nationality

Natur, -en *f.* [*na-toor'*] nature

natürlich *adj.* [*na-tühr'-liç*] natural, genuine

Natürlich! [*na-tühr'-liç*] Of course!, Naturally!

Neapel *n.* [*ne-ah'-pəl*] Naples

Nebel, - *m.* [*neh'-bəl*] fog

nebelig [*neh'-bə-liç*] foggy

neben *prep.* (plus dat.; acc. for motion) [*neh'-bən*] next to, beside, alongside

nebenan [*neh-bə-nan'*] next door

nebeneinander [*neh'-bən-ai-nan-dər*] side by side

Nebenstrasse, -n *f.* [*neh'-bən-shtrah-sə*] side street

Neffe, -n *f.* [*ne'-fə*] nephew

negativ [*neh'-ga-teef*] negative

Neger, - *m.* [*neh'-gər*] Negro

Negerin, -nen *f.* [*neh'-gə-rin*] Negro woman

nehmen *v. irreg.* [*neh'-mən*] take

　Nehmen Sie Platz! [*neh'-mən zee plats*] Take a seat!

　(einem etwas) nehmen *v. irreg.* [(*ai'-nəm et'-vas*) *neh'-mən*] deprive [someone of something]

　Er nimmt mir die Hoffnung [*ehr nimt meer dee hof'-nung*] He deprives me of hope

Neigung, -en *f.* [*nai'-gung*] inclination, incline

nein [*nain*] no

Nelke, -n *f.* [*nel'-kə*] carnation

nennen *v. irreg.* [*ne'-nən*] name, call

Nerv, -en *m.* [*nerf*] nerve

nervenkrank [*ner'-vən-krank*] neurotic, nervous

nervös [*ner-vöhs'*] nervous

Nerz, -e *m.* [*nerts*] mink, mink coat

Nest, -er *n.* [*nest, ne'-stər*] nest

nett [*net*] nice, cute

Netz, -e *n.* [*nets*] net [fishing]

neu [*noi*] new, fresh; modern, recent

Neugier *f.* [*noi'-geer*] curiosity

neugierig [*noi'-gee-riç*] curious

Neuheit, -en *f.* [*noi'-hait*] novelty

Neuigkeit, -en *f.* [*noi'-iç-kait*] news

Neujahr, -e *n.* [*noi'-yahr*] New Year

　Prosit Neujahr! [*proh'-zit noi'-yahr*] Happy New Year!

neulich [*noi'-liç*] recently, the other day

neun [*noin*] nine
neunt [*noint*] ninth
neunzehn [*noin'-tsehn*] nineteen
neunzig [*noin'-tsiç*] ninety
neutral [*noi-trahl'*] neutral
nicht [*niçt*] not, no
   nicht einer [*niçt ai'-nər*] not one
   nicht mehr [*niçt mehr*] no more
Nichte, -n *f.* [*niç'-tə*] niece
Nichtraucher, - *m.* [*niçt'-rou-khər*] nonsmoker [special car
   for non-smokers]
nichts [*niçts*] nothing
   nichts Besonderes [*niçts bə-zon'-də-rəs*] nothing special
   nichts Neues [*niçts noi'-əs*] nothing new
   überhaupt nichts [*üh-bər-houpt' niçts*] nothing at all
nie [*nee*] never
niedergeschlagen *adj.* [*nee'-dər-gə-shlah-gən*] downhearted
Niederkunft, ⸗e *f.* [*nee'-dər-kunft, nee'-dər-künf-tə*] childbirth
Niederlage, -n *f.* [*nee'-dər-lah-gə*] defeat
Niederlegung, -en *f.* [*nee'-dər-leh-gung*] resignation [of an
   office]
niedrig [*need'-riç*] low, base
niemals [*nee'-mahls*] never, at no time
niemand [*nee'-mant*] nobody
Niere, -n *f.* [*nee'-rə*] kidney
nirgendwo [*nir'-gənt-voh*] nowhere
noch [*nokh*] still, yet
   noch einmal [*nokh ain'-mahl*] once more
   noch nicht [*nokh niçt*] not yet
   nochmals [*nokh'-mahls*] once again
   weder . . . noch [*veh'-dər . . . nokh*] neither . . . nor
Nonne, -n *f.* [*no'-nə*] nun
Nordamerika *n.* [*nort'-a-meh-ri-ka*] North America
Norden *m.* [*nor'-dən*] north
nördlich [*nört'-liç*] northern
Nordosten *m.* [*nort'-o-stən*] northeast
Nordsee *f.* [*nort'-zeh*] North Sea
Nordwesten *m.* [*nort'-ve-stən*] northwest

Norm, -en *f.* [*norm*] standard
normal [*nor-mahl'*] normal
Norwegen *n.* [*nor'-veh-gən*] Norway
norwegisch [*nor'-veh-gish*] Norwegian
Not, ⸗**e** *f.* [*noht, nöh'-tə*] need; difficulty, distress, trouble
  in Not bringen *v. irreg.* [*in noht bring'-ən*] distress
Notar, -e *m.* [*no-tahr'*] [public] notary
Notausgang, ⸗**e** *m.* [*noht'-ous-gang, noht'-ous-geng-ə*]
  emergency exit
Note, -n *f.* [*noh'-tə*] grade [acad.]; note [music]; memorandum
Notfall, ⸗**e** *m.* [*noht'-fal, noht'-fe-lə*] emergency
  im Notfall [*im noht'-fal*] in case of emergency, if necessary
notieren *v.* [*no-tee'-rən*] note
nötig [*nöh'-tiç*] necessary
Notiz, -en *f.* [*no-teets'*] note
Notizbuch, ⸗**er** *n.* [*no-teets'-bookh, no-teets'-bü-çer*] notebook
notwendig [*noht'-ven-diç*] necessary
Notwendigkeit, -en *f.* [*noht'-ven-diç-kait*] necessity
November *m.* [*no-vem'-bər*] November
nüchtern [*nüç'-tərn*] sober, insipid
Nudel, -n *f.* [*noo'-dəl*] noodle
Null, -en *f.* [*nul*] zero
Nummer, -n *f.* [*nu'-mər*] number; issue [of magazine]
nun [*noon*] now, at present; Well!
nur [*noor*] only, nothing but, merely
Nuss, ⸗**e** *f.* [*nus, nü'-se*] nut [food]
nützen *v.* [*nü'-tsən*] be of use, be useful for
nützlich [*nüts'-liç*] useful
Nützlichkeit *f.* [*nüts'-liç-kait*] utility
nutzlos [*nuts'-los*] useless
Nylonstrümpfe *m. pl.* [*nai'-lon-shtrüm-pfə*] nylons [stockings]

O

ob [*op*] if, whether
  als ob [*als op*] as if
oben [*oh'-bən*] above; at the top; upstairs
oben auf (plus dat.; acc. for motion) [*oh'-bən ouf*] on top of
ober [*oh'-bər*] upper, superior
Ober, - *m.* [*oh'-bər*] [head] waiter
  Herr Ober! [*her oh'-bər*] Waiter!
Oberfläche, -n *f.* [*oh'-bər-fle-çə*] surface
oberflächlich [*oh'-bər-fleç-liç*] superficial
Oberhaupt, ⸗**er** *n.* [*oh'-bər-houpt, oh'-bər-hoip-tər*] head [chief]
Oberhemd, -en *n.* [*oh'-bər-hemt, oh'-bər-hem-dən*] shirt, dress
Oberkellner, - *m.* [*oh'-bər-kel-nər*] headwaiter
Oberst, -en *m.* [*oh'-bərst*] colonel
obgleich *conj.* [*op-glaiç'*] although
Objekt, -e *n.* [*op-yekt'*] object
obligatorisch [*ob-li-ga-toh'-rish*] obligatory
obschon [*op-shohn'*] although
Obst *n.* [*ohpst*] fruit
Obstgarten, ⸗ *m.* [*ohpst'-gar-tən, ohpst'-ger-tən*] orchard
Obstmarkt, ⸗**e** *m.* [*ohpst'-markt, ohpst'-merk-tə*] fruit market
Obstsalat, -e *m.* [*ohpst'-za-laht*] fruit salad
obszön [*ops-tsöhn'*] obscene, filthy
obwohl [*op-vohl'*] although
Ochse, -n *m.* [*ok'-sə*] ox
Ochsenschwanzsuppe, -n *f.* [*ok'-sən-shvants-zu-pə*] oxtail soup
oder [*oh'-dər*] or
  entweder . . . oder [*ent'-veh-dər . . . oh'-dər*] either . . . or
Ofen, ⸗ *m.* [*oh'-fən, öh'-fən*] stove, oven
offen [*o'-fən*] frank, open
offenbar [*o'-fən-bahr*] obvious, evident
öffentlich [*ö'-fent-liç*] public
offiziell [*o-fi-tsi-el'*] official

Offizier, -e *m.* [*o-fi-tseer'*] officer [mil.]

öffnen *v.* [*öf'-nən*] open

    Öffnen Sie die Tür! [*öf'-nən zee dee tühr*] Open the door!

Öffnung, -en *f.* [*öf'-nung*] opening; orifice

oft [*oft*] often

öfter, öfters [*öf'-tər, öf'-tərs*] more often, quite often

ohne *prep.* (plus acc.) [*oh'-nə*] without

ohnehin [*oh-nə-hin'*] anyway

Ohnmacht, -en *f.* [*ohn'-makht*] faint

    in Ohnmacht fallen *v. irreg.* (*Aux:* SEIN) [*in ohn'-makht fa'-lən*] faint

Ohr, -en *n.* [*ohr*] ear

Ohrring, -e *m.* [*ohr'-ring*] earring

Oktober *m.* [*ok-toh'-bər*] October

Öl, -e *n.* [*öhl*] oil

Ölbohrloch, ⸗er *n.* [*öhl'-bohr-lokh, öhl'-bohr-lö-çər*] oil well

Ölfeld, -er *n.* [*öhl'-felt, öhl'-fel-dər*] oil field

Ölgemälde, - *n.* [*öhl'-gə-mehl-də*] oil painting

Olive, -n *f.* [*o-lee'-və*] olive

Olivenöl *n.* [*o-lee'-vən-öhl*] olive oil

Omelett, -e *n.* [*o-mə-let'*] omelet

Omnibus, -se *m.* [*om'-ni-bus*] bus

Onkel, - *m.* [*on'-kəl*] uncle

Oper, -n *f.* [*oh'-pər*] opera

Operation, -en *f.* [*o-pə-ra-tsi-ohn'*] operation

Operette, -n *f.* [*o-pə-re'-tə*] operetta

operieren *v.* [*o-pə-ree'-rən*] operate

Opfer, - *n.* [*o'-pfər*] sacrifice, victim

Optiker, - *m.* [*op'-ti-kər*] optician

Optimist, -en *m.* [*op-ti-mist'*] optimist

optimistisch [*op-ti-mi'-stish*] optimistic

Orangensaft *m.* [*o-rahn'-zhən-zaft*] orange juice

Orchester, - *n.* [*or-ke'-stər*] orchestra

Orchidee, -n *f.* [*or-çi-dee'-ə*] orchid

Orden, - *m.* [*or'-dən*] medal; order [religious]

ordentlich [*or'-dent-liç*] tidy; respectable

ordnen *v.* [*ord'-nən*] arrange, set in order

Ordnung, -en *f.* [*ord'-nung*] order [regularity]; arrangement
   Das ist in Ordnung [*das ist in ord'-nung*] That is all right
   in Ordnung bringen *v. irreg.* [*in ord'-nung bring'-ən*] put
     in order
   Zur Ordnung! [*tsur ord'-nung*] Order! Order!, Chair!
Organisation, -en *f.* [*or-ga-ni-za-tsi-ohn'*] organization
organisch [*or-gah'-nish*] organic
Orgel, -n *f.* [*or'-gəl*] organ [music]
orientalisch [*o-ri-en-tah'-lish*] oriental
originell [*o-ri-gi-nel'*] original
Ort, -e *m.* [*ort*] place, site, spot
örtlich [*ört'-liç*] local
Osten *m.* [*o'-stən*] east
   der Ferne Osten [*dehr fer'-nə o'-stən*] the Far East
   der Nahe Osten [*dehr nah'-ə o'-stən*] the Near East
Osterhase, -n *m.* [*oh'-stər-hah-zə*] Easter bunny
Ostern *n. pl.* [*oh'-stərn*] Easter
   zu Ostern [*tsu oh'-stərn*] at Easter, for Easter
Österreich *n.* [*öh'-stə-raiç*] Austria
Österreicher, - *m.* [*öh'-stə-rai-çər*] Austrian [male]
Österreicherin, -nen *f.* [*öh'-stə-rai-çə-rin*] Austrian [female]
österreichisch [*öh'-stə-rai-çish*] Austrian
Ostsee *f.* [*ost'-zeh*] Baltic Sea
Ozean, -e *m.* [*oh'-tse-ahn*] ocean
Ozeandampfer, - *m.* [*oh'-tse-ahn-dam-pfər*] liner [ship]

P

Paar, -e *n.* [*pahr*] pair, couple
   ein paar [*ain pahr*] some, a few
   ein paarmal [*ain pahr'-mahl*] several times
packen *v.* [*pa'-kən*] pack
Packen *n.* [*pa'-ken*] packing
Paket, -e *n.* [*pa-keht'*] parcel, package
Palast, ⸗e *m.* [*pa-last'*, *pa-le'-stə*] palace

Palme, -n *f.* [*pal'-mə*] palm [bot.]

Pampelmuse, -en *f.* [*pam'-pəl-moo-zə*] grapefruit

Panne, -n *f.* [*pa'-nə*] breakdown, mishap, puncture

Pantoffel, -n *m.* [*pan-to'-fəl*] slipper

Panzerwagen, - *m.* [*pan'-tsər-vah-gən*] tank [mil.]

Papagei, -en *m.* [*pa-pa-gai'*] parrot

Papier, -e *n.* [*pa-peer'*] paper

Papiere *n. pl.* [*pa-pee'-re*] papers, documents

Papierkorb, ꞊e *m.* [*pa-peer'-korp, pa-peer'-kör-be*]
    wastepaper basket

Pappel, -n *f.* [*pa'-pəl*] poplar

Papst, ꞊e *m.* [*pahpst, pehp'-stə*] Pope

Parade, -n *f.* [*pa-rah'-də*] parade

Paradies, -e *n.* [*pa-ra-dees'*] paradise

parallel [*pa-ra-lehl'*] parallel

Parfüm, -e *n.* [*par-fühm'*] perfume

Park, -s *m.* [*park, parks*] park

parken *v.* [*par'-kən*] park

  Kein Parken!, Parken verboten! [*kain par'-kən, par'-kən
    fer-boh'-tən*] No parking!

Parkett *n.* [*par-ket'*] orchestra [seats]

Parkplatz, ꞊e *m.* [*park'-plats, park'-plet-sə*] parking lot,
    parking spot

Parlament, -e *n.* [*par-la-ment'*] parliament

Partei, -en *f.* [*par-tai'*] party [politics, law]

Parterre *n.* [*par-te'-rə*] ground floor, first floor [Amer.];
    pit [theatre]

Parzelle, -n *f.* [*par-tse'-lə*] lot [real estate]

Pass, ꞊e *m.* [*pas, pe'-sə*] passport; pass

Passagier, -e *m.* [*pa-sa-zheer'*] passenger

passen *v.* [*pa'-sən*] fit, suit

  auf-passen *v.* [*ouf'-pa-sən*] look out, watch

  Passen Sie auf! [*pa'-sən zee ouf*] Look out!

passend (für) [*pa'-sənt (führ)*] suitable, convenient (for)

passieren *v.* [*pa-see'-ren*] happen

passiv [*pa'-seef*] passive

Passkontrolle, -n *f.* [*pas'-kon-tro-lə*] passport control

Pastor, -en *m.* [*pa'-stor, pa-stoh'-rən*] pastor, minister

Pate, -n *m.* [*pah'-tə*] godfather

Patenkind, -er *n.* [*pah'-tən-kint, pah'-tən-kin-dər*] godchild

Patent, -e *n.* [*pa-tent'*] patent

Patient, -en *m.* [*pa-tsi-ent'*] patient [male]

Patientin, -nen *f.* [*pa-tsi-en'-tin*] patient [female]

Patin, -nen *f.* [*pah'-tin*] godmother

Patriot, -en *m.* [*pa-tri-oht'*] patriot

patriotisch [*pa-tri-oh'-tish*] patriotic

Patrone, -n *f.* [*pa-troh'-nə*] cartridge

Pause, -n *f.* [*pou'-zə*] pause

Pech *n.* [*peç*] bad luck; pitch, tar

Pedal, -e *n.* [*pe-dahl'*] pedal

Pein *f.* [*pain*] anguish

peinlich [*pain'-liç*] painful, embarrasing

Peitsche, -n *f.* [*pai'-chə*] whip

Pelz, -e *m.* [*pelts*] fur

Pelzmantel, ⁼ *m.* [*pelts'-man-təl, pelts'-men-təl*] fur coat

Pension, -en *f.* [*pahn-zi-ohn'*] boardinghouse

pensionieren *v.* [*pahn-zi-o-nee'-rən*] pension off, retire

perfekt [*per-fekt'*] perfect

Perle, -n *f.* [*per'-lə*] pearl, bead

Perlenkette, -n *f.* [*per'-lən-ke-tə*] pearl necklace

persisch [*per'-zish*] Persian

Person, -en *f.* [*per-zohn'*] person

Personal *n.* [*per-zo-nahl'*] personnel

Personalausweis, -e *m.* [*per-zo-nahl'-ous-vais*] identification card

Personenzug, ⁼e *m.* [*per-zoh'-nən-tsook, per-zoh'-nən-tsüh-gə*] passenger train

persönlich [*per-zöhn'-liç*] personal

Persönlichkeit, -en *f.* [*per-zöhn'-liç-kait*] personality

Pessimist, -en *m.* [*pe-si-mist'*] pessimist

pessimistisch [*pe-si-mi'-stish*] pessimistic

Petersilie, -n *f.* [*pe-tər-zee'-li-ə*] parsley

Pfad, -e *m.* [*pfaht, pfah'-də*] trail, path

Pfanne, -n *f.* [*pfa'-nə*] [frying] pan

Pfannkuchen, - *m.* [*pfan'-koo-khən*] pancake

Pfarrer, - *m.* [*pfa'-rə*] priest, clergyman

Pfau, -en *m.* [*pfou*] peacock
Pfeffer *m.* [*pfe'-fər*] pepper
Pfefferminz *f.* [*pfe-fər-mints'*] peppermint
Pfeife, -n *f.* [*pfai'-fə*] pipe [smoking]; whistle
Pfeifen *v. irreg.* [*pfai'-fən*] whistle
Pfeiler, - *m.* [*pfai'-lər*] pillar; pier [of bridge]
Pfennig, -e *m.* [*pfe'-niç, pfe'-ni-gə*] penny
Pferd, -e *n.* [*pfehrt, pfehr'-də*] horse
Pferderennen, - *n.* [*pfehr'-də-re-nən*] horse race
Pfingsten *pl.* [*pfing'-stən*] Pentecost, Whitsuntide
Pfirsich, -e *m.* [*pfir'-ziç*] peach
Pflanze, -n *f.* [*pflan'-tsə*] plant
pflanzen *v.* [*pflan'-tsən*] plant
Pflaster, - *n.* [*pfla'-stər*] plaster [remedy]; pavement
Pflaume, -n *f.* [*pflou'-mə*] plum, prune
Pflege, -n *f.* [*pfleh'-gə*] care, nursing
pflegen *v.* [*pfleh'-gən*] nurse, take care of
Pflicht, -en *f.* [*pfliçt*] duty, obligation
pflücken *v.* [*pflü'-kən*] pluck, gather
Pflug, ⸗e *m.* [*pflook, pflüh'-ge*] plow
pflügen *v.* [*pflüh'-gən*] plough
Pförtner, - *m.* [*pfört'-nər*] janitor
Pfote, -n *f.* [*pfoh'-tə*] paw
Pfund, -e *n.* [*pfunt, pfun'-də*] pound [weight, money]
   drei Pfund Fleisch [*drai pfunt flaish*] three pounds of meat
Phantasie, -n *f.* [*fan-ta-zee'*] imagination
phantastisch [*fan-ta'-stish*] fantastic
Phase, -n *f.* [*fah'-zə*] phase
Philosoph, -en *m.* [*fi-lo-zohf'*] philosopher
Philosophie, -n *f.* [*fi-lo-zo-fee'*] philosophy
Photo, -s *n.* [*foh'-toh, foh'-tohs*] photograph
Photograph, -en *m.* [*fo-to-grahf'*] photographer
photographieren *v.* [*fo-to-gra-fee'-rən*] photograph, take
   a picture
Physik *f.* [*fi-zeek'*] physics
physisch [*füh'-zish*] physical
Pianist, -en *m.* [*pi-a-nist'*] pianist [male]
Pianistin, -nen *f.* [*pi-a-ni'-stin*] pianist [woman]

Pille, -n *f.* [*pi′-lə*] pill
Pilot, -en *m.* [*pi-loht′*] pilot [plane, boat]
Pilz, -e *m.* [*pilts*] mushroom
Pinsel, - *m.* [*pin′-zəl*] paintbrush
Pistole, -n *f.* [*pi-stoh′-lə*] pistol
Plage, -n *f.* [*plah′-gə*] bother, misery
plagen *v.* [*plah′-gən*] afflict
Plakat, -e *n.* [*pla-kaht′*] poster, bill
Plakatsäule, -n *f.* [*pla-kaht′-zoi-lə*] advertisement pillar
Plan, ⸗e *m.* [*plahn, pleh′-nə*] plot, intrigue; plan; design
planen *v.* [*plah′-nən*] plan
Planet, -en *m.* [*pla-neht′*] planet
Platin *n.* [*plah′-teen*] platinum
platt [*plat*] flat, plain, level
Platte, -n *f.* [*pla′-te*] record [phono]; plate
Platz, ⸗e *m.* [*plats, ple′-tsə*] place; square; seat
  Es gibt keinen Platz hier [*es gipt kai′-nən plats heer*]
    There's no room here
  Bitte, nehmen Sie Platz! [*bi′-tə neh′-mən zee plats*]
    Please have a seat!
plaudern *v.* [*plou′-dərn*] chat
plötzlich [*plöts′-liç*] suddenly
plus [*plus*] plus
Pocken *f. pl.* [*po′-kən*] smallpox
Pol, -e *m.* [*pohl*] pole [astronomy, physics]
Pole, -n *m.* [*poh′-lə*] Pole [male]
Polen *n.* [*poh′-lən*] Poland
Police, -n *f.* [*po-lee′-sə*] policy [insurance]
polieren *v.* [*po-lee′-rən*] polish
Polin, -nen *f.* [*poh′-lin*] Pole [woman]
Politik *f.* [*po-li-teek′*] politics; policy [gov.]
politisch [*po-lee′-tish*] political
Polizei *f.* [*po-li-tsai′*] police
Polizeiwache, -n *f.* [*po-li-tsai′-va-khə*] police station
Polizist, -en *m.* [*po-li-tsist′*] policeman
polnisch [*pol′-nish*] Polish
Polster, - *n.* [*pol′-stər*] cushion, bolster
Polsterung, -en *f.* [*pol′-stə-rung*] upholstery, stuffing

populär [*po-pu-lehr'*] popular

Portion, -en *f.* [*por-tsi-ohn'*] portion, helping [of food]
  zwei Portionen Kaffee [*tsvai por-tsi-oh'-nən ka-feh'*]
    coffee for two

Porto *n.* [*por'-to*] postage

Porträt, -e *n.* [*por-treht'*] portrait

Portugal *n.* [*por'-tu-gal*] Portugal

portugiesisch [*por-tu-gee'-zish*] Portuguese

Porzellan, -e *n.* [*port'-se-lahn*] chinaware, porcelain

positiv [*poh'-zi-teef*] positive

Post *f.* [*post*] mail, post office

Postamt, ⸗er *n.* [*post'-amt, post'-em-tər*] post office

Postanweisung, -en *f.* [*post'-an-vai-zung*] postal money order

Postkarte, -n *f.* [*post'-kar-tə*] postcard

postlagernd [*post'-lah-gərnt*] general delivery

postwendend [*post'-ven-dənt*] by return mail

prächtig [*preç'-tiç*] gorgeous, splendid

prahlen *v.* [*prah'-lən*] brag

Prahler, - *m.* [*prah'-lər*] braggart

praktisch [*prak'-tish*] practical

Prämie, -n *f.* [*preh'-mi-ə*] bonus, premium

Präsident, -en *m.* [*pre-zi-dent'*] president

Predigt, -en *f.* [*preh'-diçt*] sermon

Preis, -e *m.* [*prais, prai'-zə*] cost, price; prize; praise
  zum Preise von [*tsum prai'-zə fon*] at the rate of

preisen *v.* [*prai'-zən*] praise

Preislage, -n *f.* [*prais'-lah-gə*] price range

Preisliste, -n *f.* [*prais'-li-stə*] price list

Preisnachlass *m.* [*prais'-nakh-las*] price discount

preiswert [*prais'-vert*] reasonable [price]

Presse, -n *f.* [*pre'-sə*] press, newspapers

Pressefreiheit *f.* [*pre'-sə-frai-hait*] freedom of the press

pressen *v.* [*pre'-sən*] squeeze, press

Priester, - *m.* [*pree'-stər*] priest

prima [*pree'-ma*] first-rate

primitiv [*pri-mi-teef'*] primitive

Prinz, -en *m.* [*prints*] prince

Prinzessin, -nen *f.* [*prin-tse'-sin*] princess

Prinzip, -ien *n.* [*prin-tseep', prin-tsee'-pi-ən*] principle [moral]
   aus Prinzip [*ous prin-tseep'*] on principle
privat [*pri-vaht'*] private
Probe, -n *f.* [*proh'-bə*] test; rehearsal
probieren *v.* [*proh-bee'-rən*] try, test
Problem, -e *n.* [*pro-blehm'*] problem
Produkt, -e *n.* [*pro-dukt'*] product
Produktion, -en *f.* [*pro-duk-tsi-ohn'*] production
Professor, -en *m.* [*pro-fe'-sor, pro-fe-soh'-rən*] professor
Programm, -e *n.* [*pro-gram'*] program
Pronomen *n. sing.* **Pronomina** *pl.* [*pro-noh'-mən,*
   pro-noh'-mi-na] pronoun
Propaganda *f.* [*pro-pa-gan'-da*] propaganda
Propeller, - *m.* [*pro-pe'-lər*] propeller
Prophezeiung, -en *f.* [*pro-fe-tsai'-ung*] prophecy
prosaisch [*pro-zah'-ish*] prosaic
Prosit! [*proh'-zit*] To your health!, Here's to you!
Protest, -e *m.* [*pro-test'*] protest
Protestant, -en *m.* [*pro-te-stant'*] Protestant
protestieren *v.* [*pro-tes-tee'-rən*] protest
Protokoll, -e *n.* [*pro-to-kol'*] protocol; record; minutes
   [of a meeting]
Provinz, -en *f.* [*pro-vints'*] province
provinziell [*pro-vin-tsi-el'*] provincial
Provision, -en *f.* [*pro-vi-zi-ohn'*] commission
Prozent, - *n.* [*pro-tsent'*] percent
Prozentsatz, ⁼e *m.* [*pro-tsent'-zats, pro-tsent'-ze-tsə*]
   percentage
Prozess, -e *m.* [*pro-tses'*] lawsuit, process, trail
prüfen *v.* [*prüh'-fən*] examine, test, search
Prüfer, - *m.* [*prüh'-fər*] examiner
Prüfung, -en *f.* [*prüh'-fung*] examination, trail
PS *abbr.* [*peh es*] horsepower
Psychiater, - *m.* [*psii-çi-ah'-ter*] psychiatrist [male]
Psychiatrie *f.* [*psii-çi-a-tree'*] psychiatry
Psychiatrin, -nen *f.* [*psii-çi-aht'-rin*] psychiatrist [female]
Psychoanalyse *f.* [*psii-ço-a-na-lüh'-zə*] psychoanalysis
Psychologie *f.* [*psii-ço-lo-gee'*] psychology

psychologisch [*psü-ço-loh'-gish*] psychological
Publikum *n.* [*poo'-bli-kum*] (the) public, audience
Pudel, - *m.* [*poo'-dəl*] poodle
Puder *m.* [*poo'-dər*] powder
Puls, -e *m.* [*puls, pul'-zə*] pulse
Pulsschlag, ⸗e *m.* [*puls'-shlahk, puls'-shleh-gə*] beat [pulse]
Pult, -e *n.* [*pult*] desk
Pulver *n.* [*pul'-vər*] [gun] powder
Pumpe, -n *f.* [*pum'-pə*] pump
Pumpernickel *m.* [*pum'-pər-ni-kəl*] Westphalian rye bread
Punkt, -e *m.* [*punkt*] period [punctuation]; point, dot
pünktlich [*pünkt'-liç*] punctual, on time
Puppe, -n *f.* [*pu'-pə*] doll
purpurn [*pur'-purn*] purple
Pute, -n *f.* [*poo'-tə*] turkey [hen]
putzen *v.* [*pu'-tsən*] clean, polish, shine [shoes], brush [teeth]
Putzfrau, -en *f.* [*puts'-frou*] cleaning woman
Pyjama *m.* [*pü-dzah'-mah*] pyjamas
Pyramide, -n *f.* [*pü-ra-mee'-də*] pyramid

Q

Qual, -en *f.* [*kvahl*] agony
quälen *v.* [*kveh'-lən*] torture
Qualität, -en *f.* [*kva-li-təht'*] quality
Qualm *m.* [*kvalm*] thick smoke
Quarantäne *f.* [*kva-ran-teh'-nə*] quarantine
Quelle, -n *f.* [*kve'-lə*] spring, source, fountainhead
quer [*kvehr*] across
  kreuz und quer [*kroits unt kvehr*] in all directions, zigzag
Querstrasse, -n *f.* [*kvehr'-shtrah-sə*] crossroad
quetschen *v.* [*kve'-chən*] squeeze; bruise
Quetschung, -en *f.* [*kve'-chung*] bruise
Quittung, -en *f.* [*kvi'-tung*] receipt

R

Rabbiner, - *m.* [*ra-bee'-nər*] rabbi
Rabe, -n *m.* [*rah'-bə*] raven
Rache *f.* [*ra'-khə*] vengeance, revenge
rächen *v.* [*re'-çən*] avenge
Rad, ⸗er *n.* [*raht, reh'-dər*] wheel; bike
Radfahrer, - *m.* [*raht'-fah-rər*] cyclist
radieren *v.* [*ra-dee'-rən*] erase; etch
Radiergummi, -s *m.* [*ra-deer'-gu-mee, ra-deer'-gu-mees*]
    eraser
Radieschen, - *n.* [*ra-dees'-çən*] red radish
Radio, -s *n.* [*rah'-di-oh, rah'-di-ohs*] radio
Rahm *m.* [*rahm*] cream
Rahmen, - *m.* [*rah'-mən*] frame
Rakete, -n *f.* [*ra-keh'-tə*] rocket
Rand, ⸗er *m.* [*rant, ren'-dər*] border, rim, margin
Rang, ⸗e *m.* [*rang, reng'-ə*] rank
rannte *past tense of* RENNEN [*ran'-tə*] ran
rar [*rahr*] rare, scarce
rasch [*rash*] quick, swift
rasen *v.* (*Aux:* SEIN) [*rah'-zən*] speed, race
Rasen, - *m.* [*rah'-zən*] lawn
rasend [*rah'-zənt*] raving, frenzied
Rasierapparat, -e *m.* [*ra-zeer'-a-pa-raht*] razor
rasieren *v.* [*ra-zee'-rən*] shave
    sich rasieren [*ziç ra-zee'-rən*] shave [oneself]
Rasieren *n.* [*ra-zee'-rən*] shave
Rasierklinge, -n *f.* [*ra-zeer'-kling-ə*] razor blade
Rasierkrem, -e *m.* [*ra-zeer'-krehm*] shaving cream
Rasiermesser, - *n.* [*ra-zeer'-me-sər*] razor
Rasierpinsel, - *m.* [*ra-zeer'-pin-zəl*] shaving brush
Rasse, -n *f.* [*ra'-sə*] race [human]
Rat *m. sing.* **Ratschläge** *pl.* [*raht, raht'-shleh-gə*] advice

264

Rate, -n *f.* [*rah'-tə*] rate; installment
raten *v. irreg.* [*rah'-tən*] advise, counsel; guess
Ratgeber, - *m.* [*raht'-geh-bər*] adviser
Rathaus, ⸗er *n.* [*raht'-hous, raht'-hoi-zər*] city hall, town hall
rationell [*ra-tsi-o-nel'*] rational
Rätsel, - *n.* [*reht'-səl*] riddle, puzzle
Ratte, -n *f.* [*ra'-tə*] rat
rauben *v.* [*rou'-bən*] rob
Räuber, - *m.* [*roi'-bər*] robber
Rauch *m.* [*roukh*] smoke
rauchen *v.* [*rou'-khən*] smoke
   Rauchen verboten! [*rou'-khən fer-boh'-tən*] No smoking!
Raucher, - *m.* [*rou'-khər*] smoker
rauh [*rou*] rough
Raum, ⸗e *m.* [*roum, roi'-mə*] room, space
Raumanzug, ⸗e *m.* [*roum'-an-tsook, roum'-an-tsüh-gə*]
   space suit
Raupe, -n *f.* [*rou'-pə*] caterpillar
Rausch, ⸗e *m.* [*roush, roi'-shə*] intoxication, drunkenness
Rauschgift, -e *n.* [*roush'-gift*] drug [narcotic]
Reaktion, -en *f.* [*re-ak-tsi-ohn'*] reaction
rechnen *v.* [*reç'-nən*] count, calculate
Rechnung, -en *f.* [*reç'-nung*] calculation; bill, invoice
Recht, -e *n.* [*reçt*] right; justice; law
   recht haben *v. irreg.* [*reçt hah'-bən*] be right
   Ist es Ihnen recht? [*ist es ee'-nən reçt*] Is it all right
     with you?
rechtfertigen *v.* [*reçt'-fer-ti-gən*] justify, defend
rechts [*reçts*] right [direction]
   Rechts fahren [*reçts fah'-rən*] Keep to the right
Rechtsanwalt, ⸗e *m.* [*reçts'-an-valt, reçts'-an-vel-tə*] lawyer,
   attorney [male]
Rechtsanwältin, -nen *f.* [*reçts'-an-vel-tin*] lawyer, attorney
   [female]
rechtzeitig [*reçt'-tsai-tiç*] in good time
Redakteur, -e *m.* [*re-dak-töhr'*] editor
Rede, -n *f.* [*reh'-də*] speech
   eine Rede halten *v. irreg.* [*ai'-nə reh'-də hal'-tən*] make

a speech

reden *v.* [*reh'-dən*] talk, speak

Redner, - *m.* [*rehd'-nər*] speaker, orator

Referenz, -n *f.* [*re-fe-rents'*] reference

Reform, -en *f.* [*re-form'*] reform

Regal, -e *n.* [*re-gahl'*] shelf

Regel, -n *f.* [*reh'-gəl*] rule

regelmässig [*reh'-gəl-meh-siç*] regular

Regen, - *m.* [*reh'-gən*] rain

Regenbogen, ⸗ *m.* [*reh'-gən-boh-gən, reh'-gen-böh-gən*] rainbow

regendicht [*reh'-gən-diçt*] rainproof

Regenmantel, ⸗ *m.* [*reh'-gən-man-təl, reh'-gən-men-təl*] raincoat

Regenschirm, -e *m.* [*reh'-gən-shirm*] umbrella

regieren *v.* [*re-gee'-rən*] rule, reign

Regierung, -en *f.* [*re-gee'-rung*] government, administration

Regiment, -er *n.* [*re-gi-ment', re-gi-men'-tər*] regiment

Regisseur, -e *m.* [*re-zhi-söhr'*] stage manager; director

Register, - *n.* [*re-gi'-stər*] register, index

registrieren *v.* [*re-gi-stree'-rən*] register

regnen *v.* [*rehg'-nən*] rain

 Regnet es? [*rehg'-nət es*] Is it raining?

 Es regnet in Strömen [*es rehg'-nət in shtröh'-mən*] It's pouring rain

Reh, -e *n.* [*reh*] deer, doe

reiben *v. irreg.* [*rai'-bən*] rub

reich [*raiç*] rich

Reich, -e *n.* [*raiç*] empire, kingdom

reichen *v.* [*rai'-çən*] hand, pass; reach; last

reichlich [*raiç'-liç*] ample

Reichtum, ⸗**er** *m.* [*raiç'-toom, raiç'-tüh-mər*] wealth, riches

reif [*raif*] mature, ripe

Reifen, - *m.* [*rai'-fən*] tire; ring, hoop

Reifeprüfung, -en *f.* [*rai'-fə-prüh-fung*] graduation [from high school]

Reifezeugnis, -se *n.* [*rai'-fə-tsoik-nis*] high school certificate

Reihe, -n *f.* [*rai'-ə*] row, series

Reim, -e *m.* [*raim*] rhyme

rein [*rain*] pure

reinigen *v.* [*rai'-ni-gən*] clean

Reinigung, -en *f.* [*rai'-ni-gung*] cleaning

Reinigungsanstalt, -en *f.* [*rai'-ni-gungs-an-shtalt*] cleaner's shop

Reis *m.* [*rais*] rice

Reise, -n *f.* [*rai'-zə*] travel, trip

    Glückliche Reise! [*glük'-li-çə rai'-zə*] Have a nice trip!

Reisebüro, -s *n.* [*rai'-zə-bü-roh, rai'-zə-bü-rohs*] travel agency

reisen *v.* (*Aux:* SEIN) [*rai'-zən*] travel

Reisende, -n *m.*, *f.* [*rai'-zən-də*] traveler

Reiseplan, ⸗**e** *m.* [*rai'-zə-plahn, rai'-zə-pleh-nə*] itinerary

Reisescheck, -s *m.* [*rai'-zə-shek, rai'-zə-sheks*] traveler's check

reissen *v. irreg.* [*rai'-sən*] tear, rend

Reissverschluss, ⸗**e** *m.* [*rais'-fer-shlus*] zipper

reiten *v. irreg.* (*Aux:* SEIN) [*rai'-tən*] ride a horse

Reiter, - *m.* [*rai'-tər*] horseman

Reiz, -e *m.* [*raits*] charm; stimulus

reizen *v.* [*rait'-sən*] charm, tempt; irritate

reizend [*rait'-sənt*] charming

Reizung, -en *f.* [*rait'-sung*] irritation

Reklame, -n *f.* [*re-klah'-mə*] advertisement, publicity

    Reklame machen für (plus acc.) *v.* [*re-klah'-mə ma'-khən führ*] advertise

Rekord, -e *m.* [*re-kort', re-kor'-də*] record [sports]

Rekrut, -en *m.* [*re-kroot'*] recruit

relativ *adj.* [*re-la-teef'*] relative

Religion, -en *f.* [*re-li-gi-ohn'*] religion

rennen *v. irreg.* (*Aux:* SEIN) [*re'-nən*] race, run

Rennen, - *n.* [*re'-nən*] race

Rente, -n *f.* [*ren'-tə*] pension

Reparatur, -en *f.* [*re-pa-ra-toor'*] repair

reparieren *v.* [*re-pa-ree'-rən*] repair, fix

Reproduktion, -en *f.* [*re-pro-duk-tsi-ohn'*] reproduction; copy

Republik, -en *f.* [*re-pu-bleek'*] republic

reservieren *v.* [*re-zer-vee'-rən*] reserve

Reservierung, -en *f.* [*re-zer-vee'-rung*] reservation [hotel, plane, etc.]

Respekt *m.* [*re-shpekt'*] respect

Rest, -e *m.* [*rest*] remainder

Restaurant, -s *n.* [*re-sto-rant'*, *re-sto-rants'*] restaurant

Resultat, -e *n.* [*re-zul-taht'*] result

retten *v.* [*re'-tən*] save [life], rescue

Rettich, -e *m.* [*re'-tiç*] radish

Rettungsboot, -e *n.* [*re'-tungz-boht*] lifeboat

Revolution, -en *f.* [*re-vo-lu-tsi-ohn'*] revolution

Revolver, - *m.* [*re-vol'-vər*] revolver

Rezept, -e *n.* [*re-tsept'*] prescription [medical]; recipe
   [cooking]

Rheumatismus, -ismen *m.* [*roi-ma-tis'-mus, roi-ma-tis'-mən*]
   rheumatism

Richter, - *m.* [*riç'-tər*] judge

richtig [*riç'-tiç*] correct, right, true

Richtung, -en *f.* [*riç'-tung*] direction

riechen *v. irreg.* [*ree'-çən*] smell

Riemen, - *m.* [*ree'-mən*] strap

Riese, -n *m.* [*ree'-zə*] giant

riesig [*ree'-ziç*] gigantic, immense

Rinder *n. pl.* [*rin'-dər*] cattle

Rindfleisch *n.* [*rint'-flaish*] beef

Rindfleischbrühe, -n *f.* [*rint'-flaish-brüh-ə*] beef broth

Ring, -e *m.* [*ring*] ring [on finger]

ringen *v.* [*ring'-ən*] wrestle

Rippchen *n. pl.* [*rip'-çən*] spareribs

Rippe, -n *f.* [*ri'-pə*] rib

Risiko *n. sing.* **Risiken** *pl.* [*ree'-zi-koh, ree'-zi-kən*] risk

riskieren *v.* [*ris-kee'-rən*] risk

Ritt, -e *m.* [*rit*] ride [horseback]

Ritter, - *m.* [*ri'-tər*] knight

Ritz, -e *m.* [*rits*] scratch [skin], crack

Rival, -en *m.* [*ri-vahl'*] rival

Rizinusöl *n.* [*ree'-tsi-nuz-öhl*] castor oil

Rock, ⸗e *m.* [*rok, ro'-kə*] skirt; coat, jacket

Roggen *m.* [*ro'-gən*] rye

roh [*roh*] coarse, raw; rare [meat]

Röhre, -n *f.* [*röh'-rə*] pipe [water]

Rohstoff, -e *m.* [*roh'-stof*] raw material
Rolle, -n *f.* [*ro'-lə*] part [in a play]; roll [list]; roller
Rolltreppe, -n *f.* [*rol'-tre-pə*] escalator
Rom *n.* [*rohm*] Rome
Roman, -e *m.* [*ro-mahn'*] novel
Romanschriftsteller, - *m.* [*ro-mahn'-shrift-shte-lər*] novelist
romantisch [*ro-man'-tish*] romantic
römisch [*röh'-mish*] Roman
Röntgenstrahlen *m. pl.* [*rönt'-gən-shtrah-lən*] X-rays
rosa [*roh'-za*] pink
Rose, -n *f.* [*roh'-zə*] rose
Rosine, -n *f.* [*ro-zee'-nə*] raisin
Rost *m.* [*rost*] rust
Rost, -e *m.* [*rost*] grate, gridiron
rösten *v.* [*rö'-stən*] roast, toast
rostig [*ro'-stiç*] rusty
rot [*roht*] red
Rotkohl, -e *m.* [*roht'-kohl*] red cabbage
Rotwein, -e *m.* [*roht'-vain*] red wine
Rübe, -n *f.* [*rüh'-bə*] turnip, beet, carrot
Rubin, -e *m.* [*ru-been'*] ruby
Rücken, - *m.* [*rü'-kən*] back [anat.]
Rückfahrkarte, -n *f.* [*rük'-fahr-kar'-tə*] round trip ticket
Rückgrat, -e *n.* [*rük'-graht*] spine
Rückkehr *f.* [*rük'-kehr*] return
rückständig [*rük'-shten-diç*] backward
Ruder, - *n.* [*roo'-dər*] oar, rudder
rudern *v.* [*roo'-dərn*] row
Ruf, -e *m.* [*roof*] call
rufen *v. irreg.* [*roo'-fən*] call
   ab-rufen [*ap'-roo-fən*] call off
   auf-rufen [*ouf'-roo-fən*] call up
   aus-rufen [*ous'-roo-fən*] call out, exclaim;
     proclaim
Ruhe *f.* [*roo'-ə*] silence, calm; repose, sleep
   Ruhe! [*roo'-ə*] Silence!
   Angenehme Ruhe! [*an'-gə-neh-mə roo'-ə*] Sleep well!
   Lassen Sie ihn in Ruhe! [*la'-sən zee een in roo'-ə*] Leave

him alone!

ruhen *v.* [*roo'-ən*] rest

ruhig [*roo'-iç*] quiet, tranquil, calm

   Seien Sie ruhig! [*zai'-ən zee roo'-iç*] Keep quiet!

Ruhm *m.* [*room*] glory, fame

rühmen *v.* [*rüh'-mən*] praise

   sich rühmen [*ziç rüh'-mən*] boast, brag

Ruhr *f.* [*roor*] dysentery

Rührei, -er *n.* [*rüh'-rai*] scrambled egg

rühren *v.* [*rüh'-rən*] stir; touch, move

rührend [*rüh'-rənt*] touching

Ruine, -n *f.* [*ru-ee'-nə*] ruin

Rumänien *n.* [*ru-meh'-ni-ən*] Rumania

rumänisch [*ru-meh'-nish*] Rumanian

rund [*runt*] round

Rundfunk *m.* [*runt'-funk*] radio

Rundfunksendung, -en *f.* [*runt'-funk-zen-dung*] broadcast

rundherum [*runt'-he-rum*] [all] around

Rundreise, -n *f.* [*runt'-rai-zə*] round trip

Rundschau *f.* [*runt'-shou*] review [periodical]

Russe, -n *m.* [*ru'-sə*] Russian [male]

Russin, -nen *f.* [*ru'-sin*] Russian [female]

russisch [*ru'-sish*] Russian

Russland *n.* [*rus'-lant*] Russia

rutschen *v.* (*Aux:* SEIN) [*rut'-shən*] slip, slide

S

Saal, ⁼e *m.* [*zahl, zeh'-lə*] hall

Sabotage, -n *f.* [*za-bo-tah'-zhə*] sabotage

sabotieren *v.* [*za-bo-tee'-rən*] sabotage

Sache, -n *f.* [*za'-khə*] matter, thing, affair; cause

sachlich [*zakh'-liç*] matter-of-fact, objective, businesslike

Sack, ⁼e *m.* [*zak, ze'-kə*] sack

Saft, ⁼e *m.* [*zaft, zef'-tə*] juice, sap

saftig [*zaf'-tiç*] juicy

Säge, -n *f.* [*zeh'-gə*] saw [tool]

sägen *v.* [*zeh'-gən*] saw

sagen *v.* [*zah'-gən*] say, tell

   Sagen Sie mir! [*zah'-gən zee meer*] Tell me!

   Sagen Sie uns (ihr, ihm) [*zah'-gən zee uns (eer, eem)*]
     Tell us (her, him)

sah *past tense of* SEHEN [*zah*] saw

Sahne *f.* [*zah'-nə*] cream

Salat, -e *m.* [*za-laht'*] salad, lettuce

Salbe, -n *f.* [*zal'-bə*] ointment

Salon, -s *m.* [*za-lohn', za-lohns'*] parlor

Salz, -e *n.* [*zalts*] salt

Salzfass, =er *n.* [*zalts'-fas, zalts'-fe-sər*] salt cellar

salzig [*zal'-ziç*] salty

Samen, - *m.* [*zah'-mən*] seed

sammeln *v.* [*za'-məln*] gather, collect

Sammlung, -en *f.* [*zam'-lung*] collection

Samstag, -e *m.* [*zams'-tahk, zams'-tah-gə*] Saturday

Samt, -e *m.* [*zamt*] velvet

sämtlich [*zemt'-liç*] all, all of them

Sanatorium *n. sing.* **Sanatorien** *pl.* [*za-na-toh'-ri-um,*
   za-na-toh'-ri-ən] sanatorium

Sand *m.* [*zant*] sand

sanft [*zanft*] gentle

sang *past tense of* SINGEN [*zang*] sang

Sänger, - *m.* [*zeng'-ər*] singer [male]

Sängerin, -nen *f.* [*zeng'-ə-rin*] singer [female]

sank *past tense of* SINKEN [*zank*] sank

Saphir, -e *m.* [*za'-fir, za-fee'-rə*] sapphire

Sardelle, -n *f.* [*zar-de'-lə*] anchovy

Sardine, -n *f.* [*zar-dee'-nə*] sardine

sarkastisch [*zar-ka'-stish*] sarcastic

sass *past tense of* SITZEN [*zahs*] sat

Satire, -n *f.* [*za-tee'-rə*] satire

satirisch [*za-tee'-rish*] satirical

satt [*zat*] sated, full

   Ich bin satt [*iç bin zat*] I've had enough

Sattel, ⁼ *m.* [*za'-təl, ze'-təl*] saddle

Satz, ⁼e *m.* [*zats, zet'-sə*] sentence; movement [music]; set [tennis]; leap

sauber [*zou'-bər*] tidy, clean

säubern *v.* [*zoi'-bərn*] clean

sauer [*zou'-ər*] sour

Sauerbraten *m.* [*zou'-ər-brah-tən*] sauerbraten

Sauerkraut *n.* [*zou'-ər-krout*] sauerkraut

Sauerstoff *m.* [*zou'-ər-shtof*] oxygen

Säule, -n *f.* [*zoi'-lə*] column [arch.]

Saum, ⁼e *m.* [*zoum, zoi'-mə*] hem

Säure, -n *f.* [*zoi'-rə*] acid

Schach *n.* [*shakh*] chess

Schachtel, -n *f.* [*shakh'-təl*] box [container]

Schade!, Wie schade! *interj.* [*shah'-də, vee shah'-də*] What a pity!

schaden *v.* [*shah'-dən*] harm, damage

Schaden, ⁼ *m.* [*shah'-dən, sheh'-dən*] damage, injury

schadhaft [*shaht'-haft*] defective, damaged; decayed [tooth]

schädlich [*sheht'-liç*] harmful

Schäfer, - *m.* [*sheh'-fər*] shepherd

schaffen *v. irreg.* [*sha'-fən*] create

Schaffner, - *m.* [*shaf'-nər*] conductor [bus, etc.]

Schal, -s *m.* [*shahl, shahls*] scarf

Schale, -n *f.* [*shah'-lə*] shell [egg]; bowl

schälen *v.* [*sheh'-lən*] peel [foods]

schalldicht [*shal'-diçt*] soundproof

Schallplatte, -n *f.* [*shal'-pla-tə*] [phonograph] record

Schalter, - *m.* [*shal'-tər*] switch [electric]; window [ticket, teller]

Scham *f.* [*shahm*] shame

(sich) schämen *v.* [*(ziç) sheh'-mən*] be ashamed

schamlos [*shahm'-lohs*] shameless

Schande *f.* [*shan'-də*] shame

schändlich [*shent'-liç*] shameful

Schar, -en *f.* [*shahr*] troop; flock [geese]

scharf [*sharf*] sharp, keen, shrill

Schärfe *f.* [*sher'-fə*] sharpness; edge

scharfsinning [*sharf'-zi-niç*] shrewd, sagacious

Scharlachfieber *n.* [*shar'-lakh-fee-bər*] scarlet fever

Schatten, - *m.* [*sha'-tən*] shade, shadow

schattig [*sha'-tiç*] shady

Schatz, ⸚e *m.* [*shats, shet'-sə*] sweetheart; treasure

schätzen *v.* [*shet'-sən*] value, estimate, appreciate

Schatzkammer, -n *f.* [*shats'-ka-mər*] treasury

Schatzmeister, - *m.* [*shats'-mai-stər*] treasurer

schauen *v.* [*shou'-ən*] look, gaze

    Schauen Sie! [*shou'-ən zee*] Look!

Schaufel, -n *f.* [*shou'-fəl*] shovel

Schaufenster, - *n.* [*shou'-fen-stər*] shopwindow

Schaum, ⸚e *m.* [*shoum, shoi'-mə*] foam

Schauspiel, -e *n.* [*shou'-shpeel*] play [theatre], show

Schauspieler, - *m.* [*shou'-shpee-lər*] actor

Schauspielerin, -nen *f.* [*shou'-shpee-lə-rin*] actress

Schaustellung, -en *f.* [*shou'-shte-lung*] exhibition, show

Scheck, -s *m.* [*shek, sheks*] check [money]

Scheibe, -n *f.* [*shai'-bə*] slice; disk; target

scheiden *v. irreg.* [*shai'-dən*] separate, part

    sich scheiden lassen von (plus dat.) *v. irreg.* [*ziç shai'-dən
la'-sən fon*] divorce

    Er liess sich von seiner Frau scheiden [*er lees ziç fon
zai'-nər frou shai'-dən*] He divorced his wife

Scheidung, -en *f.* [*shai'-dung*] divorce

scheinen *v. irreg.* [*shai'-nən*] shine; seem, appear

    Es scheint mir, dass . . . [*es shaint meer das*] It seems
to me that . . .

Scheinwerferlicht *n.* [*shain'-ver-fər-liçt*] spotlight

schellen *v.* [*she'-lən*] ring

schelten *v. irreg.* [*shel'-tən*] scold, rebuke

Schenkel, - *m.* [*shen'-kəl*] leg, thigh

schenken *v.* [*shen'-kən*] present [a gift], give, donate

Schere, -n *f.* [*sheh'-rə*] scissors

Scherz, -e *m.* [*sherts*] joke

scherzen *v.* [*shert'-sən*] joke

scheu [*shoi*] timid, shy

Scheune, -n *f.* [*shoi'-nə*] barn

scheusslich [*shois'-liç*] hideous

schicken *v.* [*shi'-kən*] send

Schicksal, -e *n.* [*shik'-sahl*] fate, destiny

schieben *v. irreg.* [*shee'-bən*] push, shove; shift

Schiedsrichter, - *m.* [*sheets'-riç-tər*] referee

schief [*sheef*] crooked, leaning; wry

Schiene, -n *f.* [*shee'-nə*] rail

schiessen *v. irreg.* [*shee'-sən*] shoot [to fire]

Schiff, -e *n.* [*shif*] ship, boat

　Wann fährt das Schiff ab? [*van fehrt das shif ap*] When
　　does the ship sail?

Schiffahrtslinie, -n *f.* [*shif'-fahrts-lee-ni-ə*] steamship line

Schild, -er *n.* [*shilt, shil'-dər*] signboard [shop]; signpost
　　[traffic]

schimpfen *v.* [*shim'-pfən*] scold

Schinken, - *m.* [*shin'-kən*] ham

Schinkenbrot, -e *n.* [*shin'-kən-broht*] ham sandwich

Schirm, -e *m.* [*shirm*] umbrella; protection

Schlacht, -en *f.* [*shlakht*] battle

Schlachtschiff, -e *n.* [*shlakht'-shif*] battleship

Schlaf *m.* [*shlahf*] sleep

Schläfchen *n.* [*shlehf'-çən*] nap

　ein Schläfchen machen *v.* [*ain shlehf'-çən ma'-khən*] take
　　a nap

schlafen *v. irreg.* [*shlah'-fən*] sleep, be asleep

schlafen gehen *v. irreg.* (*Aux:* SEIN) [*shlah'-fən geh'-ən*]
　　go to bed, retire

schlafend [*shlah'-fənt*] asleep

schläfrig [*shlehf'-riç*] sleepy

Schlafsaal *m. sing.* **Schlafsäle** *pl.* [*shlahf'-zahl, shlahf'-zeh-lə*]
　　dormitory

Schlafwagen, - *m.* [*shlahf'-vah-gən*] sleeping car

Schlafzimmer, - *n.* [*shlahf'-tsi-mər*] bedroom

Schlag, ⸚**e** *m.* [*shlahk, shleh'-gə*] blow

schlagen *v. irreg.* [*shlah'-gən*] strike, slap, beat

Schlagsahne *f.* [*shlahk'-zah-nə*] whipped cream

Schlamm *m.* [*shlam*] mud

Schlange, -n *f.* [*shlang'-ə*] snake

schlank [*shlank*] slender, slim

schlau [*shlou*] cunning

schlecht [*shleçt*] bad, poor

schlechtgelaunt [*shleçt'-gə-lount*] in a bad temper

Schleier, - *m.* [*shlai-'ər*] veil

schlief *past tense of* SCHLAFEN [*shleef*] slept

schliessen *v. irreg.* (*Aux:* SEIN) [*shlee'-sən*] shut, close, conclude [treaty]

Schliessfach, ⸗er *n.* [*shlees'-fakh, shlees'-fe-çər*] post-office box

schliesslich [*shlees'-liç*] finally, in conclusion

schlimm [*shlim*] bad, evil

Schlittschuh laufen *v. irreg.* (*Aux:* SEIN) [*shlit'-shoo lou'-fən*] skate

Schlittschuhläufer, - *m.* [*shlit'-shoo-loi-fər*] skater

Schloss, ⸗er *n.* [*shlos, shlö'-sər*] castle

schloss *past tense of* SCHLIESSEN [*shlos*] shut; concluded

Schlosser, - *m.* [*shlo'-sər*] locksmith; mechanic

schlucken *v.* [*shlu'-kən*] swallow

schlug *past tense of* SCHLAGEN [*shlook*] struck, hit

schlummern *v.* [*shlu'-mərn*] doze

schlüpfen *v.* (*Aux:* SEIN) [*shlü'-pfən*] slip, slide

schlüpfrig [*shlüpf'-riç*] slippery; piquant

Schluss, ⸗e *m.* [*shlus, shlü'-sə*] conclusion, end

Schlüssel, - *m.* [*shlü'-səl*] key

Schlüsselloch, ⸗er *n.* [*shlü'-səl-lokh, shlü'-səl-lö-çər*] keyhole

schmal [*shmahl*] narrow

schmecken *v.* [*shme'-kən*] taste

    Wie schmeckt es? [*vee shmekt es?*] How does it taste?, Is it good?

    Das schmeckt gut [*das shmekt goot*] This tastes good

schmeicheln *v.* [*shmai'-çəln*] flatter

Schmeichler, - *m.* [*shmaiç'-lər*] flatterer

Schmelzen *v. irreg.* (*Aux:* SEIN) [*shmel'-tsən*] melt

Schmerz, -en *m.* [*shmerts*] ache, pain

schmerzen *v.* [*shmert'-sən*] hurt [ache]

schmerzhaft [*shmerts'-haft*] painful

schmerzlos [*shmerts'-lohs*] painless

Schmetterling, -e *m.* [*shme'-tər-ling*] butterfly

Schmied, -e *m.* [*shmeet, shmee'-də*] (black)smith

schmieren *v.* [*shmee'-rən*] lubricate; bribe

Schmieren *n.* [*shmee'-rən*] lubrication

Schminke, -n *f.* [*shmin'-kə*] rouge

Schmuck *m.* **Schmuckstücke** *pl.* [*shmuk, shmuk'-shtü-kə*] jewelry

schmücken *v.* [*shmü'-kən*] adorn, decorate

schmutzig [*shmut'-siç*] dirty, filthy

Schnabel, ⸗ *m.* [*shnah'-bəl, shneh'-bəl*] beak, bill [of birds]

Schnalle, -en *f.* [*shna'-lə*] buckle

Schnaps, ⸗e *m.* [*shnaps, shnep'-sə*] liquor

Schnapsidee, -n *f.* [*shnaps'-i-deh*] crazy idea

schnarchen *v.* [*shnar'-çən*] snore

Schnecke, -n *f.* [*shne'-kə*] snail

Schnee *m.* [*shneh*] snow

Schneeflocke, -n *f.* [*shneh'-flo-kə*] snowflake

Schneesturm, ⸗e *m.* [*shneh'-shturm, shneh'-shtür-mə*] snowstorm, blizzard

schneiden *v. irreg.* [*shnai'-dən*] cut

Schneider, - *m.* [*shnai'-dər*] tailor

Schneiderin, -nen *f.* [*shnai'-də-rin*] dressmaker

schneien *v.* [*shnai'-ən*] snow

schnell [*shnel*] fast, rapid, speedy

Schnelligkeit *f.* [*shne'-liç-kait*] speed

Schnellzug, ⸗e *m.* [*shnel'-tsook, shnel'-tsüh-gə*] express [train]

Schnitt, -e *m.* [*shnit*] cut [dress], style, pattern

Schnitzel *n.* [*shnit'-səl*] veal cutlet

schnitzen *v.* [*shnit'-sən*] carve

Schnitzerei, -en *f.* [*shnit'-sə-rai*] carving

Schnur, ⸗e *f.* [*shnoor, shnüh'-rə*] string

schnüren *v.* [*shnüh'-rən*] lace, tie

Schnurrbart, ⸗e *m.* [*shnur'-bahrt, shnur'-behr-tə*] mustache

Schnürsenkel, - *m.* [*shnühr'-zen-kəl*] shoelace

Schock, -s *m.* [*shok, shoks*] shock

Schokolade, -n *f.* [*sho-ko-lah'-də*] chocolate

Scholle, -n *f.* [*sho'-lə*] sole [fish]

schon [*shohn*] already

schön [*shöhn*] beautiful; fine [weather]; very well

Danke schön! [*dan'-kə shöhn*] Thanks very much!
Schönheit *f.* [*shöhn'-hait*] beauty
Schönheitsmittel, - *n.* [*shöhn'-haits-mi-təl*] cosmetic
Schöpfung, -en *f.* [*shöh'-pfung*] creation
Schornstein, -e *m.* [*shorn'-shtain*] chimney
Schottland *n.* [*shot'-lant*] Scotland
schottisch [*sho'-tish*] Scotch
Schrank, ˵e *m.* [*shrank, shren'-kə*] cupboard, closet
Schraube, -n *f.* [*shrou'-bə*] screw
Schraubenschlüssel, - *m.* [*shrou'-bən-shlü-səl*] wrench
Schraubenzieher, - *m.* [*shrou'-bən-tsee-ər*] screwdriver
Schrecken, - *m.* [*shre'-kən*] terror
schrecklich [*shrek'-liç*] horrible, dreadful
Schrei, -e *m.* [*shrai*] scream
schreiben *v. irreg.* [*shrai'-bən*] write
Schreibmaschine, -n *f.* [*shraip'-ma-shee-nə*] typewriter
Schreibpapier, -e *n.* [*shraip'-pa-peer*] writing paper
Schreibtisch, -e *m.* [*shraip'-tish*] desk
Schreibwaren *f. pl.* [*shraip'-vah-rən*] stationery
Schreibwarengeschäft, -e *n.* [*shraip'-vah-rən-gə-sheft*]
    stationery shop
schreien *v. irreg.* [*shrai'-ən*] cry, scream
Schreiner, - *m.* [*shrai'-nər*] carpenter
Schrift, -en *f.* [*shrift*] writing
schriftlich [*shrift'-liç*] in writing, written
Schriftsteller, - *m.* [*shrift'-shte-lər*] writer
Schritt, -e *m.* [*shrit*] step, pace
    Schritt für Schritt [*shrit führ shrit*] step by step
Schublade, -n *f.* [*shoop'-lah-də*] drawer
Schuft, -e *m.* [*shuft*] scoundrel
Schuh, -e *m.* [*shoo*] shoe
Schuhgeschäft, -e *n.* [*shoo'-gə-sheft*] shoe store
Schuhmacher, - *m.* [*shoo'-ma-khər*] shoemaker
Schuhputzer, - *m.* [*shoo'-put-sər*] shoeshine boy
Schuld, -en *f.* [*shult*] guilt; debt
    eine Schuld bezahlen *v.* [*ai'-nə shult bə-tsah'-lən*] pay a debt
schulden *v.* [*shul'-dən*] owe
    Wieviel schulde ich Ihnen? [*vee-feel' shul'-də iç ee'-nən*]

How much do I owe you?

schuldig [*shul'-diç*] guilty

Schule, -n *f.* [*shoo'-lə*] school

Schüler, - *m.* [*shüh'-lər*] pupil [male], student

Schülerin, -nen *f.* [*shüh'-lə-rin*] pupil [female], student

Schulter, -n *f.* [*shul'-tər*] shoulder

Schulzeugnis, -se *n.* [*shool'-tsoik-nis*] school certificate, report card

Schürze, -n *f.* [*shürt'-sə*] apron

Schuss, ⸗e *m.* [*shus, shü'-sə*] shot [from gun]

Schüssel, -n *f.* [*shü'-səl*] pan, dish, bowl

schütteln *v.* [*shü'-təln*] shake

Hände schütteln [*hen'-də shü'-təln*] shake hands

Schutz *m.* [*shuts*] protection

schützen *v.* [*schüt'-sən*] protect

schwach [*shvakh*] weak, feeble

Schwäche, -n *f.* [*shve'-çə*] weakness

Schwager, ⸗ *m.* [*shvah'-gər, shveh'-gər*] brother-in-law

Schwägerin, -nen *f.* [*shveh'-gə-rin*] sister-in-law

Schwalbe, -n *f.* [*shval'-bə*] swallow [bird]

Schwamm, ⸗e *m.* [*shvam, shve'-mə*] sponge

schwamm *past tense of* SCHWIMMEN [*shvam*] swam

Schwan, ⸗e *m.* [*shvahn, shveh'-nə*] swan

schwanger [*shvang'-ər*] pregnant

Schwangerschaft, -en *f.* [*shvang'-ər-shaft*] pregnancy

Schwanz, ⸗e *m.* [*shvants, shven'-tsə*] tail

schwarz [*shvarts*] black

Schwarzbrot, -e *n.* [*shvarts'-broht*] rye bread, brown bread

schwatzen *v.* [*shvat'-sən*] gossip, chatter

Schweden *n.* [*shveh'-dən*] Sweden

schwedisch [*shveh'-dish*] Swedish

Schwefel *m.* [*shveh'-fəl*] sulphur

Schweigen *n.* [*shvai'-gən*] silence

schweigen *v. irreg.* [*shvai'-gən*] be silent

Schwein, -e *n.* [*shvain*] pig, hog

Schweinefleisch *n.* [*shvai'-nə-flaish*] pork

Schweiss *m.* [*shvais*] perspiration

die Schweiz *f.* [*dee shvaits*] Switzerland

in der Schweiz [*in dər shvaits*] in Switzerland
schweizerisch [*shvai'-tsə-rish*] Swiss
schwellen v. irreg. (*Aux:* SEIN) [*shve'-lən*] swell
schwer [*shvehr*] hard, heavy
schwerfällig [*shvehr'-fe-liç*] clumsy
schwerhörig [*shvehr'-höh-riç*] hard-of-hearing
Schwerindustrie, -n f. [*shvehr'-in-du-stree*] heavy industry
Schwert, -er n. [*shvehrt, shvehr'-tər*] sword
Schwester, -n f. [*shve'-stər*] sister, nurse
Schwiegereltern pl. [*shvee'-gər-el-tərn*] parents-in-law
Schwiegermutter, ¨ f. [*shvee'-gər-mu-tər, shvee'-gər-mü-tər*]
    mother-in-law
Schwiegersohn, ¨e m. [*shvee'-gər-zohn, shvee'-gər-zöh-nə*]
    son-in-law
Schwiegertochter, ¨ f. [*shvee'-gər-tokh-tər, shvee'-gər-töç-tər*]
    daughter-in-law
Schwiegervater, ¨ m. [*shvee'-gər-fah-tər, shvee'-gər-feh-tər*]
    father-in-law
schwierig [*shvee'-riç*] difficult
Schwierigkeit, -en f. [*shvee'-riç-kait*] difficulty
Schwimmbad, ¨er n. [*shvim'-baht, shvim'-beh-dər*] swimming
    pool
schwimmen v. irreg. (*Aux:* SEIN) [*shvi'-mən*] swim; float
Schwimmer, - m. [*shvi'-mər*] swimmer [male]
Schwimmerin, -nen f. [*shvi'-mə-rin*] swimmer [female]
schwindeln v. [*shvin'-dəln*] swindle; fib
schwindlig sein v. irreg. [*shvind'-liç zain*] be dizzy
schwitzen v. [*shvit'-sən*] perspire, sweat
schwören v. irreg. [*shvöh'-rən*] swear, vow
schwül [*shvühl*] muggy
Schwur, ¨e m. [*shvoor, shvüh'-rə*] oath, vow
sechs [*zeks*] six
sechst [*zekst*] sixth
sechzehn [*zeç'-tsehn*] sixteen
sechzig [*zeç'-tsiç*] sixty
See, -n m. [*zeh*] lake
See, -en f. [*zeh*] sea, ocean
Seehafen, ¨ m. [*zeh'-hah-fən, zeh'-heh-fən*] seaport

Seehund, -e m. [*zeh'-hunt, zeh'-hun-də*] seal

seekrank [*zeh'-krank*] seasick

Seele, -n f. [*zee'-lə*] soul

Seemann m. sing. **Seeleute** pl. [*zeh'-man, zeh'-loi-tə*] sailor

Seereise, -n f. [*zeh'-rai-zə*] sea voyage

Segel, - n. [*zeh'-gəl*] sail

Segelboot, -e n. [*zeh'-gəl-boht*] sailboat

segeln v. [*zeh'-gəln*] sail

Segen m. [*zeh'-gən*] blessing

segnen v. [*zehg'-nən*] bless

sehen v. irreg. [*zeh'-ən*] see, watch

    Sehen wir! [*zeh'-ən veer*] Let's see

sich sehnen nach (plus dat.) v. [*ziç zeh'-nən nakh*] long for

Sehnsucht f. [*zehn'-zukht*] longing

sehr [*zehr*] very, very much

    Sehr angenehm [*zehr an'-gə-nehm*] How do you do?
      [upon introductions]

Seide, -n f. [*zai'-də*] silk

Seidenpapier n. [*zai'-dən-pa-peer*] tissue paper

Seife, -n f. [*zai'-fə*] soap

Seil, -e n. [*zail*] rope, cord

sein v. irreg. (*Aux:* SEIN) [*zain*] be

Sein n. [*zain*] being, existence

sein m. & n. pron. [*zain*] his, it(s)

seine f. pron. [*zai'-nə*] her(s), it(s)

seit (plus dat.) [*zait*] since

    Seit wann? [*zait van*] Since when?

seitdem [*zait-dehm'*] ever since

Seite, -n f. [*zai'-tə*] side; page [of book]

Seitenstrasse, -n f. [*zai'-tən-shtrah-sə*] side street

seitwärts [*zait'-verts*] sideways

Sekretär, -e m. [*ze-kre-tehr'*] secretary [male]

Sekretärin, -nen f. [*ze-kre-teh'-rin*] secretary [female]

Sekunde, -n f. [*ze-kun'-də*] second [of time]

selbst adv. [*zelpst*] even

Selbst, -n n. [*zelpst*] ego; [one's own] self

selbständig [*zelp'-shten-diç*] independent, self-supporting

selbstlos [*zelpst'-lohs*] unselfish

Selbstmord, -e m. [*zelpst'-mort, zelpst'-mor-də*] suicide
selbstverständlich [*zelpst'-fer-shtent-liç*] naturally, of course
selbstzufrieden [*zelpst'-tsu-free-dən*] smug
selig [*zeh'-liç*] blissful, blessed
Sellerie, -s m. [*ze'-lə-ree, ze'-lə-rees*] celery
selten adj. [*zel'-tən*] rare, scarce
selten adv. [*zel'-tən*] rarely, seldom; exceptionally
Senat, -e m. [*ze-naht'*] senate
Senator, -en m. [*ze-nah'-tor, ze-na-toh'-rən*] senator
senden v. irreg. [*zen-dən*] send; mail; broadcast
Sender, - m. [*zen'-dər*] radio station
Senf m. [*zenf*] mustard
sentimental [*zen-ti-men-tahl'*] sentimental, soft-hearted, corny
September m. [*zep-tem'-bər*] September
Serie, -n f. [*zeh'-ri-ə*] series
Service, -e n. [*zer-vees'*] service set
Serviette, -n f. [*zer-vi-e'-tə*] napkin
Sessel, - m. [*ze'-səl*] armchair
setzen v. [*zet'-sən*] set, put; raise [monument]
  sich setzen [*ziç zet'-sən*] sit down
  Setzen Sie sich, bitte! [*zet'-sən zee ziç, bi'-tə*] Sit down,
    please
Shampoo, -s n. [*sham-poo', sham-poos'*] shampoo
Sherry, -s m. [*she'-ri, she'-ris*] sherry
sich dat. & acc. [*ziç*] oneself, himself, herself, itself,
    themselves; yourself, yourselves; to himself, etc.
sicher [*zi'-çər*] sure, certain; safe, secure
  Sind Sie sicher? [*zint zee zi'-çər*] Are you sure?
Sicherheit, -en f. [*zi'-çər-hait*] safety, security; certainty
sicherlich [*zi'-çər-liç*] surely
sichern v. [*zi'-çərn*] secure
Sicht f. [*ziçt*] view, visibility
sichtbar [*ziçt'-bahr*] visible
sie pers. pron. [*zee*] she, her, it; they, them
Sie [*polite form*] [*zee*] you
  Haben Sie die Zeitung? Ja, ich habe sie [*hah'-bən zee
    dee tsai'-tung? yah iç hah'-bə zee*] Have you the
    newspaper? Yes, I have it

sieben [*zee'-bən*] seven
siebent [*zee'-bənt*] seventh
siebzehn [*zeep'-tsehn*] seventeen
siebzig [*zeep'-tsiç*] seventy
sieden v. [*zee'-dən*] boil
Sieg, -e m. [*zeek, zee'-gə*] victory
Siegel, - n. [*zee'-gəl*] seal [document]
siegreich [*zeek'-raiç*] triumphant
Silbe, -n f. [*zil'-bə*] syllable
Silber n. [*zil'-bər*] silver
singen v. irreg. [*zing'-ən*] sing
sinken v. irreg. [*zin'-kən*] sink
Sinn, -e m. [*zin*] sense, mind
sinnlich [*zin'-liç*] sensual
sinnlos [*zin'-lohs*] senseless, futile
Sirene, -n f. [*zi-reh'-nə*] siren
Sitte, -n f. [*zi'-tə*] custom, manners
Sitz, -e m. [*zits*] seat
sitzen v. irreg. [*zit'-sən*] sit
Sizilien n. [*zi-tsee'-li-ən*] Sicily
sizilisch [*zi-tsee'-lish*] Sicilian
Skandal, -e m. [*skan-dahl'*] scandal
Skelett, -e n. [*ske-let'*] skeleton
Ski, Schi, -er m. [*skee, shee, skee'-ər, shee'-ər*] ski
skilaufen v. irreg. (*Aux:* SEIN) [*shee'-lou-fən*] ski
Skiläufer, - m. [*shee'-loi-fər*] skier
Skizze, -n f. [*skit'-sə*] sketch
Sklave, -n m. [*sklah'-və*] slave
Sklaverei f. [*sklah-ve-rai'*] slavery
Skulptur, -en f. [*skulp-toor'*] sculpture
Smaragd, -e m. [*sma-rakt', sma-rak'-də*] emerald
so [*zoh, zo*] so, thus; therefore
so . . . wie [*zoh . . . vee*] as . . . as
sobald wie [*zo-balt' vee*] as soon as
Socke, -n f. [*zo'-kə*] sock
Soda n. [*zoh'-dah*] soda
sodass [*zo-das'*] so that
Sofa, -s n. [*zoh'-fa, zoh'-fas*] sofa

sofort [*zo-fort'*] at once, immediately

sogar [*zo-gahr'*, *zo-gar'*] even

  sogar ich [*zo-gar' iç*] even I

Sohle, -n *f.* [*zohl'-lə*] sole [of shoe or foot]

Sohn, ⸗e *m.* [*zohn*, *zöh'-nə*] son

solch; solcher, solche, solches [*zolç*, *zol'-çər*, *zol'-çə*, *zol'-çəs*] such

Soldat, -en *m.* [*zol-daht'*] soldier

sollen *mod. aux.* [*zo'-lən*] be obliged to; have to; be said to; ought to; should

  ich, er, sie, es sollte [*iç*, *er*, *zee*, *es zol'-tə*] I, he, she, it should

  Ich sollte es eigentlich tun [*iç zol'-tə es ai'-gənt-liç toon*] I really ought to do it

  wir, Sie, sie sollten [*veer*, *zee*, *zee zol'-tən*] we, you [formal], they should

Sommer, - *m.* [*zo'-mər*] summer

sonderbar [*zon'-dər-bahr*] odd, unusual

sondern [*zon'-dərn*] but

Sonnabend, -e *m.* [*zon'-ah-bənt*, *zon'-ah-bən-də*] Saturday

Sonne, -n *f.* [*zo'-nə*] sun

Sonnenaufgang, ⸗e *m.* [*zo'-nən-ouf-gang*, *zo'-nən-ouf-geng-ə*] sunrise

Sonnenbrille, -n *f.* [*zo'-nən-bri-lə*] sunglasses

Sonnenschein *m.* [*zo'-nən-shain*] sunshine

Sonnenuntergang, ⸗e *m.* [*zo'-nən-un-tər-gang*, *zo'-nən-un-tər-geng-ə*] sunset

sonnenverbrannt [*zo'-nen-fer-brant*] sunburned

Sonntag, -e *m.* [*zon'-tahk*, *zohn'-tah-gə*] Sunday

sonst [*zonst*] else, otherwise

  sonst nichts [*zonst niçts*] nothing else

  Sonst noch etwas? [*zonst nokh et'-vas*] Anything else?

Sorgen *f. pl.* [*zor'-gən*] cares

sorgen (für) *v.* [*zor'-gən führ*] care (for)

  sich Sorgen machen [*ziç zor'-gən ma'-khən*] worry

sorgfältig [*zork'-fel-tiç*] careful, attentive

sorglos [*zorg'-lohs*] careless

Sorte, -n *f.* [*zor'-tə*] kind, sort

Sosse, -n *f.* [*zoh'-sə*] sauce, gravy
soviel wie [*zo-veel' vee*] as much as
   soviel ich weiss [*zo-veel' iç vais*] so far as I know
sowieso [*zoh-vee-zoh'*] anyway, at any rate
Sowjetunion *f.* [*so-vi-et'-un-i-ohn*] Soviet Union
sozial [*zo-tsi-ahl'*] social
Sozialist, -en *m.* [*zo-tsi-a-list'*] socialist
sozusagen [*zoh-tsu-zah'-gən*] so to speak, as it were
spähen *v.* [*shpeh'-ən*] spy, peer, pry
spalten *v.* [*shpal'-tən*] split
Spanien *n.* [*shpah'-ni-ən*] Spain
Spanier, - *m.* [*shpah'-ni-ər*] Spaniard [male]
Spanierin, -nen *f.* [*shpah'-ni-ə-rin*] Spaniard [female]
spanisch [*shpah'-nish*] Spanish
sparen *v.* [*shpah'-rən*] save [money]
Spargel, - *m.* [*shpar'-gəl*] asparagus
Sparkasse, -n *f.* [*shpahr'-ka-sə*] savings bank
Sparkonto *n. sing.* **Sparkonten** *pl.* [*shpahr'-kon-to,*
   shpahr'-kon-tən] savings account
sparsam [*shpar'-zam*] thrifty
Spass, ⸗e *m.* [*shpahs, shpeh'-sə*] joke; fun
spät [*shpeht*] late
   Wie spät ist es? [*vee shpeht ist es*] What time is it?
später [*shpeh'-tər*] later, afterwards
spätestens [*spheh'-tə-stəns*] at the latest
Spazierfahrt, -en *f.* [*shpa-tseer'-fahrt*] drive [in car], ride
Spaziergang, ⸗e *m.* [*shpa-tseer'-gang, shpa-tseer'-geng-ə*] walk
   einen Spaziergang machen *v.* [*ai'-nən shpa-tseer'-gang*
   mah'-khən] take a walk
Speck *m.* [*shpek*] bacon
Speise, -n *f.* [*shpai'-zə*] food, meal, dish
Speisekarte, -n *f.* [*shpai'-zə-kar-tə*] menu
speisen *v.* [*shpai'-zən*] eat, take food
Speiseschrank, ⸗e *m.* [*shpai'-zə-shrank, shrai'-zə-shren-kə*]
   cupboard
Speisewagen, - *m.* [*shpai'-zə-vah-gən, shpai'-zə-veh-gən*]
   dining car
Speisezimmer, - *n.* [*shpai'-zə-tsi-mər*] dining room

Sperling, -e *m.* [*shper'-ling*] sparrow
sperren *v.* [*shpe'-rən*] bar; stop [a check]
spezial [*shpe-tsi-ahl'*] special
Spezialist, -en *m.* [*shpe-tsi-a-list'*] specialist
Spezialität, -en *f.* [*shpe-tsi-a-li-teht'*] specialty
Spiegel, - *m.* [*shpee'-gəl*] mirror
Spiegelung, -en *f.* [*shpee'-gə-lung*] reflection; mirage
Spiel, -e *n.* [*shpeel*] play [theatre]; game, match
    ein Spiel Karten [*ain shpeel kar'-tən*] a pack of playing
    cards
spielen *v.* [*shpee'-lən*] play; gamble
Spielkarten *f. pl.* [*shpeel'-kar-tən*] playing cards
Spielwaren *f. pl.* [*shpeel'-vah-rən*] toys
Spielzeug *n. sing.* **Spielsachen** *pl.* [*shpeel'-tsoik,*
    shpeel'-za-khən] toy
Spinat *m.* [*shpi-naht'*] spinach
Spinne, -n *f.* [*shpi'-nə*] spider
spinnen *v. irreg.* [*shpi'-nən*] spin
Spion, -e *m.* [*shpi-ohn'*] spy
Spitze, -n *f.* [*shpit'-sə*] point [land, knives]; lace
spitzig [*shpit'-siç*] pointed
Spitzname, -n *m.* [*shpits'-nah-mə*] nickname
Sport, -e *m.* [*shport*] sport [athletics]
sportlich [*shport'-liç*] sporting
Spott *m.* [*shpot*] scorn, ridicule
sprach *past tense of* SPRECHEN [*shprahkh*] spoke
Sprache, -n *f.* [*shprah'-khə*] language, speech
sprachlos [*shprahkh'-lohs*] speechless
sprang *past tense of* SPRINGEN [*shprang*] sprang
sprechen *v. irreg.* [*shpre'-çən*] speak, talk
    Sprechen Sie deutsch? [*shpre'-çən zee doich*] Do you
    speak German?
Sprecher, - *m.* [*shpre'-çər*] speaker, spokesman
Sprichwort, ¤er *n.* [*shpriç'-vort, shpriç'-vör-tər*] proverb
springen *v. irreg.* (*Aux:* SEIN) [*shpring'-ən*] jump, leap;
    dive [swimming]
Spritze, -n *f.* [*shprit'-sə*] injection; syringe
spritzen *v.* [*shprit'-sən*] spray, squirt

Sprung, ⸗e *m.* [*shprung, shprüng'-ə*] leap, jump

spucken *v.* [*shpu'-kən*] spit

spülen *v.* [*shpüh'-lən*] wash, rinse

Spur, -en *f.* [*shpoor*] trace, track; vestige

Staat, -en *m.* [*shtaht*] state, country; government

Staatsangehörigkeit, -en *f.* [*shtahts'-an-gə-höh-riç-kait*] nationality, citizenship

Staatsanwalt, ⸗e *m.* [*shtahts'-an-valt, shtahts'-an-vel-tə*] district attorney, prosecutor

Staatsmann, ⸗er (*m*) [*shtahts'-man, shtahts'-me-nər*] statesman

Stadion *n. sing.* **Stadien** *pl.* [*shtah'-di-on, shtah'-di-ən*] stadium

Stadt, ⸗e *f.* [*shtat, shte'-tə*] town, city

städtisch [*shte'-tish*] urban, municipal

Stahl, ⸗e *m.* [*shtahl, shteh'-lə*] steel

stahl *past tense of* STEHLEN [*shtahl*] stole

Stall, ⸗e *m.* [*shtal, shte'-lə*] stable

Stamm, ⸗e *m.* [*shtam, shte'-mə*] tribe; stem, trunk [bot.]

stand *past tense of* STEHEN [*shtant*] stood

Standesamt, ⸗er *n.* [*shtan'-dəs-amt, shtan'-dəs-em-tər*] registrar's office

Standpunkt, -e *m.* [*shtant'-punkt*] standpoint

Stange, -n *f.* [*shtang'-ə*] pole, rod

stark [*shtark*] strong, stout; intense

Stärke *f.* [*shter'-kə*] strength; starch

stärken *v.* [*shter'-kən*] strengthen; starch

starten *v.* [*shtar'-tən*] start

Station, -en *f.* [*shta-tsi-ohn'*] station

Statistik *f.* [*shta-ti'-stik*] statistics

statt *prep.* (plus gen.) [*shtat*] instead of

statt-finden *v. irreg.* [*shtat'-fin-dən*] take place

Staub *m.* [*shtoup*] dust

staubig [*shtou'-biç*] dusty

Staubsauger, - *m.* [*shtoup'-zou-gər*] vacuum cleaner

staunen *v.* [*shtau'-nən*] be astonished

Steak, -s *n.* [*stehk, stehks*] steak

stechen *v. irreg.* [*shte'-çən*] prick, sting

Steckdose, -n *f.* [*shtek'-doh-zə*] outlet [electric]

stecken v. [shte'-kən] stick; put [into]

stecken-bleiben v. irreg. (Aux: SEIN) [shte'-kən-blai-bən] be stuck

Steckenpferd, -e n. [shte'-kən-pfehɪt, shte'-kən-pfehr-də] hobby; hobbyhorse

Stecknadel, -n f. [shtek'-nah-dəl] pin

stehen v. irreg. [shteh'-ən] stand

stehen-bleiben v. irreg. (Aux: SEIN) [shteh'-ən-blai-bən] remain standing, stop

stehlen v. irreg. [shteh'-lən] steal

steif [shtaif] stiff

steigen v. irreg. (Aux: SEIN) [shtai'-gən] mount, ascend, climb

steil [shtail] steep

Stein, -e m. [shtain] stone, rock

Stelle, -n f. [shte'-lə] place; job; passage [in book]
   auf der Stelle [auf dehr shte'-lə] on the spot, at once
   die Stelle auf-geben v. irreg. [dee shte'-lə ouf'-geh-bən] resign [from job]

stellen v. [shte'-lən] put, place, set

Stellenvermittlungsbüro, -s m. [shte'-lən-fer-mit-lungs-bü-roh, shte'-lən-fer-mit-lungs-bü-rohs] employment agency

Stellung, -en f. [shte'-lung] position, attitude; job

stempeln v. [shtem'-pəln] stamp [letters]

stenografieren v. [shte-no-gra-fee'-rən] write in shorthand

Stenograph, -en m. [shte-no-grahf'] stenographer

Stenotypistin, -nen f. [shte-no-tü-pi'-stin] typist [shorthand]

sterben v. irreg. (Aux: SEIN) [shter'-bən] die

sterilisiert [shte-ri-li-zeert'] sterilized

Stern, -e m. [shtern] star

Steuer, - n. [shtoi'-ər] rudder, helm

Steuer, -n f. [shtoi'-ər] tax

steuerfrei [shtoi'-ər-frai] tax-free

Steuerrad, ⁼er n. [shtoi'-ər-raht, shtoi'-ər-reh-dər] steering wheel

Steward, -s m. [styoo'-ərt, styoo'-ərts] steward

Stewardess, -en f. [styoo'-ər-des] stewardess

sticken v. [shti'-kən] embroider

Stickerei, -en f. [shti-kə-rai'] embroidery

Stiefel, - *m.* [*shtee'-fəl*] boot
Stiefmutter, = *f.* [*shteef'-mu-tər, shteef'-mü-tər*] stepmother
Stiefvater, = *m.* [*shteef'-fah-tər, shteef'-feh-tər*] stepfather
Stier, -e *m.* [*shteer*] bull
Stierkampf, =e *m.* [*shteer'-kampf, steer'-kem-pfə*] bullfight
stiften *v.* [*shtif'-tən*] donate
Stil, -e *m.* [*shteel*] style
still [*shtil*] silent, quiet
Stimme, -n *f.* [*shti'-mə*] voice; vote
stimmen *v.* [*shti'-mən*] vote; tune
   Stimmt! [*shtimt*] Correct!
Stimmung *f.* [*shti'-mung*] mood, humor
Stirn, -en *f.* [*shtirn*] forehead
Stock, =e *m.* [*shtok, shtö'-kə*] stick, cane, baton
Stoff, -e *m.* [*shtof*] matter; fabric
stolpern (über plus acc.**)** *v.* (*Aux:* SEIN) [*shtol'-pərn (üh'-bər)*] trip (over)
stolz [*shtolts*] proud
Stolz *m.* [*shtolts*] pride
Stopplicht, -er *n.* [*shtop'-liçt, shtop'-liç-tər*] stoplight
Storch, =e *m.* [*shtorç, shtör'-çə*] stork
stören *v.* [*shtöh'-rən*] disturb
   Stören Sie mich nicht! [*shtöh'-rən zee miç niçt*] Don't bother me!
Störung, -en *f.* [*shtöh'-rung*] disturbance; breakdown
stossen *v. irreg.* [*shtoh'-sən*] push, shove, kick
Strafe, -n *f.* [*shtrah'-fə*] fine, penalty, punishment
Sträfling, -e *m.* [*shtrehf'-ling*] convict
strahlen *v.* [*shtrah'-lən*] shine, radiate; beam
Strand, -e *m.* [*shtrant, shtran'-də*] beach, shore
Strasse, -n *f.* [*shtrah'-sə*] street, road
Strassenbahn, -en *f.* [*shtrah'-sən-bahn*] streetcar
Strecke, -n *f.* [*shtre'-kə*] route; distance
Streichholz, =er *n.* [*straiç'-holts, straiç'-höl-tsər*] match [cigarette]
Streife, -n *f.* [*shtrai'-fə*] patrol
Streik, -s *m.* [*shtraik, shtraiks*] strike
streiken *v.* [*shtrai'-kən*] strike

Streit, -e *m.* [*shtrait*] dispute, quarrel

streiten *v.* [*shtrai'-tən*] fight, dispute

streitsüchtig [*shtrait'-züç-tiç*] quarrelsome

streng [*shtreng*] severe, stern, strict
   streng gegen einen sein *v.* [*shtreng geh'-gən ai'-nən zain*] be down on a person

streuen *v.* [*shtroi'-ən*] spread, strew, scatter

stricken *v.* [*shtri'-kən*] knit

Stroh *n.* [*shtroh*] straw

Strom, ⸗e *m.* [*shtrohm, shtröh'-mə*] stream; large river

Struktur, -en *f.* [*shtruk-toor'*] structure

Strumpf, ⸗e *m.* [*shtrumpf, shtrüm'-pfə*] stocking

Stube, -n *f.* [*shtoo'-bə*] room [in house]

Stubenmädchen, - *n.* [*shtoo'-bən-meht-çən*] housemaid

Stück, -e *n.* [*shtük*] piece; play [theatre]

Student, -en *m.* [*shtu-dent'*] student [male]

Studentin, -nen *f.* [*shtu-den'-tin*] student [female]

studieren *v.* [*shtu-dee'-rən*] study; go to college

Studierstube, -n *f.* [*shtu-deer'-shtoo-bə*] study

Stufe, -n *f.* [*shtoo'-fə*] step, stair

stufenweise [*shtoo'-fən-vai-zə*] gradually

Stuhl, ⸗e *m.* [*shtool, shtüh'-lə*] chair

stumm [*shtum*] dumb, mute

Stunde, -n *f.* [*shtun'-də*] hour; lesson

stundenlang [*shtun'-dən-lang*] for hours

stündlich [*shtünt'-liç*] hourly

Sturm, ⸗e *m.* [*shturm, shtür'-mə*] storm

Sturz, ⸗e *m.* [*shturts, shtür'-tsə*] downfall; fall

stürzen *v.* [*shtür'-tsən*] fall down; plunge

stützen *v.* [*shtü'-tsən*] support, prop up

subtil [*zup-teel'*] subtle

Suche *f.* [*zoo'-khə*] search

suchen *v.* [*zoo'-khən*] seek, look for
   suchen nach [*zoo'-khən nakh*] search for

Sucher, - *m.* [*zoo'-khər*] view-finder

Süden *m.* [*züh'-dən*] south

Südamerika *n.* [*züht'-a-meh-ri-ka*] South America

südamerikanisch [*züht'-a-me-ri-kah-nish*] South American

Sühne *f.* [*züh'-nə*] atonement
Summe, -n *f.* [*zu'-mə*] sum
Sünde, -n *f.* [*zün'-də*] sin
Suppe, -n *f.* [*zu'-pə*] soup
süss [*zühs*] sweet
sympathisch [*züm-pah'-tish*] congenial
Symphonie, -n *f.* [*züm-fo-nee'*] symphony
Symptom, -e *n.* [*zümp-tohm'*] symptom
synthetisch [*zün-teh'-tish*] synthetic
System, -e *n.* [*zü-stehm'*] system
systematisch [*zü-ste-mah'-tish*] systematic
Szene, -n *f.* [*stseh'-nə*] scene

T

Tabak, -e *m.* [*tah'-bak*] tobacco
Tabelle, -n *f.* [*ta-be'-lə*] chart, table
Tablett, -e *n.* [*ta-blet'*] tray
Tablette, -n *f.* [*ta-ble'-tə*] tablet [med.], pill
tadellos [*tah'-dəl-lohs*] excellent, perfect
tadeln *v.* [*tah'-dəln*] blame
Tafel, -n *f.* [*tah'-fəl*] blackboard; bar [of chocolate];
    dinner table
Tag, -e *m.* [*tahk, tah'-gə*] day
    den ganzen Tag [*dehn gant'-sən tahk*] all day long
    jeden Tag [*yeh'-dən tahk*] every day
Tagebuch, ⸗er *n.* [*tah'-gə-bookh, tah'-gə-bü-çər*] diary
Tageszeitung, -en *f.* [*tah'-gəs-tsai-tung*] daily paper
täglich [*tehk'-liç*] daily
    zweimal täglich [*tsvai'-mahl tehk'-liç*] twice a day
Tagung, -en *f.* [*tah'-gung*] meeting, session
Takt, -e *m.* [*takt*] beat, measure, bar [music]; tact
taktlos [*takt'-lohs*] tactless
Tal, ⸗er *n.* [*tahl, teh'-lər*] valley
Tank, -s *m.* [*tank, tanks*] tank

tanken v. [*tan'-kən*] get gasoline

Tankstelle, -n f. [*tank'-shte-lə*] gasoline station

Tanne, -n f. [*ta'-nə*] fir tree

Tante, -n f. [*tan'-tə*] aunt

Tanz, ⸗e m. [*tants, ten'-tsə*] dance

   Darf ich um den Tanz bitten? [*darf iç um dehn tants bi'-tən*] May I have this dance?

tanzen v. [*tan'-tsən*] dance

Tänzer, - m. [*ten'-tsər*] dancer [male]

Tänzerin, -nen f. [*ten'-tsə-rin*] dancer [female]

Tapete, -n f. [*ta-peh'-tə*] wallpaper

tapfer [*ta'-pfər*] brave

Tapferkeit f. [*ta'-pfər-kait*] bravery

Tarif, -e m. [*ta-reef'*] tariff; wage scale

Tasche, -n f. [*ta'-shə*] pocket; [hand] bag

Taschendieb, -e m. [*ta'-shən-deep, ta'-shən-dee-bə*] pickpocket

Taschengeld n. [*ta'-shən-gelt*] allowance

Taschenlampe, -n f. [*ta'-shən-lam-pə*] flashlight

Taschentuch, ⸗er n. [*ta'-shən-tookh, ta'-shən-tüh-çər*] handkerchief

Tasse, -n f. [*ta'-sə*] cup

Tat, -en f. [*taht*] deed, act

Tätigkeit, -en f. [*teh'-tiç-kait*] activity

Tatsache, -n f. [*taht'-za-khə*] fact

tatsächlich [*taht-zeç'-liç*] actually, in fact

Tau m. [*tou*] dew

taub [*toup*] deaf

Taube, -n f. [*tou'-bə*] pigeon

taubstumm [*toup'-shtum*] deaf-mute

tauchen v. (*Aux:* SEIN) [*tou'-khən*] dive, plunge

Taufe, -n f. [*tou'-fə*] baptism

Taufname, -n m. [*touf'-nah-mə*] Christian name

täuschen v. [*toi'-shən*] deceive, cheat

Täuschung, -en f. [*toi'-shung*] deceit, delusion

tausend [*tou'-zənt*] thousand

Taxi, -s n. [*tak'-see, tak'-sees*] cab, taxi

Technik, -en f. [*teç'-nik*] technique, workmanship

technisch [*teç'-nish*] technical

Tee, -s *m.* [*teh, tehs*] tea
Teekanne, -n *f.* [*teh'-ka-nə*] teapot
Teelöffel, - *m.* [*teh'-lö-fəl*] teaspoon
Teetasse, -n *f.* [*teh'-ta-sə*] teacup
Teich, -e *m.* [*taiç*] pool, pond
Teil, -e *m.* [*tail*] part, share
   zum Teil [*tsum tail*] partly
teilen *v.* [*tai'-lən*] divide, share
Teilhaber, - *m.* [*tail'-hah-bər*] associate
teil-nehmen an (plus dat.) *v. irreg.* [*tail'-neh-mən an*]
   participate in; be present at; join
teilweise [*tail'-vai-zə*] partially
Teint, -s *m.* [*taint, taints*] complexion
Telegram, -e *n.* [*te-le-gram'*] telegram
telegraphieren *v.* [*te-le-gra-fee'-rən*] cable, wire
Telephon, -e *n.* [*te-le-fohn'*] telephone
   am Telephon [*am te-le-fohn'*] on the telephone
   ans Telephon gehen *v. irreg.* (*Aux:* SEIN) [*ans te-le-fohn'*
   geh'-ən] answer the telephone
telephonieren *v.* [*te-le-fo-nee'-rən*] telephone
telephonisch [*te-le-foh'-nish*] by phone
Telephonist, -en *m.* [*te-le-fo-nist'*] telephone operator [male]
Telephonistin, -nen *f.* [*te-le-fo-ni'-stin*] telephone operator
   [female]
Telephonzelle, -n *f.* [*te-le-fohn'-tse-lə*] telephone booth
Teller, - *m.* [*te'-lər*] plate [dish]
Tempel, - *m.* [*tem'-pəl*] temple
Temperatur, -en *f.* [*tem-pə-ra-toor'*] temperature
Teppich, -e *m.* [*te'-piç*] rug, carpet
Terrasse, -n *f.* [*te-ra'-sə*] terrace
teuer [*toi'-ər*] expensive, dear
   Wie teuer ist es? [*vee toi'-ər ist es*] How much is it?
Teufel, - *m.* [*toi'-fəl*] devil
Text, -e *m.* [*tekst*] text
Textilwaren *f. pl.* [*teks-teel'-vah-rən*] textiles
Theater, - *n.* [*te-ah'-tər*] theater
Theaterkasse, -n *f.* [*te-ah'-tər-ka-sə*] box office
Thema *n. sing.* **Themen** *pl.* [*teh'-ma, teh'-mən*] topic,

theme, subject

Theorie, -n *f.* [*te-o-ree'*] theory

Thermometer, - *n.* [*ter-mo-meh'-tər*] thermometer

Thron, -e *m.* [*trohn*] throne

tief [*teef*] deep, profound

Tiefe, -n *f.* [*tee'-fə*] depth

Tier, -e *n.* [*teer*] animal

Tierarzt, ⸗e *m.* [*teer'-ahrst, teer'-ehrts-tə*] veterinary

Tiger, - *m.* [*tee'-gər*] tiger

Tinte, -n *f.* [*tin'-tə*] ink [for pen]

Tisch, -e *m.* [*tish*] table

Tischdecke, -n *f.* [*tish'-de-kə*] tablecloth

Titel, - *m.* [*tee'-təl*] title

Toast, -e *m.* [*tohst*] toast [for breakfast; to health]

Tochter, ⸗ *f.* [*tokh'-tər, töç'-tər*] daughter

Tod *m. sing.* **Todesfälle** *pl.* [*toht, toh'-dəs-fe-lə*] death

tödlich [*töht'-liç*] fatal, deadly

Toilette, -n *f.* [*to-a-le'-tə*] toilet

Toilettenpapier *n.* [*to-a-le'-tən-pa-peer*] toilet paper

Tomate, -n *f.* [*to-mah'-tə*] tomato

Tomatensaft *m.* [*to-mah'-tən-zaft*] tomato juice

Ton, ⸗e *m.* [*tohn, töh'-nə*] tone, sound, note

Tonfilm, -e *m.* [*tohn'-film*] sound film, talkie

Tonleiter, -n *f.* [*tohn'-lai-tər*] scale [music]

Tonne, -n *f.* [*to'-nə*] ton [weight]; barrel

Topf, ⸗e *m.* [*topf, tö'-pfə*] pan, pot

Töpferware, -n *f.* [*tö'-pfər-vah-rə*] pottery

Tor, -e *n.* [*tohr*] gate; goal [football]

Torte, -n *f.* [*tor'-tə*] pie; layer cake

tot [*toht*] dead

total [*to-tahl'*] total, whole, entire

töten *v.* [*töh'-tən*] kill

Tourist, -en *m.* [*tu-rist'*] tourist [male]

Touristin, -nen *f.* [*tu-ri'-stin*] tourist [female]

Tradition, -en *f.* [*tra-di-tsi-ohn'*] tradition

traditionell [*tra-di-tsi-o-nel'*] traditional

traf *past tense of* TREFFEN [*trahf*] met [definite appointment];
hit [target]

tragen *v. irreg.* [*trah'-gən*] bear, carry; wear

Träger, - *m.* [*treh'-gər*] porter; bearer [of name]; wearer [of dress]

tragisch [*trah'-gish*] tragic

Tragödie, -n *f.* [*tra-göh'-di-ə*] tragedy

Trainer, - *m.* [*treh'-nər*] coach

Träne, -n *f.* [*treh'-nə*] tear(drop)

Traube, -n *f.* [*trou'-bə*] bunch [of grapes]

trauern um (plus acc.) *v.* [*trou'-ərn um*] mourn
  in Trauer [*in trou'-ər*] in mourning

Traum, ⸗e *m.* [*troum, troi'-mə*] dream

träumen *v.* [*troi'-mən*] dream

traurig [*trou'-riç*] sad

Traurigkeit *f.* [*trou'-riç-kait*] sadness

treffen *v. irreg.* [*tre'-fən*] meet [definite appointment];
  strike [target]; guess

Treibstoff, -e *m.* [*traip'-shtof*] fuel

trennen *v.* [*tre'-nən*] separate; disconnect

Trennung, -en *f.* [*tre'-nung*] separation

Treppe, -n *f.* [*tre'-pə*] stairs, staircase

treten *v. irreg.* (*Aux:* SEIN) [*treh'-tən*] tread, step, walk
  ins Haus treten [*ins hous treh'-tən*] enter the house

treu [*troi*] faithful, loyal

Tribut, -e *m.* [*tri-boot'*] tribute

Trick, -s *m.* [*trik, triks*] trick

trinken *v. irreg.* [*trin'-kən*] drink

Trinkgeld, -er *n.* [*trink'-gelt, trink'-gel-dər*] tip

Trinkspruch, ⸗e *m.* [*trink'-shprukh, trink'-shprü-çə*] toast
  [to one's health]

Tritt, -e *m.* [*trit*] step, pace, kick

trocken [*tro'-kən*] dry, arid

trocknen *v.* [*trok'-nən*] dry

Trommel, -n *f.* [*tro'-məl*] drum

Trompete, -n *f.* [*trom-peh'-tə*] trumpet

Tropen *f. pl.* [*troh'-pən*] tropics

tröpfeln *v.* [*trö'-pfəln*] drip

Tropfen, - *m.* [*tro'-pfən*] drop

tropisch [*troh'-pish*] tropical

Trost *m.* [*trohst*] comfort
trotz *prep.* (plus gen.) [*trots*] in spite of
trotzdem [*trots-dehm'*] nevertheless
trotzend [*trot'-sənt*] defiant
trüb, trübe [*trühp, trüh'-bə*] muddy, dull, gloomy
Trümmer *f. pl.* [*trü'-mər*] ruins, debris
Tuberkulose *f.* [*tu-ber-ku-loh'-zə*] tuberculosis
Tuch, ⸗er *n.* [*tookh, tüh'-çər*] cloth, fabric
tüchtig [*tüç'-tiç*] efficient, able
Tugend, -en *f.* [*too'-gənt, too'-gən-dən*] virtue
tugendhaft [*too'-gənt-haft*] virtuous
Tulpe, -n *f.* [*tul'-pə*] tulip
Tumult, -e *m.* [*tu-mult'*] commotion, riot
tun *v. irreg.* [*toon*] do
   Was tun Sie? [*vas toon zee*] What are you doing?
Tunnel, - *m.* [*tu'-nəl*] tunnel
Tür, -en *f.* [*tühr*] door
die Türkei *f.* [*dee tür-kai'*] Turkey
türkisch [*tür'-kish*] Turkish
Turm, ⸗e *m.* [*turm, tür'-mə*] tower
turnen *v.* [*tur'-nən*] do gymnastics
Turnen *n.* [*tur'-nən*] gymnastics
Turnhalle, -n *f.* [*turn'-ha-lə*] gymnasium
Turnier, -e *n.* [*tur-neer'*] tournament
tut *3d pers. sing. pres. tense of* TUN [*toot*] does
Tüte, -n *f.* [*tüh'-tə*] paper bag
Typ, -en *m.* [*tühp*] type [pattern]
typisch [*tüh'-pish*] typical
Tyrann, -en *m.* [*tü-ran'*] tyrant
Tyrannei *f.* [*tü-ra-nai'*] tyranny

U

übel [*üh'-bəl*] evil, bad
übel-nehmen *v. irreg.* [*üh'-bəl-neh-mən*] take amiss; resent

üben *v.* [*üh'-bən*] exercise [body or mind]; practice
über *prep.* (plus dat.; acc. for motion) [*üh'-bər*] over; above; across; by way of
  über Bord [*üh'-bər bort*] overboard
überall [*üh'-bər-al*] everywhere, anywhere
überarbeiten *v.* [*üh-bər-ar'-bai-tən*] retouch [painting]; revise [book]
überein-stimmen *v.* [*üh-bər-ain'-shti-mən*] agree
Übereinstimmung *f.* [*üh-bər-ain'-shti-mung*] agreement, accord
überfahren *v. irreg.* [*üh-bər-fah'-rən*] run over
Überfahrt, -en *f.* [*üh'-bər-fahrt*] crossing
Überfall, ⸗e *m* [*üh'-bər-fal, üh'-bər-fe-lə*] robbery, holdup; raid
überfliegen *v. irreg.* [*üh-bər-flee'-gən*] fly over
Überfluss *m.* [*üh'-bər-flus*] abundance
überflüssig [*üh'-bər-flü-siç*] superfluous
überführen (plus gen.) *v. irreg.* [*üh-bər-füh'-rən*] convict of
Übergang, ⸗e *m.* [*üh'-bər-gang, üh'-bər-geng-ə*] crossing
überhaupt [*üh-bər-houpt'*] generally; at all; really
Überheblichkeit, -en *f.* [*üh-bər-hehp'-liç-kait*] arrogance
überholen *v.* [*üh-bər-hoh'-lən*] overtake
überleben *v.* [*üh-bər-leh'-bən*] survive
Überlebende, -n *m., f.* [*üh-bər-leh'-bən-də*] survivor [male, female]
überlegen *v.* [*üh-bər-leh'-gən*] reflect on, weigh
  Ich habe es mir anders überlegt [*iç hah'-bə es meer an'-dərs üh-bər-lehkt'*] I changed my mind
Überlegenheit *f.* [*üh-bər-leh'-gən-hait*] superiority
Übermass *n.* [*üh'-bər-mahs*] excess
übermorgen [*üh'-bər-mor-gən*] the day after tomorrow
übernehmen *v. irreg.* [*üh-bər-neh'-mən*] take over
überraschen *v.* [*üh-bər-ra'-shən*] surprise
überrascht sein *v.* [*üh-bər-rasht' zain*] be surprised
Überraschung, -en *f.* [*üh-bər-ra'-shung*] surprise
überreden *v.* [*üh-bər-reh'-dən*] persuade
Überschwemmung, -en *f.* [*üh-bər-shve'-mung*] flooding, inundation

Übersee *f.* [*üh'-bər-zeh*] overseas

übersetzen *v.* [*üh-bər-zet'-sən*] translate

Übersetzer, - *m.* [*üh-bər-zet'-sər*] translator

Übersetzung, -en *f.* [*üh-bər-zet'-sung*] translation

überspannt [*üh-bər-shpant'*] extravagant; eccentric

übertragen *v.* [*üh-bər-trah'-gən*] carry forward; transmit [a broadcast]

Übertragung, -en *f.* [*üh-bər-trah'-gung*] transmission

übertreffen *v. irreg.* [*üh-bər-tre'-fən*] beat; exceed

übertreiben *v. irreg.* [*üh-bər-trai'-bən*] exaggerate

Übertreibung, -en *f.* [*üh-bər-trai'-bung*] exaggeration

überweisen *v. irreg.* [*üh-bər-vai'-zən*] remit

Überweisung, -en *f.* [*üh-bər-vai'-zung*] remittance

überwinden *v. irreg.* [*üh-bər-vin'-dən*] overcome

überzeugen *v.* [*üh-bər-tsoi'-gən*] convince

üblich [*ühp'-liç*] usual, customary

übrig [*üh'-briç*] leftover, remaining

übrigens [*üh'-bri-gəns*] incidentally

Übung, -en *f.* [*üh'-bung*] exercise

Ufer, - *n.* [*oo'-fər*] shore, coast; bank

Uhr, -en *f.* [*oor*] clock; watch

   Es ist zehn Uhr [*es ist tsehn oor*] It's ten o'clock

   Wieviel Uhr ist es? [*vee-veel' oor ist es*] What time is it?

um *prep.* (plus acc.) [*um*] around, about; near; for

um zu *conj.* [*um tsu*] in order to

   Die Stunde ist um [*dee shtun'-də ist um*] The lesson is over

umarmen *v.* [*um-ar'-mən*] embrace

Umarmung, -e *f.* [*um-ar'-mung*] embrace

(sich) um-drehen *v.* [*(ziç) um'-dreh-ən*] turn around

Umfang *m.* [*um'-fang*] size, volume, extent; girth

Umgang haben (mit) *v.* [*um'-gang hah'-bən (mit)*] associate (with)

umgeben *v. irreg.* [*um-geh'-bən*] surround

Umgebung, -en *f.* [*um-geh'-bung*] surroundings

um-gehen *v. irreg.* (*Aux:* SEIN) [*um'-geh-ən*] circulate

umgehen *v. irreg.* (*Aux:* HABEN) [*um-geh'-ən*] elude, evade; turn [flank]

umgekehrt [*um'-gə-kehrt*] reverse, contrary

Umlauf, ⁼e *m.* [*um'-louf, um'-loi-fə*] circulation, turn, revolution

Umleitung, -en *f.* [*um'-lai-tung*] detour

Umschlag, ⁼e *m.* [*um'-shlahk, um'-shleh-gə*] envelope, wrapper; sudden change

umsonst [*um-zonst'*] in vain; gratis

Umstand, ⁼e *m.* [*um'-shtant, um'-shten-də*] circumstance; formality

    Machen Sie keine Umstände! [*ma'-khen zee kai'-nə um'-shten-də*] Don't put yourself out!

um-steigen *v. irreg.* (*Aux:* SEIN) [*um'-shtai-gən*] change train, plane

um-stürzen *v.* [*um'-shtür-tsən*] overturn

um-tauschen *v.* [*um'-tou-shən*] change (for)

um-wandeln in (plus acc.) *v.* [*um'-van-dəln in*] transform (into)

Umweg, -e *m.* [*um'-vehk, um'-veh-gə*] detour

Umwelt *f.* [*um'-velt*] environment

um-ziehen *v. irreg.* (*Aux:* SEIN) [*um'-tsee-ən*] move [one's dwelling]

unabhängig [*un'-ap-heng-iç*] independent

Unabhängigkeit *f.* [*un'-ap-heng-iç-kait*] independence

unähnlich [*un'-ehn-liç*] unlike, dissimilar

unangenehm [*un'-an-gə-nehm*] unpleasant, disagreeable

unanständig [*un'-an-shten-diç*] indecent, obscene

unbedingt [*un'-bə-dinkt*] implicit, unconditional; absolutely

Unbehagen *n.* [*un'-bə-hah-gən*] discomfort

unbekannt [*un'-bə-kant*] unknown

unbequem [*un'-bə-kvehm*] uncomfortable

unbeschreiblich [*un-bə'-shraip-liç*] indescribable

unbesetzt [*un'-bə-zetst*] unoccupied

unbesorgt [*un'-bə-zorkt*] unconcerned, carefree

unbestimmt [*un'-bə-shtimt*] indefinite, uncertain

unbewusst [*un'-bə-vust*] unconscious

unbrauchbar [*un'-broukh-bahr*] useless

und [*unt*] and

    und so weiter [*unt zoh vai'-tər*] et cetera

undankbar [*un'-dank-bahr*] ungrateful

undenkbar [*un'-denk-bahr*] unimaginable
unehrlich [*un'-ehr-liç*] dishonest
unendlich [*un-ent'-liç*] infinite
unentschieden [*un'-ent-shee-dən*] undecided, open, drawn
unermesslich [*un'-er-mes-liç*] immense
unerträglich [*un'-er-trehk-liç*] intolerable
unerwartet [*un'-er-var-tət*] unexpected
unfähig [*un'-feh-iç*] unable, incapable
unfair [*un'-fehr*] unfair
unfreundlich [*un'-froint-liç*] unkind, unfriendly
ungarisch [*ung'-ga-rish*] Hungarian
Ungarn *n.* [*ung'-garn*] Hungary
ungeachtet *prep.* (plus gen.) [*un'-ge-akh-tət*] regardless of
Ungeduld *f.* [*un'-gə-dult*] impatience
ungeduldig [*un'-gə-dul-diç*] impatient
ungefähr [*un'-gə-fehr*] approximately
ungeheuer [*un'-ge-hoi-ər*] monstrous, vast, huge, enormous
ungekürzt [*un'-gə-kürtst*] unabridged
ungerade [*un'-gə-rah-də*] odd [uneven]
ungerecht [*un'-gə-reçt*] unjust
Ungerechtigkeit, -en *f.* [*un'-gə-reç-tiç-kait*] injustice
ungern [*un'-gern*] unwillingly
ungeschickt [*un'-gə-shikt*] awkward
ungesund [*un'-gə-zunt*] unhealthy, unwholesome
Ungewitter, - *n.* [*un'-gə-vi-tər*] thunderstorm
ungewöhnlich [*un'-gə-vöhn-liç*] unusual
unglaublich [*un-gloup'-liç*] incredible
ungleich [*un'-glaiç*] unequal
Unglück *n. sing.* **Unglücksfälle** *pl.* [*un'-glük, un'-glüks-fe-lə*]
   misfortune, ill luck; accident
unglücklich [*un'-glük-liç*] unhappy, unlucky
Ungnade *f.* [*un'-gnah-də*] disgrace
ungünstig [*un'-gün-stiç*] unfavorable
unhöflich [*un'-höhf-liç*] impolite
Uniform, -en *f.* [*u-ni-form'*] uniform
uninteressant [*un'-in-tə-re-sant*] uninteresting
universal [*un-i-ver-zahl'*] universal
Universität, -en *f.* [*u-ni-ver-zi-teht'*] university

Unkosten *pl.* [*un'-kos-tən*] expenses, costs
Unkraut, ⸗**er** *n.* [*un'-krout, un'-kroi-tər*] weed
unleserlich [*un'-leh-zər-liç*] illegible
unlogisch [*un'-loh-gish*] illogical
unmittelbar [*un'-mi-təl-bahr*] immediate, direct
unmöglich [*un-möhk'-liç*] impossible
unmoralisch [*un'-mo-rah-lish*] immoral
unnötig [*un'-nöh-tiç*] unnecessary
unordentlich [*un'-or-dənt-liç*] sloppy, untidy
Unordnung *f.* [*un'-ord-nung*] disorder
Unrecht *n.* [*un'-reçt*] injustice, wrong
  Unrecht haben *v.* [*un'-reçt hah'-bən*] be wrong
unregelmässig [*un'-reh-gəl-meh-siç*] irregular
unreif [*un'-raif*] immature, unripe
unrichtig [*un'-riç-tiç*] incorrect
unruhig [*un'-roo-iç*] uneasy
uns [*uns*] us, to us; ourselves, to ourselves
unsäglich [*un-zehk'-liç*] unspeakable
Unschuld *f.* [*un'-shult*] innocence
unschuldig [*un'-shul-diç*] innocent
unser, unsere [*un'-zər, un'-zə-rə*] our, ours
unsicher [*un'-zi-çər*] uncertain, unsteady, unsafe
unsichtbar [*un'-ziçt-bar*] invisible
Unsinn *m.* [*un'-zin*] nonsense
unsympathisch [*un'-züm-pah-tish*] unpleasant
untauglich [*un'-touk-liç*] unfit, unsuitable
unten [*un'-tən*] below, downstairs
unter *prep.* (plus dat.; acc. for motion) [*un'-tər*] among; below, under
unterbrechen *v. irreg.* [*un-tər-bre'-çən*] interrupt
Unterbrechung, -en *f.* [*un-tər-bre'-çung*] intermission
unterdrücken *v.* [*un-tər-drü'-kən*] oppress, suppress
unter-gehen *v. irreg.* (*Aux:* SEIN) [*un'-tər-geh-ən*] go down; set; sink
Untergrundbahn, -en *f.* [*un'-tər-grunt-bahn*] subway
unterhalb [*un'-tər-halp*] below
unterhalten *v. irreg.* [*un-tər-hal'-tən*] entertain
  sich unterhalten [*ziç un-tər-hal'-tən*] converse; amuse oneself

Unterhaltung, -en *f.* [*un-tər-hal'-tung*] entertainment, amusement, conversation

unterirdisch [*un'-tər-ir-dish*] underground

Unterkleid, -er *n.* [*un'-tər-klait, un'-ter-klei-dər*] slip

Unterkunft, ⸗e *f.* [*un'-tər-kunft, un'-tər-künf-tə*] lodging, accommodation

unterlassen *v. irreg.* [*un-tər-la'-sən*] omit

Unterlassung, -en *f.* [*un-tər-la'-sung*] omission

unternehmen *v. irreg.* [*un-tər-neh'-mən*] undertake

Unterricht, -e *m.* [*un'-tər-riçt*] instruction, lessons

unterrichten *v.* [*un-tər-riç'-tən*] instruct, teach

Unterschätzung, -en *f.* [*un-tər-she'-tsung*] undervaluation

unterscheiden (von) *v. irreg.* [*un-tər-shai'-dən (fon)*] distinguish (from)

Unterschied, -e *m.* [*un'-tər-sheet, un'-tər-shee-də*] difference

unterschreiben *v. irreg.* [*un-tər-shrai'-bən*] sign

Unterschrift, -en *f.* [*un'-tər-shrift*] signature

Unterseeboot, -e *n.* [*un'-tər-zeh-boht*] submarine

unterstützen *v.* [*un-tər-shtü'-tsən*] support

untersuchen *v.* [*un-tər-zoo'-khən*] investigate, examine

Untersuchung, -en *f.* [*un-tər-zoo'-khung*] investigation; examination

Untertasse, -n *f.* [*un'-tər-ta-sə*] saucer

Unterwäsche *f.* [*un'-tər-ve-shə*] underwear

unterwegs [*un-ıər-vehks'*] on the way

Unterwelt *f.* [*un'-tər-velt*] underworld

Unterzeichnung, -en *f.* [*un-tər-tsaiç'-nung*] signature; ratification

untreu [*un'-troi*] unfaithful, disloyal

untröstlich [*un-tröhst'-liç*] disconsolate

unverantwortlich [*un-fer-ant'-vort-liç*] irresponsible, inexcusable

unvergesslich [*un-fer-ges'-liç*] unforgettable

unvergleichlich [*un-fer-glaiç'-liç*] incomparable

unverheiratet [*un'-fer-hai-rah-tət*] single, unmarried

unvermeidlich [*un-fer-mait'-liç*] inevitable

unvernünftig [*un'-fer-nünf-tiç*] unreasonable

unverschämt [*un'-fer-shehmt*] shameless, impudent

unversehrt [*un'-fer-zehrt*] uninjured, intact, safe
unversöhnlich [*un-fer-zöhn'-liç*] implacable, irreconcilable
unverständlich [*un'-fer-shtent-liç*] unintelligible
unvollkommen [*un'-fol-ko-mən*] imperfect
unvollständig [*un'-fol-shten-diç*] incomplete
unvorbereitet auf (plus acc.) [*un'-fohr-bə-rai-tət ouf*]
    unprepared for
unvorsichtig [*un'-fohr-ziç-tiç*] careless, incautious
unwahr [*un'-vahr*] untruthful, false, untrue
unwichtig [*un'-viç-tiç*] unimportant
unwillig [*un'-vi-liç*] unwilling
unwillkommen [*un'-vil-ko-mən*] unwelcome
unwissend [*un'-vi-sənt*] ignorant
unwohl [*un'-vohl*] not well, indisposed
Unze, -n *f.* [*un'-tsə*] ounce
unzeitig [*un'-tsai-tiç*] untimely
unzufrieden [*un'-tsu-free-dən*] dissatisfied
unzweifelhaft [*un-tsvai'-fəl-haft*] unquestionable
uralt [*oor'-alt*] ancient
Urlaub, -e *m.* [*oor'-loup, oor'-lou'-bə*] furlough, leave of
    absence
Ursache, -n *f.* [*oor'-za-khə*] cause
ursprünglich [*oor'-shprüng-liç*] originally, at first
Urteil, -e *n.* [*ur'-tail*] sentence [legal], judgment
urteilen *v.* [*ur'-tai-lən*] judge
Urteilsspruch, ⸗e *m.* [*ur'-tails-shprukh, ur'-tails-shprü-çə*]
    sentence, verdict

V

Vater, ⸗ *m.* [*fah'-tər, feh'-tər*] father
Vaterland, -er *n.* [*fah'-tər-lant, fah'-tər-len-dər*] native land
Veilchen, - *n.* [*fail'-çən*] violet
(sich) verabreden *v.* [(*ziç*) *fer-ap'-reh-dən*] make an
    appointment

verantwortlich [*fer-ant'-vort-liç*] responsible
Verantwortung, -en *f.* [*fer-ant'-vor-tung*] responsibility
verbessern *v.* [*fer-be'-sərn*] improve; correct
Verbesserung, -en *f.* [*fer-be'-sə-rung*] improvement; correction
sich verbeugen vor (plus dat.) *v.* [*ziç fer-boi'-gən fohr*] bow to
verbinden *v. irreg.* [*fer-bin'-dən*] bandage; connect, join
  Sehr verbunden! [*zehr fer-bun'-dən*] Much obliged!
verbindlich [*fer-bint'-liç*] obligatory; courteous
verboten [*fer-boh'-tən*] prohibited, banned
verbracht *past part. of* VERBRINGEN [*fer-brakht'*] spent [time]
verbrachte *past tense of* VERBRINGEN [*fer-brakh'-tə*] spent
  [time]
Verbrauch, ⸗e *m.* [*fer-broukh', fer-broi'-çə*] consumption
verbrauchen *v.* [*fer-brou'-khən*] consume; wear out
Verbrechen, - *n.* [*fer-bre'-çən*] crime
Verbrecher, - *m.* [*fer-bre'-çər*] criminal [male]
Verbrecherin, -nen *f.* [*fer-bre'-çə-rin*] criminal [female]
verbrennen *v. irreg.* [*fer-bre'-nən*] burn
verbringen *v. irreg.* [*fer-bring'-ən*] spend [time]
verbunden (mit) *past part. of* VERBINDEN [*fer-bun'-dən (mit)*]
  allied, connected (with)
Verdacht *m.* [*fer-dakht'*] suspicion
verdanken *v.* (plus dat.) [*fer-dan'-kən*] owe something to
  someone
verdauen *v.* [*fer-dou'-ən*] digest
verderben *v. irreg.* [*fer-der'-bən*] spoil
verdienen *v.* [*fer-dee'-nən*] deserve; earn [money]
Verdienst, -e *m.* [*fer-deenst'*] gain, profit, earnings
verdoppeln *v.* [*fer-do'-pəln*] double
verehren *v.* [*fer-eh'-rən*] worship, respect
Verein, -e *m.* [*fer-ain'*] association, club
vereinigen *v.* [*fer-ai'-ni-gən*] unite, combine
  (die) Vereinigten Staaten *pl.* [(*dee*) *fer-ai'-niç-tən shtah'-tən*]
    (the) United States
  (die) Vereinten Nationen *pl.* [(*dee*) *fer-ain'-tən na-tsi-oh'-nən*]
    (the) United Nations
Verfassung, -en *f.* [*fer-fa'-sung*] constitution; condition
verfolgen *v.* [*fer-fol'-gən*] pursue; persecute

verführen v. [fer-füh'-rən] seduce
vergangen adj. [fer-gang'-ən] past
Vergangenheit, -en f. [fer-gang'-ən-hait] past
Vergaser, - m. [fer-gah'-zər] carburetor
vergass past tense of VERGESSEN [fer-gahs'] forgot
vergeben v. irreg. [fer-geh'-bən] forgive
vergessen v. irreg. [fer-ge'-sən] forget
vergessen past part. of VERGESSEN [fer-ge'-sən] forgotten
vergleichen mit (plus dat.) v. irreg. [fer-glai'-çən mit] compare
    with
Vergnügen n. [fer-gnüh'-gən] pleasure; entertainment
vergrössern v. [fer-gröh'-sərn] enlarge, magnify
Verhältnis, -se n. [fer-helt'-nis] proportion;
    relations; condition
verhältnismässig [fer-helt'-nis-meh-siç] relative(ly)
sich verheiraten v. [ziç fer-hai'-rah-tən] get married
verhindern v. [fer-hin'-dərn] prevent
sich verirren v. [ziç fer-i'-rən] lose one's way
Verkauf, ⁼e m. [fer-kouf', fer-koi'-fə] sale
verkaufen v. [fer-kou'-fən] sell
Verkäufer, - m. [fer-koi'-fər] salesclerk [male]
Verkäuferin, -nen f. [fer-koi'-fə-rin] salesclerk [female]
Verkehr, -e m. [fer-kehr'] traffic; dealings
verkehrt [fer-kehrt'] wrong, upside down, reverse
verlangen v. [fer-lang'-ən] demand
verlassen adj. [fer-la'-sən] forsaken
verlassen v. irreg. [fer-la'-sən] leave, abandon, desert
verlassen past part. of VERLASSEN [fer-la'-sən] left
verlegen adj. [fer-leh'-gən] embarrassed
verlegen v. [fer-leh'-gən] misplace; publish
Verleger, - m. [fer-leh'-gər] publisher
verletzen v. [fer-let'-sən] hurt [somebody]; injure; violate
sich verlieben v. [ziç fer-lee'-bən] fall in love
verlieren v. irreg. [fer-lee'-rən] lose
verliess past tense of VERLASSEN [fer-lees'] left
sich verloben v. [ziç fer-loh'-bən] become engaged
Verlobte, -n m., f. [fer-lohp'-tə] fiance
verlor past tense of VERLIEREN [fer-lohr'] lost

verloren *past part. of* VERLIEREN [*fer-loh'-rən*] lost

Verlust *m.* [*fer-lust'*] loss; casualty

vermieten *v.* [*fer-mee'-tən*] rent, lease, let

Vermögen, - *n.* [*fer-möh'-gən*] fortune; property

vermuten *v.* [*fer-moo'-tən*] suppose, guess

vernachlässigen *v.* [*fer-nahkh'-le-si-gən*] neglect

vernichten *v.* [*fer-niç'-tən*] destroy; dash [hopes]

Vernunft *f.* [*fer-nunft'*] reason

vernünftig [*fer-nünf'-tiç*] rational, sensible

veröffentlichen *v.* [*fer-ö'-fənt-li-çən*] publish

verpacken *v.* [*fer-pa'-kən*] wrap up

Verrat *m.* [*fer-raht'*] treason; betrayal

Verräter, - *m.* [*fer-reh'-tər*] traitor

verrenken *v.* [*fer-ren'-kən*] sprain

verrückt [*fer-rükt'*] crazy, mad

verschieden *adj.* [*fer-shee'-dən*] different

verschwenden *v.* [*fer-shven'-dən*] waste, squander

Versehen, - *n.* [*fer-zeh'-en*] oversight, mistake, slip

versichern *v.* [*fer-zi'-çərn*] assure, insure

versöhnen *v.* [*fer-zöh'-nən*] reconcile

versorgen *v.* [*fer-zor'-gən*] supply; take care of

versprechen *v. irreg.* [*fer-shpre'-çən*] promise

Verstand *m.* [*fer-shtant'*] mind, understanding

Verständnis, -se *n.* [*fer-shtent'-nis*] understanding

verstecken *v.* [*fer-shte'-kən*] hide

versteckt *past part. of* VERSTECKEN [*fer-shtekt'*] hidden

verstehen *v. irreg.* [*fer-shteh'-ən*] understand

verstorben [*fer-shtor'-bən*] deceased, late

Versuch, -e *m.* [*fer-zookh'*] experiment, test, try

versuchen *v.* [*fer-zoo'-khən*] attempt; tempt

verteidigen *v.* [*fer-tai'-di-gən*] defend

Verteidiger, - *m.* [*fer-tai'-di-gər*] counsel for the defense

verteilen *v.* [*fer-tai'-lən*] distribute

Vertrag, ∸e *m.* [*fer-trahk'*, *fer-treh'-gə*] treaty, contract

Vertrauen *n.* [*fer-trou'-ən*] trust, confidence

vertraut [*fer-trout'*] intimate, familiar

vertreten *v. irreg.* [*fer-treh'-tən*] substitute [for a person];
    represent

Vertreter, - *m.* [*fer-treh'-tər*] representative, deputy, agent
verunglücken *v.* [*fer-un'-glü-kən*] have an accident
verursachen *v.* [*fer-oor'-za-khən*] cause
verurteilen *v.* [*fer-ur'-tai-lən*] condemn, sentence
Verwaltung, -en *f.* [*fer-val'-tung*] administration, management
verwandeln *v.* [*fer-van'-dəln*] turn into, change, transform
verwandt sein mit (plus dat.) [*fer-vant' zain mit*] be related
    to [family]
Verwandte, -n *m., f.* [*fer-van'-tə*] relative
Verwandtschaft, -en *f.* [*fer-vant'-shaft*] relationship [family]
verwenden *v. irreg.* [*fer-ven'-dən*] employ; use; spend [time]
verwöhnen *v.* [*fer-vöh'-nən*] spoil
verzeihen *v. irreg.* [*fer-tsai'-en*] pardon, forgive
  Verzeihung! [*fer-tsai'-ung*] Pardon me!, Excuse me!
verzichten auf (plus acc.) *v.* [*fer-ziç'-tən ouf*] renounce
verzollen *v.* [*fer-tso'-lən*] pay duty on; declare
verzweifeln *v.* [*fer-tsvai'-fəln*] despair
Vetter, -n *m.* [*fe'-tər*] cousin [male]
Vieh *n.* [*fee*] beast; cattle
Viehzucht *f.* [*fee'-tsukht*] cattle breeding
viel [*feel*] much
  sehr viel [*zehr feel*] great deal, very much
  zu viel [*tsoo feel*] too much
viele [*fee'-lə*] many
vielleicht [*fee-laiçt'*] maybe, perhaps
vier [*feer*] four
viert [*feert*] fourth
Viertel, - *n.* [*fir'-təl*] quarter
  drei Viertel zwei [*drai fir'-təl tsvai*] a quarter to two
Viertelstunde, -n *f.* [*fir'-təl-shtun-də*] quarter of an hour
vierzehn [*fir'-tsehn*] fourteen
vierzig [*fir'-tsiç*] forty
Vogel, ⸗ *m.* [*foh'-gəl, föh'-gəl*] bird
Volk, ⸗er *n.* [*folk, föl'-kər*] people, nation
Volksschule, -n *f.* [*folks'-shoo-lə*] elementary school
voll [*fol*] full
vollenden *v.* [*fo-len'-dən*] finish, complete
vollkommen [*fol-ko'-mən*] perfect; entire, complete

Vollmacht, -en *f.* [*fol'-makht*] power of attorney

vollständig [*fol'-shten-diç*] complete, whole

von *prep.* (plus dat.) [*fon*] from, of, by

vom: von dem [*fom*] from the; of the; by the

vor *prep.* (plus dat.; acc. for motion) [*fohr*] before, in front of

  vor einem Jahre [*fohr ai'-nəm yah'-rə*] a year ago

voraus [*fo-rous'*] ahead, in front

  im voraus [*im foh'-rous*] in advance

voraussichtlich [*fo-rous'-ziçt-liç*] presumably

vorbei [*fohr-bai'*] along, by [space]; over [time]

vorbei-gehen *v. irreg.* (*Aux:* SEIN) [*fohr-bai'-geh-ən*] pass; blow over [storm]

vor-bereiten *v.* [*fohr'-bə-rai-tən*] prepare

Vorfall, ⸗e *m.* [*fohr'-fal, fohr'-fe-lə*] incident, event

vorgestern [*fohr'-ge-stərn*] the day before yesterday

Vorhang, ⸗e *m.* [*fohr'-hang, fohr'-heng-ə*] curtain

vorher *adv.* [*fohr'-hehr*] before, beforehand

vor-kommen *v. irreg.* (*Aux:* SEIN) [*fohr'-ko-mən*] occur

vorn [*forn*] before, in front

Vorname, -n *m.* [*fohr'-nah-mə*] first name

vornehm [*fohr'-nehm*] distinguished

Vorort, -e *m.* [*fohr'-ort*] suburb

Vorrat, ⸗e *m.* [*fohr'-raht, fohr'-reh-tə*] supply, stock

Vorschlag, ⸗e *m.* [*fohr'-shlahk, fohr'-shleh-gə*] proposal, suggestion

vor-schlagen *v. irreg.* [*fohr'-shlah-gən*] suggest, propose

Vorsicht *f.* [*fohr'-ziçt*] caution, precaution

  Vorsicht! [*fohr'-ziçt*] Be careful!, Beware!

Vorspeise, -n *f.* [*fohr'-shpai-zə*] appetizer

vor-stellen *v.* [*fohr'-shte-lən*] introduce [people]; imagine

  Das kann ich mir vorstellen [*das kan iç meer fohr'-shte-lən*] I can imagine that

  Darf ich mich vorstellen? [*darf iç miç fohr'-shte-lən*] May I introduce myself?

Vorstellung, -en *f.* [*fohr'-shte-lung*] introduction; performance [theatre]; idea

Vorteil, -e *m.* [*for'-tail*] advantage

Vortrag, ⸗e *m.* [*fohr'-trahk, fohr'-treh-gə*] lecture; recitation

vorüber [*fo-rüh'-bər*] finished, over, past
vorüber-gehen v. *irreg.* (*Aux:* SEIN) [*fo-rüh'-bər-geh-ən*]
   go by, pass
Vorurteil, -e n. [*fohr'-ur-tail*] prejudice
Vorwand, ⁼e m. [*fohr'-vant, fohr'-ven-də*] pretext
vorwärts [*fohr'-verts*] forward
vor-ziehen v. *irreg.* [*fohr'-tsee-ən*] prefer
vorzüglich [*fohr-tsühk'-liç*] excellent, superior
vulgär [*vul-gehr'*] vulgar

W

Waage, -n f. [*vah'-gə*] scale [for weighing]
waagerecht [*vah'-gə-reçt*] horizontal
wach [*vakh*] awake
wachen v. [*va'-khən*] (keep) watch, be awake
Wachs, -e n. [*vaks*] wax
wachsam [*vakh'-zam*] vigilant, watchful
wachsen v. *irreg.* (*Aux:* SEIN) [*vak'-sən*] grow
Waffe, -n f. [*va'-fə*] weapon
Waffenstillstand m. [*va'-fən-shtil-shtant*] armistice
wagen v. [*vah'-gən*] dare
Wagen, - m. [*vah'-gən*] car, coach
wägen v. [*veh'-gən*] balance
Wahl, -en f. [*vahl*] election, choice
wählen v. [*veh'-lən*] elect, choose, vote for; dial [phone]
Wahlstimme, -n f. [*vahl'-shti-mə*] vote
wahr [*vahr*] true, real
   Ist es wahr? [*ist es vahr*] Is it true?
   Nicht wahr? [*niçt vahr*] Don't you think so?
während *prep.* (plus gen.) [*veh'-rənt*] during
Wahrheit, -en f. [*vahr'-hait*] truth
wahrscheinlich [*vahr-shain'-liç*] likely, probable
Währung, -en f. [*veh'-rung*] currency [money]
Waisenkind, -er n. [*vai'-zən-kint, vai'-zən-kin-dər*] orphan

Wald, ⸗er m. [valt, vel'-dər] forest, wood(s)
Walzer, - m. [valt'-sər] waltz
Wand, ⸗e f. [vant, ven'-də] wall
wandern v. (*Aux:* SEIN) [van'-dərn] wander, hike
Wanderung, -en f. [van'-də-rung] excursion, trip
Wandschrank, ⸗e m. [vant'-shrank, vant'-shren-kə] closet
Wandteppich, -e m. [vant'-te-piç] tapestry
Wange, -n f. [vang'-ə] cheek
wann [van] when
Wanne, -n f. [va'-nə] tub, bath
war *past tense of* SEIN [vahr] was
Ware, -n f. [vah'-rə] goods, merchandise
waren *past tense of* SEIN [vah'-rən] were
Warenhaus, ⸗er n. [vah'-rən-hous, vah'-rən-hoi-zər] department store
warm [varm] warm
wärmen v. [ver'-mən] warm, heat
warnen v. [var'-nən] warn
Warnung, -en f. [var'-nung] admonition, warning
warten v. [var'-tən] wait
warum [va-rum'] why
was [vas] what; that, whatever, which
Wäsche, -n f. [ve'-shə] lingerie; laundry, wash
waschen v. *irreg.* [va'-shən] wash
   Ich wasche mir die Hände [iç va'-shə meer dee hen'-də] I wash my hands
Waschmaschine, -n f. [vash'-ma-shee-nə] washing machine, washer
Wasser, ⸗ n. [va'-sər, ve'-sər] water
wasserdicht [va'-sər-diçt] waterproof
weben v. *irreg.* [veh'-bən] weave
Weber, - m. [veh'-bər] weaver [male]
Weberin, -nen f. [veh'-bə-rin] weaver [female]
Wechsel, - m. [vek'-səl] exchange, bill of exchange
wechseln v. [vek'-səln] change, vary
wecken v. [ve'-kən] awaken
Wecker, - m. [ve'-kər] alarm clock
weder . . . noch [veh'-dər . . . nokh] neither . . . nor

Weder Sie noch ich [*veh'-dər zee nokh iç*] Neither you nor I

weg [*vek*] away, off

   Geh weg! [*geh vek*] Be off!

Weg, -e *m.* [*vehk, veh'-gə*] way, road

wegen *prep.* (plus gen.) [*veh'-gən*] because of, on account of

weg-fahren *v. irreg.* (*Aux:* SEIN) [*vek'-fah-rən*] drive away

weg-gehen *v. irreg.* (*Aux:* SEIN) [*vek'-geh-ən*] go away

Wehe! [*veh'-ə*] Woe!, Alas!

Wehrdienst *m.* [*vehr'-deenst*] military service

Weib, -er *n.* [*vaip, vai'-bər*] woman, wife

weiblich [*vaip'-liç*] female, feminine

weich [*vaiç*] soft, tender, weak

Weihnachten *f. pl.* [*vai'-nakh-tən*] Christmas

   Fröhliche Weihnachten! [*fröh'-li-çə vai'-nakh-tən*]
     Merry Christmas!

Weihnachtsabend, -e *m.* [*vai'-nakhts-ah-bənt,*
   vai'-nakhts-ah-bən-də] Christmas Eve

weil [*vail*] because

Wein, -e *m.* [*vain*] wine

Weinberg, -e *m.* [*vain'-berk, vain'-ber-gə*] vineyard

weinen *v.* [*vai'-nən*] cry, weep

weise [*vai'-zə*] wise

Weise, -n *f.* [*vai'-zə*] manner, way

   auf diese Weise [*ouf dee'-zə vai'-zə*] in this way

Weisheit *f.* [*vais'-hait*] wisdom, wit

weiss *adj.* [*vais*] white

Weisswein, -e *m.* [*vais'-vain*] white wine

weit [*vait*] far, wide, vast

   Wie weit ist es? [*vee vait ist es*] How far is it?

   weit weg [*vait vek*] far away

Weite, -n *f.* [*vai'-tə*] width, size

weiter [*vai'-tər*] further

Weizen *m.* [*vait'-sən*] wheat

welcher, welche, welches [*vel'-çər, vel'-çə, vel'-çəs*] which,
   that, who, whom; what, which

Welle, -n *f.* [*ve'-lə*] wave

Welt, -en *f.* [*velt*] world

Weltall *n.* [*velt'-al*] universe

wem *dat. of* WER [*vehm*] to whom

wen *acc. of* WER [*vehn*] whom

wenden *v. irreg.* [*ven'-dən*] turn

wenig [*veh'-niç*] little
  ein wenig [*ain veh'-niç*] a little, a bit
  sehr wenig [*zehr veh'-niç*] very little

wenige [*veh'-ni-gə*] few

weniger [*veh'-ni-gər*] fewer; less; minus

wenn [*ven*] when, if

wer *interr. & rel. pron.* [*vehr*] who

werden *v. irreg.* (*Aux:* SEIN) [*vehr'-dən*] become; get; grow; shall
  Ich werde ein Kleid kaufen [*iç vehr'-də ain klait kou'-fən*] I shall buy a dress
  Er, sie, es wird [*er, zee, es virt*] He, she, it will

werfen *v. irreg.* [*ver'-fən*] throw, toss

Werk, -e *n.* [*verk*] work, deed

Werkzeug, -e *n.* [*verk'-tsoik, verk'-tsoi-gə*] tool

wert [*vehrt*] worth; worthy, esteemed

Wert, -e *m.* [*vehrt*] value, worth

Wesen, - *n.* [*veh'-zən*] nature, character, being

wesentlich [*veh'-zənt-liç*] substantial, essential

wessen *gen. of* WER [*ve'-sən*] whose

Westen *m.* [*ve'-stən*] west

westlich [*vest'-liç*] western

Wette, -n *f.* [*ve'-tə*] bet

wetten *v.* [*ve'-tən*] bet

Wetter *n.* [*ve'-tər*] weather

wichtig [*viç'-tiç*] important

wider *prep.* (plus acc.) [*vee'-dər*] against, contrary to

widmen *v.* [*vit'-mən*] dedicate

wie *conj.* [*vee*] like, as

wie *adv.* [*vee*] how
  Wie geht es Ihnen? [*vee geht es ee'-nən*] How do you do?, How are you?

wieder [*vee'-dər*] again
  hin und wieder [*hin unt vee'-dər*] now and then
  immer wieder [*i'-mər vee'-dər*] again and again

wiederholen v. [vee-dər-hoh'-lən] repeat
  Wiederholen Sie bitte! [vee-dər-hoh'-lən zee bi'-tə]
    Please repeat!
wieder-sehen v. irreg. [vee'-dər-zeh-ən] meet again
  Auf Wiedersehen! [ouf vee'-dər-zeh-ən] Goodbye!
Wiege, -n f. [vee'-gə] cradle
wiegen v. irreg. [vee'-gən] weigh
Wien n. [veen] Vienna
Wiese, -n f. [vee'-zə] meadow
wieso [vee-zoh'] why, why so
wieviel [vee-feel'] how much
  wieviele [vee-fee'-lə] how many
  Wieviel Uhr ist es? [vee-feel' oor ist es] What time is it?
wild [vilt] wild, savage
Wild n. [vilt] game; venison
Wille, -n m. [vi'-lə] will
Willkommen! [vil-ko'-mən] Welcome!
Wind, -e m. [vint, vin'-də] wind
Windel, -n f. [vin'-dəl] diaper
winken v. [vin'-kən] signal, beckon, wave
Winter, - m. [vin'-tər] winter
Wintersport m. [vin'-tər-shport] winter sports
winzig [vin'-tsiç] tiny
wir [veer] we
wird 3d pers. sing. pres. tense of WERDEN [virt] will [future];
  becomes, gets, grows
wirklich adj. [virk'-liç] real, actual, genuine
Wirklichkeit, -en f. [virk'-liç-kait] reality
wirksam [virk'-sam] effective
Wirt, -e m. [virt] landlord, host, inn-keeper
Wirtin, -nen f. [vir'-tin] landlady, hostess, inn-keeper
Wirtschaft, -en f. [virt'-shaft] economy; household
wissen v. irreg. [vi'-sən] know [a fact]; be aware of
  Ich weiss nicht, wo sie ist [iç vais niçt, voh zee ist] I don't
    know where she is
Wissen n. [vi'-sen] knowledge, learning
Wissenschaft, -en f. [vi'-sən-shaft] science
Wissenschaftler, - m. [vi'-sən-shaft-lər] scientist [male]

Wissenschaftlerin, -nen *f.* [*vi'-sən-shaft-lə-rin*] scientist [female]
wissenschaftlich [*vi'-sən-shaft-liç*] scientific
Witwe, -n *f.* [*vit'-və*] widow
Witwer, - *m.* [*vit'-vər*] widower
Witz, -e *m.* [*vits*] joke
wo [*voh*] where
woanders [*voh-an'-dərs*] somewhere else
wobei [*voh-bai'*] whereby; at which
Woche, -n *f.* [*vo'-khə*] week
   nächste Woche [*nehç'-stə vo'-khə*] next week
   vorige Woche [*foh'-ri-gə vo'-khə*] last week
wöchentlich [*vö'-çənt-liç*] weekly
wofür [*voh-führ'*] what for
woher [*voh-hehr'*] from where
wohin [*voh-hin'*] whereto
wohl [*vohl*] well; probably
   Auf Ihr Wohl! [*ouf eer vohl*] To your health!
wohnen *v.* [*voh'-nən*] live, dwell
Wohnung, -en *f.* [*voh'-nung*] apartment
Wohnzimmer, - *n.* [*vohn'-tsi-mər*] living room
Wolf, =e *m.* [*volf, völ'-fə*] wolf
Wolke, -n *f.* [*vol'-kə*] cloud
Wolkenkratzer, - *m.* [*vol'-kən-krat-sər*] skyscraper
Wolldecke, -n *f.* [*vol'-de-kə*] woolen blanket
Wolle, -n *f.* [*vo'-lə*] wool
wollen *mod. aux.* [*vo'-lən*] wish, desire; want
   Was wollen Sie machen? [*vas vo'-lən zee ma'-khən*]
     What do you want to do?
womit [*voh-mit'*] with what, with which, by which
woran [*voh-ran'*] whereon, whereat; on, of, against what
woraus [*voh-rous'*] wherefrom; of what, out of which
Wort, -e, =er *n.* [*vort, vor'-tə, vör'-tər*] word
Wörterbuch, =er *n.* [*vör'-tər-bookh, vör'-tər-büh-çər*]
   dictionary
wuchs *past tense of* WACHSEN [*vooks*] grew
Wunde, -n *f.* [*vun'-də*] sore, wound
Wunder, - *n.* [*vun'-dər*] wonder, miracle
wunderbar [*vun'-dər-bahr*] marvelous

sich wundern *v.* [*ziç vun'-dərn*] wonder, be surprised
Wunsch, ⸚e *m.* [*vunsh, vün'-shə*] wish, desire
wünschen *v.* [*vün'-shən*] desire
    Was wünschen Sie? [*vas vün'-shən zee*] What do you wish?
wünschenswert [*vün'-shəns-vehrt*] desirable
Würde, -n *f.* [*vür'-də*] dignity, honor
Würfel, - *m.* [*vür'-fəl*] die
Wurm, ⸚er *m.* [*vurm, vür'-mər*] worm
Wurst, ⸚e *f.* [*vurst, vür'-stə*] sausage
Wurstladen, ⸚ *m.* [*vurst'-lah-dən, vurst'-leh-dən*] sausage
    shop, charcuterie
Würze, -n *f.* [*vür'-tsə*] spice
würzen *v.* [*vür'-tsən*] season, spice
Wurzel, -n *f.* [*vur'-tsəl*] root
Wüste, -n *f.* [*vüh'-stə*] desert
Wut *f.* [*voot*] rage, fury
wütend [*vüh'-tənt*] furious

Z

Zahl, -en *f.* [*tsahl*] number, figure
zahlbar [*tsahl'-bahr*] payable, due
zahlen *v.* [*tsah'-lən*] pay
zählen *v.* [*tseh'-lən*] count
    zählen auf (plus acc.) [*tseh'-lən ouf*] count on
zahlreich [*tsahl'-raiç*] numerous
Zahlung, -en *f.* [*tsah'-lung*] payment
Zahlungsanweisung, -en *f.* [*tsah'-lungz-an-vai-zung*] money
    order
zahm [*tsahm*] tame
Zahn, ⸚e *m.* [*tsahn, tseh'-nə*] tooth
Zahnarzt, ⸚e *m.* [*tsahn'-ahrtst, tsahn'-ehrts-tə*] dentist [male]
Zahnärztin, -nen *f.* [*tsahn'-ehrts-tin*] dentist [female]
Zahnbürste, -n *f.* [*tsahn'-bür-stə*] toothbrush
Zahnfleisch *n.* [*tsahn'-flaish*] gum [of teeth]

Zahnpasta *f.* **Zahnpasten** *pl.* [*tsahn'-pa-stah, tsahn'-pa-stən*] toothpaste

Zahnschmerzen *m. pl.* [*tsahn'-shmer-tsən*] toothache

Zange, -n *f.* [*tsang'-ə*] tongs, pincers

zart [*tsahrt*] tender, delicate

zärtlich [*tsehrt'-liç*] fond, loving, tender

Zauber, - *m.* [*tsou'-bər*] magic; spell; glamour

zauberhaft [*tsou'-bər-haft*] magical

Zaun, ⁼e *m.* [*tsoun, tsoi'-nə*] fence

Zehe, -n *f.* [*zeh'-ə*] toe

zehn [*tsehn*] ten

zehnt [*tsehnt*] tenth

Zeichen, - *n.* [*tsai'-çən*] sign, mark; signal

zeichnen *v.* [*tsaiç'-nən*] draw [a picture]; subscribe [to a fund]

Zeichnung, -en *f.* [*tsaiç'-nung*] design, drawing

zeigen *v.* [*tsai'-gən*] show

    Zeigen Sie mir! [*tsai'-gən zee meer*] Show me!

Zeile, -n *f.* [*tsai'-lə*] line [of letters]

Zeit, -en *f.* [*tsait*] time [extent]

Zeitgenosse, -n *m.* [*tsait'-gə-no-sə*] contemporary

Zeitschrift, -en *f.* [*tsait'-shrift*] magazine, review

Zeitung, -en *f.* [*tsai'-tung*] newspaper

Zelle, -n *f.* [*tse'-lə*] cell

Zelt, -e *n.* [*tselt*] tent

Zement *m., n.* [*tse-ment'*] cement, concrete

Zentimeter, - *m.* [*tsen'-ti-meh-tər*] centimeter

Zentralheizung, -en *f.* [*tsen-trahl'-hait-sung*] central heating

Zeremonie, -n *f.* [*tse-re-mo-nee'*] ceremony

zerreissen *v. irreg.* [*tser-rai'-sən*] tear, tear up

zerrissen *past part. of* ZERREISEN [*tser-ri'-sən*] torn

zerschmettern *v.* [*tser-shme'-tərn*] smash

zerschneiden *v. irreg.* [*tser-shnai'-dən*] cut up, slice

zerstören *v.* [*tser-shtöh'-rən*] destroy

Zerstörung, -en *f.* [*tser-shtöh'-rung*] destruction

Zettel, - *m.* [*tse'-təl*] slip [of paper]

Zeug *n.* [*tsoik*] stuff

Zeugnis, -se *n.* [*tsoik'-nis*] report card, record [school]; testimony, witness

Ziege, -n *f.* [*tsee′-gə*] goat, she-goat

Ziegel, - *m.* [*tsee′-gəl*] brick

ziehen *v. irreg.* [*tsee′-ən*] pull, draw; breed

Ziel, -e *n.* [*tseel*] goal, aim; target

zielen auf (plus acc.) *v.* [*tsee′-lən ouf*] aim at

ziemlich [*tseem′-liç*] rather, pretty

Ziffer, -n *f.* [*tsi′-fər*] figure, cipher, digit

Zigarette, -n *f.* [*tsi-ga-re′-tə*] cigarette

Zigarre, -n *f.* [*tsi-ga′-rə*] cigar

Zigeuner, - *m.* [*tsi-goi′-nər*] gypsy

Zimmer, - *n.* [*tsi′-mər*] room [in house]

Zimmerdecke, -en *f.* [*tsi′-mər-de-kə*] ceiling

Zimmermann *m. sing.* **Zimmerleute** *pl.* [*tsi′-mər-man, tsi′-mər-loi-tə*] carpenter

Zimt *m.* [*tsimt*] cinnamon

Zinn *n.* [*tsin*] tin

Zinsen *m. pl.* [*tsin′-zən*] interest [money]

zirka [*tsir′-kah*] about, nearly

Zirkus, -se *m.* [*tsir′-kus*] circus

Zitat, -e *n.* [*tsi-taht′*] quotation

zitieren *v.* [*tsi-tee′-rən*] quote, cite

Zitrone, -n *f.* [*tsi-troh′-nə*] lemon

zittern *v.* [*tsi′-tərn*] shiver, tremble

Zivilisation, -en *f.* [*tsi-vi-li-za-tsi-ohn′*] civilization

Zivilist, -en *m.* [*tsi-vi-list′*] civilian

zögern *v.* [*tsöh′-gərn*] hesitate

Zoll, - *m.* [*tsol*] inch

Zoll, ⸗e *m.* [*tsol, tsö′-lə*] toll; duty [customs]

Zollbeamte, -n *m.* [*tsol′-bə-am-tə*] customs officer

zollfrei [*tsol′-frai*] duty-free

Zollgebühr, -en *f.* [*tsol′-gə-bühr*] customs duty

Zollhaus, ⸗er *n.* [*tsol′-hous, tsol′-hoi-zər*] customhouse

Zorn *m.* [*tsorn*] anger

zu *prep.* (plus dat.) [*tsu*] to, towards; at, in; on; along with
   zu Hause [*tsu hou′-zə*] at home

zu *adv.* [*tsoo*] too, all too; closed

Zucker *m.* [*tsu′-kər*] sugar

Zuckerdose, -en *f.* [*tsu′-kər-doh-zə*] sugar bowl

zuerst [*tsu-ehrst'*] at first; above all

Zufall, ⸗e *m.* [*tsoo'-fal, tsoo'-fe-lə*] chance, accident
  durch Zufall [*durç tsoo'-fal*] by chance

zufällig [*tsoo'-fe-liç*] accidental, by chance

zufrieden [*tsu-free'-dən*] satisfied, content(ed)

Zug, ⸗e *m.* [*tsook, tsüh'-gə*] train; passage; trait; draft [of air]

Zugabteil, -e *n.* [*tsook'-ap-tail*] compartment in a train

zugänglich [*tsoo'-geng-liç*] accessible

zu-geben *v. irreg.* [*tsoo'-geh-bən*] give in; admit

zu-hören *v.* [*tsoo'-höh-rən*] listen

zu-kleben *v.* [*tsoo'-kleh-bən*] paste, seal [envelope]

Zukunft *f.* [*tsoo'-kunft*] future
  in Zukunft [*in tsoo'-kunft*] in the future

zu-lassen *v. irreg.* [*tsoo'-la-sən*] admit; permit

zuletzt [*tsu-letst'*] finally, at last, eventually, last

zum: zu dem [*tsum*] to the, towards the; at the, in the;
  on the; along with the

zu-machen *v.* [*tsoo'-ma-khən*] close, shut

zunächst [*tsu-nehçst'*] next; first of all

Zuname, -n *m.* [*tsoo'-nah-mə*] surname

Zündkerze, -n *f.* [*tsünt'-ker-tsə*] sparkplug

Zunge, -n *f.* [*tsung'-ə*] tongue

zurück *adv.* [*tsu-rük'*] back

zurück-fallen *v. irreg.* (*Aux:* SEIN) [*tsu-rük'-fa-lən*] fall back

zurück-geben *v. irreg.* [*tsu-rük'-geh-bən*] give back

zurück-kommen *v. irreg.* (*Aux:* SEIN) [*tsu-rük'-ko-mən*]
  come back, return
  Wann kommt sie zurück? [*van komt zee tsu-rük'*] When
  will she return?

zusammen [*tsu-za'-mən*] together

Zusammenarbeit *f.* [*tsu-za'-mən-ar-bait*] cooperation

Zusammenfassung, -en *f.* [*tsu-za'-mən-fa-sung*] summary

zusätzlich [*tsoo'-zets-liç*] additional

Zuschauer, - *m.* [*tsoo'-shou-ər*] spectator; audience

zu-schliessen *v. irreg.* [*tsoo'-shlee-sən*] lock (up)

zu-sehen *v. irreg.* [*tsoo'-zeh-ən*] watch, look on

Zustand, ⸗e *m.* [*tsoo'-shtant, tsoo'-shten-də*] condition
  in gutem Zustande [*in goo'-təm tsoo'-shtan-də*] in good

condition

zuständig [*tsoo'-shten-diç*] competent

Zustimmung, -en *f.* [*tsoo'-shti-mung*] consent

Zutritt *m.* [*tsoo'-trit*] admittance

   Zutritt verboten! [*tsoo'-trit fer-boh'-tən*] No admittance!

zuverlässig [*tsoo'-fer-le-siç*] reliable

zuviel [*tsu-feel'*] too much

Zwang *m.* [*tsvang*] compulsion

zwanzig [*tsvan'-tsiç*] twenty

zwar [*tsvahr*] indeed, though, to be sure

   und zwar [*unt tsvahr*] namely, at that

Zweck, -e *m.* [*tsvek*] purpose

zwei [*tsvai*] two

Zweifel, - *m.* [*tsvai'-fəl*] doubt

zweifeln *v.* [*tsvai'-fəln*] doubt

zweifellos [*tsvai'-fəl-lohs*] doubtless

Zweig, -e *m.* [*tsvaik, tsvai'-gə*] branch

zweimal [*tsvai'-mahl*] twice

zweit [*tsvait*] second

zweitens [*tsvai'-təns*] secondly

Zwiebel, -n *f.* [*tsvee'-bəl*] onion; bulb [plant]

Zwielicht *n.* [*tsvee'-liçt*] twilight

Zwilling, -e *m.* [*tsvi'-ling*] twin

zwingen *v. irreg.* [*tsving'-ən*] force, compel

zwischen *prep.* (plus dat.; acc. for motion) [*tsvi'-shən*]
   between

zwölf [*tsvölf*] twelve

zwölft [*tsvölft*] twelfth

Phrases for Use Abroad

Helpful Expressions

Good morning/afternoon/evening.
Guten Tag/Nachmittag/Abend.
Goo'-tən tahk/nahkh'-mi-tahk/ah'-bənt.

Hello. How do you do?
Guten Tag./Hallo. Wie geht es Ihnen?
Goo'-tən tahk./Ha-loh'. Vee geht es ee'-nən?

Good-bye. See you later.
Auf Wiedersehen. Bis später.
Ouf vee'-dər-zeh-ən. Bis shpeh'-tər.

Thank you.
Danke (schön).
Dan'-kə (shöhn).

You're welcome.
Bitte (sehr).
Bi'-tə (zehr).

Excuse me.
Entschuldigen Sie.
Ent-shul'-di-gən zee.

This is Mr./Mrs./Miss/Ms. . . .
Das ist Herr/Frau/Fräulein/Ms. . . .
Das ist Her/Frou/Froi'-lain/Miz . . .

My name is . . . .
Ich heisse . . . .
Iç hai'-sə. . . .

What is your name?
Wie heissen Sie?
Vee hai'-sən zee?

I am pleased to meet you.
Es freut mich, Sie kennenzulernen.
Es froit miç, zee ke'-nən-tsoo-ler-nən.

I don't understand.
Ich verstehe (es) nicht.
Iç fer-shteh'-ə (es) niçt.

Could you speak more slowly, please?
Könnten Sie bitte langsamer sprechen?
Kön'-tən zee bi'-tə lang'-zah-mər shpre'-çən?

Do you speak English?
Sprechen Sie englisch?
Shpre'-çən zee eng'-lish?

How much?
Wieviel?
Vee-feel'?

Where?
Wo?
Voh?

Where to?
Wohin?
Voh-hin'?

When?
Wann?
Van?

Can you help me, please?
Bitte, können Sie mir helfen?
Bi'-tə, kö'-nən zee meer hel'-fən?

How do you say . . . in German?
Wie sagt man . . . auf deutsch?
Vee zahkt man . . . ouf doitsh?

What does . . . mean?
Was bedeutet . . . ?
Vas be-doi'-tət . . . ?

Customs

May I see your passport/visa, please?
Bitte, zeigen Sie mir Ihren Pass/Ihr Visum?
Bi'-tə, zai'-gən zee meer ee'-rən pas/eer vee'-zum?

Do you have anything to declare?
Haben Sie etwas zu verzollen?
Hah'-bən zee et'-vas tsoo fer-tso'-lən?

How long are you staying?
Wie lange halten Sie sich hier auf?
Vee lan'-gə hal'-tən zee siç heer ouf?

I will be here for . . . days/weeks/months.
Ich werde mich hier auf . . . Tage/Wochen/Monate aufhalten.
Iç ver'-də miç heer ouf . . . tah'-gə/vo'-khən/moh'-na-tə ouf'-hal-tən.

Money

Where can I cash this traveler's check?
Wo kann ich diesen Reisescheck einlösen?
Voh kan iç dee'-zən rai'-zə-shek ain'-löh-zən?

When does the bank open/close?
Wann ist die Bank offen/geschlossen?
Van ist dee bank o'-fən/gə-shlo'-sən?

Please give me some small change.
Bitte, geben Sie mir etwas Kleingeld.
Bi'-tə, geh'-bən zee meer et'-vas klain'-gəlt.

At the Hotel

I reserved a single/double room by mail/telephone.
Ich reservierte brieflich/telephonisch ein Einzelzimmer/ein Doppelzimmer.
Iç re-zer-veer'-tə breef'-liç/te-le-foh'-nish ain ain'-tsəl-tsi-mər/ ain do'-pəl-tsi-mər.

I want a room with/without bath.
Ich will ein Zimmer mit Bad/ohne Bad.
Iç vil ain tsi'-mər mit baht/oh'-nə baht.

How much is this room?
Wieviel kostet dieses Zimmer?
Vee-feel' ko'-stət dee'-zəs tsi'-mər?

Are meals included?
Ist das Essen eingeschlossen?
Ist das e'-sən ain'-gə-shlo-sən?

I would like something cheaper.
Ich möchte etwas Billigeres.
Iç möç'-tə et'-vas bi'-li-gə-rəs.

Where is the manager?
Wo ist der Manager?
Voh ist dehr me'-nə-dzhər?

Are there any messages for me?
Hat jemand angerufen?
Hat yeh'-mant an'-gə-roo-fən?

Laundry/Dry Cleaning

Where is a laundry/dry cleaner?
Wo ist eine Wäscherei/eine Reinigungsanstalt?
Voh ist ai'-nə ve-shə-rai'/ai'-nə rai'-ni-gungs-an-shtalt?

Please wash these clothes.
Bitte, waschen Sie diese Kleider.
Bi'-tə, va'-shən zee dee'-zə klai'-dər.

When will my clothes be ready?
Wann werden meine Kleider fertig sein?
Van ver'-dən mai'-nə klai'-dər fer'-tiç zain?

I want these clothes dry cleaned.
Ich möchte diese Kleider reinigen lassen.
Iç möç'-tə dee'-zə klai'-dər rai'-ni-gən la'-sən.

Please press these trousers/this dress.
Bitte, bügeln Sie diese Hosen/dieses Kleid.
Bi'-tə, büh'-gəln zee dee'-zə hoh'-zən/dee'-zəs klait.

Hairdresser/Barber

I would like a haircut.
Ich möchte Haarschneiden.
Iç möç'-tə hahr'-shnai-dən.

Not too short, please.
Nicht zu kurz, bitte.
Niçt tsoo kurts, bi'-tə.

I would like a shampoo and set.
Ich möchte mir die Haare waschen und frisieren lassen.
Iç möç'-tə meer dee hah'-rə va'-shən unt fri-zee'-rən la'-sən.

Getting Around

When is the next flight to . . . ?
Wann ist der nächste Flug nach . . . ?
Van ist dehr nehç'-stə flook nahkh . . . ?

I want a ticket to . . . , please.
Bitte, ich will eine Fahrkarte nach . . . .
Bi'-tə, iç vil ai'-nə fahr'-kar-tə nahkh . . .

Is lunch/dinner served on this flight?
Wird auf diesem Flug Mittagessen/Abendessen serviert?
Virt ouf dee'-zəm flook mi'-tahk-e-sən/ah'-bənt-e-sən zer-veert'?

Take my bags to my cabin, please.
Bitte, bringen Sie mein Gepäck in meine Kabine.
Bi'-tə, brin'-gən zee main gə-pek' in mai'-nə ka-bee'-nə.

When is lunch/dinner/breakfast?
Wann wird das Mittagessen/das Abendbrot/das Frühstück
  serviert?
*Wan virt das mi'-tahk-e-sən/das ah'-bənt-broht/das früh'-
  shtük zer-veert'?*

At what time/When does the boat dock?
Um wieviel Uhr/Wann wird das Schiff anlegen?
Um vee-feel' oor/Van veert das shif an'-leh-gən?

Where is the ticket window?
Wo ist der Schalter?
Voh ist dehr shal'-tər?

May I have a timetable?
Darf ich einen Fahrplan haben?
Darf iç ai'-nən fahr'-plan hah'-bən?

**How much is a one-way/round-trip first-class/second-class
  ticket to . . . ?**
Wieviel kostet eine einfache Fahrkarte/eine Rückfahrkarte
  erster Klasse/zweiter Klasse nach . . . ?
*Vee-feel' ko'-stət ai'-nə ain'-fa-khə fahr'-kar-tə/ai'-nə rük'-
  fahr-kar-tə ehr'-stər kla'-sə/tsvai'-tər kla'-sə nakh . . . ?*

From which track does the train for . . . leave?
Von welchem Gleis fährt der Zug nach . . . ab?
Fon vel'-çəm glais fehrt dehr tsook nakh . . . ap?

What time does this train leave?
Um wieviel Uhr fährt dieser Zug ab?
Um vee-feel' oor fehrt dee'-zər tsook ap?

Is this seat taken?
Ist dieser Platz besetzt?
Ist dee'-zər plats bə-zetst'?

When is the dining car open?
Wann ist der Speisewagen offen?
Van ist dehr shpai'-zə-vah-gən o'-fən?

Where is the bus station?
Wo ist die Autobus-Haltestelle?
Voh ist dee ou'-to-bus hal'-tə-shte-lə?

When is the next bus to . . . ?
Wann fährt der nächste Autobus nach . . . ?
Van fehrt dehr neç'-stə ou'-to-bus nakh . . . ?

Take me to . . . .
Bringen Sie mich zum/zu der . . . .
Brin'-gən zee miç tsoom/tsoo dehr . . . .

I am in a hurry to catch a bus/train/plane.
Ich bin in Eile einen Autobus/einen Zug/ein Flugzeug zu erreichen.
Iç bin in ai'-lə ai'-nən ou'-to-bus/ai'-nən tsook/ain flook'-tsoik tsoo er-rai'-çən.

Where can I rent a car?
Wo kann ich ein Auto mieten?
Voh kan iç ain ou'-to mee'-tən?

Do you charge by the day or by the mile?
Wie wird das gerechnet? Pro Tag oder pro Distanz?
Vee virt das gə-reç'-nət? Proh tahk oh'-dər proh di-stants'?

Where is the nearest gas station?
Wo ist die nächste Tankstelle?
Voh ist dee neç'-stə tank'-shte-lə?

Please check the oil/tires.
Bitte, prüfen Sie das Öl/die Reifen.
Bi'-tə, prüh'-fən zee das öhl/dee rai'-fən.

Fill it up with regular/premium.
Bitte voll tanken mit Normalbenzin/Superbenzin.
Bi'-tə fol tan'-kən mit nor-mahl'-ben-tseen/zoo'-pər-ben-tseen

Is there a mechanic here?
Gibt es hier einen Mechaniker?
Gipt es heer ai'-nən me-çah'-ni-kər?

I am having trouble with . . . .
Ich habe Schwierigkeiten mit . . . .
Iç hah'-bə shvee'-riç-kai-tən mit . . . .

When will my car be ready?
Wann wird mein Auto bereit sein?
Van veert main ou'-to bə-rait' zain?

Shopping

How much does this cost?
Wieviel kostet das?
Vee-feel' ko'-stət das?

Have you anything better/cheaper?
Haben Sie irgend etwas Besseres/Billigeres?
Hah'-bən zee ir'-gənt et'-vas be'-sə-rəs/bi'-li-gə-rəs?

Is this hand-made?
Ist das handgearbeitet?
Ist das hant'-gə-ar-bai-tət?

Does this come in another color?
Kommt das in noch einer anderen Farbe?
Komt das in nokh ai'-nər an'-də-rən far'-bə?

This is too large/small.
Das ist zu gross/klein.
Das ist tsoo grohs/klain.

Do you accept checks/traveler's checks?
Nehmen Sie Schecks/Reiseschecks an?
Neh'-mən zee sheks/rai'-zə-sheks an?

Sightseeing

I would like a tour of the city.
Ich möchte eine Stadttour.
Iç möç'-tə ai'-nə shtat'-toor.

How long will the tour last?
Wie lange dauert die Tour?
Vee lan'-gə doi'-ərt dee toor?

Where is the museum/zoo?
Wo ist das Museum/der Tiergarten?
Voh ist das mu-zeh'-um/dehr teer'-gar-tən?

Do we have to pay to go in?
Kostet es Eintritt?
Ko'-stət es ain'-trit?

What hours are the museums open?
Wann sind die Museen offen?
Van zint dee mu-zeh'-ən o'-fən?

Entertainment

I would like to see an opera/a play.
Ich möchte eine Oper/ein Schauspiel sehen.
Iç möç'-tə ai'-nə oh'-pər/ain shou'-shpeel zeh'-ən.

I want to eat breakfast/lunch/dinner.
Ich wünsche Frühstück/Mittagessen/Abendessen zu essen.
Iç vün'-shə früh'-shtük/mi'-tahk-e-sən/ah'-bənt-e-sən tsoo e'-sən.

We would like a table for two, please.
Wir möchten einen Tisch für zwei Personen, bitte.
Veer möç'-tən ai'-nən tish führ tsvai per-soh'-nən, bi'-tə.

May we have a menu/wine list, please?
Dürfen wir um Ihre Speisekarte/Weinkarte bitten?
Dürf'-ən veer um ee'-rə shpai'-zə-kar-tə/vain'-kar-tə bi'-tən?

What do you recommend?
Was empfehlen Sie?
Vas emp-feh'-lən zee?

I didn't order this.
Das habe ich nicht bestellt.
Das hah'-bə iç niçt bə-shtelt'.

Please bring the check.
Bitte, bringen Sie mir die Rechnung.
Bi'-tə, brin'-gən zee meer dee reç'-nung.

Is the tip included?
Ist das Trinkgeld eingeschlossen?
Ist das trink'-gəlt ain'-gə-shlo-sən?

Where do I pay?
Wo bezahlt man?
Voh bə-tsahlt' man?

There is a mistake in the bill.
Hier ist ein Fehler in der Rechnung.
Heer ist ain feh'-lər in dehr reç'-nung.

Health

I don't feel well.
Ich fühle mich nicht wohl.
Iç füh'-lə miç niçt vohl.

I need a doctor/dentist.
Ich brauche einen Artz/einen Zahnarzt.
Iç brou'-çə ai'-nən ahrtst/ai'-nən tsahn'-ahrts.

I have a headache/stomachache/toothache.
Ich habe Kopfschmerzen/Magenschmerzen/Zahnschmerzen.
Iç hah'-bə kopf'-shmer-tsən/mah'-gən-shmer-tsən/tsahn'-shmer-tsən.

I have a fever/a bad cold.
Ich habe Fieber/mich schwer erkältet.
Iç hah'-bə fee'-bər/miç shvehr er-kel'-tət.

My . . . is burned/hurt/bleeding.
Mein/meine . . . ist verbrannt/tut mir weh/blutet.
Main/mai'-nə . . . ist fer-brant'/toot meer veh/bloo'-tət.

Please make up this prescription.
Bitte, fertigen Sie dieses Rezept.
Bi'-tə, fer'-ti-gən zee dee'-zəs re-tsept'.

Emergencies

Help!
Hilfe!
Hil'-fə!

Police!
Polizei!
Po-li-tsai'!

Please call a policeman/an ambulance.
Bitte, rufen Sie einen Polizisten/einen Krankenwagen an.
Bi'-tə, roo'-fən zee ai'-nən po-li-tsi'-stən/ai'-nən kran'-kən-vah-gən an.

I need a lawyer.
Ich brauche eine Rechtsanwält.
Iç brou'-çə ai'-nə reçts'-an-valt.

I've been robbed.
Man hat mich bestohlen.
Man hat miç bə-shtoh'-lən.

Is there anyone here who speaks English?
Spricht hier jemand Englisch?
Shpriçt heer yeh'-mant eng'-lish?

I am lost.
Ich habe mich verlaufen.
Iç hah'-bə miç fer-lou'-fən.

Someone is injured.
Jemand ist verletzt.
Yeh'-mant ist fer-letst'.

Menu Reader

Beverages

Bier [*beer*] beer
   Fassbier [*fas'-beer*] draft beer
Kaffee [*ka'-fə*] coffee
   Eiskaffee [*ais'-ka-fə*] iced coffee
Milch [*milç*] milk
Milchmischgetränk [*milç'-mish-gə-trenk*] milkshake
Saft [*zaft*] juice
   Orangensaft [*o-rahn'-zhən-zaft*] orange juice
   Tomatensaft [*to-mah'-tən-zaft*] tomato juice
Schokolade [*sho-ko-lah'-də*] chocolate, hot chocolate
Tee [*teh*] tea
Wasser [*va'-sər*] water
Sodawasser [*zoh'-da-va-sər*] soda water
Wein [*vain*] wine
   Weisswein [*vaiz'-vain*] white wine
   Rotwein [*roht'-vain*] red wine

The Menu

Aal [*ahl*] eel
Ananas [*a'-na-nas*] pineapple
Apfel [*ap'-fəl*] apple
Apfelstrudel [*ap'-fəl-shtroo-dəl*] thin pastry filled with apples,
   almonds and raisins
Aprikose [*ap-ri-koh'-zə*] apricot
Artischocke [*ar'-ti-sho-kə*] artichoke
Austern [*ou'-stərn*] oysters

Backpflaume [*bak'-pflou-mə*] prune
Banane [*ba-nah'-nə*] banana
Barsch [*barsh*] perch
Beefsteak [*beef'-stehk*] chopped steak
belegtes Butterbrot [*bə-lehk'-təs bu'-tər-broht*] sandwich
Blumenkohl [*bloo'-mən-kohl*] cauliflower
Bohnen [*boh'-nən*] beans
   dicke Bohnen [*di'-kə boh'-nən*] broad beans
   grüne Bohnen [*grüh'-nə boh'-nən*] green beans
Braten [*brah'-tən*] roast
braten [*brah'-tən*] sautéed, fried
Brathuhn mit Reis [*braht'-hoon mit rais*] chicken with rice
Brot [*broht*] bread
   geröstetes Brot [*gə-röh'-stə-təs broht*] toast
   Schwarzbrot [*shvarts'-broht*] dark bread
Brötchen [*bröt'-çən*] roll
Butter [*boo'-tər*] butter

Creme [*krehm*] cream or mousse

durchgebraten [*durç'-gə-brah-tən*] well done

Ei(er) [*ai'-(ər)*] egg(s)
   hart gekocht [*hart gə-kokht'*] hard-boiled
   weich gekocht [*vaiç gə-kokht'*] soft-boiled
   Rühreier [*rühr'-ai-ər*] scrambled eggs
   Spiegeleier [*shpee'-gəl-ai-ər*] fried eggs
eingelegt [*ain'-gə-lehkt*] pickled
Eintopf(gericht) [*ain'-topf (gə-riçt')*] stew
Eis [*ais*] ice cream
Eisbein [*ais'-bain*] pig's feet
englische Art (gekocht) [*eng'-li-shə ahrt (gə-kokht')*] broiled,
   very rare
Ente [*en'-tə*] duck
Erbsen [*erp'-sən*] green peas
Erdbeeren [*ehrt'-beh-rən*] strawberries
(Wein)Essig [*(vain)'-e-siç*] vinegar
   und Öl [*unt öhl*] vinegar and oil salad dressing

Fische [*fi'-shə*] fish
Fischgericht [*fish'-gə-riçt*] seafood dish
Fleisch [*flaish*] meat
   mit Fleisch gefüllt [*mit flaish gə-fült'*] stuffed with meat
Fleischpasteten [*flaish'-pa-steh-tən*] meat pies
Flundern [*floon'-dərn*] flounder
Forelle blau [*fo-re'-lə blou*] very fresh trout, steamed
französische Art (in Butter gekocht) [*fran-tsöh'-zi-shə ahrt (in bu'-tər gə-kokht')*] French style (cooked in butter)

Gans [*gans*] goose
Garnele [*gar-neh'-lə*] shrimp
gebraten (in der Pfanne) [*gə-brah'-tən (in dehr pfa'-nə)*] (pan) broiled
Geflügel [*gə-flüh'-gəl*] poultry
Geflügelpastete [*gə-flüh'-gəl-pa-steh-tə*] baked poultry pie topped with truffles
gegrillt [*gə-grilt'*] grilled
gekocht [*gə-kokht'*] cooked, stewed, boiled
gekochte Kartoffelklösse [*gə-kokh'-tə kar-to'-fəl-klöh-sə*] potato dumplings
Gemüse [*gə-müh'-zə*] vegetables
Gemüseplatte [*gə-müh'-zə-pla-tə*] vegetable plate of cauliflower, tomatoes, endive and dressing
Gurken [*gur'-kən*] cucumbers

Hammelfleisch [*ha'-məl-flaish*] lamb
   Hammelbraten [*ha'-məl-brah-tən*] leg of lamb
   Hammelkoteletten [*ha'-məl-ko-tə-le-tən*] lamb chops
Hase [*hah'-zə*] rabbit
Hasenpfeffer [*hah'-zən-pfe-fər*] rabbit stew
Hausbacken [*hous'-ba-kən*] home-made
Heilbutt [*hail'-but*] halibut
Heringe [*heh'-rin-gə*] herring
Honig [*hoh'-niç*] honey
Huhn [*hoon*] hen
Hummer [*hoo'-mər*] lobster

italienische Art (mit Pasta) [*i-tah-li-ə'-ni-shə ahrt (mit pas'-ta)*] Italian style (with pasta)

Kalbsbrust (gefüllte) [*kalps'-brust (gə-fül'-tə)*] breast of veal (stuffed)

Kalbskotelett [*kalps'-ko-tə-let*] veal cutlet

Kalbs- und Schweinefleisch Bratwurst [*kalps- unt shvai'-nə-flaish braht'-vurst*] veal and pork sausage

kalter Aufschnitt [*kal'-tər ouf'-shnitt*] cold cuts

Kammuschel [*kahm'-moo-shəl*] scallops

Karfreitagssemmel [*kahr-frai'-tahks-ze-məl*] hot cross bun

Karotte [*ka-ro'-tə*] carrot

Kartoffeln [*kar-to'-fəln*] potatoes
   gebraten [*gə-brah'-tən*] home fries
   Kartoffelbrei [*kar-to'-fəl-brai*] mashed potatoes

Käse [*keh'-zə*] cheese
   Quarkkäse [*kvark'-keh-zə*] creamed cottage cheese

Kasseler Rippenspeer [*ka'-se-lər ri'-pən-shpehr*] roast ribs of pork

Keks [*kehks*] cookie

Kirschen [*kir'-shən*] cherries

Klösse, Knödel [*klöh'-sə, knöh'-dəl*] dumplings

Knoblauch [*knohp'-loukh*] garlic

Kohl [*kohl*] cabbage
   Rotkohl, Rotkraut [*roht'-kohl, roht'-krout*] red cabbage

Kotelett [*ko-tə-let'*] chop

Krabbe [*kra'-bə*] crab, crabmeat, shrimp

Kraut [*krout*] cabbage
   Sauerkraut [*zou'-ər-krout*] boiled cabbage and potato with wine or cream

Kuchen [*koo'-khən*] cake

Leber [*leh'-bər*] liver

leicht gebraten [*laiçt gə-brah'-tən*] rare

Lendenschnitten [*len'-dən-shni-tən*] fillet

Mais [*mais*] corn

Makrele [*ma-kreh'-lə*] mackerel

Mandeln [*man'-dəln*] almonds
mariniert [*ma-ri-neert'*] marinated
Marmelade [*mar-mə-lah'-də*] jam
Meerrettich [*mehr'-re-tiç*] horseradish
Melone [*me-loh'-nə*] melon
Mus [*moos*] mousse or cream
Muschel [*moo'-shəl*] clams

Nachtische [*nahkh'-ti-shə*] desserts, sweets
Nudeln [*noo'-dəln*] noodles

Obst [*ohpst*] fruit
Öl [*öhl*] oil
Oliven [*o-lee'-vən*] olives
Omelett [*o-mə-let'*] omelet

Pampelmuse [*pam'-pəl-moo-zə*] grapefruit
paniert [*pa-neert'*] breaded
Paprika Huhn [*pah'-pri-ka hoon*] fried chicken with paprika
   cream sauce
Paprika Rahmschnitzel [*pah'-pri-ka rahm'-shnit-səl*] veal cutlet
   with paprika cream sauce
Pfannkuchen [*pfan'-koo-khən*] pancakes
Pfirsiche [*pfir'-zi-çə*] peaches
Pflaume [*pflou'-mə*] plum
Pichelsteiner [*pi'-çəl-shtai-nər*] mixed meat stew
Pilze [*pil'-tsə*] mushrooms
Plätzchen [*plets'-çən*] cookie

Rahmstrudel [*rahm'-shtroo-dəl*] thin pastry filled with sour
   cream, cottage cheese, almonds and raisins
Rehrücken [*reh'-rü-kən*] loin of venison
Rinderfilet, gegrillt [*rin'-dər-fi-leh, gə-grilt'*] tenderloin, grilled
Rinderrouladen [*rin'-dər-roo-lah-dən*] rolled beef stuffed with
   bacon and onion, served with cream sauce
Rindfleisch [*rint'-flaish*] beef
Rostbraten [*rost'-brah-tən*] beef pan-broiled with onions

Salat [*za-laht'*] *salad*
  Kopfsalat [*kopf'-za-laht*] Boston lettuce
  Gurkensalat [*gur'-kən-za-laht*] cucumber salad
  Kartoffelsalat [*kar-to'-fəl-za-laht*] potato salad
Salm [*zalm*] salmon
Salz [*zalts*] salt
Salzburger Nockerln [*zalts'-bur-gər no'-kərln*] sweet omelet-soufflé
Sardellen [*zar-de'-lən*] anchovies
Sardinen [*zar-dee'-nən*] sardines
Sauerbraten [*zou'-ər-brah-tən*] beef marinated in wine
Schaltier [*shahl'-teer*] shellfish
Schellfisch [*shel'-fish*] haddock
Schinken [*shin'-kən*] ham
Schinkenbrötchen [*shin'-kən-bröt-çən*] ham sandwich
Schlagsahne [*shlahk'-zah-nə*] whipped cream
Schnitzel [*shnit'-səl*] cutlet
schwarzer Pfeffer [*shvart'-sər pfe'-fər*] black pepper
Schweine (Brat)Würste [*shvai'-nə (braht)'-vür-stə*] pork sausages
Schwertfisch [*shvert'-fish*] swordfish
Seezunge [*zeh'-tsun-gə*] sole
Semmel [*ze'-məl*] roll
Senf [*zenf*] mustard
spanische Art (mit Tomaten) [*shpah'-ni-shə ahrt (mit to-mah'-tən)*] Spanish style (with tomatoes)
Spargel [*shpar'-gəl*] asparagus
Spargelkohl [*shpar'-gəl-kohl*] broccoli
Spätzle [*shpets'-əl*] small noodle dumplings served with meat and vegetables
Speck [*shpek*] bacon
Spinat [*shpi-naht'*] spinach
Steak [*stehk*] steak
Suppe [*zoo'-pə*] soup
  gewürzte Gemüsesuppe [*gə-vürts'-tə gə-müh'-zə-zu-pə*] seasoned vegetable soup
  Gulaschsuppe [*goo'-lash-zu-pə*] goulash
  Kraftbrühe [*kraft'-brüh-ə*] consommé

Tomatensuppe [*to-mah'-tən-zu-pə*] tomato soup
Süsskartoffeln [*zühs'-kar-to-fəln*] sweet potatoes

Thunfisch [*toon'-fish*] tuna
Toast [*tohst*] toast
Tomate [*to-mah'-tə*] tomato
Torte [*tor'-tə*] tart, pie

ungarischer Gulasch-Eintopf [*oon'-gah-ri-shər goo'-lash ain'-topf*] Hungarian goulash

Vanillesosse, gekocht [*va-nil'-ə-zoh-sə, gə-kokht'*] custard, boiled
Vorspeisen [*fohr'-shpai-zən*] appetizers; first course

Weintraube [*vain'-trou-bə*] bunch of grapes
weisse Rübe [*vai'-sə rüh'-bə*] turnip
Wiener Schnitzel [*vee'-nər shnit-səl*] breaded veal cutlet Viennese style

Zucker [*tsoo'-kər*] sugar
Zwiebel [*tsvee'-bəl*] onion

A Concise German Grammar

Indo-European, the ancestor of most modern European languages, distinguished three genders of nouns — masculine, feminine, and neuter. Whereas modern English has lost this distinction, German has retained it. Articles, pronouns, and adjectives modifying nouns still show this gender difference most clearly, since the form of many German nouns no longer identifies the gender. Gender, in German, is a grammatical, not a biological term. Every noun, whether referring to an animate or inanimate object, takes a masculine, feminine or neuter article. Therefore it is of the utmost importance that you learn the article with every noun.

The Article

The definite article is declined for the three genders, two numbers (singular and plural), and four cases (nominative, accusative, dative, and genitive).

	Singular			Plural
	Masc.	*Fem.*	*Neut.*	*Masc., Fem., Neut.*
Nom.	der	die	das	die
Acc.	den	die	das	die
Dat.	dem	der	dem	den
Gen.	des	der	des	der

Other "limiting" words declined like *der*, *die*, *das* are *dieser*, this; *jeder*, each, every; *mancher*, many a; *solcher*, such; *welcher*, which, that. These "limiting" words follow the feminine declension of the article when modifying feminine nouns (*diese Frau*) and the neuter declension when modifying neuter nouns (*dieses Mädchen*).

The indefinite article *ein*, a, an; the negative *kein*, not a, not any, no; the possessive adjectives *mein*, my; *dein*, your (familiar); *sein*, his; *ihr*, her; *unser*, our; *euer*, your (familiar plural); *Ihr*, your (formal); are declined according to the form of the indefinite article.

| | *Singular* | | | *Plural* |
	Masc.	*Fem.*	*Neut.*	*Masc., Fem., Neut.*
Nom.	ein	eine	ein	keine
Acc.	einen	eine	ein	keine
Dat.	einem	einer	einem	keinen
Gen.	eines	einer	eines	keiner

Kein and the possessive adjectives are declined in the plural forms; *ein* is not.

Both the definite and indefinite articles must agree in gender, number, and case with the noun they modify.

The Noun

Nouns are either masculine, feminine, or neuter. And all nouns have number (singular and plural) and case: the nominative (subject of a sentence); the accusative (direct object of the verb); the dative (indirect object of the verb); and the genitive (possessive). Nouns are capitalized.

The *strong noun declension*, comprising mostly masculine and neuter nouns, is distinguished by an -(*e*)*s* in the genitive singular and no -*n* in the nominative plural. (The few feminine nouns are invariable in the singular.) Plurals take an ending or an umlaut or both.

Masculine:

| | Singular | Plural |
	the father	the fathers
Nom.	der Vater	die Väter
Acc.	den Vater	die Väter
Dat.	dem Vater	den Vätern
Gen.	des Vaters	der Väter

Feminine:

	the mother	the mothers
Nom.	die Mutter	die Mütter
Acc.	die Mutter	die Mütter
Dat.	der Mutter	den Müttern
Gen.	der Mutter	der Mütter

Neuter:

	the house	the houses
Nom.	das Haus	die Häuser
Acc.	das Haus	die Häuser
Dat.	dem Haus(e)	den Häusern
Gen.	des Hauses	der Häuser

The *weak noun declension* is composed primarily of feminine nouns, the singular being invariable, the plural always ending in *-n* or *-en*. Masculine nouns end in *-n* or *-en* in all cases except the nominative singular. There are no neuter nouns in this declension.

Masculine:

	Singular	Plural
	the student	the students
Nom.	der Student	die Studenten
Acc.	den Studenten	die Studenten
Dat.	dem Studenten	den Studenten
Gen.	des Studenten	der Studenten

Feminine:

	the woman, wife	the women, wives
Nom.	die Frau	die Frauen
Acc.	die Frau	die Frauen
Dat.	der Frau	den Frauen
Gen.	der Frau	der Frauen

	the sister	the sisters
Nom.	die Schwester	die Schwestern
Acc.	die Schwester	die Schwestern
Dat.	der Schwester	den Schwestern
Gen.	der Schwester	der Schwestern

The *mixed noun declension*, which forms the genitive with -*s* but the plural with an -*(e)n*, is a combination of the other two declensions, the singular being strong, the plural weak.

Neuter:

	Singular	Plural
	the eye	*the eyes*
Nom.	das Auge	die Augen
Acc.	das Auge	die Augen
Dat.	dem Auge	den Augen
Gen.	des Auges	der Augen

The plural form of a noun cannot be predicted accurately from the singular form, since plurals are formed in a variety of ways. However, when the singular ends in -*ung*, -*heit*, -*keit*, the plural adds -*en;* and when the singular ends in -*in*, the plural adds -*nen*.

Among the ways of forming the plurals of nouns are the following:

(*a*) The singular and the plural are the same:

der Lehrer the teacher **die Lehrer** the teachers

In the dictionary, a dash after the entry word indicates that the noun does not change in the plural:

Lehrer, - *m.*

(*b*) The vowel stem changes; that is, it takes an umlaut:

der Garten the garden **die Gärten** the gardens

In the dictionary, this plural is shown as follows:

Garten, = *m.*

(*c*) An ending, -*e*, -*er*, -*n*, -*en*, is added:

der Tisch the table **die Tische** the tables
das Kind the child **die Kinder** the children

Such plural endings appear in the dictionary as follows:

Tisch, -e *m.*   **Kind, -er** *n.*

(*d*) The stem takes an umlaut and an ending is added:

das Buch the book **die Bücher** the books

This plural is shown in the dictionary as follows:

Buch, ⸗er *n*.

(*e*) An *-s* is added to certain borrowings from modern foreign languages:

das Hotel the hotel   **die Hotels** the hotels

(*f*) In other foreign borrowings ending in *-a, -is, -us, -um*, the ending *-en* is substituted; others add *-n, -en,* or *-ien:*

das Drama the drama   **die Dramen** the dramas
das Material the material   **die Materialien** the materials

In the dictionary, plurals substituting *-en* are spelled out; additions are indicated as for (*c*) above.

Proper names are generally not declined in German, except in the genitive, where an *-s* without apostrophe is added:

Goethes Gedicht   Goethe's poem

The Adjectives

German has three declensions of adjectives: strong, weak, and mixed. The *strong adjective declension* is used when neither an article nor possessive adjective precedes the adjective.

Masculine:

	Singular	Plural
	good man	good men
Nom.	guter Mann	gute Männer
Acc.	guten Mann	gute Männer
Dat.	gutem Mann(e)	guten Männern
Gen.	guten Mannes	guter Männer

Feminine:

	good daughter	good daughters
Nom.	gute Tochter	gute Töchter
Acc.	gute Tochter	gute Töchter
Dat.	guter Tochter	guten Töchtern
Gen.	guter Tochter	guter Töchter

Neuter:

	good child	good children
Nom.	gutes Kind	gute Kinder
Acc.	gutes Kind	gute Kinder
Dat.	gutem Kind(e)	guten Kindern
Gen.	guten Kindes	guter Kinder

With the exception of the masculine and neuter genitive singulars, the adjective is declined like the definite article *der*.

The *weak adjective declension* is used when a definite article (such as *der, dieser, jener*) precedes the adjective. Note that all cases, excepting the nominative singular in all three genders and the accusative singular in feminine and neuter, end in *-en*.

Masculine:

	Singular	Plural
	the good husband	*the good husbands*
Nom.	der gute Mann	die guten Männer
Acc.	den guten Mann	die guten Männer
Dat.	dem guten Mann(e)	den guten Männern
Gen.	des guten Mannes	der guten Männer

Feminine:

	the good wife	*the good wives*
Nom.	die gute Frau	die guten Frauen
Acc.	die gute Frau	die guten Frauen
Dat.	der guten Frau	den guten Frauen
Gen.	der guten Frau	der guten Frauen

Neuter:

	the good girl	*the good girls*
Nom.	das gute Mädchen	die guten Mädchen
Acc.	das gute Mädchen	die guten Mädchen
Dat.	dem guten Mädchen	den guten Mädchen
Gen.	des guten Mädchens	der guten Mädchen

The *mixed adjective declension* is used when the adjective is preceded by *ein, kein,* or a possessive adjective. The adjective is declined as in the weak declension with three exceptions.

The nominative singular masculine and the nominative and accusative singular neuter take strong endings.

Masculine:

	Singular	*Plural*
	my good husband	*my good husbands*
Nom.	mein guter Mann	meine guten Männer
Acc.	meinen guten Mann	meine guten Männer
Dat.	meinem guten Mann(e)	meinen guten Männern
Gen.	meines guten Mannes	meiner guten Männer

Feminine:

	my good wife	*my good wives*
Nom.	meine gute Frau	meine guten Frauen
Acc.	meine gute Frau	meine guten Frauen
Dat.	meiner guten Frau	meinen guten Frauen
Gen.	meiner guten Frau	meiner guten Frauen

Neuter:

	my good child	*my good children*
Nom.	mein gutes Kind	meine guten Kinder
Acc.	mein gutes Kind	meine guten Kinder
Dat.	meinem guten Kind(e)	meinen guten Kindern
Gen.	meines guten Kindes	meiner guten Kinder

An adjective must agree with the noun it modifies in gender, number, and case. After the verbs *sein*, to be, and *werden*, to become, to get, the adjective is not inflected.

> **Das Wetter ist schön.** The weather is beautiful.
> **Es wird heiss.** It's getting hot.

Adjectives used as adverbs are not inflected.

> **Sie fährt schnell.** She's driving fast.

Adjectives may also be used as nouns:

> **der Alte** the old man   **ein Armer** a poor man

The comparative is formed by adding *-er* to the adjective, and the superlative *-(e)st* or by using the idiomatic *am -sten*.

klein small   **kleiner** smaller   **(der) kleinste** smallest
                                          am kleinsten smallest

The comparative and superlative take the appropriate case endings.

> **Der älteste Wagen war klein.**
> The oldest car was small.
> **Der kleinere Tisch gehört mir.**
> The smaller table belongs to me.

Monosyllabic adjectives generally take an umlaut in the comparative and superlative. The *a*, *o*, or *u* change to *ä*, *ö*, or *ü*.

alt	**älter**	**(der) älteste** *or* **am ältesten**
jung	**jünger**	**(der) jüngste** *or* **am jüngsten**
kurz	**kürzer**	**(der) kürzeste** *or* **am kürzesten**

The irregular forms of adjectives are:

Positive		*Comparative*		*Superlative*	
gut	good	**besser**	better	**(der) beste**	best
				am besten	best
gross	large	**grösser**	larger	**(der) grösste**	largest
				am grössten	largest
hoch	high	**höher**	higher	**(der) höchste**	highest
				am höchsten	highest
nah	near	**näher**	nearer	**(der) nächste**	nearest
				am nächsten	nearest
viel	much	**mehr**	more	**(die) meisten**	most
				am meisten	most

The positive comparison of equality is expressed by *so . . . wie*, as . . . as:

> **Anna ist so gross wie ich.**
> Anna is as tall as I am.

The comparative adjective plus *als*, then, expresses the comparison of inequality.

> **Anna ist grösser als ich.**
> Anna is taller than I am.

The Pronoun

The *personal pronouns* have the following forms:

		Singular			
	I	*you*	*he*	*she*	*it*
Nom.	ich	du	er	sie	es
Acc.	mich	dich	ihn	sie	es
Dat.	mir	dir	ihm	ihr	ihm
Gen.	meiner	deiner	seiner	ihrer	seiner

		Plural		
	we	*you*	*they*	*you* (polite)
Nom.	wir	ihr	sie	Sie
Acc.	uns	euch	sie	Sie
Dat.	uns	euch	ihnen	Ihnen
Gen.	unser	euer	ihrer	Ihrer

When referring to a noun previously mentioned, the personal pronoun possesses the same gender as the noun.

> **Der Brief ist von Hans. Er ist von ihm.**
> The letter is from Hans. It's from him.

In German there are three ways of saying *you: du, ihr,* and *Sie.* The familiar forms, *du* in the singular and *ihr* in the plural, are used in addressing God, one's family, friends, and pets.

> **Wo bist du, Mutti?** Where are you, Mother?

Sie, singular and plural, is the formal address used with strangers, acquaintances, doctors, etc.

When the pronouns *ihm, ihn, ihr, sie, es,* and *ihnen* would occur after prepositions and refer to inanimate objects, they are replaced by *da* or *dar* (if the preposition begins with a vowel).

> **Klara kommt mit dem Zug. Sie kommt damit.**
> Klara comes by train. She comes by it.

Es can be used as an indefinite pronoun.

> **Es regnet.** It's raining.
> **Es klopft.** There's a knock on the door.

Personal pronouns may be used reflexively when they refer back to the subject of a sentence. They are used in their dative and accusative forms:

Ich wasche mich.   I'm washing (myself).

When the verb takes only the dative case (as indicated in the dictionary), the dative form of the personal pronoun must be used.

Ich helfe mir ...   I help myself ...

Only the third person, singular and plural, has a special reflexive pronoun, *sich.*

Er hilft sich ...   He helps himself ...

Sich may also mean *each other.*

Verbs are used reflexively more often in German than in English. The reflexive pronoun is often not translated.

Bitte, setzen Sie sich!   Please sit down.
Er freut sich.   He's glad.

The *possessive pronouns and adjectives* are:

	Masculine	*Singular* *Feminine*	*Neuter*
my	mein	meine	mein
your (*familiar*)	dein	deine	dein
his	sein	seine	sein
her	ihr	ihre	ihr

		Plural	
our	unser	uns(e)re	unser
your (*familiar*)	euer	eu(e)re	euer
their	ihr	ihre	ihr
your (*formal*)	Ihr	Ihre	Ihr

The possessive adjectives are inflected like *ein.*

Hier ist Ihre Zeitung.   Here is your newspaper.
Ist das dein Buch?   Is that your book?

A possessive pronoun not followed by a noun takes the endings of *dieser:* the nominative singular masculine takes the ending *-er;* the nominative and accusative singular feminine take the ending *-e;* and the nominative and accusative singular neuter take the ending *-es.*

Mein Buch liegt auf dem Tisch. Wo ist Ihres?
  My book lies on the table. Where is yours?
Ihr Bruder wohnt in der Stadt. Meiner wohnt auf dem Lande.
  Her brother lives in the city. Mine lives in the country.

The *demonstrative pronouns* most frequently used are *dieser, der, die,* and *das.* They are declined like the definite article and correspond in English to the personal pronoun. The demonstrative pronouns *jener,* that one; *derselbe,* the same; and *derjenige,* those, he, she, it, are rarely used.

  Die ist nicht hier. She is not here.
  Der versteht nichts. He understands nothing.

The interrogative pronouns are:

	Masc., Fem., Neut. (*used for people*)	(*used for objects*)
Nom.	wer, *who*	was, *what*
Acc.	wen, *whom*	was, *what*
Dat.	wem, *to whom*	
Gen.	wessen, *whose*	

When formulating a question with the word *what* in conjunction with a preposition, the prefix *wo-* replaces the pronoun (*wor-* if the preposition begins with a vowel):

  Worauf warten Sie For what are you waiting?
  Wovon sprichst du? About what are you speaking?

The *relative pronouns, who, which, that,* are similar to the definite article, except in the genitive and in the dative plural.

	Singular			*Plural*
	Masc.	*Fem.*	*Neut.*	*All genders*
Nom.	der	die	das	die
Acc.	den	die	das	die
Dat.	dem	der	dem	denen
Gen.	dessen	deren	dessen	deren

The *indefinite pronouns einer*, one; *keiner*, none, nobody; *jeder*, each one; are declined like the definite article.

> **Karl und Ernst sind Brüder. Einer ist sehr gescheit.**
> Karl and Ernest are brothers. One is very clever.

Some indefinite pronouns are not declined: *etwas*, something; *nichts*, nothing; and *ein paar*, a few, some.

Man, one, you, people, they, is declined in the following manner:

Nom.	man
Acc.	einen
Dat.	einem

Jemand, someone, somebody; *niemand*, no one, nobody; and *jedermann*, everyone, everybody, are inflected only in the genitive case.

The Preposition

German prepositions require either the dative, accusative, or genitive case. Prepositions that always require the dative case when followed by a noun or pronoun are *aus*, out of, from; *ausser*, except, besides; *bei*, at, near, at the house of; *mit*, with; *nach*, to, after; *seit*, since, for (expresses time); *von*, from, of, by; and *zu*, to, at.

> **Wir fliegen nach Deutschland.**
> We are flying to Germany.
> **Sie wohnt bei ihren Eltern.**
> She lives with her parents.
> **Er geht zum Arzt.**
> He's going to the doctor.

Note that prepositions followed by the definite article in the dative case may be contracted: *an dem — am; in dem — im; von dem — vom; zu dem — zum; zu der — zur; bei dem — beim.*

Prepositions which always require the accusative case when followed by a noun or pronoun are *durch*, through; *für*, for; *gegen*, against; *ohne*, without; *um*, around, at; *wider*, against; *bis*, up to, as far as; and *entlang*, along.

Sie fährt um die Stadt.   She drives around the city.
Diese Zeitung ist für dich.   This newspaper is for you.
Wir bleiben bis September.   We're staying until September.

(*Bis* may be used alone when followed by an expression of time or place. Otherwise, it is generally used with another preposition, and this preposition determines the case.)

Contractions of prepositions followed by the definite article in the accusative case are *an das — ans; in das — ins; auf das — aufs; für das — fürs.*

Prepositions that always require the genitive case are *anstatt, statt,* instead of; *trotz,* in spite of; *während,* during; *wegen,* because of; *ausserhalb,* outside of; *innerhalb,* inside of; *oberhalb,* above; *unterhalb,* below.

> **Trotz des Regens sind sie gekommen.**
>   They came in spite of the rain.
> **Während des Sommers haben wir Ferien.**
>   We have vacation during the summer.

Prepositions that require either the dative or accusative case are *an,* at, to, up to (an object); *auf,* on, on top of, upon; *hinter,* behind, in back of; *in,* in, into; *neben,* beside, next to; *über,* over, above; *unter,* under, among; *vor,* before, in front of, ago; *zwischen,* between. These prepositions use the dative case in answer to the question *Wo?,* Where?, indicating the place where an object or person is located or an action is taking place. They use the accusative case in answer to the question *Wohin?,* Where to?, when they imply motion to a place or a goal (and this includes direction of thought). Note that verbs of motion are used in the latter case.

  Sie geht ans Fenster.   She is going to the window.
  Jetzt ist sie am Fenster.   Now she is at the window.

Prepositions are often used idiomatically with certain verbs and adjectives followed by either the dative or accusative case. Such expressions must simply be learned. Examples are:

> **bestehen aus** (plus dat.)
> > **Das Haus besteht aus vier Zimmern.**
> > The house consists of four rooms.
> **sich erinnern an** (plus acc.)
> > **Ich erinnere mich an die Vergangenheit.**
> > I remember the past.

The Conjunction and Word Order

Word order is extremely important in German. When using the coordinating conjunctions *aber*, but; *oder*, or; *sondern*, but (on the contrary); *und*, and; *entweder . . . oder*, either . . . or; *weder . . . noch*, neither . . . nor; the subject is followed by the verb in both independent clauses.

Die Studentin trinkt Kaffee aber der Student bestellt ein Glas Bier.

> The (female) student drinks coffee but the (male) student orders a glass of beer.

After subordinating conjunctions, the verb comes at the end of the subordinate clause and at the beginning of the independent clause. The most common of these conjunctions are *dass*, that; *wann*, when; *wenn*, if, when; *ob*, whether; *obgleich*, *obschon*, although; *als ob*, as if; *falls*, in case; *bevor*, before; *indem*, while; *nachdem*, after; *seitdem*, since (used with time); *weil*, because; *während*, while; *wie*, how, as; *wo*, where.

Sie weiss, dass niemand gekommen ist.

> She knows that no one has come.

Obgleich er kein Geld hat, will er ihr doch ein Geschenk geben.

> Although he has no money, he nevertheless wants to give her a present.

Because German is a case language, the word order in a simple declarative statement is extremely flexible. The sentence may begin with an adverb, a time expression, with the dative or accusative case as well as with the nominative case, but *the verb is always in second position*. Note the rearrangement of the following sentence, which is equally correct in all versions.

> **Heute gehe ich ins Kino.**
> **Ich gehe heute ins Kino.**
> **Ins Kino gehe ich heute.**
> I'm going to the movies today.

When using both an indirect (dative) and direct object (accusative) in a simple statement, if the objects are both nouns, the indirect object precedes the direct.

> **Er gibt dem Studenten die Zeitung.**
> He gives the student the newspaper.

If the indirect and direct objects are both pronouns, the reverse is true.

> **Er gibt sie ihm.**   He gives it to him.

Expressions of time precede place.

> **Das Kind geht morgen zur Schule.**
> The child is going to school tomorrow.

The Adverb

In form, the German adverb looks like the adjective. There is no special ending for the adverb.

> **Das Essen ist gut.**   The food is good.
> **Sie schreibt gut.**   She writes well.

Almost any adjective can be used as an adverb. Only a few adverbs, such as *gern*, like to, and *bald*, soon, can never be used as adjectives. Adverbs, like adjectives, form the comparative and superlative degrees by adding *-er* and *am -sten* to the stem. Common irregular forms are:

> **gern** like to   **lieber** rather
> **am liebsten**   like best of all
> **bald** soon   **früher/eher** sooner
> **am frühesten/am ehesten**   soonest

When used with the verb *haben*, *gern* expresses enjoyment.

Ich habe Bier gern. I like beer.
Ich habe Wein lieber. I prefer wine.
Ich habe Wasser am liebsten. I like water best of all.

The Verb

The German verb must agree with the subject in number and in person.

Here is the present tense of the verb *kommen*. Note that in the dictionary the verb is always given in the infinitive form, i.e., the verb ends in *-en* or *-n* (*gehen*, to go; *nehmen*, to take).

> **ich komme** I come, I do come, I am coming
> **du kommst** you come (familiar)
> **er, sie, es kommt** he, she, it comes
> **wir kommen** we come
> **ihr kommt** you come (plural familiar)
> **sie, Sie kommen** they, you (formal) come

The familiar form *du* (the plural is *ihr*) is used in addressing the immediate family, children, relatives, close friends and animals. The form *Sie* (capitalized and not to be confused with *sie*, she, or *sie*, they) is used in all other cases.

Of twelve tenses, five are most frequently used in conversational German. Except for the modals (see p. 360), auxiliaries (p. 356), and *wissen*, to know, conversational German uses the present perfect tense to indicate the past. The simple past is used in newspapers, books, and articles.

PRESENT: **ich sehe** I see, I do see, I am seeing
PAST: **ich sah** I saw or was seeing
PRESENT PERFECT: **ich habe gesehen** I saw or I have seen
PAST PERFECT: **ich hatte gesehen** I had seen
FUTURE: **ich werde sehen** I shall see
CONDITIONAL: **ich würde sehen** I would see

German verbs divide into two groups for conjugation. The weak or regular forms correspond closely to the English regular verbs; *tanzen*, to dance; *tanzte*, danced; *getanzt*, danced. A *-te* ending is added to the stem of the verb to form the past tense: *machen*, to do; *machte*, did; and a prefix *ge-* and the ending *-t* to form the past participle, *gemacht*, did; *brauchen*, to need; *brauchte*, needed; *gebraucht*, needed. See p. 358 for the conjugation of weak verbs.

The strong or irregular verbs correspond to the English irregular verbs: *singen*, to sing; *sang*, sang; *gesungen*, sung. The stem vowel of these verbs changes to form the different tenses, so that they must be learned in the three principal parts immediately: *laufen*, to run; *lief*, ran; (*ist*) *gelaufen*, run. The formation of the past of these verbs is irregular, but they form the past participle by adding the prefix *ge-* and the ending *-en: essen*, to eat; *ass*, ate; *gegessen*, eaten. See p. 359 for the conjugation of strong verbs. Both strong and weak verbs use the same endings for the present tense.

As in English, German uses *sein*, to be, and *haben*, to have, as auxiliary verbs to form the present and past perfect tenses. *Haben* is more frequently used to form the perfect tenses: *sagen*, to say; *ich habe gesagt*, I said *or* I have said; excepting for those verbs which use *sein* when they indicate motion or a change of condition: *kommen*, to come; *ich bin gekommen*, I came *or* I have come; *sterben*, to die; *er ist gestorben*, he died *or* he has died.

The verb *werden* is used to form the future and future perfect tenses: *ich werde kommen*, I shall come; *sie wird gekommen sein*, she will have come. The future may also be indicated by using the present tense of the verb with a time expression:

Morgen gehe ich nach Hause.
I'm going home tomorrow.

Werden plus the past participle of a verb is also used to form the passive voice. The passive voice indicates that the subject is being acted upon. When human, the agent performing the action is indicated by *von* plus the dative. Otherwise, the agent is indicated by *durch* plus the accusative.

Der Brief wird von mir geschrieben.
The letter is being written by me.

In summary, *werden* functions in three different ways: as a verb meaning *to become;* as an auxiliary to indicate the future and future perfect tenses; and to form the passive voice.

The modal auxiliaries are: *dürfen*, to be allowed, may; *können*, can, to be able; *mögen*, may, to like; *müssen*, must, have to, to be compelled; *sollen*, shall, be said to; *wollen*, will, to want, to desire. They are inflected and precede the infinitive form of the main verb.

> **Sie kann heute nicht schlafen.**
> She can't sleep today.
> **Wollen Sie ins Konzert gehen?**
> Do you want to go to the concert?

The *subjunctive mood* is used in indirect discourse, in unreal conditions, after *als ob*, as if, and to express wishes, polite requests, and doubts. The endings *-e*, *-est*, *-e*, *-en*, *-et*, *-en* are added to the stem. Weak verbs that add *-te* to the stem to form the past indicative use this same form for the past subjunctive. Strong verbs which change their stem vowels in the past indicative to *a, o, u,* form the past subjunctive with *ä, ö, ü*.

> **Er sagte, er habe (*or* hätte) kein Geld.**
> He said he had no money.
> **Hätte ich nur ein Glas Wein!**
> If I only had a glass of wine!
> **Sie sah aus, als ob sie reich wäre.**
> She looked as if she were rich.
> **Möchten Sie Tee oder Kaffee?**
> Would you like tea or coffee?

SUBJUNCTIVE

PRESENT:

ich sage	ich fahre	ich freue mich
du sagest	du fahrest	du freuest dich
er, sie, es sage	er fahre	er freue sich
wir sagen	wir fahren	wir freuen uns
ihr saget	ihr fahret	ihr freuet euch
sie, Sie sagen	sie fahren	sie freuen sich

PAST:

ich sagte	ich führe	ich freute mich
du sagtest	du führest	du freutest dich
er, sie, es sagte	er führe	er freute sich
wir sagten	wir führen	wir freuten uns
ihr sagtet	ihr führet	ihr freutet euch
sie, Sie sagten	sie führen	sie freuten sich

The *conditional*, using a form of *würden*, like the subjunctive expresses contrary-to-fact conditions and polite requests. The past conditional is to be avoided.

PRESENT:

Wenn sie hier wäre, (so) würde sie ins Theater gehen.
If she were here, she would go to the theater.

CONDITIONAL

PRESENT:

ich würde sagen, etc.	Ich würde fahren, etc.	ich würde mich freuen, etc.

The *imperative* uses a separate form to express the familiar singular, the familiar plural, and the polite form (singular and plural).

IMPERATIVE

Mache!	Geh!	Amüsiere dich!
Macht!	Geht!	Amüsiert euch!
Machen Sie!	Gehen Sie!	Amüsieren Sie sich!

Reflexive verbs are followed by the appropriate reflexive personal pronoun.

Ich wasche mich.	Wir waschen uns.
Du wäscht dich.	Ihr wascht euch.
Er wäscht sich.	Sie waschen sich.

Separable and inseparable prefixes. Certain German verbs have prefixes before the main part of the verb, which in the present tense, simple past, and imperative form are separated and placed at the end of the sentence or clause. In the past participle the *-ge-* comes between the prefix and the stem. In pronunciation the prefix is stressed.

an-fangen   **Sie fängt an.**   She begins.   **angefangen**
            Sie fing an.   She began.
            Fangen Sie an!   Begin!

Other verbs bearing prefixes are inseparable. They do not add a *ge-* to form the past participle.

verstehen   **Er versteht.**   He understands
           Er verstand.   He understood
           Er hat verstanden.   He (has) understood.

The Auxiliaries

SEIN, to be

PRESENT:

ich bin	wir sind
du bist	ihr seid
er, sie, es ist	sie, Sie sind

PAST:

ich war	wir waren
du warst	ihr wart
er, sie, es war	sie, Sie waren

PRESENT PERFECT:

ich bin gewesen	wir sind gewesen
du bist gewesen	ihr seid gewesen
er, sie, es ist gewesen	sie, Sie sind gewesen

PAST PERFECT:

ich war gewesen	wir waren gewesen
du warst gewesen	ihr wart gewesen
er, sie, es war gewesen	sie, Sie waren gewesen

FUTURE:

ich werde sein	wir werden sein
du wirst sein	ihr werdet sein
er, sie, es wird sein	sie, Sie werden sein

FUTURE PERFECT:

ich werde gewesen sein	wir werden gewesen sein
du wirst gewesen sein	ihr werdet gewesen sein
er, sie, es wird gewesen sein	sie, Sie werden gewesen sein

CONDITIONAL:

ich würde sein	wir würden sein
du würdest sein	ihr würdet sein
er, sie, es würde sein	sie, Sie würden sein

IMPERATIVE:

Sei . . . !   Seid . . . !   Seien Sie . . . !

HABEN, to have

PRESENT:

ich habe	wir haben
du hast	ihr habt
er, sie, es hat	sie, Sie haben

PAST:

ich hatte	wir hatten
du hattest	ihr hattet
er, sie, es hatte	sie, Sie hatten

PRESENT PERFECT:

ich habe gehabt	wir haben gehabt
du hattest gehabt	ihr habt gehabt
er, sie, es hatte gehabt	sie, Sie haben gehabt

PAST PERFECT:

ich hatte gehabt	wir hatten gehabt
du hattest gehabt	ihr hattet gehabt
er, sie, es hatte gehabt	sie, Sie hatten gehabt

FUTURE:

ich werde haben	wir werden haben
du wirst haben	ihr werdet haben
er, sie, es wird haben	sie, Sie werden haben

FUTURE PERFECT:

ich werde gehabt haben	wir werden gehabt haben
du wirst gehabt haben	ihr werdet gehabt haben
er, sie, es wird gehabt haben	sie, Sie werden gehabt haben

CONDITIONAL:

ich würde haben	wir würden haben
du würdest haben	ihr würdet haben
er, sie, es würde haben	sie, Sie, würden haben

IMPERATIVE:
Habe . . . !   Habt . . . !   Haben Sie . . . !

The Weak or Regular Verbs

LIEBEN, to love

PRESENT:

ich liebe	wir lieben
du liebst	ihr liebt
er, sie, es liebt	sie, Sie lieben

PAST:

ich liebte	wir liebten
du liebtest	ihr liebtet
er, sie, es liebte	sie, Sie liebten

PRESENT PERFECT:

ich habe geliebt	wir haben geliebt
du hast geliebt	ihr habt geliebt
er, sie, es hat geliebt	sie, Sie hatten geliebt

PAST PERFECT:

ich hatte geliebt	wir hatten geliebt
du hattest geliebt	ihr hattet geliebt
er, sie, es hatte geliebt	sie, Sie hatten geliebt

FUTURE:

ich werde lieben	wir werden lieben
du wirst lieben	ihr werdet lieben
er, sie, es wird lieben	sie, Sie werden lieben

FUTURE PERFECT:

ich werde geliebt haben	wir werden geliebt haben
du wirst geliebt haben	ihr werdet geliebt haben
er, sie, es wird geliebt haben	sie, Sie werden geliebt haben

CONDITIONAL:

ich würde lieben	wir würden lieben
du würdest lieben	ihr würdet lieben
er, sie, es würde lieben	sie, Sie würden lieben

IMPERATIVE:
Liebe!   Liebt!   Lieben Sie!

The Strong or Irregular Verbs

GEHEN, to go

PRESENT:

ich gehe	wir gehen
du gehst	ihr geht
er, sie, es geht	sie, Sie gehen

PAST:

ich ging	wir gingen
du gingst	ihr gingt
er, sie, es ging	sie, Sie gingen

PRESENT PERFECT:

ich bin gegangen	wir sind gegangen
du bist gegangen	ihr seid gegangen
er, sie, es ist gegangen	sie, Sie sind gegangen

PAST PERFECT:

ich war gegangen	wir waren gegangen
du warst gegangen	ihr wart gegangen
er, sie, es war gegangen	sie, Sie waren gegangen

FUTURE:

ich werde gehen	wir werden gehen
du wirst gehen	ihr werdet gehen
er, sie, es wird gehen	sie, Sie werden gehen

FUTURE PERFECT:

ich werde gegangen sein	wir werden gegangen sein
du wirst gegangen sein	ihr werdet gegangen sein
er, sie, es wird gegangen sein	sie, Sie werden gegangen sein

CONDITIONAL:

ich würde gehen	wir würden gehen
du würdest gehen	ihr würdet gehen
er, sie, es würde gehen	sie, Sie würden gehen

IMPERATIVE:
Geh!   Geht!   Gehen Sie!

The Modal Auxiliaries

MÜSSEN, must, have to

PRESENT:

ich muss	wir müssen
du musst	ihr müsst
er, sie, es muss	sie, Sie müssen

PAST:
ich musste, etc.

PRESENT PERFECT:
ich habe gemusst, etc.

FUTURE:
ich werde müssen, etc.

MÖGEN, may, to like

PRESENT:

ich mag	wir mögen
du magst	ihr mögt
er, sie, es mag	sie, Sie mögen

PAST:
ich mochte, etc.

PRESENT PERFECT:
ich habe gemocht, etc.

FUTURE:
ich werde mögen, etc.

DÜRFEN, may, be allowed

PRESENT:

ich darf	wir dürfen
du darfst	ihr dürft
er, sie, es darf	sie, Sie dürfen

PAST:
ich durfte, etc.

PRESENT PERFECT:
ich habe gedurft, etc.

FUTURE:
ich werde dürfen, etc.

KÖNNEN, can, to be able

PRESENT:

ich kann	wir können
du kannst	ihr könnt
er, sie, es kann	sie, Sie können

PAST:
ich konnte, etc.

PRESENT PERFECT:
ich habe gekonnt, etc.

FUTURE:
ich werde können, etc.

WOLLEN, will, to want

PRESENT:

ich will	wir wollen
du willst	ihr wollt
er, sie, es will	sie, Sie, wollen

PAST:
ich wollte, etc.

PRESENT PERFECT:
ich habe gewollt, etc.

FUTURE:
ich werde wollen, etc.

SOLLEN, ought to, to be to, be said to

PRESENT:
ich soll	wir sollen
du sollst	ihr sollt
er, sie, es soll	sie, Sie sollen

PAST:
ich sollte, etc.

PRESENT PERFECT:
ich habe gesollt, etc.

FUTURE:
ich werde sollen, etc.

The Verb List

This list includes strong or irregular verbs only and gives their principal parts: the infinitive and its meaning, the third person singular of the present indicative, the imperative if it is irregularly formed (in italics), the third person singular of the past indicative, and the past participle. The third person singular presents the irregularity in the present tense. A past participle preceded by *ist* in parentheses is conjugated in the perfect tenses with an appropriate form of *sein;* otherwise the auxiliary is *haben*.

The imperative singular form is given only when the vowel of the stem changes from *e* to *i*. The modal auxiliaries and some verbs obviously do not have imperatives.

From this basic list of verbs, many new verbs can be formed by the addition of a prefix. For example, *schreiben*, to write, with the addition of *be-* becomes *beschreiben*, to describe. *Kommen*, to come, with the addition of *an-* becomes *ankommen*, to arrive. Such new compounds are conjugated according to the original verb forms.

STRONG VERBS:

backen, bake: bäckt, buk, gebacken
befehlen, command: befiehlt, *befiehl*, befahl, befohlen
beginnen, begin: beginnt, begann, begonnen
beissen, bite: beisst, biss, gebissen
bersten, burst: birst, *birst*, barst, (ist) geborsten
betrügen, deceive: betrügt, betrog, betrogen
bewegen, induce: bewegt, bewog, bewogen
biegen, bend: biegt, bog, gebogen
binden, bind: bindet, band, gebunden
bitten, beg, ask: bittet, bat, gebeten
blasen, blow: bläst, blies, geblasen
bleiben, remain: bleibt, blieb, (ist) geblieben
braten, roast: brät, briet, gebraten
brechen, break: bricht, *brich*, brach, gebrochen
brennen, burn: brennt, brannte, gebrannt
bringen, bring: bringt, *bring*, brachte, gebracht
denken, think: denkt, dachte, gedacht
ein-laden, invite: lädt ein, lud ein, eingeladen
empfehlen, recommend: empfiehlt, *empfiehl*, empfahl, empfohlen
erschrecken, be frightened: erschrickt, *erschrick*, erschrak, (ist) erschrocken
essen, eat: isst, *iss*, ass, gegessen
fahren, drive, ride: fährt, fuhr, (ist) gefahren
fallen, fall: fällt, fiel, (ist) gefallen
fangen, catch: fängt, fing, gefangen
finden, find: findet, fand, gefunden
fliegen, fly: fliegt, flog, (ist) geflogen
fliehen, flee: flieht, floh, (ist) geflohen
fliessen, flow: fliesst, floss, (ist) geflossen
fressen, eat (of animals): frisst, *friss*, frass, gefressen
frieren, freeze: friert, fror, gefroren
gebären, bear, give birth: gebiert, gebar, (ist) geboren
geben, give: gibt, *gib*, gab, gegeben
gehen, go: geht, ging, (ist) gegangen
gelingen, succeed: gelingt, gelang, (ist) gelungen

gelten, be worth: gilt, galt, gegolten
geniessen, enjoy: geniesst, genoss, genossen
geschehen, happen: geschieht, geschah, (ist) geschehen
gewinnen, gain, get: gewinnt, gewann, gewonnen
giessen, pour: giesst, goss, gegossen
gleichen, resemble: gleicht, glich, geglichen
graben, dig: gräbt, grub, gegraben
greifen, seize: greift, griff, gegriffen
haben, have: hat, hatte, gehabt
halten, hold: hält, hielt, gehalten
hängen, hang, be suspended: hängt, hing, gehangen
heben, lift: hebt, hob, gehoben
heissen, bid, be called: heisst, hiess, geheissen
helfen, help: hilft, *hilf*, half, geholfen
kennen, know, be acquainted with: kennt, kannte, gekannt
klingen, sound: klingt, klang, geklungen
kommen, come: kommt, kam, (ist) gekommen
kriechen, creep: kriecht, kroch, (ist) gekrochen
lassen, let, leave: lässt, liess, gelassen
laufen, run: läuft, lief, (ist) gelaufen
leiden, suffer: leidet, litt, gelitten
leihen, lend: leiht, lieh, geliehen
lesen, read: liest, *lies*, las, gelesen
liegen, lie: liegt, lag, gelegen
lügen, tell a lie: lügt, log, gelogen
messen, measure: misst, *miss*, mass, gemessen
nehmen, take: nimmt, *nimm*, nahm, genommen
nennen, name: nennt, nannte, genannt
preisen, praise: preist, pries, gepriesen
raten, advise: rät, riet, geraten
reiben, rub: reibt, rieb, gerieben
reissen, tear: reisst, riss, gerissen
reiten, ride: reitet, ritt, (ist) geritten
rennen, run, race: rennt, rannte, gerannt
riechen, smell: riecht, roch, gerochen
rufen, call, shout: ruft, rief, gerufen
schaffen, create: schafft, schuf, geschaffen
scheiden, separate, divorce: scheidet, schied, geschieden

scheinen, appear, shine: scheint, schien, geschienen
schelten, scold: schilt, *schilt*, schalt, gescholten
schieben, shove, push: schiebt, schob, geschoben
schiessen, shoot: schiesst, schoss, geschossen
schlafen, sleep: schläft, schlief, geschlafen
schlagen, strike: schlägt, schlug, geschlagen
schliessen, shut: schliesst, schloss, geschlossen
schmelzen, melt: schmilzt, *schmilz*, schmolz, (hat *or* ist) geschmolzen
schneiden, cut: schneidet, schnitt, geschnitten
schreiben, write: schreibt, schrieb, geschrieben
schreien, cry out, shout: schreit, schrie, geschrieen
schweigen, be silent: schweigt, schwieg, geschwiegen
schwellen, swell: schwillt, schwoll, (ist) geschwollen
schwimmen, swim: schwimmt, schwamm, (hat *or* ist) geschwommen
schwören, swear: schwört, schwor *or* schwur, geschworen
sehen, see: sieht, *sieh*, sah, gesehen
sein, be: ist, *sei*, war, (ist) gewesen
senden, send: sendet, sandte, gesandt *or* gesendet
sieden, simmer, seethe: siedet, sott, gesotten
singen, sing: singt, sang, gesungen
sinken, sink: sinkt, sank, (ist) gesunken
sitzen, sit: sitzt, sass, gesessen
spinnen, spin: spinnt, spann, gesponnen
sprechen, speak: spricht, *sprich*, sprach, gesprochen
springen, spring: springt, sprang, (ist) gesprungen
stechen, prick: sticht, *stich*, stach, gestochen
stehen, stand: steht, stand, gestanden
stehlen, steal: stiehlt, *stiehl*, stahl, gestohlen
steigen, ascend: steigt, stieg, (ist) gestiegen
sterben, die: stirbt, *stirb*, starb, (ist) gestorben
stossen, push, kick: stösst, stiess, gestossen
streiten, argue: streitet, stritt, gestritten
tragen, carry: trägt, trug, getragen
treffen, hit, meet: trifft, *triff*, traf, getroffen
treten, step: tritt, trat, (ist) getreten
trinken, drink: trinkt, trank, getrunken

tun, do: tut, tat, getan
verderben, spoil: verdirbt, *verdirb,* verdarb, verdorben
vergessen, forget: vergisst, *vergiss,* vergass, vergessen
verlieren, lose: verliert, verlor, verloren
verzeihen, pardon: verzeiht, verzieh, verziehen
wachsen, grow: wächst, wuchs, (ist) gewachsen
wägen, weigh: wägt, wog, gewogen
waschen, wash: wäscht, wusch, gewaschen
weben, weave: webt, wob, gewoben
wenden, turn: wendet, wandte *or* wendete, gewandt *or*
  gewendet
werden, become, get: wird, wurde, (ist) geworden
werfen, throw: wirft, *wirf,* warf, geworfen
wiegen, weigh: wiegt, wog, gewogen
ziehen, draw, pull: zieht, zog, gezogen
zwingen, force: zwingt, zwang, gezwungen

MODAL AUXILIARIES AND "WISSEN":

dürfen, be allowed, may: darf, durfte, gedurft
können, can, be able: kann, konnte, gekonnt
mögen, may, like: mag, mochte, gemocht
müssen, must, have to, be compelled: muss, musste, gemusst
sollen, shall, be said to: soll, sollte, gesollt
wollen, will, want: will, wollte, gewollt
wissen, know (a fact): weiss, wusste, gewusst